GLOBAL
SOUTH
ASIA

Padma Kaimal

K. Sivaramakrishnan

Anand A. Yang

SERIES EDITORS

BANARAS
RECONSTRUCTED

ARCHITECTURE AND SACRED SPACE
IN A HINDU HOLY CITY

Madhuri Desai

UNIVERSITY OF WASHINGTON PRESS

Seattle and London

Banaras Reconstructed was made possible in part by a generous grant from the George Dewey and Mary J. Krumrine Endowment, administered by the Department of Art History and the College of Arts and Architecture at the Pennsylvania State University.

UNIVERSITY OF WASHINGTON PRESS
www.washington.edu/uwpress

LIBRARY OF CONGRESS CATALOGING-IN-PUBLICATION DATA
Names: Desai, Madhuri (Madhuri Shrikant), author.
Title: Banaras reconstructed : architecture and sacred space in a Hindu holy city / Madhuri Desai.
Description: Seattle : University of Washington Press, 2017. | Series: Global South Asia | Includes
   bibliographical references and index.
Identifiers: LCCN 2016050496| ISBN 9780295741604 (hardcover : alk. paper) |
   ISBN 9780295741994 (pbk. : alk. paper)
Subjects: LCSH: Hindu architecture—India—Varanasi (Uttar Pradesh) | Sacred space—India—
   Varanasi (Uttar Pradesh) | Architecture and society—c (Uttar Pradesh) | Varanasi (Uttar
   Pradesh, India)—Buildings, structures, etc.
Classification: LCC NA1508.V37 D47 2017 | DDC 720.954—DC23
LC record available at https://lccn.loc.gov/2016050496]

For my parents
and for Nandu

CONTENTS

Color plates appear after page 166.

ACKNOWLEDGMENTS

So many people have helped me during the course of this project. My colleagues in the Department of Art History at the Pennsylvania State University, especially Craig Zabel, Nancy Locke, Elizabeth Smith, Robin Thomas, Brian Curran, and Sarah Rich, were staunchly supportive and encouraging. The late Kumkum Chatterjee was a lively and insightful interlocutor. My teachers at the University of California–Berkeley gave me the foundational tools to become an architectural and urban historian. Professor Stephen Tobriner has been a generous advisor and steadfast mentor as I developed this project, as well as in other areas of academic life. Professors Greig Crysler and Lawrence Cohen gave me critical guidance and encouragement. Professors Vasudha Dalmia, Muzaffar Alam, and Kathleen James-Chakraborty were thoughtful and unstinting with their advice. Professor Nalini Thakur consistently provided help and direction besides imparting her infectious and discerning passion for all things historical. At the University of Washington Press, Ranjit Arab believed in this book from the very beginning, and I am grateful to him as well as to Larin McLaughlin, Margaret Sullivan, Whitney Johnson, Beth Fuget, and my editor, Amy Smith Bell. My thanks also to the editors of the Global South Asia series as well as the two anonymous reviewers for giving the manuscript a close reading and for their many suggestions for its improvement.

Many institutions and individuals have supported this research by providing archival and visual source material. My thanks to the staff of the National Museum (New Delhi), the National Archives (New Delhi), the British Library (London), the Bancroft Library (Berkeley), the Royal Academy (London), the Maharaja Sawai Mansingh II Museum (Jaipur), and the Maharana of Mewar Charitable Foundation and Research Institute (Udaipur). In Banaras, my sincere thanks to His Highness, Maharaja Anantnarain Singh. My thanks also to Dr. T. K. Biswas, Dr. R. P. Singh, Dr. Lakshmi Dutt Vyas, J. P. Pathak, and all the management and staff at the following institutions—Bharat Kala Bhawan, Regional Archives (Banaras), Sampurnanand Sanskrit Library, Saraswati Bhandar and Purana Department (Ramnagar), the Jangambadi Muth, the Kumarswamy Muth, the Annapurna Chattra Trust, the Holkar Trust, the Ramakrishna Mission, Nagari Pracharini Sabha, Abhimanyu Pustakalaya, and the Carmichael Library.

Special thanks are due to Rai Anand Krishna, Dr. O. P. Kejariwal, Dr. Dhirendranath Singh, Dr. Om Prakash Sharma, Dr. Bhanushankar Mehta, Dr. Nilkanth Purushottam Joshi, the Peshwa family, the Sahi family, Shashank Singh, the Shah family of Azmatgarh palace, the Basu family, Swami Jaikishan Puri, Abdul Batin sahib, Sadiq Ali sahib, Sanghamitra Sarkar, Mohammad Khalil, Aftab Ali, Istiyak Ali, Al Qamar, Klaus Rotzer, Jyotima, M.B. Bajre, K. S. Khushwaha, Harishanker Singh, the Bharadwaj family, and the Agarwal family of the Banaras Art Gallery. In Allahabad, my thanks to Dr. O. P. Srivastava, Dr. Ghulam Sarwar, and Rajesh Sonkar of the Regional Archives, and Dr. Shailaja Pandey of the Ganganath Jha Institute. I am grateful also to Dr. David Curley, Dr. Stewart Gordon, David Moffat, Judy Loeven, and Cynthia Col.

My research assistants—Nanditha Veeraraghavelu, Gretta Tritch Roman, and Rohan Haksar—were invaluable as well as technically proficient in creating maps and architectural drawings, and Jennifer Shontz shared her aesthetic judgment and graphic skills. Any remaining errors or lacunae are entirely mine. Initial research funding was provided through the IDRF program of the Social Science Research Council. Additional support was provided by a fellowship from the Paul Mellon Centre for British Art, London, and research grants provided by the College of Arts and Architecture and the Institute for Arts and Humanities at the Pennsylvania State University. Publication support was provided through generous grants from the George Dewey and Mary J. Krumrine Endowment, administered by the Department of Art History and the College of Arts and Architecture at the Pennsylvania State University.

Shikha Jain and her family have helped me in innumerable ways, and my father-in-law, Mohandas Desai, was untiring as he acquired editions of rare Sanskrit texts on my request. My family has sustained me in this research over the years, especially my late father, Shrikant Malhar Nandgaonkar; my mother, Padma Nandgaonkar; and my brothers, Ujjval Nandgaonkar and Girish Nandgaonkar. I am grateful to Dad and Ujjval for their stoic and unwavering support. I am forever indebted to Girish for his unconditional faith and active assistance. I am grateful for Mom's intellectual interests—they have molded and shaped my own. Although Dad left us all before this book was published, his enthusiasm and indomitable spirit have sustained its completion. My husband, Nandkishore Desai, has been a source of strength and always "in my corner"; without his support this book would not have become reality. Much love and heartfelt thanks to you all.

BANARAS RECONSTRUCTED

FIG. I.1   Riverfront at Banaras.

THE PARADOX OF BANARAS

OST visitors to the north Indian pilgrimage center of Banaras (also known by the names Kashi and Varanasi) expect to find a city of ancient temples and ritual sites along the sacred Ganges River (Map I.1). Some general truisms used to describe Banaras are "continuously inhabited for two thousand years" and "the quintessential Hindu city." A rich textual corpus in Sanskrit and various regional vernacular languages sustains such narratives, supported by a thriving religious life of pilgrimage routes and festivals in a built environment of temples, riverfront edifices, and monasteries. As the subject of numerous pilgrimage maps, paintings, and photographs, images of hoary sanctity are reinforced through visual media. Yet, as one takes a closer look at this city, there are hints of a more complex story. Several of the temple towers, though archaic in appearance, are supported on Mughal columns that first appeared in northern India during the seventeenth century. The riverfront ghats bear an uncanny resemblance to the Mughal fortress-palaces that line the Jamuna River at Delhi and Agra. One of the city's most significant institutions, the Sampurnanand Sanskrit University, is housed in a gothic revival–style building, more reminiscent of a college in nineteenth-century Britain than a traditional Indian *gurukul* (scholarly retreat). Such details belie both the city's age as well as conventional expectations from the appearance of a "Hindu" city. No significant building on the riverfront can be dated to earlier than the year 1600 (Fig. I.1), and the city's skyline is punctuated by two visually dominant, seventeenth-century mosques. Kashi may be an ancient site, but it is a reconstructed Banaras that contemporary pilgrims and visitors encounter. This book investigates the circumstances of this regeneration, through the motives and actions of significant historical actors.

The disjuncture between its appearance and its representations is the key to such an inquiry. Much evidence for the city's antiquity is derived from textual sources that are viewed as static and ahistorical. This perspective has a basis in general impressions of the city as "eternal," "timeless," and "unchanging" that are simultaneously and contradictorily sustained through accounts of its repeated rebuilding after several instances of invasion and destruction at the hands of Islamic rulers. These repeated assaults purportedly begin with the Ghurids in the twelfth century and end with the specific policies and actions of the Mughal emperor Aurangzeb in the seventeenth century. The presence of significant mosques lends credence to such theories, although only a few of these structures were

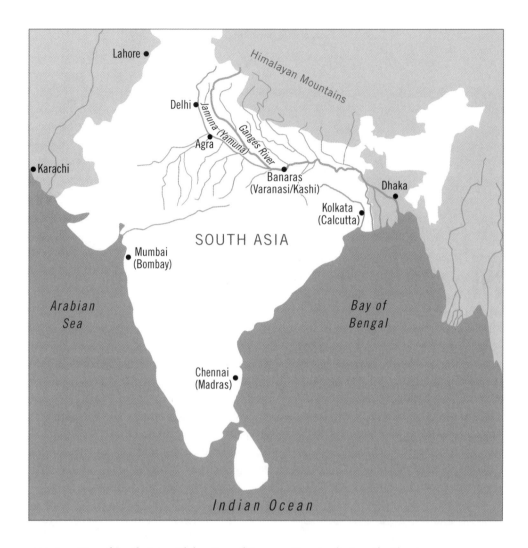

MAP I.I   Map of South Asia with location of Banaras. Drawing by Jennifer Shontz.

actually built on or near former temple sites. Scholars also concede that Banaras underwent an upheaval after the Ghurid encounters, although the precise nature of this shift is
still debated.[1]

They observe, for instance, that many features of its sacred landscape (such as the practice of pilgrimage routes around the Vishweshwur temple) evolved after the twelfth century. Yet these new elements and their religious, textual, and spatial characteristics are
rarely, if ever, discussed in historical terms. Furthermore, abstract ideas regarding a sacred
zone with boundaries and a center were sustained in a reciprocal relationship with tangible
buildings and urban spaces—a connection that remains unexplored in its political and
cultural dimensions. The motives of individuals and groups who shaped this environment
also remain obscure beyond simplistic explanations of patronage for a "timeless" Banaras.

INTRODUCTION

Textual references to Banaras can be traced back at least to the sixth century of the Common Era. However, even a preliminary critical overview of the textual corpus reveals that despite certain shared elements (such as defined boundary and center), the authors of each text held differing views on the overall configuration as well as details of its sacred landscape. At least since the twelfth century, its ritual geography was conceptualized as a sacred zone (the Kashikshetra), spreading outward from its physical and ritual center (a *linga*), the aniconic symbol of the Hindu deity Shiva. This geography was the basis of a pilgrimage zone that existed simultaneously as imagined configuration as well as lived experience. If authors of religious texts defined it as an idealized circle or square, in practice the extents and contours of this zone were always irregular and contingent. Moreover, the identity of the central, anchoring Shivalinga remained on shifting ground, altered and adjusted through the centuries.

Philological studies and analyses suggest that ideas regarding a sacred zone centered on a Vishweshwur *linga* were first conceptualized and summarized in a Sanskrit text called the *Kashikhand*. A compendium of pilgrimage routes, individual sacred sites, and their related myths, this text was actually composed as late as the fourteenth century. The *Kashikhand* does not contain any mention of the outermost pilgrimage route, the Panchkroshi, which surrounds Banaras and by extension also circumscribes the Vishweshwur *linga*.[2] This route was mentioned in pilgrimage texts only as late as the fifteenth century and was first described in some detail in a sixteenth-century Sanskrit text, the *Kashirahasya*.[3] Since then, successive generations of Brahmin scholars have assessed and reinterpreted the *Kashikhand* as well as the *Kashirahasya*. In subsequent centuries both texts were incorporated into the *purana* textual literature on the city and the prescriptions contained within each were folded into the formal cannon of pilgrimage and ritual worship connected with Kashikshetra. As Wendy Doniger and Velcheru Narayana Rao have explicated, "folk" narratives or texts were often folded into the enveloping narrative of a *purana* text and therefore these should be viewed as processes in which multiple traditions merged together.[4] Such augmentation could often indicate the fact that a localized tradition or practice had been incorporated into an encompassing Brahminical social and narrative structure.[5]

In essence, both the *Kashikhand* (incorporated within the *Skandapurana*) and the *Kashirahasya* (incorporated within the *Brahmavaivartapurana*) are spatial texts. Their authors were preoccupied with the significance of sacred sites and also their location and physical disposition, and their merger with the formal *purana* tradition had consequences for the city's spaces and built environment. Their continued reinterpretations (in particular, those undertaken between the fifteenth and nineteenth centuries) were the basis for the city's evolving sacred landscape over the past four centuries as a temple dedicated to house the Vishweshwur *linga* that was visualized as a central and monumental manifestation of its connection to Shiva. The city's riverfront was a visible marker of its function as a site for ritual cleansing and cremation, and patrons reinforced this role through spectacular architecture.

Besides texts, pilgrimage *pata* (schematic charts) and maps were powerful tools that allowed pilgrims to visualize complex connections described within texts. The spatial dimensions and characteristics of sacred zones and pilgrimage routes could be conveyed through a single painting or map and had the advantage of being accessible as a collection of easily comprehended images and symbols. Their creators adapted a variety of pictorial and cartographic devices from the larger worlds of Mughal and colonial survey techniques and visual representation. This suggests the existence of a continually evolving relationship between the religious imagination and its contingent political and cultural contexts. Patronage was key to the gradual development of ritual and spatial practices as in the case of specific pilgrimage routes, particularly the Panchkroshi *yatra* and the Antargriha *yatra*. Patronage was channeled through support for temples and monasteries.

To understand the city's evolution in historical terms, this book relies on the earliest architectural vestiges of its sacred landscape, the most significant of which are datable to the reign of the Mughal emperor Akbar. Mughal state patronage and state-sponsored interventions between the late sixteenth and early eighteenth centuries shaped the religious environment of Banaras including its principal shrines, such as the ones dedicated to Vishweshwur and Bindu Madhav, as well as the edifices built along the city's riverfront that lent this space its distinct character. The term "state-sponsored" is used here to indicate tacit support through land grants (substantiated in many cases by *farmans*, or orders) as well as to the enabling role of the Mughal *mansabdar*, or general/administrator, than many high-ranking Hindu courtiers flaunted through architectural patronage. As Catherine Asher has explained, these roles reinforced the authority of a multilayered Mughal governance structure where imperial, familial, and individual interests were closely aligned and mutually reinforced.[6]

Mughal interventions during the reign of the emperor Aurangzeb also resulted in the creation of the city's most prominent mosques. Through direct imperial actions, the Gyan Vapi mosque was built to replace the Vishweshwur temple and the Dharhara mosque replaced the Bindu Madhav temple. Aurangzeb was keen to establish new norms for his reign, which included a redefinition of the relationship between the emperor, his court, and his subjects. His interventions in Banaras may be more accurately analyzed in light of his personal compulsions and political agenda, rather than as expressions of religious bigotry.[7] Significant elements that define the city's architectural and urban character were added over the course of the eighteenth century. The new temples and their associated ritual traditions were overlaid on an existing sacred landscape that augmented it in complex and often spectacular ways.

The histories of rebuilding and the tensions around the proximity of temple and mosque in the heart of the city have shaped its sacred landscape and its built environment. Their adjacent sites have largely been viewed as both the result and the cause of unadulterated antagonism between Hindus and Muslims, even though this proximity could just as easily be viewed as being the result of a compromise or even a shared notion of sacred space. The twin and somewhat simplistic accounts of timelessness and destruction, centered as they tend to be on the architectural history of Banaras as manifest in its most visible mosques, become general narratives about Indian (read Hindu) civilization and its vicissitudes at the whims of "Muslim" invaders and rulers. Moreover, the specter of "Islamic" destruction looms far beyond the actual instances of disruption instigated by Indo-Islamic regimes. A closer examination of complex interventions by successive regimes, as well as their place within collective memories and representations, reveals a more nuanced story.

This book is an assessment of various interventions and their consequences for the city in both material and imaginative terms. The city's built environment is a rich and revealing archive of its ritual and spatial history. The urban experience at Banaras was shaped by public spaces and institutions that were inexorably linked to its religious identity. New buildings were overlaid on a ritual geography of sacred associations that was summarized in *purana* texts and perpetuated through practice. The focus of this book, therefore, is on the city's built forms, ritual landscapes, and their representations. It is a story of patrons, priests, and pilgrims who created a city based in an imagination of the past and connected it to their immediate cultural and political realities. It is an inquiry into the city's so-called eternal character and raises questions about the assumption that Hindu pilgrimage centers can be understood independent of their Indo-Islamic and subsequent colonial lives.

This study understands early modern and modern Hindu practices as transformed through their changing political and cultural contexts, rather than as vestiges of an unchanging pre-Islamic past. In essence, Hinduism was reconceptualized in terms of its forms and practices even as its relationship with its own past was reimagined. The period under study begins ca. 1590—a time that coincided with the beginnings of Mughal interest and patronage for the ritual and literary traditions of Banaras. It concludes ca. 1930 with the crystallization of an antiquarian discourse for its riverfront under a colonial regime. In a larger context, this book is significant because it explores the cumulative role of Mughal, post-Mughal, and colonial regimes in redefining the built forms and spatial practices of modern Hinduism.

HISTORIES

Because material changes in the spatial environment of Banaras or Kashi are at the heart of this project, the city's political history is of particular interest. Politics were critical to the religious and cultural transitions that shaped the city's sacred environment. The focus of this book remains primarily on the city's Indo-Islamic past and the resulting rich history of cultural exchange across religious groups and identities broadly classified as "Hindu" and "Muslim." At the same time, the consolidation of various ritual and religious practices into what became known as Hinduism is equally significant. An overview of the history of Banaras starting with the last pre-Islamic rulers of Kashi, the Gahadavalas of Kannauj (whose reign saw the beginning of this process), and ending with British colonial rule (when religious ideas were recast in their modern guise) is therefore pertinent.

Kashi was designated as a second capital by the Gahadavala ruler Govindchandra in 1093. The Gahadavalas followed this move with more than five hundred grants to Brahmins in 1093 and in 1100.[8] They saw this as a means to consolidate political and spiritual authority in a newly conquered territory, and their minister, Lakshmidhara, set out to summarize ritual traditions and sacred sites in his monumental twelfth-century text, the *Krutyakalpataru*. The Gahadavalas may have contemplated major building projects in Kashi, but material interventions dating from their reign are minimal, if not entirely absent. Gahadavala rule was disrupted by the Ghurid invasion of 1193, and between the late twelfth and mid-sixteenth centuries Banaras and its vicinity were first part of the territories of the Delhi sultanate, followed by incorporation into the territories of the Sharqi sultanate with its political center in Jaunpur. This book includes an overview and analysis of the evolving sacred landscape and pilgrimage practices and routes in a changing political climate of Indo-Islamic regimes.

Banaras came firmly under Mughal rule between 1574 and 1576, with the emperor Akbar's conquest of the eastern regions of Bengal, Bihar, and Orissa.[9] Mughal rule was characterized by the political and cultural incorporation of various regional Hindu Rajput rulers, many of whom became office bearers and generals or *mansabdars* of the empire.[10] Mughal *mansabdars* combined the imperial mandate to promote and uphold the authority of the Mughal state with a desire to bolster familial lineages and promote personal agendas. As a political and cultural device, architectural patronage was a favored medium for successive emperors.[11] In keeping with this spirit and with tacit and often overt imperial support, Hindu courtiers channeled patronage toward refurbishing several key Hindu pilgrimage sites, including Banaras. Mughal support for Banaras and its ritual traditions remained vibrant during the reign of Akbar (d. 1605) and continued in varying degrees, through the reigns of the emperors Jahangir (1605–1627) and Shahjahan (1628–1658). A turn toward Islamic orthodoxy under the emperor Aurangzeb (1658–1707) initially meant a withdrawal of state support followed by the dismantling of major temples that had previously enjoyed tacit Mughal support and patronage. Even so, several religious institutions and practices remained undisturbed and were selectively supported, and even enhanced.

The early eighteenth century witnessed the gradual unraveling of Mughal authority and the emergence of a number of regional contenders with ambitions to control South Asia.[12] Among the more successful and noteworthy of this group were the Marathas, a loose federation of chiefs under the Peshwas at Pune. From the 1720s on, several Maratha chiefs successfully drove northward and conquered territories once firmly under the Mughals.[13] The Mughal Empire began to implode from within. By the 1750s, provincial governors at Awadh became virtually independent under Safdar Jung and his Shiite successors.[14] Furthermore, the Nawabs came under onslaught from competing and subordinate Rajput and Bhumihar chiefs. However, there were significant political and cultural continuities between the older Mughal Empire and the many emergent powers in the eighteenth century.[15] Mughal ideals and administrative systems continued to have currency, and many of these new groups relied, albeit to varying degrees, on Mughal social and artistic forms to derive political and cultural legitimacy.[16]

At Banaras a Bhumihar chief named Mansa Ram challenged and then replaced Meer Rustam Ali, the local representative and revenue agent of the Nawabs of Awadh. Maratha chiefs such as Malharrao Holkar and the Peshwas were interested in gaining control over principal Hindu pilgrimage centers, particularly the *tristhali* (literally, three sites) that was comprised of the three northern sacred sites of Kashi (Banaras), Prayag (Allahabad), and Gaya. Among these, Banaras remained a significant and sought-after site, and Maratha chiefs often sought control over the city in their territorial campaigns and negotiations. Politics and religion, however, did not necessarily align either perfectly or conveniently, and Maratha efforts were often stymied by other Hindu factions.

In 1738, Balwant Singh (Mansa Ram's son) was established at Banaras as a feudal subordinate of the Nawabs of Awadh, and the house of the Rajas of Banaras was created.[17] Balwant Singh took on the title "Kashi Naresh," thus implying a link between his family's lineage and the city's mythical and hoary past. In keeping with this notion, Balwant Singh sponsored religious activities in the city and patronized Brahmins and their literary activities at his court. His stated loyalties to and active employment by the Nawabs of Lucknow meant that his religious gestures were played out against more complex regional and even transregional political maneuverings.[18] Moreover, the city was governed by a *qazi* (judge) who administered it directly on the basis of legal mores derived from Mughal practices. By 1774 the Raja of Banaras's dominions were ceded to another emerging power, the English East India Company. Following the company's incursions into Awadh, Balwant Singh's successor, Chet Singh, became embroiled with its governor-general, Warren Hastings, over payment of land revenue.

In 1781 the East India Company under Hastings took direct control of the city, dethroned Chet Singh, and established his relative, the young Mahipnarain Singh, as "Raja" at Ramnagar, across the river from Banaras. In a continuation of Mughal systems of governance followed by the earlier regime, administration of the city remained under the direct control of the regional power, now the East India Company. As it set its sights on the entire subcontinent, the company gradually eliminated several of its rivals over the following two decades. By 1800 the company and the Marathas remained the principal contenders for subcontinental hegemony, and their competing interests had significant consequences for the material environment of Banaras. The emerging elites who benefited from these political and economic trends engaged in religious and artistic patronage as means of consolidating nascent positions of power and wealth. The century saw a proliferation of patronage for architecture, painting, and literature, as Mughal cultural mores and social behaviors were mimicked and adopted as signifiers of cultivated tastes and refinement.[19] The newer patrons, however, had different religious and social agendas than their Mughal predecessors, and they made a mark by incorporating archaic elements and ideas while also experimenting with innovative forms.

Alongside these political and cultural developments, historians have characterized the eighteenth century as a time of mercantile reorganization and urban expansion in the towns and cities of the Gangetic plains.[20] Banaras was a central location within banking and trading networks that stretched across South Asia. Mercantile prosperity had direct consequences for the city's sacred geography as patrons provided patronage and support for religious rituals and practices as well as architecture. Even as earlier layers of ritual association such as pilgrimage routes were partially or wholly renewed, temples and ritual tanks that anchored new and invented forms of religious practices were established to configure and refresh the role of Kashikshetra. Organized groups of mendicants acquired property and invested in *muths* (monasteries) in several religious centers across northern India including Banaras. As the nineteenth century progressed, many of these projects were motivated by regenerative Hindu movements that often had an emphasis on orthodox social practices and temple ritual.[21] Reformulated religious ideas usually required the transformation of rituals as well as spaces in keeping with the simultaneous demands of archaic tradition and impulses of transformative modernity. The results could mean something as simple as modifications to a pilgrimage path or as elaborate as the building of one of the city's temples.

Early colonial administrators in Banaras perpetuated precolonial architectural and urban forms, even as they gradually altered the institutional structures that governed the city. Many of the changes that they enacted pertained to rules regarding the ownership and management of urban land and real estate. Company officials were also determined to address what they saw as "Hindu" and "Muslim" interests equitably. In addition, to Warren Hastings's way of thinking, turning Banaras into a safe haven for Brahminical ritual and pilgrimage would draw support for the East India Company from the indigenous Hindu population of the entire subcontinent.[22] The formation of colonial knowledge has been extensively studied, as have the often simplistic and predetermined conclusions of colonial administrators and amateur scholars that altered South Asian society.[23] This project pays close attention to the consequences of colonial assumptions for the buildings, spaces, and experiences of Banaras. By the late nineteenth century, the city saw architectural and spatial interventions being enabled through an emergent civic sphere, forged through Indian agency as well as colonial instigation.

The colonial apparatus created a chronological history for the subcontinent, thereby also creating a historical timeline for the city. This new positivist perspective on the past was creatively incorporated and accounts of attacks on the city by Muslim armies were situated within a larger colonial historiography of a "Hindu" India laid siege to by invading "Muslims."[24] Paradoxically, the notion of timelessness lived on alongside stories of destruction, and positivist histories merged with accounts based in the *puranas*. Whereas the colonial government was committed to preserving what it viewed as "tradition," elites in the city channeled patronage through transformed institutions and forms of association and assembly that could simultaneously satisfy the demands of orthodoxy in a climate of emerging nationalism. The ritual landscape was assessed, altered, and managed to reflect these contingencies. New forms of architecture and urban space were devised for institutions that represented a transformed religious identity.

SOURCES, METHODS, AND SCHOLARLY ENGAGEMENTS

The Kashi that contemporary visitors experience largely evolved after the twelfth century, as pilgrimage routes and a growing city were configured around the principal Vishweshwur shrine. The rich literature on architectural and urban history, particularly studies that address the role of discursive processes in the creation of buildings and cities, has been instructive. Their authors explore the relationship between ideas, ideologies, and architectural and urban form across space and time.[25] Taking Foucault's idea of "discursive formations" as a point of departure, these studies have been valuable models for exploring connections between urban built environments, ideologies, and political intentions.[26]

The many built layers of Banaras are separated from a tangle of mythologies, texts, and beliefs. In so doing, several mapping exercises undertaken by late Mughal and colonial regimes between the late seventeenth and late nineteenth centuries provided insights into the ways that urban spaces, land uses, and social patterns shaped Banaras. Simultaneous analyses of pilgrimage texts, maps, and guidebooks aided in understanding convergences between this built environment and the ritual landscape. Banaras was reconstructed alongside evolving ideas about the nature of political authority, social and cultural spheres, urban space and religious identity. It was regenerated by several generations of Brahmin scholars who shaped the textual corpus of Kashi.

In recent years art historians have focused on cultural encounter as a mediating force in the shaping of material culture.[27] Scholars have tended to concentrate on shared forms in coinage, dress, architecture, and urban planning as evidence of a cultural negotiation along a continuum of relationships that veered between animosity, diplomacy, and trade resulting in various forms of appropriation and incorporation. Patrons and artisans made conscious choices from a palette of forms that they designated as either traditional or contemporary and engaged in formal choices informed by processes of selective amnesia.[28] The role of "tradition" in Banaras has been intimately involved in the re-creation of sites as well as rituals. In addressing similar concerns, art historians viewed such engagement as the consequence of deliberate and informed choice, when a conscious and often selective deployment of tradition is based in the exercise of active agency as cultures encounter differences that instigate and even compel change but also engender anxieties about identities and a sense of the past.[29] These varied perspectives have provided valuable guidance for this book.

In this context it may be simple to think of regenerated religious practices and the city's extant sacred architecture as "syncretic," standing in opposition to the expectations of unsullied Hindu forms such as those identified by nineteenth-century colonial scholars. However, as the historian of religion Tony Stewart has pointed out, the idea of "syncretism" is inherently flawed, since it is the end result of a union that is analyzed, rather than elements from two separate and mutually unconnected entities.[30] In other words, when brought together, each strand is irreversibly transformed and therefore impossible to understand in its "pristine" form. While conceding this stance, art historians Alka Patel and Karen Leonard have extended this idea to suggest that artistic forms are more appropriately designated as being products of an "Indo-Muslim culture" where they play "fluid" rather than static roles.[31]

In Banaras such forms included elements derived from an Indo-Islamic environment that were deliberately combined with archaic choices. This built environment could be labeled as "revivalist," understood as an occasional and often partial engagement with the past. More significantly, in this book, emphasis is placed on understanding the nature of human agency, as architects, artists, and their patrons drew on signifiers from multiple and often overlapping worlds, to define and express aspirations and religious identities that although inflected with contemporary cultural concerns could also be deeply personal. This book is concerned with understanding the role of individual agency and expression through the urban and architectural interventions undertaken by a diverse group of patrons. If formal and spatial confluences between discrete works of art or architecture determine style, they also mark religious, social, and political alliances and divergences. Moving beyond mere distillation and analyses of forms and spaces, this book addresses them as active social and political agents in the regeneration of Banaras.

The broader implications are concerned with religious sites across the subcontinent that were refurbished, enhanced, and even newly established between the fifteenth and eighteenth centuries. Examples include the temple complexes and ritual centers built, expanded, and supported by the Vijayanagara kings and their Nayaka successors.[32] In northern India, Mughal support and patronage were extended to diverse cultural and linguistic traditions such as those located in Brindavan-Mathura in the Braj region.[33] During the eighteenth century, Maratha patrons focused their attention on regenerating religious sites within and beyond their domains. It is highly pertinent that many such instances of successful patronage occurred in a larger Indo-Islamic political and cultural context. As Banaras was regenerated in recent centuries, this book has revealed much about the nature of patronage and its political role in shaping religious centers. Beyond political conciliations, patrons also addressed anxieties about religious identity and narratives of "self" and "other." As scholars of Indo-Islamic South Asia have pointed out, the intersections of religious, cultural, and political identities across several centuries were always in "transition."[34] Such confluences must be examined within particular and specific circumstances rather than through broad generalizations. This was certainly the case for Banaras and a modified picture of the city aids in understanding South Asian religious sites and their architecture beyond ideas of cultural exclusion or impermeability as well as those of "hybridity" or "syncretism." Instead, one can begin to think of these sites as evolving through the actions and expediencies of imaginative devotees, pilgrims, priests, and patrons.

This book can be placed in relation to three overlapping subfields within scholarship on South Asia. A large corpus of scholarly literature on South Asian culture and society (and more specifically on its religion and religious practices at pilgrimage centers) was produced within Orientalist frameworks. Philological studies of texts as well as cultural studies of ritual sites were conducted and concluded often without adequate attention to the political and cultural environments in which they were created. In the case of Banaras, themes of unchanging continuity and a sense of timelessness have been consistently reiterated through travel narratives and visual representations. Much of the scholarship produced on the city by Indologists in the twentieth century reflects this position.[35] Whereas general scholarly perspectives on this crutch of ahistorical "timelessness" have been challenged, a comprehensive historical study of Banaras has not been undertaken.[36] Authors such as Diana Eck and Jonathan Parry have been criticized for their approaches, yet their studies remain in academic and popular circulation as authentic and in-depth views of the city's religious landscape and funerary practices.[37]

Over the past two decades historians of Britain's South Asian empire have become interested in the interdependence of colonial interests and Indian social and mercantile networks. Among historians of South Asia, a growing number of studies were focused on the late eighteenth and nineteenth centuries and were deeply influenced by postcolonial and subaltern perspectives. Changes in the South Asian economic landscape as well as its society and culture throughout the colonial period were emphasized across several disciplines. Although these studies conclusively overturned narratives based in timelessness and exclusive social categorization, they also succeeded in overemphasizing the role of the colonial experience in shaping South Asian society. In keeping with such trends, scholarship on colonial urbanism in South Asia evolved from an initial focus on analyzing structures of colonial power through studies of built environments, to interest in the nuances inherent to the complex relationship between colonizer and colonized.[38]

This latter trend has resulted in the publication of several enlightening monographs on colonial urbanism in nineteenth-century South Asia that have redefined the terms of scholarship on colonial urbanism by moving away from analyses of the colonial city and its architecture as irreconcilably dichotomous.[39] Where Banaras is concerned, Sandria Freitag has examined political phenomenon such as conflict and protest as occurring within a "public arena" where political and social hierarchies and relationships could be articulated and defined.[40] In a similar vein, other scholars have addressed the city's recent colonial history as a major determinant in its contemporary forms and culture.[41] Predictably, perhaps, colonial Orientalists viewed temple architecture in South Asia as the direct product of religious, racial, and cultural categories that were understood as distinct and irreconcilable.[42] These perspectives have also been overturned in recent years with more attention being paid to the forging of shared cultures and built forms.[43] Although scholars have also paid attention to transformations within Hindu traditions, the overwhelming emphasis on general instances of syncretism remains, with inadequate attention to individual initiatives and possible tensions among religious and social groups.

More recently, connections to South Asia's deeper past, once relegated to the category of the "precolonial," have begun to receive scholarly attention. Much current scholarship is devoted to emphasizing the cosmopolitan environments of early modern South Asian elite cultures.[44] To an extent, this is a counter to both the legacies of Orientalism as well as the recent emphasis (perhaps overemphasis) on South Asia's colonial past.[45] Scholarship on early modern South Asia has taken a turn toward understanding the rich place of religion and literature in the city. Studies on Banaras have emphasized the role of Brahmin networks in reviving the city's religious life and highlighted the role of the Mughal state as a patron, with the focus being on shared cultural values. Usually less attention is paid to the tensions and anxieties that shape these relationships.[46]

This research owes and acknowledges a debt to the above-mentioned scholarship on South Asia. It is equally informed by the philological contributions of Orientalists and the perspectives of historians of the nineteenth century. Scholars of early modern South Asia and their critical engagement with textual sources have been inspiring models, as have studies on the integration of a "Perso-Turkic" imaginative and material ethos within South Asia's cultural landscape.[47] However, as a comprehensive overview and analysis of the configuration of sacred and urban spaces and their relationship to the textual histories and architectural forms of Banaras, this book breaks new ground. In a larger context, it forges connections between evolving religious ideas and their simultaneous and related expressions through texts, spatial practices, and architecture.

ORGANIZATION

By the turn of the twentieth century, the sacred landscape of Kashi was centered on the Vishweshwur temple and included numerous ritual sites around this central shrine that were linked together by pilgrimage routes. The most significant among these were the Antargriha *yatra* and the Panchkroshi *yatra*, and their sacred provenance was based respectively in two significant texts: the *Kashikhand* and the *Kashirahasya*. Scholars and pilgrims alike have consistently assumed that the spaces, deities, and ritual links described in these texts capture an image of a sacred urban landscape from a distant past. Contemporary visitors who approach the city either as academics or tourists continue to indulge in this illusion. This book presents an alternate reading of Banaras/Kashi. As religious practices and pilgrimage routes altered and multiplied over the centuries, texts and sites were transformed, as were their material expressions as architecture and urban space. Besides responding to change in religious practices, pilgrimage routes evolved in conjunction with trends in urbanization and spatial politics. Indeed, continued investment in architecture and urbanization was a way to lend contemporary relevance to a valued past. Given this relationship, each chapter in this book addresses a layer of engagement that has shaped the sacred zones and built environment of Banaras.

Chapter 1, "Authenticity and Pilgrimage," is a preamble to the chapters that follow. It is an overview of the evolving pilgrimage landscape between the twelfth and sixteenth centuries and draws attention to the role of the initial Islamic Ghurid incursions in disrupting and altering the city's sacred landscape. Many of the texts that were written after this event, including the comprehensive *Kashikhand,* were based in reassessments of sacred sites. Significantly, the pilgrimage routes that were a defining characteristic of the city's sacred landscape by the late nineteenth century became current only after the Ghurid invasion. During more established rule by successive Indo-Islamic sultanate regimes over the subsequent three centuries, these routes were codified within religious texts. In short, active sultanate engagement with Banaras ushered in a phase of evolution and consolidation for its ritual practices and sacred spaces.

Chapter 2, "Palimpsests and Authority," is an exploration of Mughal Banaras at the intersection of imperial policy and specific interest from Mughal grandees that influenced urban growth and architectural aesthetics. The city's ritual landscapes, and by extension its buildings and spaces, were shaped by the distinct policies pursued by each Mughal emperor. The often complex and shifting nature of Mughal interventions is examined through the concerns of the many prominent Brahmin scholars who received imperial support. Brahmin scholars were interested in consolidating and enhancing critical ritual sites and worked to garner Mughal support for their aims. They composed new texts in Sanskrit, liberally citing an older *purana* corpus, while placing their visions for the city within contemporary social and political networks. They synchronized such activities with prevalent trends in imperial policy and patronage. Despite the dramatic contrast in the policies pursued by the emperors Akbar and Aurangzeb, as a general trend the Mughals maintained political and cultural hegemony through policies of assimilation and accommodation. Architecture remained a powerful medium for expressing affiliations, alliances, and even degrees of distance from the imperial center. Mughal interventions were critical in shaping Banaras for succeeding centuries.

Chapter 3, "Expansion and Invention," is an exploration of the city in the eighteenth century, as Mughal power began to fade. The multiple power centers and emerging elites who gradually replaced the Mughals were a diverse group that included ambitious Maratha chiefs, aspiring Bengali aristocrats, and various comprador partners of the English East India Company. Despite their social and sectarian diversity, they arrived at a common consensus regarding the city's ritual landscape and its organization, including its principal shrines as well as the relevance of the Panchkroshi and Antargriha pilgrimage routes. The catalyst for such initiatives was a new generation of scholarship and activism by Brahmins intent on consolidating ritual traditions. Mughal architectural precedents became aspirational symbols alongside experiments in architectural revivalism as aristocrats oriented their efforts at self-fashioning through religious patronage. Besides investment in architecture, festivals and celebrations were avenues for elites to preside over a new socioreligious sphere, constituted through an intersection of politics, patronage, and public celebrations. The city's Mughal urban framework remained the foundation for a reconstructed city of archaic temple *shikharas* (towers) and robust pilgrimage practices.

Chapter 4, "Spectacle and Ritual," is a close look at the city's iconic riverfront as it developed during the eighteenth century. Consistently treated as a sacred space, its contemporary visual image owes much to the proliferation of the idea of the Mughal fortress-palace. Numerous such complexes based on this idea, colloquially called ghats, were overlaid on a Hindu ritual geography as patrons jostled for a place in the city's socioreligious sphere. Mughal baluster columns with lotus-bell capitals and foliated arches were employed as signifiers of elite taste and supported temple *shikharas*, the whole encased within towering sandstone fortress walls, lending the riverfront its distinctive character. The eventual decline of the socioreligious sphere by the turn of the nineteenth century made such investment less meaningful. Together, chapters 3 and 4 summarize shifts in religious practices and their physical manifestation as buildings and ritual spaces during the eighteenth century.

Chapter 5, "Order and Antiquity," is a revelation of the role played by colonial mediation and the emergence of a new civic sphere. As the East India Company gained control of South Asia, Banaras became subject to a modern discourse of spatial order, visual embellishment, and antiquarianism as desirable objectives. This interest extended to the city's sacred sites and significant pilgrimage routes. Orientalist endeavors at creating a positivist historical timeline for Banaras had consequences for its religious symbolism and its built environment. By the end of the nineteenth century, Hindu elites had selectively adopted colonial practices, and the city and its spaces were imagined through nascent ideas of a Hindu civic identity and perceived through an antiquarian lens. Nevertheless, given their intrusive and disruptive nature, colonial interventions engendered significant anxieties regarding the sacred landscape of Banaras. Brahmin priests combined colonial survey techniques with the cumulative legacy of textual knowledge on the city to imagine a Kashikshetra crowded with ritual sites and pilgrimage routes, each with irrefutable provenance.

Chapter 6, "Visions and Embellishments," returns to the riverfront and its representations. Artists and photographers often subtly, and occasionally blatantly, juxtaposed this recently created built environment and the city's textual traditions, using the former to substantiate narratives of antiquity. The discourses of urban order and antiquarianism extended to the riverfront, as did the city's association with a unified Hindu identity. Picturesque views, panoramas, and photographs reiterated its representations as an antique yet timeless built environment. The book traces a trajectory of individual agendas and actions that have shaped urban space and architecture over three centuries of the city's recent history. The association of Banaras with a unified and robust Hindu national culture is explained as the result of multiple revisions and fresh interpretations of underlying religious beliefs, narratives, and built form. The intricate connections between Hindu religious places and South Asia's complex and dynamic politics and culture become more transparent as this story unfolds.

CHAPTER ONE

AUTHENTICITY AND PILGRIMAGE

NOTIONS regarding static religious practices and associations in an unchanging city were certainly reiterated by scholars, residents, and visitors seduced by Orientalist perspectives. Yet the city's status as a preeminent *tirtha* (pilgrimage site) and center of Sanskrit scholarship lies beyond the confines and interpretations of this relatively recent intersection of colonial politics and knowledge. While the city's sacred role is closely connected to a deep textual history, the sheer volume and diversity of this literature speaks to a corresponding complexity of beliefs. To understand the city, sites and myths were consolidated through texts whose authors maintained a sharp focus on the religious landscape of the sacred zone of Kashikshetra. The fact that texts had to be continuously assessed, recompiled, and summarized suggests that their authors were concerned with altering notions of religion and sanctity as textual visions and sacred zones became intertwined, consistent with the ever-changing nature of all human societies.

Since at least the late eighteenth century, colonial archaeologists have consolidated a Buddhist identity for early Banaras. Vestiges of this past include the Dhamek stupa at Sarnath, the adjoining monastery, and various sculptural remains that date from as early as the second century of the Common Era. Stone sculpture and sculptural fragments from as early as the fifth century have also been discovered in the northern sections of the city. Some of these images, such as a fifth-century stone image of Krishna Govardhanadhara, are currently housed in the Bharat Kala Bhavan museum.[1] Other fragments of sculptures and miniature shrines have been incorporated within eighteenth-century temples and temple precincts. Taken together, these various findings certainly establish the city's antiquity. Yet substantial evidence for its role as a Shaiva Hindu sacred landscape, centered moreover on a significant temple, remains elusive.

In 1904 and 1905 the Royal Asiatic Society published (in two volumes) an English-language translation of the travel narratives of the Chinese Buddhist monk Yuan Chwang (Xuanzang/Hiouen Thsang) by one of its member-scholars, Thomas Watters. He concluded that Yuan Chwang left seventh-century China (during the Tang period) to travel to the "Western" lands and visited the "Varanasi district" that had a capital city of the same name.[2] The visiting Chinese monk described a city populated by some Buddhist scholars and several more who believed in "other systems." The four manuscripts (block-printed texts) consulted by Watters provide varying descriptions of the temples within the city.

They range from descriptions of a single large temple to twenty or more temples, to more than a hundred temples, variously located either within the city or the entire district. Their principal deity is represented as an enormous image in only one manuscript but more generally as a *linga*. Watters suspected that the passage describing an enormous image may actually have been a later interpolation within this text.[3]

While Yuan Chwang's account provides evidence for Varanasi being a center for Buddhists well as for Shaiva scholarship and religious practices, the precise nature of its sacred landscape at this time (and particularly its temples) remains uncertain. Scholars tend to use these mostly Buddhist material fragments to suggest that these vestiges can directly reflect and conform to the contours and significant nodes of contemporary ritual zones, pilgrimage routes, and sacred sites in Banaras. To project the notion of a consolidated and unified Hinduism onto the religious landscape of seventh-century or even twelfth-century Kashi would certainly constitute an anachronism since the religious beliefs, ritual practices, and their related spaces and locales would have to remain unchanged for centuries.[4]

The *puranas* (collection of myths) on Banaras or Kashi are often representations of negotiated pasts. Since the *Kashikhand* (first composed in the fourteenth century) was incorporated into the textual tradition of the *puranas*, it has been cast as a source of religious authority and ritual continuity within medieval and, to some extent, modern Hinduism. More significant, the *Kashikhand* is viewed as a summary of religious traditions within the *purana* tradition, rather than as an expression of the contemporary concerns of its authors.[5] The authors of the *Kashikhand* defined multiple pilgrimage routes and sacred zones, most of them centered on the preeminent Vishweshwur temple. If any discrepancies between the *Kashikhand* and older texts are ever noted, they are usually seen as a result of the repeated destruction of temples and shrines and consequently of the disruption of pilgrimage and ritual practices by successive Islamic regimes.[6] Certainly on the face of it, the physical proximity of temple and mosque at several sites in the contemporary city tends to substantiate such theories.

A contemporary visitor to the Vishweshwur temple cannot fail to notice the Mughal period Gyan Vapi mosque next door. Visitors also learn about the Adi-Vishweshwur temple, a little distance away, that stands next door to another mosque from the sultanate period, more commonly known as "Razia's mosque" (Fig. 1.1). Adi-Vishweshwur (the Ur-Vishweshwur), as its name suggests, is supposedly the original site of the Vishweshwur temple. They are informed that the Vishweshwur *linga* was uprooted and eventually relocated at least twice—the first time to the Gyan Vapi precinct and subsequently to its present location. Visitors cannot miss the Dharhara mosque on the riverfront that was built to replace the Bindu Madhav temple, and they learn of the Alamgiri mosque built on the foundations of the Krittivaseshwur temple. The presence of such visible signifiers of ritual disruption lends credence to the widespread conclusion that if it were not for these interruptions, the ritual landscape of the sacred zone of Kashikshetra would have remained constant and unchanged. Such assumptions, however, are not borne out by evidence either through texts or by the history of activism engaged in by their Brahmin authors. Texts and sacred zones were formed through a gradual and mutually contingent evolution. Furthermore, spatial formations were sustained through an urban environment

FIG. 1.1   "Razia's mosque."

that evolved through complex relationships between politics and patronage. If a first wave of Ghurid intervention in the twelfth century did indeed disrupt the city's ritual rhythms, a settled period of Indo-Islamic regimes also saw the emergence of elaborate sacred geographies and, more significant, robust new ritual traditions.

TEXTS AND THE SACRED LANDSCAPE

Sacred regions, sacred sites, pilgrimage routes, and their multiple interpretations intersected with the processes and experiences of urbanization in Banaras. Theories regarding perfectly shaped sacred zones and the religious significance of particular sites were articulated through texts that were composed by successive generations of Brahmins. The lived experience of pilgrimage, however, was molded by the physical reality of the city of Banaras, where urban interventions could often alter sacred configurations as the city was continually and often quite prosaically transformed. An overview of the *purana* textual corpus that is dated between the sixth and twelfth centuries suggests that eventually a number of sacred sites connected to diverse streams within an evolving Hinduism converged to form the basis of a sacred region.[7]

Some shared ideas that came to anchor notions of sanctity for the city include the *tirtha* (pilgrimage destination) and the *tirtha yatra* (pilgrimage). The *tirtha* is a sacred site that affords the pilgrim an opportunity to glimpse, indeed to "cross over" and make tangible contact with, the divine. The *tirtha yatra* can be a pilgrimage to one or several *tirthas*. These concepts are intimately linked to definitions of sacred regions and routes. An idea that was repeatedly addressed and defined was that of the entire city and its immediate environs as the sacred region of Kashikshetra.[8] This idea was closely aligned with another concept: that of the Muktikshetra. Textual and popular traditions (these latter constitute a range of everyday practices related to but also distinguishable from prescriptions in texts) maintain that living and ultimately dying within the Muktikshetra would result in salvation from the endless cycle of reincarnation and rebirth. This Muktikshetra was variously imagined either as a perfect circle or square with a Shivalinga at its center and with well-defined edges. While the concept of such a zone has remained consistent, definitions of its overall shape, boundaries, and center have altered over the centuries. Among these, the Vishweshwur temple evolved as a central anchor for multiple sacred zones since at least the fourteenth century.

Shiva's connection with the city was and is a theme in several *purana* texts. Shiva is a supreme deity, one of the Hindu "trinity" (along with Brahma and Vishnu), and his connection to the Ganges River is crystallized through a myth in which he tames the ferocious, heavenly, and life-sustaining river by binding her in his hair locks before letting her flow gently on earth.[9] At Banaras, Shiva is celebrated both as an ascetic and in his *grihastha* (householder) aspect, and the city is a home for the deity and his consort Parvati. Shiva's simultaneous ascetic identity is also celebrated by the various Shaiva *muths* (monasteries) and mendicant sects connected to the city. The most extensive myths related to Shiva as Vishweshwur (Lord of the Universe) and his connection with the city were certainly elaborated in the *Kashikhand* that became part of the *purana* tradition when it was added to the sixth century *Skandapurana*.[10] This text came to play a hegemonic role in the city's ritual life by the late eighteenth century. In addition, the authors of the *Kashirahasya*, which was added to another text, the *Brahmavaivartapurana*, prescribed the Panchkroshi pilgrimage—a route that was also focused on the Vishweshwur *linga*.[11] Patronage in the city between the late sixteenth and late eighteenth centuries has been directed towards constructing two successive temples to house this *linga*. In popular perception the contours of the Panchkroshi route merged with the idea of the sacred zone of Kashikshetra.

Kashikshetra and the city of Kashi or Banaras are, at least conceptually, imagined as distinct but intimately entangled entities. Given the belief that residence within the sacred zone is a means to accruing religious merit, the urban zone of Banaras has remained confined within the limits of Kashikshetra for much of its history. In both perception and practice the zone is bound by the Panchkroshi pilgrimage, and pilgrims followed this irregular route in an act of circumambulation around the sacred zone. The banks of the Ganges between its two feeder streams—the Varuna to the north and the Assi to the south—provide the other sacred edges. The confluence of each stream with the river was deemed significant, as were numerous sites along this stretch.

The extensive literature on Kashikshetra that defined the sanctity of sites through myths and divine associations was incorporated into the *puranas* through contingent, historical circumstances. Distinct versions of a *purana* text can vary in length and content, as material was often added or removed in response to changing political and cultural conditions. Given their following across South Asia, as well as their interactions with various local and vernacular practices and traditions, different recensions of the same *purana* could differ in terms of length and content.[12] To remain meaningful, *purana* texts had to be contextualized by Brahmin scholars who were intent on finding contemporary relevance for established practices. Considering the diversity, voluminous nature, and sheer numbers of *purana* texts, Brahmin scholars concentrated on specific sites and sacred zones that they considered immediately relevant to their circumstances. Individual Brahmin scholars could differ in terms of the weight and relevance that they granted to a particular deity or sacred site. They debated the relative merits of sites as well as religious traditions and practices. Several scholars summarized personal opinions in a type of text called a *nibandha* that although concise was composed with due regard to textual citation.

From a historian's perspective, *nibandha* texts provide glimpses into historical debates regarding religious practices and sites. By extension, they provide valuable clues about the trajectories of developing sacred zones and their urbanization. More recently, particularly since the late nineteenth century, Brahmin scholars began to write guidebooks in vernacular languages, providing visiting pilgrims with selective information about sites drawn from *purana* texts along with their locations within the contemporary city accompanied by precise and current directions and addresses. It is noteworthy that scholars continued to refer to the *puranas* as repositories of religious authority and tradition and cited them within the bodies of their *nibandha* with the intention of authenticating current concerns.

Such variation in opinion extended to definitions of the Muktikshetra or Kashikshetra sacred zones. These had already been on shifting ground, at least since the twelfth century, as Bhatta Lakshmidhara, the Gahadavala minister and scholar, revealed in his twelfth-century text, the *Krtyakalpataru*.[13] Lakshmidhara consolidated diverse traditions that were associated with twelfth-century Kashi and tried to define its sacred limits. Hans Bakker has evaluated some of Lakshmidhara's interpretations and summaries.[14] According to Bakker's general analysis, the region of Kashikshetra in the *Skandapurana* was defined as extending one *krosa* (unit of measurement roughly equivalent to a mile and a half) in each direction with its center in the shrine of Madhyameshwur. The authors of the *Matsyapurana* defined it as extending half a *yojana* (or two *krosa*) across, whereas authors of the *Brahmapurana* defined it as five *krosas* across (suggesting a circumference). The authors of the *Lingapurana* defined it as one *krosa* in each direction from the shrine of Madhyameswur, and this last definition actually suggested a circle with a circumference that is longer than five *krosas*.[15] As Bakker concludes, Lakshmidhara did not indicate any definite preference for any single definition of the sacred zone over all the others. He may instead have been making a case for the concept of a sacred zone rather than trying to fix its shape or dimensions.

If the edges and contours of an imagined sacred region were the subject of multiple interpretations, it follows that the religious mythology and significance associated with various *linga*, shrines, and sacred sites in Banaras has also changed over the centuries. A tradition that is generally considered fixed and unchanging had in fact passed through multiple interpretations and inventions. It is pertinent to note that although Lakshmidhara was preoccupied with the idea of the *tirtha*, he did not mention the *Kashikhand*, nor was he overly concerned with the Vishweshwur tradition. More significant, he made no mention of prescribed pilgrimage routes within and around the city. It is clear that Lakshmidhara's Kashi was a place fairly different from the one many contemporary pilgrims know and recognize.

TEXTS AND THE PILGRIMAGE ROUTE

Lakshmidhara's *Krtyakalpataru* is a significant *nibandha*, since it provides a basis for any initial assessment of the pre-Islamic ritual landscape of Kashikshetra. The need for such an interpretive text originally arose in the context of enhanced support for Brahminical ideologies and practices in the eleventh and twelfth centuries that occurred under Gahadavala patronage.[16] The Gahadavala ruler Govindchandra had moved his capital to Kashi at this time of political and cultural consolidation, and the sacred city was central to this initiative. Andrew Nicholson has discussed various initiatives undertaken at this time, to unify streams of religious and philosophical thought that came to be known as Hinduism.[17] In light of these developments, it is probable that Lakshmidhara's intended audience were the Brahmin scholars of his day who were faced with making choices between competing traditions and practices, some of which were encapsulated within multiple *purana* texts. They had to acknowledge popular beliefs and evaluate them in relation to formal textual traditions and practices. Indeed, some members of the Gahadavala royal family remained active supporters of Buddhist beliefs and practices.

Whereas the *Krtyakalpataru* underscored a Brahminical resurgence under the Gahadavala rulers, the *Kashikhand* was composed in a political context where rule by Indo-Islamic Tughlaq and Sharqi sultans was conducive to the growth and proliferation of pilgrimage in Banaras (Fig. 1.2).[18] Architectural and urban interventions in Banaras included mosques and tombs erected in the northern areas of Kashikshetra, including the Arhai Kangura mosque and the Rajghat mosque that may have been erected for a garrison stationed to the north of the city.[19] The pilgrimage zones of the city, particularly the inner Antargriha zone, developed to the south of the sultanate center. It is equally significant that the authors of the *Kashikhand* placed particular emphasis on pilgrimage routes and their related rituals, thereby underlining a shift in the physical configuration as well as everyday practices that asserted sanctity.[20]

In short, a comparison between the *Krtyakalpataru* and the *Kashikhand* reveals that besides a physical shift in the sacred landscape, practices had also altered within the intervening two centuries, resulting in a concentration of sacred sites around the Vishweshwur *linga*. Given that the authors of the *Kashikhand* referred to a number of sites that were not mentioned by Lakshmidhara, it is possible that this shift may have been as much the result of changing practices as the result of a deliberate disruption or invasion.[21] As Aiyangar has pointed out, the conventions of pilgrimage held that all "resident divinities" at a *tirtha* must be visited, which consequently meant that newer (often popular) practices could be incorporated within older traditions and pilgrimage routes.[22] This meant that pilgrimage practices and texts were periodically realigned.

FIG. 1.2   *Lal Shah's Tomb and Ghazimeea Ke Durgah, near Benares*, 1831–1833, by James
Prinsep. British Library Board.

The practice of pilgrimage routes itself indicates an aspect of religious consolidation. Many of the divinities that are mentioned in the *Kashikhand* (or for that matter, the
Krtyakalpataru) can be related to diverse streams and traditions within Hinduism. There
may be a twofold reason for the proliferation of pilgrimage routes in an Indo-Islamic context. On the one hand, by visiting deities from different arenas of religious practice within
a single route, pilgrims and priests could participate in the idea of unification while also
acknowledging the distinct role of each deity. In addition, Indo-Islamic rulers could more
easily be persuaded to patronize pilgrimage routes than to support the construction of a
grand temple. In his discussion on the political role of temples, Richard Eaton has drawn
a connection between the authority of a ruler and the temple within the Hindu tradition. As Eaton has discussed, a similar relationship between an Islamic ruler and a place
of worship would not ever be considered viable in either theological or political terms.[23]
Pilgrimage routes lacked a direct association with the person of a ruler and could be more
easily supported by observant, but inclusive-minded Indo-Islamic rulers. It is significant,

therefore, that the authors of the *Kashikhand* emphasize the essence of deities rather than engage in descriptions of temples or shrines. Yet the role of the temple has been central to its identity as a pilgrimage destination, as have narratives of repeated temple destruction and reconstruction.

A QUESTION OF TEMPLE DESTRUCTION

The shifting sites of temples and mosques in Banaras have usually been explained through simplistic narratives of Islamic invasions that resulted in inflexible animosities between Hindus and Muslims in the city and indeed in the entire subcontinent. Indo-Islamic rule in northern India elicited a number of responses in terms of religious practices and their spatial and architectural expression. This is largely a history of adaptation and transformation, accompanied by a few memorable instances of the actual destruction or desecration of religious sites, particularly temples. Lakshmidhara's text, the *Krtyakalpataru*, can be productively assessed against narratives of temple destruction and images of an ancient city of temples. Lakshmidhara referred to numerous *lingas* rather than temples, and the only *linga* that he described as being housed in a large building or *mahalaya* was Kedareshwur.[24] He mentioned "Vishweshwur" as one among several other *lingas*.[25]

Many of the major sites that were significant to the authors of the fourteenth-century *Kashikhand*, such as Lolark, were not mentioned by Lakshmidhara.[26] He placed the center of Kashikshetra at Madhyameshwur to the north of the contemporary location of the Vishweshwur temple. Both Kubernath Sukul and Diana Eck have suggested that the authors of the *Kashikhand* may have been describing a ritual landscape that was actually much older and that in ignoring many of its elements, Lakshmidhara was deliberately being selective, emphasizing traditions that he considered significant.[27] However, the ritual landscape of the *Kashikhand* could not have entirely existed in Lakshmidhara's Kashi since he would have described some salient features of this landscape in his own writings.

If they are correlated with contemporary sites with similar names, Lakshmidhara's sites were scattered all across Kashikshetra and all along the riverbank. Specific pilgrimages routes were neither emphasized nor described. The role of temples in this ritual scene is unclear and may have been marginal. Since the focus on the Vishweshwur shrine was a later development, the assumption that the invading Ghurids may have destroyed a temple in the city that housed the Vishweshwur *linga* is another likely anachronism. While it is a fact that the Gahadavalas were contemporaries of the great temple-building dynasties of South Asia such as the Cholas in the south (Thanjavur) or the Gangas in the east (Bhuvaneshwur) or even their neighbors, the Chandelas (Khajuraho), their role as patrons of monumental temple architecture was relatively insignificant.[28]

Temples were relatively small in scale if they existed at all, as suggested by some authors of secular Sanskrit literature, such as the Gahadavala-period *Uktivyaktiprakarana*.[29] For its author, Pandit Damodar, it was the urban environment of Kashikshetra that remained relevant, and he described a city of Brahmin scholars, their students, and merchants. Damodar referred to a shrine (*deul*) built through the support of a merchant named Dhanapal and urged his royal patron to build a substantial temple (*prasada*) in

Banaras. This suggests that although the building of a major temple was being discussed, it may not have existed at the time that this text was composed.[30] Damodar does mention religious activity and the worship of deities (*devapuja*) as well as a "Kedarasya *mutha*" as an educational institution.[31] Hence, while it is fairly possible that the Ghurids attacked the city and disrupted its ritual rhythms, it is equally possible that in this period the city may not have actually had a principal temple for them to destroy. In light of these contingencies, the existence of a role (to say nothing of architectural form) for a Vishweshwur temple before the twelfth century is questionable. Although the spaces or *mandapas* and the finial of a Vishweshwur temple are mentioned in the fourteenth-century *Kashikhand*, these details refer to a period after the Ghurid incursions. Furthermore, a direct correspondence between apocryphal descriptions of ritual spaces and the material architecture of a temple is fairly intangible.

Although an inscription mentioning the building of a Padmeshwur temple in 1296 survives as spolia in the Sharqi Lal Darwaza mosque (built in 1449) at Jaunpur, a direct account or incident related to the destruction of a Vishweshwur temple does not exist.[32] Indeed, there is no explicit record of any Vishweshwur temple being destroyed before the seventeenth century. However, most recent accounts of the city include a litany of repeated destruction. The presence of the Adi-Vishweshwur temple built ca. 1700 at the initiative of Sawai Jai Singh II of Amber and Jaipur certainly suggests that a prior location for the Vishweshwur *linga* may have existed in collective memory at least at the turn of the eighteenth century when this building was constructed. Sawai Jai Singh's act in regenerating this "ur" tradition also instigates speculation about a shrine that may have housed a Vishweshwur *linga* between the twelfth and fourteenth centuries. The presence of the sultanate period "Razia's mosque" at a location adjacent to Sawai Jai Singh's Adi-Vishweshwur temple is usually cited as evidence for the destruction of a Vishweshwur temple that once likely occupied its site. The mosque is commonly associated with Sultana Raziyyat (r. 1236–1239) of the Delhi sultanate.[33] Given the late emergence of the Vishweshwur tradition, these dates are too early to coincide with the presence of a Vishweshwur temple prominent enough to attract the attention of the nascent sultanate in Delhi, despite its territorial expansion across the Gangetic plains and conquest of Banaras under Razia's father, Sultan Iltutmish (r. 1210–1236).

Narratives of early Ghaznavid and Ghurid iconoclasm, however, survived into subsequent centuries, and the sixteenth-century Mughal chronicler Abul Fazl described a principal temple at Banaras and credited Mahmud of Ghazni with disrupting the "old faith." Yet he did not explicitly describe him or any successive Indo-Islamic ruler as the destroyer of this temple.[34] The role of the Vishweshwur *linga* as the preeminent *linga* of the city was debated well into the mid-fifteenth century.[35] Taken together, these cumulative uncertainties regarding a clear history for a Vishweshwur temple before the sixteenth century suggest that the Adi-Vishweshwur temple may have been an anachronistic creation. Indeed, the term "Adi-Vishweshwur" has been in use only since the turn of the eighteenth century. Neither the sixteenth-century scholar Narayan Bhatt nor any of his contemporaries or successors mentioned any such *linga* or temple. And yet its location at a site adjacent to a mosque in the heart of the city underlines tensions and collective memories or at least perceptions of temple desecration and ritual disruption.

Detailed studies of the evolution of pilgrimage routes can reveal the nature of the transformation of religious ideas as well as notions of sacred space. The two pilgrimage routes discussed in this book are each a collection of diverse deities located around the Vishweshwur *linga*. The practice of pilgrimage and pilgrimage routes has remained on shifting ground through its history. By the late nineteenth century, the Panchkroshi route started at the Manikarnika ghat, went on to the Vishweshwur shrine, and pilgrims proceeded along the banks of the Ganges until its confluence with the Assi River. Pilgrims would then circle the city in a clockwise fashion, eventually visiting 108 *tirthas*, with designated overnight stops on the way, at Kardameshwur (Kandwa), Bhimchandi, Rameshwur, Kapildhara, and Sheopur, ending again at the Vishweshwur temple.[36] The evolution of this route is the result of a complex interplay between text, practice, cartography, and patronage. The pilgrimage was initialized sometime during the late sultanate period and was first incorporated within a vernacular religious text, the fifteenth-century *Gurucharitra*, as a practice associated with the pilgrimage center of Kashi. As mentioned earlier, the route was formalized in the *Kashirahasya,* and this text was incorporated within the *Brahmavaivarta purana* by the sixteenth century.[37] However, its wide acceptance in this period is doubtful since neither the sixteenth-century scholar Narayan Bhatt nor any of his prominent Brahmin contemporaries especially emphasized the practice in their *nibandha* texts.

The inclusion of this pilgrimage tradition within the *Gurucharitra* suggests that it was a relevant practice for pilgrims from the Deccan regions of South Asia. Composed in the larger political and social context of a Deccan ruled by Indo-Islamic regimes, the authors of the *Gurucharitra* established a series of negotiated equations between a lay Hindu population, spiritual leaders, and sultanate regimes.[38] Within the narrative space of this text, political authority almost always resided with a Muslim ruler or governor, "a Nawab." Therefore, a "good Nawab" was sympathetic to his Hindu subjects and often supported the Brahmin priestly class and facilitated Hindu ritual practices. The outer extent of the route was consistently determined by a Dehli Vinayaka shrine—the name itself suggests an orientation toward a new center of power, Delhi, the capital of sultanate northern India.

The authors of the *Gurucharitra* accepted reconciliations between various Shaiva and Vaishnava traditions associated with the city.[39] Although they recommended the Panchkroshi pilgrimage and mentioned some of its sites that were located within the city, they were less specific about sites along the section of the route that circumscribed the urban area. They also did not provide any details about the route itself. This exchange between a vernacular tradition and its incorporation within a formal Sanskrit corpus suggests the prevalence of an ongoing conversation between popular practices and their canonization within a *purana*. Philologists have noticed several variations in the enumeration of actual deities among authors of different manuscripts of the *Kashirahasya* as well.[40] This interplay between texts, popular ritual practices, and spatial boundaries was to continue well into the nineteenth century and had an active role in shaping the built environment of Banaras.

Further, the authors of the *Kashirahasya* describe deities along the route, without any clear reference to the shrines or temples that may have housed them. The only structure along the route that can be dated to the fifteenth century is the Kardameshwur temple, currently in Kandwa village.[41] It is also the oldest extant structure on the Panchkroshi. As is explained further in chapter 3, this temple was refurbished in the mid-eighteenth century, and its relative significance during the sixteenth century remains unclear. It would therefore be reasonable to conclude that the Panchkroshi route, as described within the *Kashirahasya*, had selective appeal among patrons, priests, and pilgrims. The authors of the *Kashikhand* delineated several pilgrimages around the Vishweshwur *linga*, and the evolution of a critical route, the Antargriha *yatra*, is equally significant.

ENDURING ROUTES: THE ANTARGRIHA PILGRIMAGE

The Antargriha *yatra* remains one of the most significant pilgrimages around the Vishweshwur *linga*. The term "Antargriha" is a reference to the "inner sanctum" of the city surrounding the immediate vicinity of this *linga*. Consequently, pilgrims are expected to visit and concentrate on a sequence of deities established within the city's religious and commercial center. As other pilgrimages in Kashi, it has evolved over the centuries and had developed into a spiral string of approximately seventy-six shrines and ritual bathing sites situated around the Vishweshwur temple by the late nineteenth century.[42] The route was first mentioned by the authors of the *Kashikhand*, and they paid a lot of attention to an area of the sacred zone of Kashikshetra that is more or less congruent with the urban zone of the contemporary city, commonly known as the *pucca maholl*. It was and continues to be an area that largely coincided with the vicinity of the Vishweshwur temple, and the route effectively demarcated an Antargriha zone.

Although some of the sites along this route were mentioned by Lakshmidhara, as with the Vishweshwur tradition, the complete route either did not exist or remained relatively insignificant for him. Before there was a complete route, however, there were individual sites. As discussed earlier, much of the area contained within the limits of the Antargriha *yatra* emerged as a prominent sacred zone between the twelfth and fourteenth centuries—that is, after the composition of the *Krtyakalpataru*. It is possible, therefore, that Lakshmidhara may have ignored certain ritual practices in the city, including ones connected with Vishweshwur, as he emphasized and highlighted the ones that he considered significant. The authors of the fourteenth-century *Kashikhand*, however, could no longer ignore this zone of popular ritual or the religious practices that were established here in the intervening two centuries.

A relatively recent instance of such an exchange between formal texts and popular practice is apparent in relation to the shrine of Annapurna, located in the immediate vicinity of the Vishweshwur *linga* and its temple. Annapurna is not mentioned by the authors of the *Kashikhand*, yet the authors of the *Gurucharitra* encouraged readers to pay homage at her shrine.[43] However, for the fifteenth-century compilers of this text, the Antargriha route and the Annapurna shrine remained separate entities. While they recommended that pilgrims undertake the Antargriha pilgrimage, they also specified specific and separate occasions for paying homage to the goddess Annapurna. Over the next three centuries Annapurna was incorporated into the Antargriha pilgrimage, and the authors of several nineteenth-century guidebooks included a visit to this shrine in their lists of pilgrimage destinations along the route. In a pattern similar to that of the Panchkroshi route, the Antargriha *yatra* evolved through a dialogue between practice, patronage, and texts. In sum, powerful traditions remained the focus of popular practice and active patronage well into the nineteenth century.

SACRED FOUNDATIONS

A close evaluation of texts on Kashi composed in the centuries before Indo-Islamic rule was established in northern India revealed that the sacred landscape of Kashi was vastly different from the one described by the authors of the fourteenth-century *Kashikhand*. Several scholars have noted this change and have also concluded that this occurred solely as a result of conquest and disruption. They assumed that in an attempt to rebuild this sacred city, priests concentrated on re-creating a Kashi that was a close approximation of the one that had been destroyed. Such conclusions, however, are based in anachronisms and are built on the premise that Hindu practices remained static for several centuries. They are also predicated on an idea of sustained hostilities between various sultanate regimes and adherents of a monolithic set of "Hindu" practices.

Contrary to such ideas, many of the pilgrimage traditions of Kashi emerged and flourished in the Indo-Islamic context of sultanate regimes in northern India. Their nature was often determined by efforts at consolidating diverse religious streams that laid the foundations of later Hindu practices. Vishweshwur, previously one of numerous Shaiva sites, emerged as a prominent *linga* and pilgrimage destination sometime between the twelfth and fourteenth centuries. A detailed social and political context that could explain the rise in the popularity of this *linga* and its associated pilgrimage practices is not clearly discernible through texts. However, its insignificant status in Lakshmidhara's *Krtyakalpataru* was certainly altered through popular practice. Vishweshwur's role was incorporated within the city's textual traditions by the authors of the fourteenth-century *Kashikhand*, as were many of the pilgrimage traditions associated with this *linga*. This text gradually became the basis for definition of the city's sanctity well into subsequent centuries, including the twenty-first.

The continued evolution and transformation of this sacred landscape is equally evident in the centuries following the composition of the *Kashikhand*. Although this text was ensconced within the *purana* tradition, the role of Vishweshwur and its pilgrimage routes as significant elements in Kashi's pilgrimage practices was neither firm, solitary, nor prominent for many centuries after its composition. It was only through a confluence of Brahminical scholarly activism and state support and patronage during a century of Mughal rule that Vishweshwur's role as the principal *linga* of Kashi was established. The crystallization of its position at the heart of the city's religious life meant that the pilgrimage practices prescribed by the authors of the *Kashikhand* had gained wider acceptance.

As the myths, rituals, and routes encouraged by its authors became more widely accepted, their material presence was equally reflected in the city's built environment. Temples, bathing tanks, and riverfront embankments (known as ghats) were created by several patrons between the late sixteenth and early twentieth centuries and represented the sites and deities discussed primarily in the *Kashikhand* and the *Kashirahasya*. Alongside the promotion of the *purana* tradition encompassed within these texts, popular and sectarian traditions were reflected in the city's built environment. Patronage for temples, monasteries, and other built elements was connected to contemporary cultural conditions. Consequently, the built environment of the city's sacred zones altered along with urbanization and politics. Visiting pilgrims always experienced Kashi simultaneously as pilgrimage landscape as well as contemporary city.

PALIMPSESTS AND AUTHORITY

BANARASIDAS, the Hindu merchant-protagonist of a sixteenth-century autobiography, the *Ardhakathanak (A Half Story)*, traveled between Delhi, Agra, Allahabad, Banaras, Ayodhya, Jaunpur, and Patna. As he detailed in this narrative, Banarasidas visited several urban religious centers that were sustained through Mughal commercial networks and administrative mechanisms.[1] Imperial and regional politics equally impacted trade and pilgrimage. Such accounts as the *Ardhakathanak* provide a glimpse into the complex relationship between regenerated sites of Hindu pilgrimage and Mughal urbanism. In recent years several historians have underlined the nature of Mughal cosmopolitanism as it played out at the imperial court as well as in various regional centers. Many of these studies have elucidated the religious and artistic negotiations undertaken by various participants as they became part of an imperial structure and cosmopolitan court culture. Such efforts have undoubtedly ushered in a more nuanced understanding of the empire, extending beyond simplistic characterizations of the Mughals as a Central Asian, Islamic dynasty that largely remained distant from the religious and cultural traditions of their South Asian Hindu subjects.

The Mughals traced their familial origins to Central Asia. Ethnically Turkic, they began incursions into northern India under Babur, the first ruler and acknowledged founder of the dynasty. Both Babur and his son Humayun held fleeting control of northern India. Emperor Akbar, the third Mughal ruler, can be credited with the effective conquest of Hindustan through a combination of military success, diplomacy, and marital alliances. Although the Mughals had an affinity for the Persian language and Persian culture that they adopted at their court, Akbar's policies were flexible enough to accommodate the cultural and religious diversity of his empire in South Asia. Simultaneously, the Hindu and Muslim South Asians who became part of the Mughal structure adopted aspects of an international Persian cosmopolitanism. Beginning in the mid-sixteenth century, Akbar incorporated courtiers and officials from varied religious and linguistic backgrounds into his administration. He encouraged and supported expressions of ethnic and religious identities in the cause of imperial expansion and its continued sustainability.[2]

Akbar also remained intellectually curious about diverse religious beliefs, an interest that developed into a personal belief system that he practiced and perpetuated among an intimate circle of family members and courtiers. Beyond Akbar's personal inclinations,

Mughal patronage for cultural, religious, and linguistic traditions was aimed at strengthening the empire through a policy of inclusion.[3] For instance, direct patronage for Sanskrit learning and textual production as well as support for various vernacular traditions enhanced the Mughal state's profile among its various constituents and communities.[4] At least three generations of Mughal emperors played an active role in sustaining, reviving, and enhancing scholarly activity.[5] Beyond the inclinations of individual emperors, Mughal imperial policy was formed through interactions between a number of other actors and agents. These included prominent religious figures, both Hindu and Muslim, besides Central Asian, Persian, Indian Muslim, and Hindu Rajput courtiers and grandees with a variety of religious beliefs, tastes, and inclinations. Seen against this context, Banaras was a potent site where Mughal interests could be successfully aligned with regenerated yet relevant religious traditions.

The Mughal legacy of contemporary Banaras is prominently visible in its built environment and also through its visual representations. Beginning in the late sixteenth century, several significant buildings and urban spaces were created through the patronage of Hindu Mughal *mansabdars* (or grandees) who had been incorporated into the Mughal imperial system. These patrons and builders had clear affinities for Mughal architectural fashions, particularly imperial trends and the temples, monasteries, and mansions that they built or supported, resulted in modifying the ritual landscape of Kashi. In the late sixteenth century, Mughal attention was focused on constructing two major temples, the first dedicated to the Shaiva Vishweshwur *linga* and the second to a Vaishnava deity, Bindu Madhav. Contemporary accounts suggest that when completed, each temple was equally substantial in size and significance.[6]

Such accounts also suggest that the two temples were celebrated destinations in the city, on the itineraries of pilgrims as well as lay visitors from within and beyond the empire. Simultaneous and equivalent support for a Vaishnava temple alongside a Shaiva shrine suggests an effort at consolidating diverse beliefs and practices. At the very least, it indicated the beginnings of a conversation across sectarian divisions that could be mediated through the city's sacred landscape. Such consolidation was critical to forging shared identities and was encouraged through a state-sponsored built environment. The consolidation between its Shaiva identity and various Vaishnava traditions that were bolstered and highlighted in Kashi was achieved through investment in architecture and urbanism initiated by prominent patrons. In the political sphere an initial phase of consolidation was followed by a withdrawal of Mughal support in the late seventeenth century, and major temples that had enjoyed Mughal support were dismantled. Patrons who initiated projects to either rebuild temples or establish new religious institutions adjusted to this shift in imperial policy. The entwined character of Mughal politics and the built environment is evident in the varied architecture of the city over a century of shifting imperial policies and tastes.

VISHWESHWUR

The Mughal state regenerated and reshaped Banaras for more than a century, and much of this effort was centered on the Vishweshwur tradition. Many of the dominant features of the contemporary city, including the central role of this temple as well as the noteworthy significance of the Manikarnika, Dashashwamedha, and Panchganga ghats, were further consolidated during the Mughal period. Their place and roles within the city's ritual landscape were enhanced through textual, spatial, and architectural interventions. The Mughal role in Hindu religious life was mediated by prominent Brahmin scholars. Brahmins from the Maratha regions had forged connections with Kashi in the sixteenth century, and major advocates for its Vishweshwur tradition included the scholar Narayan Bhatt, a leading member of this community. He was at the core of a Brahmin circle that promoted a vision centered on a monumental Vishweshwur temple (Fig. 2.1).[7] Several of its members were participants in an intellectual sphere that had a subcontinental reach through a network of scholarly connections and familial lineages.[8] Through their

FIG. 2.1

Temple of Vishveshvur, Benares, 1831–1833, by James Prinsep. British Library Board.

engagement with diverse textual and philosophical traditions, they played a critical role in the city's intellectual life and generated novel and innovative philosophies in a fertile environment of religious and scholarly exchange.[9] Their approaches and investigations influenced their interpretations of the sacred landscape of Kashi. Mughal officials and grandees encouraged and supported the city's religious establishment through this circle.

Not unexpectedly, Bhatt and other scholars each maintained slightly differing visions of the city. In spatial terms this meant that each scholar emphasized a slightly different group of sacred sites and deities that he drew and reinterpreted from an eclectic mix of *purana* texts.[10] Moreover, each scholar often had a slightly different interpretation of the sacred landscape of Kashi and its provenance as based in the *puranas*. Bhatt remained the most influential of this group as is clear from his activist role in reinforcing the Vishweshwur tradition. As scholars between the fifteenth and seventeenth centuries distilled *purana* texts, their efforts were concentrated on summarizing a vast, inherited corpus of scholarship on sacred sites.[11]

In this stimulating intellectual environment, each scholar wrote his own *nibandha* on the ritual traditions of Kashi. Of the large numbers of *nibandha* texts produced, the more prominent ones include the *Tirthachintamani* (1460) by Vacaspati Misra, the *Tirthaprakasha* (of the *Viramitrodaya*, 1620) by Mitra Misra, the *Tristhalisetusarsangraha* (also known as the *Tristhalisetu)* by Bhattoji Dikshit (1620), and the *Tristhalisetu* (1560) by Narayan Bhatt. Each author addressed the contents of the *puranas*, reconciling older practices and traditions with more recent realities. The debate about the location, significance, and provenance of the *linga* of Vishweshwur was an example of such ongoing concerns. Bhatt, for instance, promoted Vishweshwur and Manikarnika whereas Bhattoji Dikshit made a case for Dashashwamedha.[12] The *Kashikhand*, which was to essentially become a hegemonic rulebook on the city by the late eighteenth century, was just one among several texts for Bhatt, Dikshit, and other scholars. Its relatively minor role in the late sixteenth century is also evident since it is absent from such seventeenth-century texts as the *Girvanpadamanjari* and the *Girvanvangmanjari*. Both *Girvan* texts contain descriptions of the city's topography, ritual landscape, secular spaces, and landmarks, but their authors made no particular mention of the Vishweshwur temple or its related pilgrimage traditions.

Mughal support, however, extended to the city's traditional connection with Shaivism through the Vishweshwur tradition as well as to an emergent and transformed Vaishnava tradition. Such inclusiveness was always selective and imperial policies carefully altered the place and nature of various religious sects and practices. The Brahmin scholars of Banaras were not impervious to such changes and several of them inculcated new perspectives on Kashi. More specifically, Bhatt and his contemporaries were significantly influenced by the Mughal affinity for Vaishnava patronage. This orientation directly inflected Brahminical discourse and debate. Besides an assertion of support for the Vishweshwur tradition, the consolidation of Shaiva and Vaishnava ritual and pilgrimage practices (at least those connected to the city) remained a motive for Bhatt and his contemporaries. His *nibandha*, the *Tristhalisetu*, remains a critical source for gaining an understanding of Mughal interventions. As a compilation of selected sacred sites and their related myths sourced from multiple texts, the *Tristhalisetu* can be read as an effective blueprint for the ritual landscape of late sixteenth-century Kashi. It is also a spatial text and in it Bhatt expressed a vision that although embedded in the *purana* tradition was equally relevant for contemporary networks of patronage and imperial support. Moreover, many of these sites could be adjusted within a syncretic Shaiva-Vaishnava vision for the city.

As its textual traditions were evaluated afresh, Kashi's Shaiva antecedents underwent a shift. This was particularly the case when the provenance of the principal *linga* was in question. Ideas about the sanctity and the *swayambhu* (self-generating) nature of a *linga* were closely connected, since a "natural" *linga* was always considered more sacred than one that was man-made. At this time, many scholars relied on the twelfth-century *Krtyakalpataru* and for them the principal *linga* of Kashi was the *swayambhu* Avimukteshwur *linga*.[13] Vishweshwur had always been a relatively insignificant *linga* in this text.[14] As mentioned earlier, since this *linga* had become prominent in the intervening centuries, its evolving pilgrimage traditions were incorporated first in the *Kashikhand* and subsequently in the *Kashirahasya*. Brahmin scholars of the fifteenth and sixteenth centuries evaluated a number of texts and attempted to resolve ambiguities to focus attention on a single and dominant Shivalinga.

Vacaspati Misra, for instance, reconciled the older textual tradition with the popular practices more recently crystallized in the *Kashikhand* when he declared that "Vishweshwur" was a current and popular term for the city's most significant shrine, which was none other than the authentic Avimukteshwur.[15] These debates appear to have been satisfactorily concluded. Writing a century later, such reconciliation was no longer necessary for Narayan Bhatt, who described Vishweshwur as a unique and preeminent *linga*. Furthermore, though Bhatt valued the concept of the *swayambhu linga*, he emphasized sites rather than *lingas* and advocated their continued ritual use, sidelining memories of desecration. He took pains to suggest that *lingas* could be replaced in cases where original ones had either been confiscated, or destroyed, or were simply missing.[16] He proposed that such incidents were a sign of the times since they could usually be attributed to actions by *mleccha* (literally "outcastes," in this case, Turko-Afghan Muslims). Bhatt urged pilgrims to worship any *linga* that was located at a sacred site, without worrying too much about its provenance. All in all, he was more interested in perpetuating ritual traditions than in debating questions of authenticity. His prime motive was to consecrate a principal Vishweshwur *linga* in Banaras, house it in a prominent temple, and perpetuate its pilgrimage traditions, even if they had to be re-created.

Brahmin assessments were combined with accounts of popular practices and were frequently folded into the official histories and geographies written in Persian for the Mughal state. As Abul Fazl compiled the *Ain-i-Akbari*, he observed the role that temples had played within past constructions of South Asian kingship. Significantly, when he mentioned a temple at Banaras that had existed in centuries gone by, Abul Fazl did not actually name its presiding deity, leaving a discursive space for Narayan Bhatt and his scholar contemporaries. Since material evidence for the existence of a twelfth-century temple in Banaras was (and continues to be) scarce, by emphasizing popular beliefs, Abul Fazl created a clear opportunity for Mughal intervention and patronage. Abul Fazl made specific mention of a tradition of circumambulating this temple, although in his own writings, particularly the *Tristhalisetu*, Bhatt did not overly emphasize pilgrimage routes. Yet Abul

Fazl underlined the significance of such a practice at "Baranasi," by comparing it to the practice of circumambulation around the Kaaba at Mecca. By so doing, he articulated the Mughal state's favorable policy toward the city's ritual and pilgrimage associations. By mentioning Mahmud of Ghazni and his disruption of the "old faith," Abul Fazl distanced the Mughal state from the iconoclastic actions (whether real or perceived) of previous Indo-Islamic regimes. By implication, then, the Mughals were providing support for a renewed faith, even a transformed Hinduism. The Mughal Vishweshwur temple was built at a new location within a larger and more spacious precinct around 1590, under the aegis of Narayan Bhatt and with the direct support of the Mughal grandee Todarmal.[17]

Like many of his Brahmin contemporaries, Narayan Bhatt participated in debates and discussions concerning abstract philosophical traditions. For Bhatt these debates were also anchored to the ritual spaces of Kashi. He was committed to sustaining the city's role as a pilgrimage destination and establishing and emphasizing the provenance of its various *tirthas* and deities, a concern that he addressed in the *Tristhalisetu*. Besides Vishweshwur, the core of Mughal attention and investment were focused on select sites within the Antargriha zone. Mughal intervention established the city's forms, spaces, and land use patterns. Yet this is not intended as a story of a definitive role for the Vishwesh-wur temple at the resurgent center of a triumphant Mughal cosmopolitanism. Although Mughal architectural and urban forms enjoyed prestige within the subcontinent's courtly elite, Brahmin scholars continued to articulate anxieties about the loss of an idealized Kashi, to say nothing of its ritual purity and authenticity. Despite these tensions, the sacred landscape of Kashi and the urban environment of Banaras were inexorably altered by the actions of scholars, patrons, and pilgrims.

A SACRED LANDSCAPE FOR MUGHAL BANARAS

In the overall plan for his text, the *Tristhalisetu*, Narayan Bhatt emphasized selected textual traditions on pilgrimage sites in northern India. His larger aim was to endorse pilgrimage to the *tristhali*—that is, the three sacred sites of Kashi, Prayag (Allahabad), and Gaya. In the section on Kashi, Bhatt promoted the idea of the sacred zone of Kashikshetra that had taken firm root a few centuries earlier. Bhatt used Lakshmidhara's interpretation of the *Lingapurana* as the basis for his own definition of this sacred zone.[18] Having established its boundaries, he proceeded to describe the significant sacred sites of Kashi, selectively merging diverse textual and ritual traditions. He drew from Vaishnava *puranas* such as the *Matsyapurana* and the *Naradiyapurana*, Shaiva texts such as the *Lingapurana*, and *tirtha* texts such as the *Krtyakalpataru* and the *Kashikhand*. He paid particular attention to Vaishnava sites and deities such as the Bindumadhav (that is cursorily mentioned in the *Kashikhand*) and dwelled at some length on the liberating benefits of Manikarnika, thereby suggesting its potential as an ideal site for conducting cremations.[19]

Yet (and as mentioned earlier) Bhatt did not overly emphasize the general role of pilgrimage routes in proscribing sanctity within the city. This is an important distinction between the *Tristhalisetu* and the *Kashikhand*. Significantly, neither the *Kashikhand* nor the *Kashirahasya* played a dominant role for him. Rather, Bhatt drew from the *Bhrahma-vaivarta* and *Skanda puranas* separately and made special mention of the *Padmapurana* and the *Naradiyapurana*, both Vaishnava texts. His primary focus remained on the idea of a Vishweshwur temple and the deities and traditions associated with this *linga*.[20] Although he mentioned the merits of performing the Antargriha pilgrimage around Vishweshwur, Bhatt refrained from listing a prescribed order for visiting its constituent deities. This is not to suggest that this practice did not exist in the late sixteenth century, since Bhatt separately listed twenty-two of the deities that were associated with this route. Yet he ignored the connection of individual deities to their locations along pilgrimage routes, even if these may have been nascent relationships.[21] More significantly, Bhatt established the provenance of individual sites of deification on the basis of both Shaiva and Vaishnava texts. His attention to this literature extended beyond considerations of academic interest and bore strong links to the material fabric of the city as well as the politics and intricacies of patronage. In emphasizing the sacred nature of Kashikshetra, Bhatt (like Lakshmidhara) located its center as the *linga* of Madhyameshwur.[22]

Bhatt enumerated the various religious merits of the zone in some detail, and he emphasized the religious merit that could accrue to a pilgrim who took a ritual bath in the Ganges.[23] He mentioned the Panchkroshi route, without specifying any of the sites along the way. Although he separately mentioned two of its sites (the deity Durga and associated *kund* [tank or well] as well as Bhimchandi and its associated *kund*), he did not place them on the Panchkroshi. This indicates that this pilgrimage route may have either been a relatively new tradition in the late sixteenth century, or else that it was a popular practice that had limited currency within the formal literature on Kashi.[24] Scholars have suggested that sixteenth- and seventeenth-century manuscripts of the *Kashirahasya* often included different and shorter lists of deities and sites to be visited along the route.[25] Put together, the combination of texts and practices indicates the continually evolving nature of this pilgrimage route. It also suggests a continued transformation of this tradition as it migrated between vernacular accounts and formal Sanskrit texts.

Bhatt paid special attention to Manikarnika ghat along the river and drew on a Vaishnava text, the *Naradiyapurana*, as he made detailed references to several Vaishnava ritual elements associated with this site, including the Chakrapushkarni tank and the Vishnupada (the footprints of Vishnu). He also emphasized its potent potential as a site from where souls could attain *moksha*, or liberation from the unending cycle of rebirth. Bhatt drew his references for the provenance of Manikarnika from the *Kashikhand* but also drew on the *Naradiyapurana* and other *puranas* to emphasize its simultaneous Vaishnava identity.[26] The sacred waters of the city received equal attention from Bhatt, and besides the Ganges he focused on the Matsyodari and Mandakini catchments.[27]

In his self-motivated role as a Brahmin activist, Bhatt emphasized the merit that could accrue through patronage channeled into building and endowing *brahmapuris* (residential precincts for Brahmin scholars as well as Brahmin ritual specialists) and constructing and, more significant, renovating temples.[28] He mentioned several sacred sites in the city worthy of such attention that would fall within the physical bounds of Kashikshetra, including Krittivaseshwur, Bindu Madhav, Kedar, Lolark, Vriddhakaleshwur, Gyan Vapi, Kapalamochana, Ghantakarna, and the Assi *sangam* (confluence of the Assi stream with the Ganges).[29] Narayan Bhatt's *Tristhalisetu* became a crucial framing text for the city's regeneration, and several of the sacred sites that he mentioned became the focus of patronage and attention from Mughal courtiers. Temples, riverfront sites, and urban zones in Banaras were directly connected to his *nibandha.*

The intimate connection between the ritual spaces of Kashikshetra and Mughal urbanism was reinforced through various forms of visual representation. Survey maps, called *tarah* (as they were known within Timurid architectural practices), provided information on the urban environment of Banaras. *Tarah* encapsulated information on the placement and physical dimensions of buildings and roads. Often, they also included detailed information on ownership patterns and the social identities of building owners and occupants. Whereas *patas* and panoramas of the city were largely conceptual representations that addressed thematic concerns, the surveyors who created *tarah* concentrated on tangible building footprints and land ownership. This study is partly based on one such survey effort commissioned by Bishan Singh (1672–1699) of Amber and continued under his son and successor, Sawai Jai Singh II (1688–1743), and conducted between ca. 1690 and ca. 1720.[30] A series of survey maps or *tarah* documenting the built environment and ritual landscape of Banaras was commissioned. Interestingly, the physical environment of Banaras was spatially described in three separate *tarah*. Information on the built environment was separated from the documentation of significant *lingas* and pilgrimage sites. These three *tarah* are analyzed after their broad categorization here as "survey *tarah* 183," "survey *tarah* 191," and the "pilgrimage *tarah*."

The pilgrimage *tarah* is a snapshot on the ritual landscape that existed in the late seventeenth century.[31] Its surveyors identified eighteen sites along the Panchkroshi circuit without mentioning the actual route. This may have been a basic framework for the elaborations that were to be executed in future centuries. By the late sixteenth century, the Antargriha route demarcated a significant zone in the city and twenty-five of the sites listed in the *Kashikhand* were identified by Kacchawaha surveyors.[32] This is actually a slightly larger number than the twenty-two sites and deities mentioned by Narayan Bhatt. However, in a pattern similar to the one captured by Bhatt, most of these sites can be located in the Brahmanal, Siddheshwari, and Brahma ghat areas of the city that lie to the north of the Gyan Vapi/Vishweshwur precinct.

It is significant that the surveyors separated notable buildings located on the two survey *tarah* from the sacred sites located on the pilgrimage *tarah*. As a result, the two categories of *tarah* each have only a minimal overlap in terms of the sites depicted as well as the themes addressed. Ultimately, very few of the sites that Bhatt mentions actually appear on either survey map (*tarah*). This may have been the case because several of the sites along the Antargriha and the Panchkroshi were either small in scale or ephemeral in nature, or possibly both. Besides the Gyan Vapi mosque (also noted as the site of the dismantled Vishweshwur temple), the newly constructed Adi-Vishweshwur temple and the Kashi Karvat temple (that is often incorporated by pilgrims on the Antargriha route) were the only significant religious buildings identified on survey *tarah* 191.[33] Beyond such noteworthy sites as Vishweshwur and Manikarnika that are mentioned on both kinds of maps, the pilgrimage *tarah* captures a sacred landscape that was partially rooted in texts but also based in current practices whose material traces were too fragile to interest an architectural surveyor. This is also why the creators of these maps viewed sacred sites as inherently distinct and therefore distinguishable from the built environment of the contemporary city.

Despite the presence of diverse groups of Brahmins (scholars and ritual practitioners) from many regions of South Asia who made Mughal Banaras their home, it was Mughal grandees who actively introduced a significant religious (Vaishnava and Shaiva) built environment. If Narayan Bhatt's *Tristhalisetu* provided the textual framework for the city's regeneration, it was the forms and spaces of Mughal architecture and urbanism that lent sacred sites a formal structure. The Mughal state encouraged the development of an administrative and commercial center around the shrines and *lingas* associated with the ritual zone of the Antargriha *yatra*. Recall that Bhatt had listed twenty-two of the deities and sites along this route, and although his list was shorter than the one included in the *Kashikhand*, the area covered by the Antargriha zone remained fairly consistent for both texts.[34] The zone also defined the locus as well as the extents of urban development.[35] By the turn of the eighteenth century, the Antargriha zone was completely enveloped and sustained within an intensely urbanized center.

Evidence regarding the Vishweshwur temple and its relationship to a Mughal institutional structure is preserved in the two survey *tarahs*.[36] Their authors documented physical dimensions of buildings and spaces, land use, as well as social structure and ownership. Although their focus was the precinct and immediate vicinity of the Gyan Vapi mosque, they noted urban character as well as memory. Of the two survey maps, survey *tarah* 183 is primarily a graphic assessment of the properties owned by the family of the Mughal *mansabdar*, Raja Todarmal. Survey *tarah* 191 includes a documentation of a significant stretch of the city along the street that connected the Vishweshwur/Gyan Vapi precinct to Manikarnika ghat to the south and the Mughal administrative center to its north (Fig. 2.2). This was also the principal route into the city, and by the late seventeenth century the street connected a prime site on the sacred riverfront, Manikarnika, with the Aurangabad *saray* (inn) at its opposite end.[37]

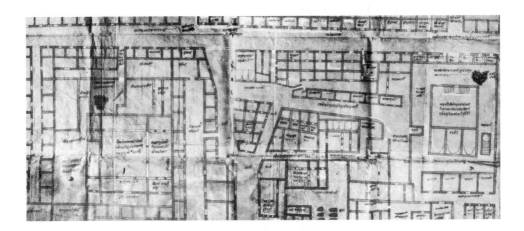

FIG. 2.2   *Tarah Kashijiki* (survey *tarah* 191, survey of Banaras), ca. 1700. Courtesy Maharaja Sawai Man Singh II Museum Trust, City Palace, Jaipur.

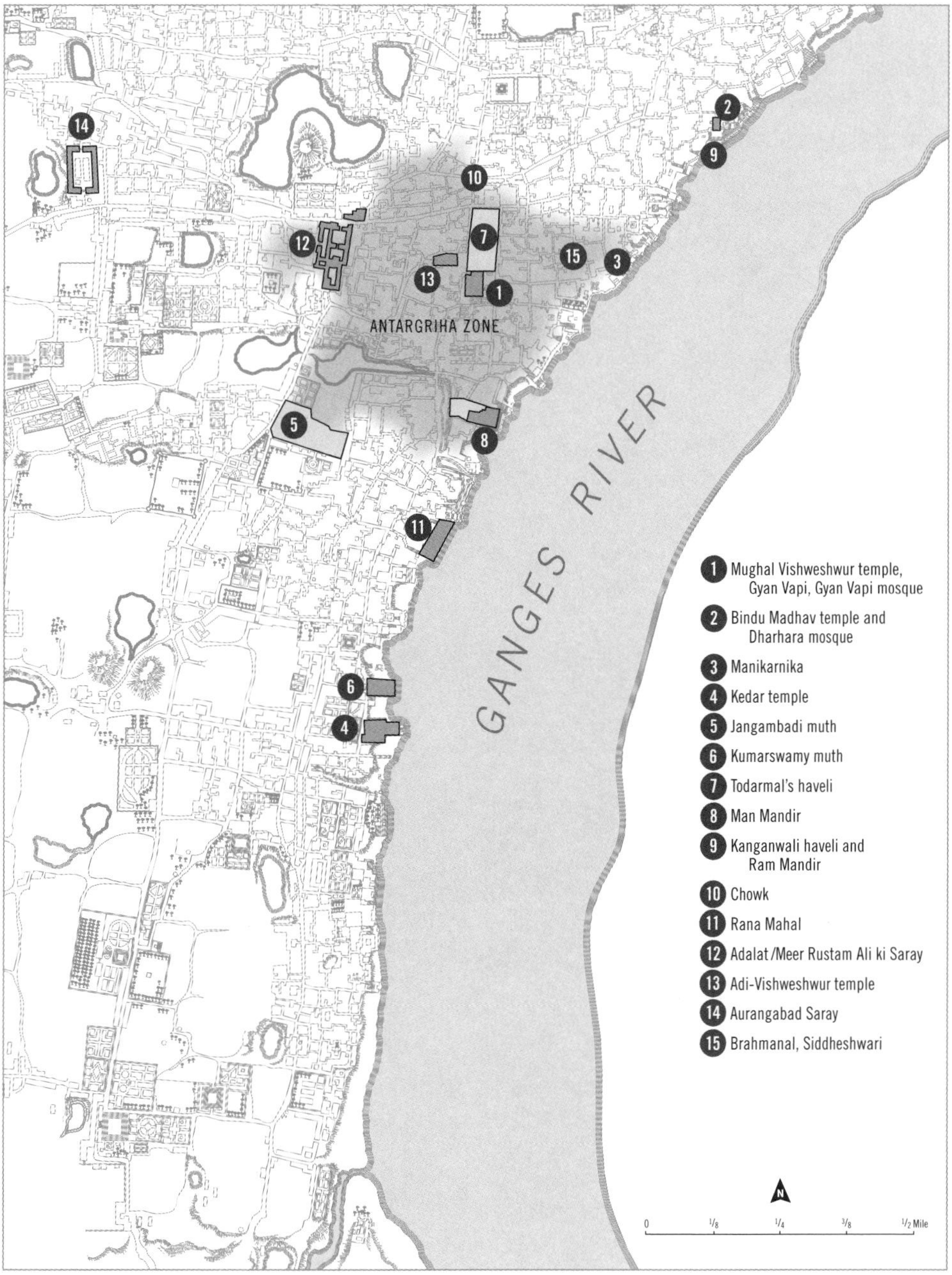
ANTARGRIHA ZONE
GANGES RIVER
1 Mughal Vishweshwur temple, Gyan Vapi, Gyan Vapi mosque
2 Bindu Madhav temple and Dharhara mosque
3 Manikarnika
4 Kedar temple
5 Jangambadi muth
6 Kumarswamy muth
7 Todarmal's haveli
8 Man Mandir
9 Kanganwali haveli and Ram Mandir
10 Chowk
11 Rana Mahal
12 Adalat/Meer Rustam Ali ki Saray
13 Adi-Vishweshwur temple
14 Aurangabad Saray
15 Brahmanal, Siddheshwari
N
0
1/8
1/4
3/8
1/2 Mile

MAP 2.1 Map of Banaras City, ca. 1600, based on *The City of Bunarus*, 1822, by James Prinsep. Drawing by Gretta Tritch Roman and Jennifer Shontz.

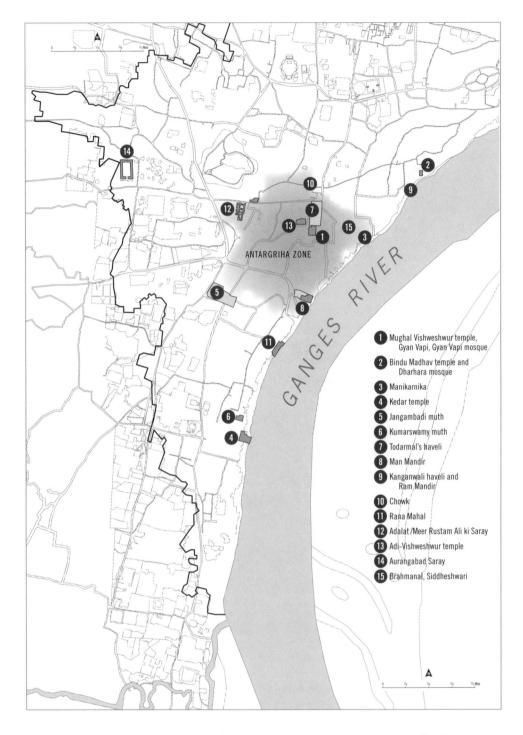

ANTARGRIHA ZONE

GANGES RIVER

1 Mughal Vishweshwur temple, Gyan Vapi, Gyan Vapi mosque
2 Bindu Madhav temple and Dharhara mosque
3 Manikarnika
4 Kedar temple
5 Jangambadi muth
6 Kumarswamy muth
7 Todarmal's haveli
8 Man Mandir
9 Kanganwali haveli and Ram Mandir
10 Chowk
11 Rana Mahal
12 Adalat /Meer Rustam Ali ki Saray
13 Adi-Vishweshwur temple
14 Aurangabad Saray
15 Brahmanal, Siddheshwari

MAP 2.2 Map of Banaras City, ca. 1600, based on *Benares City, 1928–29*. Drawing by Gretta Tritch Roman, Jennifer Shontz, Nanditha Veeraraghavelu, and Rohan Haksar.

Along the way, the *chowk* (square) bazaar was a significant urban space and an essential node in a vibrant commercial zone that was partly sustained through its proximity to the Vishweshwur temple.[38] Its prominent depiction in a late seventeenth-century pilgrimage panorama (also from the collections of the City Palace Museum) is indicative of this relationship. Until the early nineteenth century, Todarmal's *haveli* (mansion) was also known as the "Old Mint," indicating the proximity and overlap between Mughal administrative infrastructure and the Antargriha zone.[39] Consequently, the Vishweshwur temple was favorably placed in relation to a ritual geography as well as spaces of Mughal imperial authority.[40] Along with the mansions of Mughal grandees, urban spaces and buildings framed the city's religious landscape, and they were frequently represented as cartographic anchors in pilgrimage maps and panoramas. In sum, the Mughal administrative and commercial center of Banaras was established, or rather inserted, in relation to the Vishweshwur temple and its burgeoning Antargriha zone (Map 2.1 and Map 2.2).

The surveyors recorded several patrons from the previous century as well as the edifices that they had sponsored, the *haveli* of Todarmal being one such instance. Their observations indicate that developments in the late seventeenth and early eighteenth centuries were overlaid on an older, late sixteenth-century urban structure. The *mansabdari* system that was created during the reign of Akbar was continued for much of the seventeenth century, and it follows that urban morphology initiated in this earlier period formed a basic framework for Mughal cities. Considering the pattern established at many preeminent Mughal urban centers such as the new, seventeenth-century capital city of Shahjahanabad, the *haveli* was the symbolic and hierarchical center of a complex that comprised workshops, stables, living spaces for servants and dependents, and bazaars.[41] The overall disposition of *havelis* that were spread across Shahjahanabad reflected the structure and hierarchies of the Mughal imperial court, with the more important *mansabdars* being granted premium tracts of land. As noted by Stephen Blake, *havelis* occupied large sections of Shahjahanabad and were spatially and politically significant territories that extended well beyond the principal mansion at their symbolic center. *Haveli* land tracts would include income-generating rental property and were usually occupied by a diverse population of varied caste and religious backgrounds. Although caste, region, and religion could play a role in determining urban social dispersal structures, survey *tarahs* (at least in Banaras) suggest that neighborhood formations around Mughal *havelis* were socially diverse and housed a heterogeneous population.[42]

As the capital of the empire, Shahjahanabad could be created as a unified and idealized vision attributable to a singular imperial imagination. By its very nature, Banaras did not lend itself to this model of sweeping Mughal urbanism. A critical distinction between the new Mughal capital and Banaras was, as may be surmised, the sacred landscape of the pilgrimage city. The new urban structure had to be inserted around pilgrimage sites and with creative amalgamations with existing spatial conditions and ritual associations. These intersections were carefully planned and implemented. Substantial areas within and around the Antargriha zone were parceled into *havelis*, as the ideal urban unit of a Mughal city was inserted around the sacred center of Banaras. A close reading of the survey suggests that two powerful Mughal *mansabdars*, Todarmal and Man Singh, owned large tracts of urban land at prime locations.[43] Their *havelis* were significant nodes in the city, anchoring its urban life. As large complexes, they housed residential and administrative uses and were sites of production and consumption.[44]

The creators of survey *tarah* 183 noted that Todarmal owned a large tract of land around his *haveli* in close proximity to the Vishweshwur temple. As indicated on survey *tarah* 191, the mansion was built around a large courtyard and was surrounded by the residences of dependents. Mughal patronage determined the location and morphology of distinct urban areas such as the tract owned initially by Man Singh and subsequently by his descendants, the Kacchawaha Rajas of Amber (Fig. 2.3). This particular tract was referred to as Jaisinghpura in nineteenth-century colonial records.[45] Initially located in close proximity to Mughal imperial land, it included residential and commercial uses around a principal *haveli*, known as the Man Mandir (ca. 1600) after its founder. Many of the commercial and residential buildings within the *pura* were rented or leased to a diverse group of tenants with varied caste backgrounds and occupations. Todarmal's *haveli* was organized along similar ownership and management patterns, and it is likely that he provided land for the construction of the Vishweshwur temple. Yet such social diversity was not, by any means, a common characteristic across all urban areas. Harabagh, the tract awarded to Rao Surjan Hada in the late sixteenth century, may have had a more uniform social structure governed by clan-based relationships of dependence and sponsorship rather than a more general Mughal urban system.[46] The Hadas were new entrants into the Mughal courtly world, and they may have been relatively tenacious about retaining ethnic and regional affiliations within their assigned settlements.

As the Mughal state engaged diverse religious and ethnic communities and regional cultures, administrators strove to find models that could accommodate difference within an overarching yet flexible imperial structure of land ownership, taxation, and symbolic authority. In a fertile climate of religious exchange, debate, and interrogation, several Shaiva and Vaishnava sects and their institutions, particularly monasteries, found support

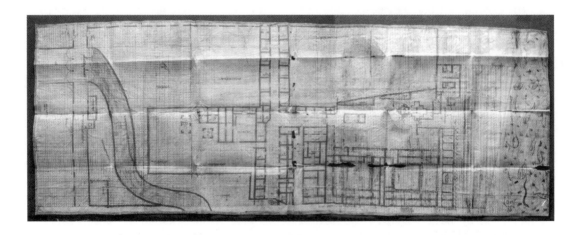

FIG. 2.3 *Map of Man Mandir* (map number 130, survey of Man Mandir and vicinity), ca. 1760. Courtesy Maharaja Sawai Man Singh II Museum Trust, City Palace, Jaipur.

from the Mughal state. *Muths* (monasteries) remained centers of intellectual activity and were powerful landowners. Systems of Mughal urbanism could be flexible and were often adapted to accommodate existing roles in shaping urban form and land ownership patterns. The Jangambadi *muth* that was endorsed by several Mughal emperors is an example of such a relationship.[47] This Lingayat (an "outlying" and egalitarian Shaiva sect) *muth* owned large tracts of land and rental properties in Banaras.[48] With its deep pre-Islamic history (substantiated through documents engraved on copper plate in addition to oral histories), the *muth* was well established on the outlying edges of the Antargriha circuit and may even have predated it. The general *haveli* pattern of landownership and management as well as building typologies was extended to such institutions. In the case of preexisting institutions such as the Jangambadi *muth*, documents were issued under Mughal imperial seals to ratify current and future ownership of land, property, and its taxation.

The urban structure of Mughal Banaras was determined through investments and ownership undertaken by courtiers and religious institutions. Beyond a zone of intense urbanization, many of the sites identified by Narayan Bhatt in his *Tristhalisetu*—including Bindu Madhav, Kedar, Krittivaseshwur, and Lolark—became the focus of indirect Mughal support well into the seventeenth century. Of these sites the Bindu Madhav temple and the Lolark *kund* were refurbished by the Kacchawahas. In the following century, the Kedar temple was refurbished by a monastic sect from southern India.

Banaras remained a vibrant center throughout the early half of the seventeenth century as patronage was continually channeled through prominent *mansabdars* and rajas. In ca. 1620, Bir Singh Deo Bundela, an intimate friend and associate of the Mughal emperor Jahangir, donated a gold casing for the pinnacle of the Vishweshwur temple.[49] Mughal support for religious and social inclusion meant that the city and some of its ritual spaces were accessible to a diverse and cosmopolitan audience. For instance, the French merchant Jean-Baptiste Tavernier's accounts of his visits to the city's temples, as well as the Central Asian visitor Balkhi's account of his visit to the Vishweshwur temple, suggest a departure from more orthodox practices of ritual and spatial exclusion based in stricter adherence to boundaries of religion and caste at temples and ritual sites.[50]

The city suffered a partial retraction of Mughal state support during the reign of the emperor Shahjahan.[51] This glitch in the city's relations with Mughal authority was successfully rectified through appeals by influential individuals such as the Brahmin scholar Kavindracharya. This religious leader was in frequent attendance at the imperial court and was successful in persuading the emperor to repeal the *jiziya* (pilgrim tax levied on Hindus) at Banaras.[52] Kavindracharya, who maintained a well-stocked and erudite library in the city, was a mentor to the Mughal prince Dara Shukoh (1615–1659), the emperor's oldest and favorite son and presumptive heir. Banaras was a critical base for the intellectual and spiritually inclined Dara Shukoh, and it was from here that he engaged in religious study and philosophical exploration as he conceptualized many of his radical religious beliefs.

Mughal support for Banaras resulted in the emergence of new religious ideas among a heterogeneous population of princes, priests, aristocrats, and merchants. At the same time that Dara Shukoh synthesized his ideas, more traditional scholars such as Bhatt and Kavindracharya questioned and reconceptualized many of their inherited notions. Some of Kavindracharya's ideas and their place in a Mughal world have filtered down through a report of a conversation that he and six of his Brahmin contemporaries had with the French merchant Francois Bernier. Although this encounter was described and published by Bernier, and not by the Brahmin scholar-interlocutors, some general nuances of content and even tone are apparent. When accused of excessive and exclusive belief in idolatry, the Brahmins emphasized their belief in the formless essence of all divinity and the existence of its true power beyond images and icons.[53] Bernier, however, remained unimpressed. He recounted having posed similar questions to a number of priests and having received vastly different answers. He remained less than charitable in his comments on the worship of idols and the nature of divinity, as conceptualized by the "Gentiles." Based on the varied accounts and opinions that he heard, Bernier concluded that Kavindracharya and his contemporaries had actually expressed unorthodox beliefs. He surmised that their ideas were forged through interactions with practitioners of other religions, particularly Christians.[54]

Bernier's skepticism aside, Banaras in the seventeenth century was a fertile arena for an exchange of ideas and the creation of new religious philosophies. In this regard, particularly given the nexus between prominent Brahmins and grandees, Banaras was a thoroughly Mughal city. Its built environment and urban spaces were a reflection of religious consolidation and transformation that was encouraged through a cosmopolitan court culture. Although tensions and differences remained, its architecture was inflected by a contemporary political climate as is borne out in the designs for riverfront fortress-palaces, major temples, and the mosques that replaced them.

RELIGION, POLITICS, AND THE RIVERFRONT

Throughout the late sixteenth and seventeenth century, the Ganges was a significant transportation route connecting the plains of northern India to urban centers in Bengal, and appearance and visibility from the river remained a major consideration for the proprietors and builders of riverfront sites in Banaras.[55] The English traveler Ralph Fitch described a riverbank with many well-built houses facing the river, where Brahmin priests presided over religious rituals.[56] Since the riverfront was valued for its ritual significance, the areas near Brahma and Durga ghat (near Panchganga) had already developed as Maratha Brahmin enclaves by the mid-sixteenth century.[57] Even so, the riverfront in the late sixteenth century was a relatively sparsely built and yet ritually significant space, and Mughal interest and intervention altered both its built environment and its sacred cartography. In a general sense, Hindu *mansabdars* at the Mughal court simultaneously straddled and molded Mughal courtly culture while fashioning themselves as pious Hindus. Yet the degree of assimilation into the Mughal world could vary with individual Rajput chiefs and their particular stance and attitude toward incorporation into the imperial system. Built interventions reflected the nature of religious change, particularly as Vaishnava deities and shrines were granted a more enhanced role within Mughal circles.

By the late sixteenth century, the riverfront fortress-palace was a symbol of a centralized political and cultural authority. Adherence to, or reluctance to reflect, imperial fashion in architectural style could be a visible statement of willingness or reluctance to be part of the Mughal imperium. Beginning in the late sixteenth century, mansions and fortress-palaces were gradually added along the ritually significant riverfront, often at sites with deep ritual and textual histories. Notably, the Mughal state owned large swathes of land in Banaras.[58] All private ownership along the river's edge, as elsewhere in the city, was ratified through Mughal *farmans* (decrees).[59] The city's sacred waters were managed through Mughal hydraulics such as the water channel at Dashashwamedha that flowed through state-owned land and was also maintained through imperial decree. Therefore, many new edifices combined the potency of a ritual site with the political overtones inherent to architectural symbolism.

Broadly speaking, Mughal architecture was based on the marriage of Iranian and Indo-Islamic precedents that were creatively reworked to create spaces and buildings meant to frame complex courtly relationships. Precedents such as the *chihil sutun* (forty-columned pavilion), the *hasht behisht* (vaulted, eight-sided pavilion), *iwans* (vaults), and *pishtaqs* (portals framing pointed arches) were reworked and combined with carved brackets, beams, and columns adapted from the sultanate architecture of western India.[60] Far from being based in a static and repetitive palette of forms, however, Mughal buildings reflected the political and cultural agenda of each emperor. Their enthusiastic engagement with Iranian forms and precedents could be replaced with a studied indifference to such choices, as individual emperors addressed domestic preoccupations or competed on the global stage of the early modern Islamic world. Their courtiers and *mansabdars* were equally alive to the opportunities provided by such cosmopolitan options.

When Man Singh Kacchawaha, Raja of Amber, constructed the Man Mandir ca. 1600, he intervened in the ritual geography of Dashashwamedha ghat.[61] The Man Mandir *haveli* reflected late sixteenth-century imperial tastes as seen in the citadel palace of Fatehpur Sikri and the Jahangiri Mahal of the Agra Fort with its architecture of columns, beams, and brackets with carved stonework, based on the regional elite architecture of western India. The *haveli* was originally designed (ca. 1600) around two courtyards, designated as the *mardana* and *zenana* courtyards (Fig. 2.4 and Fig. 2.5), the norm in elite residences where the spatial and social segregation of the sexes could be a marker of elevated family status.[62] The Mughal ceremony of the imperial *darshana* was symbolically re-created at the Man Mandir. With their intimate connection to the Mughal imperial family, the Kacchawahas were permitted to employ the symbolism of the *jharokha* (projecting window), a privilege otherwise reserved for imperial structures, indicating an extension of political authority.[63] Furthermore, imperial architectural taste was as directly reflected in the riverfront architecture at Banaras as it was at the Kacchawahas' own regional political seat, the fortress of Amber.

Several scholars of early modern South Asia have discussed Vaishnavism and its ethos of familial conviviality and domesticity as an avenue for elites to participate in a Mughal sphere.[64] They suggest that these characteristics appealed to the Mughal establishment, and they actively supported its leaders and institutions. A Hindu *mansabdar* could declare his adherence to Vaishnavism as a way to further strengthen his imperial connections, while retaining his own as well as his family's religious identity. In this climate Vaishnavism was significant for the Kacchawahas, and their patronage of the Bindu Madhav temple on Panchganga ghat was a visible sign of this affiliation. The Kanganwali

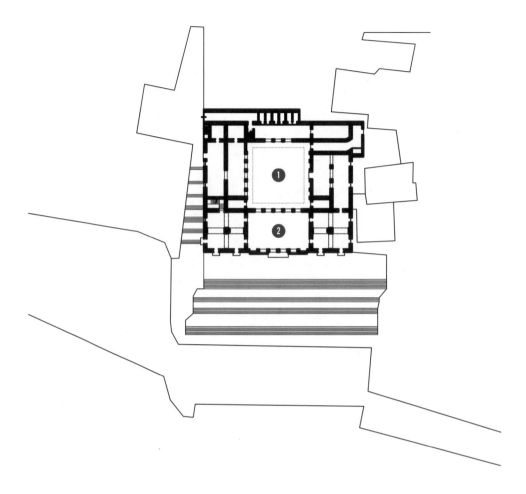

FIG. 2.4 Plan (partial) of Man Mandir. 1–*mardana* courtyard, 2–enclosed hall (added in nineteenth century). Drawing by Nanditha Veeraraghavelu and Jennifer Shontz.

haveli that was located next to it was designed and built ca. 1600 as a school for princes of the Kacchawaha family (the building also housed a temple to the deity Ram) and was, by extension, training ground for future Mughal courtiers.[65] They were schooled in diverse subjects including Sanskrit theology and early modern geography.[66] The princes would eventually either directly enter Mughal service or establish some form of political relationship with the Mughal state. A strong connection between Amber and the Mughal state was nurtured and sustained well into the middle of the eighteenth century. The presence of a Mughal institution on the riverfront further strengthened the connections between the city's ritual identity and the Mughal court. Connected to the seventeenth-century Bindu Madhav temple, its façade was punctured by *jharokha* elements arranged in a repetitive configuration—a stylistic reference to the imperial language favored by the emperor Akbar (Fig. 2.6).

FIG. 2.5   Man Mandir.

FIG. 2.6   Kanganwali *haveli*.

Spatial interventions by patrons with newly acquired Vaishanava affiliations and identities resulted in changes in the ritual role of Manikarnika ghat on the riverfront. In his *Tristhalisetu*, Narayan Bhatt emphasized an alignment of Shaiva and Vaishnava traditions with some vigor as he marked Manikarnika as an ideal site for cremation. The suggestion was put into practice by such grandees as Rao Surjan Hada, a relatively new entrant into the Mughal imperial system and its court culture. Although cremation along the riverfront had an older history, its specific association with Manikarnika ghat was the result of a newly invented tradition. The recasting of Manikarnika ghat as a prominent site served Hindu Mughal grandees seeking the integration of Vaishnava traditions, myths, and texts into the ritual life of the city and into their personal practices.

The custom of cremation on the riverfront had previously been restricted to Harishchandra ghat, mentioned as the "Mahasmashan" in a late seventeenth-century panorama. Rao Surjan's actions initiated a tradition of royal cremation at Manikarnika ghat, and his instructions that he was to be cremated there was a statement about his newly adopted religious beliefs. His political struggles against the Mughals, subsequent defeat, and the resulting issues with social and political identity are captured in an epic poem, the *Surjancharitamahakavyam*.[67] The patron and protagonist of the epic, Rao Surjan, may have cultivated an association with Vaishnavism as a way to negotiate a relationship with the Mughal court.[68] His cremation at Manikarnika ghat in the seventeenth century was a significant gesture and underlined his favorable sentiments toward Vaishnava beliefs—in particular, the Vaishnava traditions associated with the city and the specific legends that were associated with this ghat.[69] Through his association with a sect that had wide currency in the Mughal world, Rao Surjan reinforced his family's connection to the Mughal court while enabling them to retain their identity as Hindu rulers and patrons.

Besides altering the ritual character of Manikarnika ghat, the rajas of Bundi also built the Bundiparkota, a fortress-palace, immediately south of the Varuna *sangam*, the northernmost sacred site along the riverfront. This action linked their patronage to the city's sacred geography and served as a statement of dignified acquiescence rather than forcible sequestration. The central figure in a seventeenth-century illustration of the Bundiparkota ghat is a Mughal nobleman, distinguished by his turban, seated with folded hands next to a *sadhu* (mendicant), suggesting his Rajput antecedents. The artist placed both figures under a *chattri* on the terrace of one of the mansions within the fortress-palace. The image successfully marries the royal (including Mughal) symbolism associated with the *chattri* with the city's religious authority. Far from being depicted as a defeated or dejected subject, Rao Surjan is a gracious figure of royal (Rajput) lineage. A viewer can surmise that he retired to the banks of the Ganges, in full possession of his place in the world, eager and able to confer with holy men on matters of religion. The Hada fortress-palace at Bundiparkota ghat reflected contemporary Mughal architectural fashion.[70] Since imperial architecture under Akbar was closely related to Indo-Islamic (rather than Central Asian) precedents, newly incorporated rulers such as Rao Surjan could easily transition into a role within Mughal courtly circles while satisfying the requirements of ideal Hindu kingship.

The Ranas of Mewar, first defeated in 1568 by Akbar, reluctantly accepted Mughal suzerainty by the mid-seventeenth century.[71] The connection between architecture as a political statement and successful incorporation into the Mughal realm gained a new twist. By this time, Mughal imperial architecture had undergone a shift to reflect the emperor Shahjahan's tastes for a cosmopolitan idiom strongly inflected with Persianate tastes. Rajput families such as the Kacchawahas followed these trends and built a new pavilion within their fortress-palace at Amber. With its baluster columns clad in marble and its walls embellished with Persian motifs, including the flowering vase and wine pitcher, the new pavilion mirrored contemporary Mughal trends and their unique relationship with the imperial family.[72] The Ranas, however, chose to make a different statement at Banaras.

Built to maintain a distance from seventeenth-century Mughal fashion, the architecture of the Sisodia riverfront mansion, the Rana Mahal, is based in an archaic sultanate idiom that the Ranas had adopted in the mid-fifteenth century during the reign of Rana Kumbha. His master-mason, Sutradhar Mandan, devised a syncretic architectural vocabulary based in a combination of pre-Islamic and sultanate elements. Kumbha's temples and palaces at Ranakpur and Ranthambore reflect his initiative to forge a contemporary building vocabulary. As reluctant vassals of the Mughals, his descendants continued to use this language as a statement of independence and resistance, as they eschewed contemporary Mughal imperial preferences.[73] The Rana Mahal was designed with an imposing façade that was in sharp contrast to its narrow plan footprint and modest interior (Fig. 2.7). Seventeenth-century Mughal architectural trends in spatial organization and decorative detail were avoided. Although its location was close to the Dashashwamedha

FIG. 2.7   Rana Mahal.

ghat, the Sisodias placed the building within its own distinct visual frame, unmistakably identifiable from a passing boat on the river and, significantly, at a clear distance from the Man Mandir.

This persistent ambiguity in the Mewadi connections to the Mughals crept into contemporary visual representations of the city. For instance, the Rana Mahal was not depicted in a late seventeenth-century pilgrimage panorama created for Kacchawaha consumption (from the collections of the City Palace museum). Mewadi tradition holds that the fortress-palace was built ca. 1641 during the reign of Rana Jagat Singh. However, the building was not depicted in this pilgrimage panorama from the late seventeenth century, marking its uncertain place in a Mughal realm.[74] Jagat Singh and his mother traveled to several religious destinations that lay within Mughal territory and made grants and donations to temples and religious establishments. All the same, the Rana maintained his family's ambiguous relationship with the Mughals, characterized as it was by symbolic distance and occasional displays of opposition and rivalry. Contrast the absence of the Rana Mahal in this panorama with seventeenth-century representations of the Kanganwali *haveli* in the same scroll. In this panorama the *haveli* is depicted as a mansion built in a contemporary, seventeenth-century Mughal architectural language with a roofline embellished with a *bangaldar* (Bengali) roof supported in turn by four baluster columns (Fig. 2.8).

FIG. 2.8 *Pilgrimage Panorama* (map number 138), ca. 1700. Courtesy Maharaja Sawai Man Singh II Museum Trust, City Palace, Jaipur.

CHAPTER 2

This representation had no active basis in reality, since the *haveli* was never rebuilt to reflect seventeenth-century imperial fashion. Its portrayal in a current idiom emphasized the structure's ongoing significance for the Mughal court. The Kacchawahas enjoyed the privilege of imperial architectural symbols, including the *bangaldar* roof and the baluster column. By depicting the building as a contemporary imperial structure, patrons and artists could assert the *haveli*'s continuing role as a Mughal institution where future courtiers were educated and groomed. The Ranas of Mewar would not have failed to notice such blatant expressions of affiliation, and their choice of an archaic language remained a statement of their symbolic independence. With a shift in imperial policies during the reign of the emperor Aurangzeb (r. 1658–1707), the city's built environment underwent some drastic changes that reverberated well into the following two centuries.

AURANGZEB AND BANARAS

The Mughal emperor Aurangzeb's relationship with the city was, at the very least, complex. During his reign he implemented varied and often contradictory policies. For instance, in 1658 he issued a *farman* (imperial order) extending state protection to existing temples in Banaras as well as their priests.[75] At the same time, he forbade the construction of new temples. Yet in 1669 he ordered the dismantling of the Vishweshwur and Bindu Madhav temples. Aurangzeb renamed the city as "Muhammadabad" in official state documents and enhanced its urban infrastructure by adding the Aurangabad *saray*.[76] An example of Mughal state architecture, the new caravanserai was placed along the principal administrative and commercial spine in Banaras. The building was constructed around a large rectangular courtyard, surrounded by rooms and stables, with a mosque at its center. A monumental gateway announced its presence to passersby. Its various component parts, from the dimensions of rooms, the size and shape of openings, as well as the size and composition of bricks used, provide a further indication of its origins in Mughal state ateliers and workshops.

Aurangzeb's relationship with the city is also discernible through the architecture of the Gyan Vapi mosque. Built on the plinth of the dismantled Vishweshwur temple, the austere mosque abuts its lone standing wall. Since the Gyan Vapi was based on the general pattern of the triple bay South Asian mosque, this meant that a major portion of the plinth of the older temple could be left unbuilt to be reused as its courtyard. The Bindu Madhav temple was dismantled shortly after, and the Dharhara mosque was built on its site (Fig. 2.9). Also planned as a South Asian mosque with three bays surmounted by domes facing a courtyard with a tank at its center, this mosque was designed to be equally austere but significantly more monumental in scale, with towering minarets visible from a bend in the river.[77] However, the adjoining Kanganwali *haveli* and its Ram temple were left standing. Both mosques were designed to make explicit political and visual statements about Mughal control over the city's religious sphere. The choice of architectural language and materials reflected a new imperial policy of austerity, piety, and eventually orthodoxy. These mosques stand in direct contrast to the more monumental and architecturally refined imperial mosques built at Agra and Delhi by preceding emperors.

FIG. 2.9   Dharhara mosque.

Aurangzeb's policies for Banaras remained complex and contradictory well into the last decades of the seventeenth century. In a remarkable gesture, he provided support to the Jangambadi *muth*.[78] In addition, he continued and even initiated support for the establishment of a new monastery, the Kumaraswamy *muth*, as well as the renovation of the Kedar temple that the *muth* leaders undertook in 1695.[79] The memory of Mughal support is preserved in a legend recounting an encounter between the monastery's founder, Kumaraswamy, and a *padushah*. Kumaraswamy was the intellectual force and activist behind the resuscitation of the Kedar temple besides being the founder of the *muth* that bears his name. He is remembered for having impressed the *padushah* by riding into

FIG. 2.10 Kumarswamy *muth*.

court on the back of a lion. The narrative encapsulates Kumaraswamy's courageous act in confronting a powerful and intimidating Mughal ruler on terms of equality rather than supplication. It is also significant that both the *muth* and temple were constructed sixteen years after the Vishweshwur temple had been dismantled.

The designers of the Kumaraswamy *muth* drew selectively from a Mughal architectural vocabulary to reflect the close association between Mughal authority and this religious institution (Fig. 2.10). Designed around two large and six smaller courtyards, the principal

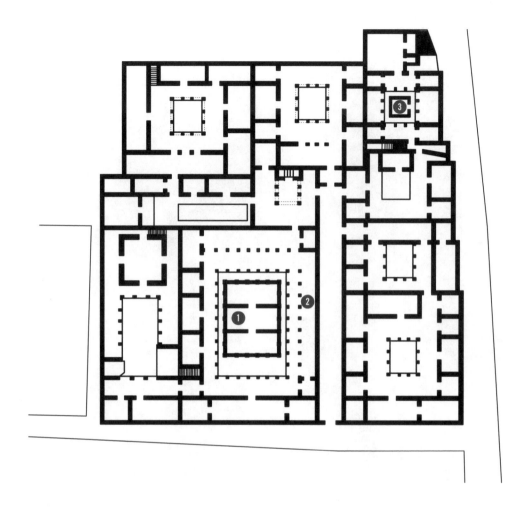

FIG. 2.11 Plan of Kumarswamy *muth*. 1–*samadhi*, 2–refectory, 3–temple. Drawing by Nanditha
Veeraraghavelu and Jennifer Shontz.

muth building is focused on the personality of its founding guru as well as the deity Shiva
(Fig. 2.11). Within the plan the founder takes precedence over Shiva, and Kumaraswamy's
samadhi (d. 1688) is located at the center of the largest courtyard.[80] Architectural details
remain austere and ornamentation is sparse (Fig. 2.12).[81] Although the more decorative
stylistic elaborations of Mughal imperial architecture were not employed in the *muth*,
certain basic building types that included the *haveli* and the tomb were reworked. Opulent *baradaris* and elaborate reception spaces were avoided in communal areas such as
the refectory. The Mughal baluster column, a seventeenth-century staple, is conspicuous
in its absence. The designers of the *muth* appropriated elements that had a stable set of
meanings attached within Mughal circles but also retained a sense of austerity that was
associated with monastic architecture.

FIG. 2.12 Refectory, Kumarswamy *muth*.

The *muth* is connected to a parent institution, the Kashi *muth*, located in the Tamil regions of South Asia. The presence of a branch of the *muth* in Banaras connects its members and adherents to the potent geography of the sacred zone of Kashikshetra. Aurangzeb successfully expanded Mughal rule to its farthest extents in South Asia by incorporating large swathes of territory in the southern Indian peninsula into his empire. He may have seen the *muth* and its preceptors as advantageous allies in this process, and he lent support for the founding of the monastery as well as for the reconstruction of the associated Kedar temple. The connection is particularly explicit through the history of the Kedar temple.[82] The temple anchored a distinct sacred zone in the city, and built as it was by an independent monastic institution, it lacked a direct connection to the shifting political alignments of Mughal *mansabdars*.[83] Thus it remained relatively isolated from the conscious cultural amalgamation and cosmopolitan environment that came to be associated with the Mughal Vishweshwur temple. The question remains as to whether Aurangzeb truly objected to Hindu practices. He merely may have been opposed to syncretism in religious matters and equally interested in preserving clear boundaries between Hinduism and orthodox Islam. His actions in lending support to the Kedar temple and Kumarswamy *muth* suggest a selective rather than totalitarian opposition.[84] All the same, Brahmin scholars continued to express reservations about their changing religious and social environment. They remained anxious and critical about unavoidable compromises and the resulting consequences of such actions for ritual authenticity and social identity.

BRAHMIN DESIRES AND KASHI

The symbiotic relationship between Indo-Islamic urbanism and the sacred landscape of pilgrimage centers that was experienced by Banarasidas can be traced to earlier times in South Asia, well before the arrival of the Mughals. Authors of medieval texts on Kashi described the presence of multiple cities within a larger Kashikshetra. Rather than seeing this as a reference to distinct zones in the city, this was an apocryphal description of its identity as a religious center that could also be a regional political center.[85] Brahmins, particularly those engaged in philosophical and scholarly pursuits, were stakeholders in perpetuating traditions and held a conflicted, even quizzical view of the nexus between religious change and Mughal patronage. In formal as well as institutional terms, ideal cities symbolized civilization, moral order, Brahminical values, and a caste hierarchy that could be sustained under the rule of a virtuous king.[86] This idealized world had to be adjusted in an environment of Indo-Islamic hegemony where the state, at least nominally, upheld differing ideologies about moral order, social hierarchies, and urban life.

Some Brahmin scholars certainly regretted this state of affairs, even as they sought support and patronage from these regimes. Their traditional expectations from kings and royal patronage were often transferred to Indo-Islamic rulers with varying results. Such patronage could be uncertain and this reality was articulated at least a century earlier by the author of the *Gurucharitra*. "Evil" nawabs, this author found, were as prevalent as "good" ones and their sympathies (or lack thereof) for Hindu pilgrimage and ritual could vary to a great degree over time and circumstances.[87] Despite his successful shepherding of the Vishweshwur temple project, Narayan Bhatt also struggled with what he perceived as the uncertain and occasionally capricious nature of Indo-Islamic patronage. He expressed a general concern about the *mleccha* (Turko-Afghan Muslims) and their interventions in the city's ritual rhythms. Securing Indo-Islamic patronage could be a daunting and uncertain enterprise.

At the same time, Brahmins remained acutely conscious of the ritual boundaries that necessarily had to be violated in order to sustain such relationships. The all-pervasive Mughal imperium was a source of political legitimacy, but its proximity and interventions could also cause a degree of anxiety. Articulating similar concerns, a mid-seventeenth-century author, Venkatadhvari, introduced two celestial beings (or *gandharvas*) as the protagonists of his *Visvagunadarasacampu*. The *gandharvas* recollected and narrated an archaic geography of the subcontinent as they flew over its landscapes. Their discussion included commentaries on its geography and cultures, with particular attention to the network of pilgrimage sites embedded within a *purana*-based cartography.[88] As they passed over Kashi, their conversation turned to the social and ritual conditions of Brahmins in the city. Surveying a subcontinent firmly under the Mughals, the *gandharvas* articulated concerns about the ability of Brahmins serving in the imperial administration to adhere to rules of ritual purity and *aachaar* (comportment and adherence to ritual prescriptions). Most elites, whether they were Hindus or Muslims, adopted Indo-Persian influences in dress, language, and comportment. Such influences could be acceptable, the *gandharvas* concluded, if elites could also garner support for the Hindu religion in "adverse" times.

This geographical consciousness should be viewed in a context in which Brahmins from different regions lived in Banaras and forged alliances within a shared Sanskrit sphere, even as they negotiated differences across boundaries of religious sect (for example, Shaiva or Vaishnava), regional culture, and language. Despite these everyday differences, Brahmins could find common intellectual interests and solidarities. Varadaraja, the author of the *Girvanpadamanjari* (ca. 1650), and Dhundiraja, the author of the *Girvanvangmanjari* (1702–1704), have described such cultural encounters in their texts. Dhundiraja's text is largely based on Varadaraja's work, and the subject is a day in the life of a Banaras Brahmin. The two texts were composed as primers for teaching the Sanskrit language to young children. Incidentally, they also provide a window into urban life and social practices in seventeenth-century Banaras.

The Kanyakubja Brahmin protagonist of the *Girvanpadmanjari*, a Vajpayee, had several Maratha Brahmin neighbors. In a variation on this idea, the Maratha Brahmin protagonist of the *Girvanvangmanjari* had studied in Bengal, and he invited a *sanyasin* (ascetic), who originally hailed from Karnataka, to his home.[89] These exchanges reflect the intersection of this diverse Brahminical world with the Indo-Persian world of the Mughals. Before he renounced worldly concerns, the *sanyasin* of the *Girvanvangmanjari* had been a Mughal grandee in imperial service. He confessed that his renunciation (in becoming a *sanyasin*) was spurred by a sense of guilt over a bout of personal indulgence that prevented him from serving his Mughal patron and mentor, Zulfikar Khan, in a satisfactory way.[90] Patronage structures were sustained through loyalty, a key ingredient in courtly relations, and the *sanyasin* had clearly suffered as a result of his lapse.

The authors of the *Girvan* texts described Banaras through an excessive use of Sanskritized terminology. Both Varadaraja and Dhundiraja used archaic place-names to describe seventeenth-century Banaras. They made deliberate references to *purana* literature rather than using names that would have referenced the contemporary Mughal city. Contemporary and vernacular terms could also be Sanskritized, such as the term *ghatta* instead of the more commonly used term *ghat* when describing the city's riverfront.[91] In addition, both authors preferred to use older Sanskritized names for particular ghats rather than names that could reference contemporary patronage. Names of ghats such as "Man Mandir" or "Bundiparkota" that were used in maps and panoramas created during the seventeenth century are conspicuously absent in the Girvan texts. A number of names for ghats were already beginning to change by the eighteenth century.[92]

Brahmin authors often employed Sanskrit terminology to define an "uncontaminated" and therefore largely imagined sphere and spaces. The authors of the Girvan texts similarly ignored newer intrusions and defined neighborhoods through religious markers and *purana* references rather than contemporary *muhalla* names.[93] Neither author mentions either a Vishweshwur *linga* or its temple, which suggests two possibilities. Dhundiraja (and possibly also Varadaraja) belonged to the Vaishnava Madhva sect that originated in southern India and a Shaiva shrine may have held marginal significance for both authors. In addition, in the case of Dhundiraja, who wrote at the turn of the eighteenth century, it may also suggest a reluctance to dwell on the dismantling of a shrine that may have been peripheral to his immediate religious concerns but was nevertheless associated with a larger world of valued beliefs and traditions. In either case, at this time, Vishweshwur did not have the universally significant place that it came to hold among all Brahmins in the nineteenth century.

The abiding concerns of Brahmin commentators were related to ritual purity and what they saw as an undesirable cultural syncretism in dress and language. At the same time, they did not explicitly articulate the physical form of an ideal Hindu city. Nor did they make overt references to descriptions within architectural and planning treatises written in Sanskrit. The syncretic Indo-Islamic architectural and urban forms of northern India were the chosen option for both Hindu and Muslim patrons. For their part, Brahmin intellectuals were more interested in spheres of influence rather than nuances of form and style, and they articulated sentiments through their privileged means of expression, the Sanskrit language. The tension between pristine imaginations articulated through Sanskrit texts and the evolving forms of religious architecture under Mughal patronage was obvious, for instance, when Narayan Bhatt reverted to spatial typologies described in the *Kashikhand* as he wrote about the Mughal Vishweshwur temple. At the same time, Mughal built forms were celebrated in visual depictions, suggesting that there were several imaginations at play in the regeneration of the city. The political role of Mughal forms is lucidly apparent in the urban assessments and temple projects that were undertaken in the wake of Aurangzeb's drastic actions.

AFTER THE TEMPLE

In 1698, Bishan Singh of Amber initiated a project to rebuild the Vishweshwur temple. Besides mapping the built environment and the ritual landscape of the city, surveyors from Amber collected information on land use and urban social patterns. In addition, they detailed various claims and controversies that surrounded the mosques. For instance, a caption labeling the Gyan Vapi mosque in the Devanagari script states, "the plinth of the Vishweshwur temple."[94] The creators of this map shrank the space of the mosque and confined it to the three covered bays before the mihrab, while the plinth retained a place within the city's ritual life. Besides the plinth of the temple/mosque, the precinct contained the sacred Gyan Vapi well. In this way an identity for this space as the original site of the Vishweshwur temple was never entirely relinquished.[95] The Amber court purchased significant pieces of land around the Vishweshwur/Gyan Vapi precinct from several persons (including many Muslim families) who lived in the area. However, they did not successfully initiate a rebuilding project for the Vishweshwur temple.[96]

The Amber survey certainly drew renewed attention to the Vishweshwur/Gyan Vapi precinct. Bishan Singh and later his successor, Sawai Jai Singh II, also resuscitated the site of the Adi-Vishweshwur temple, the supposed original site of the Vishweshwur *linga* that was located adjacent to a sultanate period mosque, also known as Razia's mosque.[97] If rebuilding Vishweshwur posed a significant challenge, an Adi-Vishweshwur temple (ca. 1700) was more easily created. Its designers and patrons chose a contemporary Mughal idiom, just as Narayan Bhatt and Todarmal had chosen an architectural language in keeping with late sixteenth-century imperial taste. Such aesthetic choices further underline connections between the Mughal state and its diverse constituencies, especially as they were expressed through temple architecture.

THREE GENERATIONS OF THE MUGHAL TEMPLE

The connection between the regenerated ritual landscape of Banaras and Mughal authority is also evident when analyzed through innovations in the city's temple architecture over the course of the long seventeenth century. As discussed earlier, the nature of Mughal support could be inconsistent, yet it was far removed from the extreme positions of either unconditional support for or the wanton desecration of principal temples in Banaras. Since Mughal interest and intervention were inflected by the individual political agendas as well as personal beliefs of each emperor, temple architecture is a window into the nature of their relations with the city. In the late sixteenth century, Emperor Akbar's interests in Sufi practices were echoed by his friend and chronicler Abul Fazl, who made special efforts to bridge the distance between Islamic and Hindu ritual. His analogy of the circumambulation of the Kaaba for pilgrimage circuits around a major temple in Banaras is consistent with Sufi motivations of understanding an unfamiliar "other." Abul Fazl's major text, the *Ain-i-Akbari*, is in essence a cultural, geographical, and economic survey of the empire. Abul Fazl and his contemporaries at Akbar's court were well aware of South Asia's pre-Islamic past and would not have failed to note the strong connection between political authority and patronage for temple architecture. The legacy of such relationships played out over a century of Mughal engagement with Banaras.

A brief recapitulation of the history of temple forms in South Asia reveals that major temples enjoyed royal patronage and that their architecture was based on a fairly mature formal and symbolic vocabulary by the twelfth century. The presiding deities of major temples, usually forms or incarnations of either of the deities Shiva or Vishnu, were directly bound to that of their royal patron through ceremonial titles, monetary and land grants, and daily as well as occasional festive rituals.[98] The intense connection between royal patronage and temple ritual also implied a corresponding relationship between religion, courtly culture, and politics. Despite regional variations, some common threads in temple design are apparent in examples across South Asia. One such shared feature was the formal distinction and spatial separation between the *garbha-griha* (sanctum) and multiple *mandapas* (ritual halls). Each of these parts was externally distinguishable through distinctive roof forms such as the *shikhara* or *vimana* (temple towers with distinctive profiles) over the sanctum and either a pyramidal or flat roof over the *mandapa*. In the centuries immediately following the encounter with Islam, designers of temples frequently incorporated what nineteenth-century art historians often described as "Indo-saracenic" elements within their schemes even as they continued to use archaic forms.[99] The "classic" form of the Hindu temple based on trabeated construction systems, *shikharas* over the sanctum, and pyramidal *mandapa* roofs was no longer the only option for expressing Hindu religious sentiments.[100]

In northern India a number of Hindu Rajput rulers patronized temple architecture between the thirteenth and sixteenth centuries. Their designs were based in well-rooted regional architectural styles and building practices but were also created using elements such as domes and arches that patrons and designers drew from the mosques, madrasas, and palaces that were being built across South Asia. Such innovations were selectively incorporated. Broadly speaking, the ritual and spatial separation of the sanctum was retained, while the *mandapa* portion of the temple was based on novel variations and interpretations. As a result, *shikhara* forms retained their symbolic association with the temple's sanctum even when liberally combined with such adopted forms as domes and vaults. The complex narrative and iconographic programs of pre-Islamic days became less common. The formerly elaborate programs of sculpture and figural embellishment were often summarized into brief and largely symbolic statements of royalty and piety. In the broader Indo-Islamic environment of these centuries, such choices extended beyond mere aesthetic preferences and brought temple architecture within contemporary symbolic frameworks and references. In other words, although patrons valued the past, they found Indo-Islamic elements compelling and meaningful as signifiers of power and prestige. In some courtly contexts, building traditions were documented, summarized, and incorporated within new architectural treatises, suggesting the continued existence of a value for tradition as knowledge as well as practice. It was understood that these were to be selectively combined with the liberal employment of innovative forms.[101]

Notwithstanding these rudimentary adaptations during the "sultanate" centuries, it was only during the reign of the Mughal emperor Akbar that Indo-Islamic forms were innovatively and completely integrated by designers of temples and their patrons. As significant temples became associated with Mughal patronage, integrated vaulted and domed spaces were increasingly preferred in place of the more traditionally placed and distinct *mandapas* of an earlier time. In examples where the Mughal state had a less direct role, such as the case of temples located within the *watan jagirs* (traditional fiefdoms) of the Kacchawahas of Amber, the older Indo-Islamic "sultanate" vocabulary continued to remain relevant as it did in the palaces built by Akbar.[102] It would be pertinent to note that in each of these cases some acknowledgment of an Indo-Islamic context was accommodated and that such acts were necessarily political.

The connection between politics and choices in temple design are evident in an example from seventeenth-century Mewar as that kingdom was incorporated within the Mughal imperium. When Rana Jagat Singh commissioned the Jagdish temple on the principal square leading to the palace gates in his new capital of Udaipur in 1651, he chose an archaic architectural language with minimal inclusion of Indo-Islamic elements (Fig. 2.13a and Fig. 2.13b).[103] Given Mewar's often fractious relationship with the Mughals, his choice of forms can be read as a statement of cultural resistance in the face of political subordination. The Kacchawahas, however, were closely aligned with the Mughal imperial family and court, and they carefully chose a Mughal architectural language for several of the major temple projects that they sponsored at Brindavan and Banaras.

These contexts and examples can allow one to filter meaning through the temple architecture of Mughal Banaras. The oldest and most significant among the temples in that city is of course the shrine dedicated to Vishweshwur. The appearance of the lone surviving wall and arch of Todarmal and Narayan Bhatt's temple suggests that this was a sandstone structure, based on a system of intersecting *iwans* (vaults in the Persian tradition) with prominent pointed arches. This innovative spatial scheme was combined with a carved

FIG. 2.13A

Jagdish temple, Udaipur.

FIG. 2.13B Figural sculpture on exterior of Jagdish temple, Udaipur.

stone exterior. Since this temple is no longer standing, other extant Mughal temples can provide a canvas for speculation on its formal and spatial characteristics. The Govind Dev temple at Brindavan, built at the same time in 1590 by Todarmal's contemporary Raja Man Singh, can provide a necessary point of comparison (Fig. 2.14a and Fig. 2.14b).

Extant remains of the Govind Dev temple indicate that it was based on a similar design. Its interior is formed with *iwans* that intersect at right angles to form a spacious tri-lobed *mandapa*, a sanctum at the end of the fourth arm, and an aniconic but carved and molded sandstone exterior. Mughal symbols of political authority such as the *jharokha* were prominently visible on the exterior of the Govind Dev temple. The French merchant Tavernier, who visited this temple ca. 1665, mentions the three *shikhara* forms that once surmounted the structure. Tavernier distinguished them as a central, taller *shikhara*, flanked by two more diminutive ones.[104] He informed his readers that each *shikhara* was embellished with sculptures of various deities. The surviving *shikharas* of the Govind Dev temple do not bear out Tavernier's description. Since the standing walls are carved and molded, but completely devoid of any figural sculpture, it is particularly difficult to ascertain the veracity of his last statement.

Tavernier recounted a visit to the Bindu Madhav temple at Banaras, also built and managed through Kacchawaha patronage. The Kacchawahas chose a Vaishnava tradition that had a deep history but insignificant ritual role within Kashikshetra.[105] By sponsoring a design for an imperial Mughal temple to celebrate this tradition, they also enhanced and celebrated the deity beyond the original confines of the *Kashikhand* or the intentions of its authors. With its monumental interior also defined by intersecting *iwans*, the design of the Bindu Madhav temple mirrored the spaces, appearance, and by extension some of the authority of the Vishweshwur tradition. The Mughal role in each building is significant since both temples were sponsored by *mansabdars* of the empire.

Tavernier described the *iwans* of the Bindu Madhav temple that intersected to form an impressive central space. An altar with an image of the presiding deity was placed at the intersection and the space was surmounted by a monumental *shikhara*.[106] He mentioned the four smaller *shikharas* that had been placed over each arm of the temple's cruciform plan.[107] As Catherine Asher has pointed out with respect to the Govind Dev temple, Persian and particularly Mughal trends and preferences were incorporated into temple design on an unprecedented scale. Thus two significant Vaishnava temples at important pilgrimage destinations in North India were designed to make a strong statement of affinity with the Mughal political and cultural world. Each was also sponsored by a well-connected Mughal *mansabdar*. The surviving elements of the Vishweshwur temple suggest a similar design. It is equally significant that the Vishweshwur and Bindu Madhav temples shared key formal attributes. This is particularly so given the connection of each temple to the Mughal court in light of Narayan Bhatt's articulation of the consolidation between Shaiva and Vaishnava practices in the *Tristhalisetu*.

Radical experiments such as the inventions undertaken in the Vishweshwur temple were then reconciled with the allegorical references already present in the *Kashikhand*. Bhatt found a way to reconcile the contemporary building with its archaic foundational text. He described the Vishweshwur temple as a collection of *mandapas* on the basis of descriptions in the *Kashikhand*.[108] He aligned descriptions of the ritual spaces contained

FIG. 2.14A Govind Dev temple, Brindavan.

FIG. 2.14B Vaulted *mandapa* in interior of Govind Dev temple, Brindavan.

within this text with the forms and spaces of the Mughal Vishweshwur temple, thereby integrating Mughal forms within descriptions of ritualized spaces. The architects for the new structure replicated these as closely as possible, while shifting a temple itself to a new location, south of its original site.[109] When Mitra Misra wrote his *nibandha* in the early seventeenth century, he also drew on the *Kashikhand* to describe and emphasize several traditions such as prescribed visits to four *mandapas* and the Gyan Vapi well within the Vishweshwur temple precinct.[110] Like his predecessor, Misra also merged the forms of the Vishweshwur temple with descriptions of ritual spaces. It is equally significant that the ca. fifteenth-century Kardameshwur temple that was eventually incorporated into the Panchkroshi pilgrimage route, and that was at least partially extant at this time, could have provided a direct model for both the Vishweshwur and Bindu Madhav temples. However, the Kardameshwur shrine was not treated as a precedent by the designer of either Mughal temple.

Ultimately, archaic forms had a limited place within the Mughal architectural idiom and contemporary Mughal attitudes were equally mediated through the Kedar temple. The edifice was associated with a venerated site and, as has been noted, was renovated with Mughal support, in this case that of the emperor Aurangzeb. In a manner similar to the Vishweshwur and Bindu Madhav temples, the Kedar temple bore a dual relationship to Mughal urbanism as well as Kashikshetra. When he reconsecrated this temple, Kuma-raswamy employed a Mughal architectural language selectively but quite emphatically.[111] Temple designers utilized contemporary imperial aesthetics and building practices.

The refurbished temple had to accommodate existing deities, pilgrimage zones, and ritual associations as well as a connection to a *muth* under Mughal patronage and protection. These multiple and symbolic layers required an appropriate architecture. In the plan a *garbha-griha* with the Kedar *linga* is preceded by an asymmetrical antechamber and surrounded by a corridor designed to accommodate a number of existing *lingas* and deities (Fig. 2.15a and Fig. 2.15b). It is preceded by a *mandapa*, unrecognizable as such from the exterior but with an impressive interior. Allegiance to Mughal authority and the support of the imperial state were often declared through its most ubiquitous built element: the baluster column. The column was re-created on a monumental scale in the Kedar temple (Fig. 2.16). Rows of such columns prominently supported a temple *mandapa* that was visited by large number of pilgrims from the southern regions of the subcontinent, particularly the Tamil country. At the same time, these were Mughal baluster columns with a difference. A base and capital derived from southern Indian and particularly Nayaka temple architecture was added to a legible Mughal shaft. The columns could indicate the existence of Mughal patronage to a visiting audience familiar with Nayaka aesthetics. In addition, the entrance to the *garbha-griha* (sanctum) was flanked by twin images of Shiva Nataraj—that is, Shiva the cosmic dancer, as he is manifest at the southern Indian temple city of Chidambaram.[112] A second and smaller Shiva temple as well as the structure enclosing Kumarswamy's *samadhi* (funerary marker) within the *muth* was based on the formal typology of a Mughal tomb. Both structures had an institutional as well as public role (similar to that of the Ram temple in the Kanganwali *haveli*). Through a deliberate choice of forms, the leaders of the *muth* chose to make a clear statement of allegiance to the Mughal state.[113]

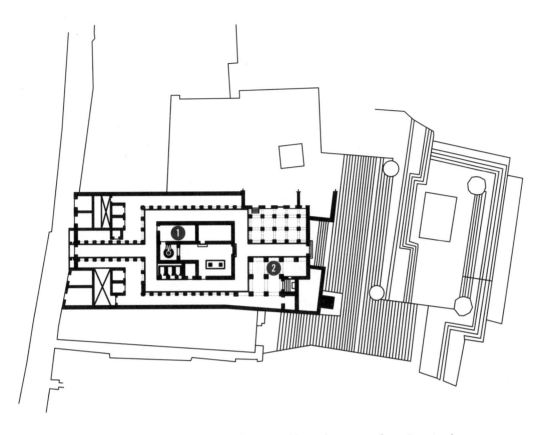

FIG. 2.15A Plan of Kedar temple and ghat. 1–*garbha-griha*, 2–*mandapa*. Drawing by
Nanditha Veeraraghavelu and Jennifer Shontz.

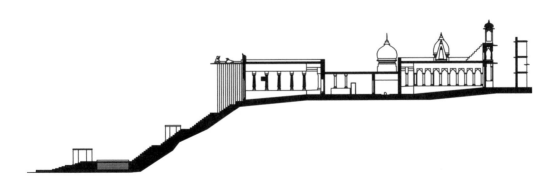

FIG. 2.15B Section through Kedar temple and ghat. Drawing by Nanditha Veeraraghavelu
and Jennifer Shontz.

FIG. 2.16 Mughal columns in the *mandapa* of Kedar temple.

This preference for a contemporary architectural language survived well up to the end of the seventeenth century in Banaras. The Adi-Vishweshwur temple (ca. 1700), initiated by Bishan Singh and completed by Sawai Jai Singh II, was designed with a conservative imperial architectural vocabulary.[114] In this austere, single-room structure, a dome was placed above a cubical sanctum, a typology more reminiscent of a Mughal tomb rather than a conventional or archaic temple plan and exterior form (Fig. 2.17 and Fig. 2.18). Indeed, the austere dome that surmounts this temple shares more in formal terms with the domes of the Dharhara mosque and also with the domes atop the shrines within the Kumaraswamy *muth*. In each case, patrons and builders underlined a connection with imperial authority.

Beginning in the late seventeenth century, the Amber court under Sawai Jai Singh II began to adopt certain overt symbols of Hindu kingship, including a public performance of the Ashwamedha *yajnya* (fire ritual), even as the rajas remained part of the Mughal imperial structure.[115] Similarly, Sawai Jai Singh II promoted careful choices in forms as he presided over the design and foundation of the city of Jaipur. He chose urban design precedents that were ostensibly derived from ancient Vedic sources, but on closer examination their origins could be equally traced to Mughal planning and design principles.[116] At Banaras the Kacchawahas stoically adhered to current imperial preferences in choosing a form

CHAPTER 2

FIG. 2.17   Adi-Vishweshwur temple.

for the Adi-Vishweshwur temple, even as they advocated the rebuilding of the Vishwesh-wur temple that Aurangzeb had dismantled. It is equally pertinent that their proposed plans for rebuilding the Vishweshwur temple did not include the destruction of the Gyan Vapi mosque.[117] Instead, they reinforced a deeper history for the Vishweshwur tradition

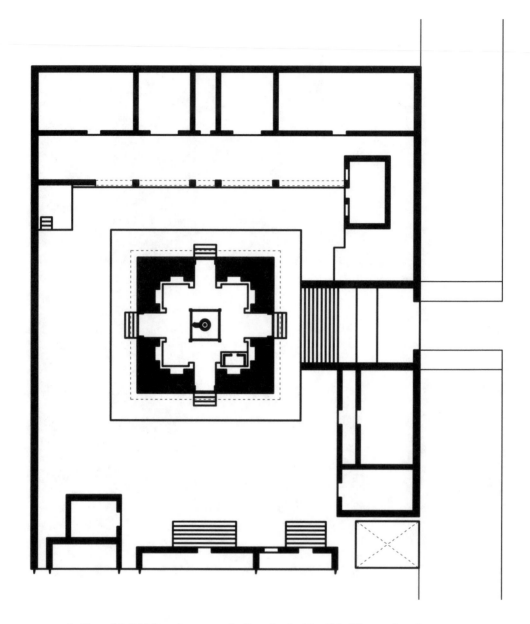

FIG. 2.18 Plan of Adi-Vishweshwur temple. Drawing by Nanditha Veeraraghavelu and Jennifer Shontz.

by tracing its ostensible roots and by emphasizing its "original site." Inadvertently, perhaps, these actions have helped to perpetuate a narrative of repeated destruction that is associated with the Vishweshwur tradition. The deliberate choice of a Mughal language for temple architecture was intended to emphasize a connection to imperial support. The currency of such a language was therefore paramount.

Aurangzeb's decision to dismantle the Vishweshwur temple reverberated in multiple and complex ways.[118] After the temple was pulled down, its western wall was converted into the *qibla* (direction toward Mecca) wall of the Gyan Vapi mosque, its walled-in central arch now supporting a mihrab.[119] The temple had been intimately connected to the urban institutions and spatial structure of the city through proximity, access, and the mechanisms of administration. These institutional, spatial, and ritual relationships did not suddenly disappear. Moreover, despite the significant vacuum at its ritual center, the city retained its role as a Hindu pilgrimage destination throughout the eighteenth century. The precinct, of what was now the Gyan Vapi mosque, continued to serve as the focal point of this network of sacred sites.[120] The act of dismantling had been almost a surgical procedure. Apart from the structure of the temple that was taken down and replaced with a mosque, the plinth of the structure as well as the surrounding buildings of the precinct was largely untouched. Oral accounts indicate that the Brahmins associated with the temple continued to reside within the precinct, to claim their priestly privileges, and to direct rituals and pilgrimages.

In a contradictory turn of events, and far from overturning religious sentiments and identities, the sheer act of dismantling may have transmuted Vishweshwur into the undisputed center and fulcrum of the city's ritual landscape. This set the stage for the *Kashikhand* in its role as the ultimate pilgrimage text on the city. As a consequence, the Shaiva vision for the city became its dominant identity. A closer look at two vastly divergent visual representations of the city in the immediate aftermath of the temple's dismantling revealed the new but firmly entrenched role of the Vishweshwur temple. The first image is a pilgrimage *pata*, created ca. 1700 in the Mewar kingdom (Plate 1). The composition includes four horizontal registers, each one corresponding to a section of the city. The lowest register is diagonally intersected by a curving river with a tributary branching down vertically to the lower edge of the frame. The next (or third) register is the largest, and it is divided into multiple squares that form a grid around a central Vishweshwur temple. Significantly, Vishweshwur is the central focus of this third register and by extension of the entire *pata*. Each square of this grid contains a shrine that corresponds to sites that are actually located in the city and some that are merely mentioned in *purana* texts. The central Vishweshwur temple is prominently associated with a Rajput patron, possibly a Sisodia, who is depicted dressed in a dhoti and Mughal turban. His dress may suggest his position in straddling the twin worlds of a Hindu ruler and patron who was also a Mughal courtier, even if ostensibly a reluctant one. This remains one of the earliest and most extensive surviving visual representations of a central Shaiva vision based to a great extent on the *Kashikhand*.

The *pata* artists included popular destinations such as the Annapurna temple.[121] They acknowledged the presence of a vibrant mercantile community in the city. Various personalities who represented political and commercial interests in the city are included as well. They are framed within individual squares, placed along the right edge of the *pata* and captioned as *labh* (profit). These "portraits" are arranged within a vertical band to the right of the Vishweshwur temple and its surrounding sacred zone. Their presence underlines the close association between religion, commerce, and politics in a Mughal city. Kashi's larger ritual role as a sacred city that enfolded other pilgrimage centers within its spaces is emphasized as well. The first and second registers contain references to Rameshwur and Gaya, *tirtha* sites that are notionally encompassed by Kashi, the mother of all *tirthas*.

The artists depicted the stretch of the Ganges between the Varuna and Assi streams as a pale blue stream surrounded by several sacred sites that are located in close proximity to the river. Included among them is the Assi *sangam* as well as the Dashashwamedha and Manikarnika ghats. The ghats are depicted as sites for ritual bathing, although their precise geographic locations are ignored and they are placed on opposite sides of the river. It is, however, the relationship of each site to the river that is significant. Each ghat is further depicted as a collection of several nested *tirthas*. Dashashwamedha, for instance, encompasses the Prayag *tirtha* and in a departure from nineteenth-century representations also includes the Chakrapushkarni *tirtha*. The Varuna *sangam* is located at the upper edge of this register. The artists cut a bow-shaped stream into the rectilinear grid of the Antargriha, to mark this critical ritual node. The creators of the *pata* acknowledge the city's significant Vaishnava shrines, although these are essentially treated as being peripheral to a predominantly Shaiva identity.[122] The Bindu Madhav temple is depicted as a relatively insignificant temple near the Varuna *sangam*. The *pata* represents a city based predominantly in the *Kashikhand* and its center, Vishweshwur. Although the physical structure of the temple was already dismantled when this *pata* was created, its inclusion as the central focus of this image suggests that its memory and site continued to dominate expectations for Banaras.[123]

Vaishnava perspectives on the city were also incorporated within visual representations such as the pilgrimage panorama discussed earlier that was produced for the Amber court in the late seventeenth century, which provides a predominantly Vaishnava view of this ritual landscape. A few of the shrines on the Antargriha route are included within the panorama, but the major deities and sites depicted reference a Vaishnava sensibility.[124] Many ritual wells and bathing tanks associated with pilgrimages in the *Kashikhand* and the *Kashirahasya* are visible, including the Lolark well and the Durga *kund*. Other easily recognizable sites that fall within the bounds of the sacred zone of Kashikshetra include the Kurukshetra ritual tank, the Vishweshwur and Kalbhairav temples, and the oversized Tilbhandeshwur *linga*. Yet other structures include the Laxmi *kund* and *muth*, labeled as "Laxmivilas mandap," its institutional role suggested by depicting a group of *sadhus* in an adjoining grove of trees.

The central role and realm of the Vishweshwur temple is captured through repetitive depictions, in this case within a Vaishnava panorama that was created at around the same time as the aforementioned *pata*. The panorama, however, is a lingering Vaishnava perspective on the city, and the central focus of the composition is a row of imagined shrines dedicated to the Dashavatar, the many reincarnations of Vishnu.[125] Vishweshwur's place is relatively marginal to this predominantly Vaishnava vision. Yet the temple is depicted twice, suggesting that given its central role in the city, artists and patrons could not ignore its role. At the same time, its dual representation implies uncertainty regarding its place within a Vaishnava vision. The panorama includes an image of the Dharhara mosque,

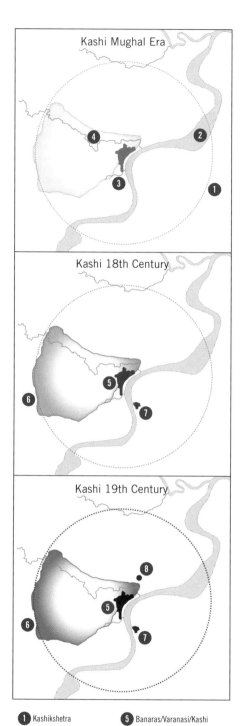

Kashi Mughal Era

Kashi 18th Century

Kashi 19th Century

1 Kashikshetra
2 Ganges River
3 Assi Stream
4 Barna (Varuna) Stream
5 Banaras/Varanasi/Kashi
6 Panchkroshi pilgrimage route
7 Ramnagar
8 Sarnath

a consistent reminder of a loss. In a short while, the towering minarets became coveted symbols of the city and, interestingly, its religious identity. In several narratives they were treated as representations of the Bindu Madhav temple that the mosque had replaced. In retrospect, Aurangzeb's decision to dismantle prominent Mughal temples resulted in a renewed focus on their sites and especially on the Vishweshwur *linga* and its pilgrimage traditions. The creators of both the *pata* and the panorama successfully merged distinct ritual landscapes based in Shaiva and Vaishnava texts, with selected and significant elements from its tangible urban environment.

Despite the fractured nature of Mughal cosmopolitanism and the varied anxieties of its participants, Mughal interventions were designed to build a careful relationship with the ritual spaces and sacred sites of Kashikshetra. Recognizable Mughal features, though placed strategically, were intended to regenerate selected elements of the ritual landscape. The choice of a Mughal architectural and spatial language for several major projects, including for the Vishweshwur temple, successfully conveyed imperial support. Although Aurangzeb's support for the Kedar temple in particular suggests selective rather than complete opposition to Hindu groups and their practices, the withdrawal of Mughal patronage and the dismantling of key temple structures during his reign resulted in an enhanced role for their deities within religious memory and the city's ritual landscape. Whether as

MAP 2.3

Pilgrimage Landscape of Kashi, ca. 1600–ca. 1900. Drawing by Gretta Tritch Roman and Jennifer Shontz.

a city with thriving temples or a city of prominent imperial mosques, its urban structure, spaces, and architectural forms constituted a distinctly Mughal Banaras.

Textual imaginations on the city were always more extensive and complex than their manifestations on the ground. In creating their inventories of the city, Sawai Jai Singh II's surveyors found, as Narayan Bhatt had more than a hundred years earlier, that the ritual imagination of texts was only partially realized on the ground (Map 2.3). But it was in the space between the imagination of the text and the material reality of the city that eighteenth-century patrons found renewed opportunities.

CHAPTER THREE

EXPANSION AND INVENTION

E NUGULA Veeraswamy, a visitor from Madras in 1831, described Banaras as a city
filled with temples, monasteries, and charitable institutions. He found a city that
enjoyed robust support for the construction of its religious buildings and public celebrations from a diverse group of patrons. The visitor from southern India described an
overall city structure that most contemporary visitors recognize, with its ritual center at
the Vishweshwur temple, surrounded by its Antargriha zone. Like Veeraswamy, they can
locate the city's sacred boundary marked by the Panchkroshi pilgrimage circuit and identify with his experience of religious rupture as they gaze on the city's prominent mosques.
Many aspects of the spatial environment of contemporary Banaras were initiated and
realized over the course of the eighteenth century, overlaid on its older Mughal framework. This was a period when festivals and fairs were abundantly supported, and the city's
role as a penultimate pilgrimage destination based primarily in the *Kashikhand* and the
Kashirahasya was reiterated.

The city received interest and investments from diverse patrons over the course of a
century that also saw the decline of the Mughal Empire. After more than two centuries
the Mughals were gradually being replaced by various regional powers. The century was
to end with large parts of South Asia under the control of the East India Company. As
marginal groups acquired political clout, they sought symbols of legitimacy and lineage.
In this competitive environment, patrons who often came from obscure beginnings saw
the city and its burgeoning religious life as an avenue to showcase patronage for both well-
established and newly invented traditions. Mughal customs, forms, and building types
were valued for their association with power, prestige, lineage, and good taste. In particular, architectural precedents provided a visible anchor for newly fashioned identities and
personas. Even so, the city's skyline was soon punctuated by numerous *shikharas*, archaic
choices for emergent elites interested in revivalist gestures while retaining a preference
for Mughal forms. The terms and contingencies of this revivalism were underlined by
consensus as well as competition.

Aristocrats in the eighteenth century were a fragmented group with multiple regional,
religious, and social (caste) affiliations. Unlike their Mughal predecessors, they had divergent goals and pursued varied political interests. With the disappearance of Mughal grandees and their patronage, Brahmins (ritual specialists and scholars) in search of livelihoods

and new patrons turned their attention to enhancing the prestige of newer rulers and power brokers. Their numbers included several members of an emergent Maratha aristocracy and Bengali landowners who had alliances with the East India Company. Brahmin priests could often have multiple and competing patrons who depended on their endorsement in this changing society. At the same time, parvenu aristocrats interested in patronizing the city's regeneration often had different motivations and perspectives than Brahmins. The Rajas of Banaras had begun their reign as *zamindars* (landowners and/or revenue collectors) under the Nawabs (Mughal governors) of Awadh. They gradually distanced themselves from that role and refashioned themselves as "Kashi Naresh" (kings of Kashi) by the early decades of the nineteenth century. Their patronage of public festivities further enhanced the city's resurgent religious role. As Banaras simultaneously became a prominent commercial center in the eighteenth century, it provided a link between the older political centers of Delhi and Agra and the newer regional centers of Patna and Murshidabad.[1] Bankers and traders became participants in the city's regeneration, forging a connection between commerce, urbanization, and religious identity.

The combination of a critical number of interested elites and a shifting idea of the ritual landscape through an emphasis on specific texts meant that the sacred zone of Kashikshetra would be imagined afresh, populated and urbanized. A consensus about a Vishweshwur temple surrounded by its Antargriha zone and a periphery demarcated by the Panchkroshi pilgrimage route were its defining features (Map 3.1, Map 3.2, and see Map 2.3). This configuration was the basis for locating architectural and urban investments. By the late eighteenth century, several elites had built mansions within the bounds of the Panchkroshi circuit and were well ensconced in semiautonomous estates. Their presence was aptly captured by James Prinsep in his 1822 map (Plate 5) and accompanying "Directory" of "principal Moosulman and Hindoo families."[2]

Prinsep depicted a city clustered along the river, with new growth extending in eastward spurs, occupying ridges and higher ground and skirting several of the lakes and pools that dotted Kashikshetra.[3] Many of these natural catchments were designated as sacred within *purana* and *nibandha* texts. Elites built walled *chahar-baghs* (quadripartite gardens) within several of these catchments, and large *havelis* (mansions) acted as development catalysts, multiplying rapidly by the late eighteenth century. If newly minted aristocrats were nostalgic about a Mughal legacy, they ostensibly also began to value a pre-Islamic past. A diverse and motley group of patrons succeeded in promoting a unified vision for the city.

BRAHMIN VISIONS AND THE SOCIORELIGIOUS SPHERE

Religious trends in Banaras were closely connected to a Brahmin intellectual sphere of scholarly exchange and advocacy. The scholarly circle around Narayan Bhatt had emphasized the idea of Kashikshetra with its center at Madhyameshwur as well as Kashi's role as an ideal site for conducting cremations. His legacy of activism and his vision for the city were perpetuated by his great-grandson, Nagesh Bhatt, who wrote his own *tirtha* text, the *Tirthendushekhara*, in the early eighteenth century.[4] Besides defining Kashikshetra and promoting Kashi's role as an ideal site for funerals, Nagesh Bhatt linked its sacred landscape to narratives in the *Mahabharata*.[5] He endorsed activities that a lay

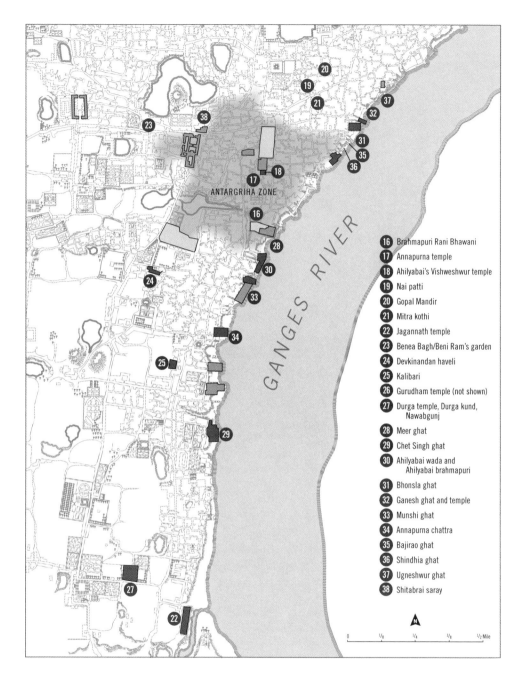

MAP 3.1   Map of Banaras City, ca. 1800, based on *The City of Bunarus*, 1822, by James Prinsep.
Drawing by Gretta Tritch Roman and Jennifer Shontz.

(rather than scholarly) population could participate in, including pilgrimage, the sponsoring and partaking of charitable meals, and inevitably funerals. He asserted Kashi's role as

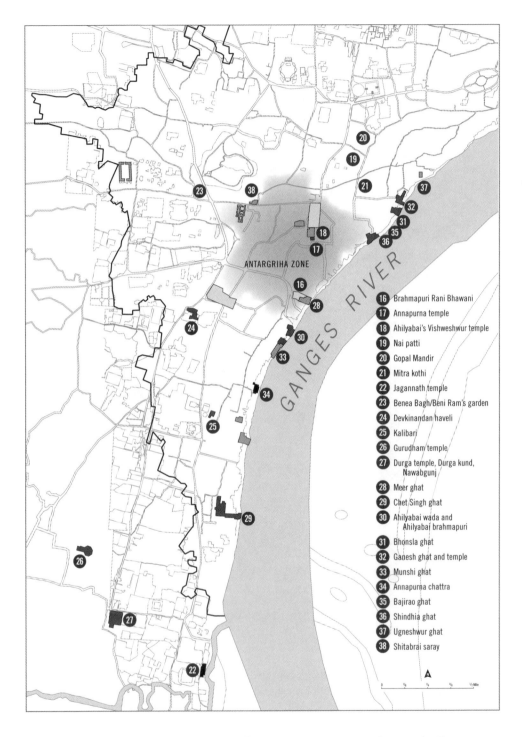

ANTARGRIHA ZONE

GANGES RIVER

16 Brahmapuri Rani Bhawani
17 Annapurna temple
18 Ahilyabai's Vishweshwur temple
19 Nai patti
20 Gopal Mandir
21 Mitra kothi
22 Jagannath temple
23 Benea Bagh/Beni Ram's garden
24 Devkinandan haveli
25 Kalibari
26 Gurudham temple
27 Durga temple, Durga kund, Nawabgunj
28 Meer ghat
29 Chet Singh ghat
30 Ahilyabai wada and Ahilyabai brahmapuri
31 Bhonsla ghat
32 Ganesh ghat and temple
33 Munshi ghat
34 Annapurna chattra
35 Bajirao ghat
36 Shindhia ghat
37 Ugneshwur ghat
38 Shitabrai saray

MAP 3.2 Map of Banaras City, ca. 1800, based on *Benares City, 1928–29*. Drawing by Gretta Tritch Roman, Jennifer Shontz, Nanditha Veeraraghavelu, and Rohan Haksar.

Avimukta (never forsaken by Shiva) and the significance of the Madhayameshwur *linga* as the center of Kashikshetra. He emphasized its topographical situation between the Varuna and Assi as well as the pilgrimage traditions associated with the Vishweshwur *linga*. While Nagesh Bhatt drew ideas and concepts from a variety of *purana* sources, he essentially described a Shaiva city determined through the *Kashikhand* and the Vishweshwur tradition. Nevertheless, a number of other deities and ritual traditions could be nested and accommodated within this overarching idea.

Since a fresh focus on the Vishweshwur temple implied renewed interest in the *Kashikhand* and the *Kashirahasya*, the sacred imagination contained within these texts became a loose blueprint that would shape the city's built environment. Several translations in vernacular languages emphasized the myths, ritual landscapes, and pilgrimage practices discussed in each text.[6] These were promoted through a sociopolitical sphere that was intimately connected to Brahmin activism. Although Brahmin scholars were part of an intellectual network of shared knowledge, individual patronage links developed with emerging or established aristocrats and other elites by ritual specialists were often forged on the basis of regional affiliations.

Patronage for religious activities and architecture were avenues for elites and nonelites to participate in this mediated sociopolitical sphere that was also connected to religion.[7] The sphere encapsulated patronage as an index of connection to the city's religious traditions and to the larger movement of its regeneration. A major component of exchange in this sphere was the acknowledgment of patronage among the city's elites as well as its nonelites. Among elites, this could occur through mutual recognition and participation in each other's rituals. Across social differentiators, acknowledgment could occur through acts of *dana* (charity) or *dakshina* (ritual gift-giving), the latter transaction taking place between elites and the city's Brahmins. The practice and public spectacle of hosting *brahmin-bhojans* (ritual feasts) remained current and robust.[8] Elites competed through acts of *dakshina* channeled toward Brahmins and also by maintaining connections to newly established or refurbished temples. Brahmins and rituals were also supported through endowments. Visible acts of patronage engendered recognition and prestige and bound patrons and beneficiaries in interdependent social and political relationships.

In a manner promoted by their predecessors both across South Asia as well as within Banaras, emerging elites were expected to have a visible urban presence as they patronized its religious life. Sponsoring rituals in a visible manner and at a conspicuous scale became critical to their quest for prominent social roles. In this crowded theater, participation in the socioreligious sphere often occurred through the invention of tradition.[9] By the early eighteenth century, and under the initiative of Narayan Dikshit Patankar (the Peshwa's Brahmin mentor), this was further transformed into robust activism that also hinged on public charity. Patankar promoted pilgrimage to Banaras, himself leading several contingents of pilgrims from the Deccan.[10] The emphasis on Brahmin practices motivated the Peshwas in the 1730s to invest primarily in those sites and activities that would foster and perpetuate the city's Brahmin-centered ritual life.

In this fragmented world, formal and aesthetic approaches to the built environment and spectacle once reserved solely for the Mughal imperial family and high-ranking members of their court became accessible to a broad group of emergent elites. Mughal models first became more widely available under the Nawabs of Awadh, who came to control the city and its region by the early eighteenth century. The Nawabs deputed Meer Rustam Ali as the provincial administrator of the Banaras region. He built a new *saray* and court-house along the major urban artery that already connected Aurangzeb's *saray* with the Vishweshwur temple and Manikarnika ghat.[11] Besides bolstering the city's administrative structure and upgrading its administrative and commercial infrastructure, Meer Rustam Ali espoused a visibly syncretic culture through support for and participation in Hindu festivals—particularly, the annual Holi celebrations.[12] Through such actions he signaled at least partial state support for Hindu rituals and pilgrimage activity. Furthermore, it was Meer Rustam Ali's patronage for built forms and celebrations rather than the early Brahmin-centric, ritually correct yet materially sparse interventions of the Marathas that ultimately molded the material and social forms of a socioreligious sphere and its anchoring architecture.

Succeeding Meer Rustam Ali, elite patrons in the mid-eighteenth century could range from ambitious Maratha chiefs (such as the Bhonslas from Central India) to established Bengali landowners (such as Rani Bhawani of Natore). Other investors included the newly established ruling house of the Rajas of Banaras. Many of them adopted and adapted Mughal architectural precedents that could provide viable and culturally relevant models that could visibly link political authority and ritual sites. Emergent Maratha aristocrats (apart from those of Brahmin origin) actively claimed Rajput descent. A Rajput identity provided an idealized source of emulation for Maratha states in the eighteenth century.[13] Other emergent elites added to this number toward the late eighteenth century and included families such as the Mitras, who were comprador partners of the East India Company. Many of the subcontinent's scribal and administrative elites made fortunes in these turbulent times and began to invest in the city. Beniram and Bishambar Pandit (active late eighteenth to early nineteenth centuries), who had worked for a number of Maratha ruling houses but had switched allegiance to the East India Company toward the late eighteenth century, belonged to this latter group. At the turn of the nineteenth century, many deposed or disenfranchised rulers such as Amrut Rao Peshwa, a failed contender to the position of Peshwa in Pune, added to their numbers.[14] Deprived of fiefdoms and power bases, patrons expressed visible piety through religious rituals and temples. Although devised as a means to reclaim status or compensate for its loss, such activities provided a significant boost to the city's religious economy.

The relationship between the subcontinent's numerous established and emergent ruling elites and the city's Brahmins was based in a reciprocal system of legitimation. Personal honor and status could be achieved by presiding over a formal audience or *sabha* of Brahmins and opinion makers. For instance, when Krishnachandra Ghoshal, head of a Bengali *zamindar* family and a partner of the East India Company, patronized a *shivasthapana* (literally, the "establishment of Shiva") ceremony on a visit to the city ca. 1768, he invited a large number of the city's Brahmins to the event.[15] A *linga* was consecrated as "Kandarpeshwur," named after his father, Kandarp Ghoshal.[16] It was an occasion for a social and material transaction between Ghoshal and the city's Bengali Brahmins. Vijayaram Sen, a scribe in Ghoshal's entourage, was careful to mention in his narrative *Tirthamangala* that rituals followed the *shastras*. After the consecration of the *linga*,

Ghoshal held an assembly and presided over a "learned debate," where the discussion, according to Sen, was centered on questions of "Smriti-sahitya, Nyaya-shastra, Vedanta-purana."[17] An emergent aristocrat and the Brahmins that he sponsored converged around an event of archaic provenance, their actions fueled by contemporary aspirations.

When elites such as Ghoshal presided over assemblies of Brahmins engaged in "shastra"-based arguments, they also conducted and directed proceedings where contemporary issues of change were debated and anxieties were articulated. Sandria Freitag has hesitated to define this as a "public sphere." Rather, she prefers the term "public arena" as a material, social, and political space where "hierarchy" played out among "unequals" through "ritual, theatre and symbol" in celebration and conflict.[18] The socioreligious sphere was characterized by relationships of mutual dependence. It was a space where socially differentiated participants were linked through acts of patronage as well as the city's ever-evolving ritual traditions. Elites, who were engaged in a quest for power and legitimacy, were equally dependent on Brahmins as well as nonelite audiences for affirmation. For their part, Brahmins and other beneficiaries acquired social and material gains.

As in Ghoshal's case, patrons often selected audiences on the basis of regional affiliation. Sen praised Ghoshal for sponsoring a ritual feast and distributed presents among a large number of the city's Brahmins. A significant number of these were Bengali Brahmins who resided in the city, who also retained links to Bengal through familial connections and patronage networks. Ghoshal's patronage was directed at this Bengali circle through which he strengthened his own and, by extension, his family's status among the diaspora in Banaras as well as a wider audience in Bengal. Vijayaram Sen's role as scribe was pivotal to this dispersal.

The widowed Rani Bhawani of Natore (r. 1748–1789) gained substantial influence and a pious reputation for her multiple charities and investments in eighteenth-century Banaras, especially among its Bengali population.[19] The Rani represented an older and more established Bengali elite family, once landowners under the Nawabs of Bengal. Her actions and charities became models for new groups who were loyal to the company but aspired to more established social roles. The Rani's munificence was deliberately mentioned by Vijayaram Sen in the *Tirthamangala*.[20] Sen dwelled at some length on the temples that she built and endowed, as well as the residences and pensions that she distributed among the city's Brahmins.[21] In his text Sen forged a direct link between the Rani's acts (and by extension her lineage) and his patron's role and actions in Banaras. The Rani was remembered well into the latter half of the nineteenth century, and several observers including the missionary Matthew Atmore Sherring mentioned the Rani as a patron responsible for enhancing the infrastructure of the Panchkroshi route.[22] Sherring wrote his account almost a century later, which suggests that the social recognition that such acts could bring had an enduring quality.

By the early nineteenth century, Veeraswamy could observe that patronage supported the large numbers of northern Indian Brahmin families who styled themselves as the Gangaputra (sons of the Ganges).[23] They considered such patronage as a ritual privilege along with the right to "collect fees" from pilgrims based on their economic means.[24] Manikarnika ghat was a locus for their activities, and pilgrims who wished to perform rituals there had to negotiate with powerful priestly networks. Instances of nonparticipation could often become widespread knowledge and lead to public embarrassment. Veera-swamy pointedly mentioned an elite visitor, "Sarbhoji," the princely ruler of Tanjore, who circumvented such obligations by bathing in the Kedar ghat and participating in an alternate ritual network that was controlled by Brahmins from southern India. Similarly, the "Raja of Vijayanagar" avoided the Gangaputra Brahmins for a year by staying away from Manikarnika ghat, a fact also remarked upon by the observant Veeraswamy.[25] Yet this nexus of elite patronage, mediating Brahmins, and ritual space was sustained because of its implications for the accumulation of social and cultural capital. Powerful individuals and families could certainly control the modes, materials, activities, and built forms of the socioreligious sphere.

The Burhvamangal festival that was patronized by the Rajas of Banaras was a direct appropriation and transformation of Meer Rustam Ali's Holi celebrations, and it depended on elite support and participation. The evening of Holi brought "crowds of people, with obscene shows" and "natives of all ranks" assembled to witness the "immoral spectacle."[26] Urban spaces including the riverfront were sites where such activities brought the elite and nonelite together, the former either as mere spectators or active participants and patrons. Patrons of the Burhvamangal festival simultaneously maintained a relationship to popular aspects of this celebration while supporting more exclusive soirees that referenced a Persianized cultural sphere. Devised as it was to provide a means to respond to changing political and social conditions, by its very nature the success of the socio-religious sphere and its supporting spaces depended on forms that had social currency across social divides. While this was partly achieved through patronage for Hindu rituals, the social demands of the late eighteenth century meant that Persianized social mores and pastimes such as *mehfils* (musical soirees) and *mushairas* (poetry readings) were also held in mansions and gardens for more select audiences.[27] The Ramlila celebrations, also sponsored by the Rajas of Banaras, provided another opportunity to invent a tradition for the city. Although performed primarily in Ramnagar across the river from Banaras, certain spaces within Kashikshetra were strategically incorporated into the active space of the performance. Philip Lutgendorf has described this celebration as a way of linking the traditions of the Ramayana to a Shaiva city.[28]

In a similar fashion, most festivals had some religious component, often through a connection to the city's textual mythology, but also included secular forms of entertainment. The missionary Sherring observed that though the ostensible purpose of such gatherings was religious, "amusement and trade" and "opportunities for vice" were equally significant objectives for participants.[29] Whereas distinctions in power and status were maintained, spectacles and festivities attracted participation from the elite as well as the nonelite and urban spaces became legible through their role in such events. In case of celebrations associated with Sufi saints, such as those at the *dargah* of Gazi Miyan, participants included Muslims as well as Hindus of all classes. The space around Bakariya *kund* was associated with the *dargah* and its festival and occupied a liminal space between Hindu and Muslim practices. Similarly, during the Kajri *mela* in the nineteenth century, when elite women bathed ritually at the Sankhudhara and Iswarganji tanks, they were "serenaded" by professional female singers who simultaneously also attracted a male audience.[30] A similar set of relationships came into play during the associated Holi celebration. "Obscene representations and the use of abusive language" as well as the circulation of "licentious pictures" might have kept some women away, but participation by males of all classes was essential for its continued popularity, not to mention its social and economic viability.[31]

The tradition of Kashibas (retiring to Kashi, especially in one's declining years) was further reinforced by the colonial government during the nineteenth century. Following its success in quelling the rebellion of 1857–58, the colonial government escalated support for this practice and encouraged visits by a number of rulers whose actual political power had been substantially diminished.[32] Most of them had lost territories and land holdings and were compelled to live on pensions granted by the colonial government. To establish a residence at Banaras and participate in its socioreligious sphere was a way to retain tangible links to established symbols and codes of prestige, if not power. The British recognized the value of such connections and facilitated the move to and residence at Banaras. The missionary James Kennedy, a pastor with the London Missionary Society, described the situation aptly when he said that it seemed "as if our Government wished to compensate them for the loss of their dominion by conferring on them special religious advantages."[33] Emergent elites sustained the socioreligious sphere well into the nineteenth century, and it lingered there alongside a new and emerging civic sphere.

VISHWESHWUR

The political, religious, and cultural transitions that the city experienced in the eighteenth and early nineteenth centuries had significant implications for the Vishweshwur tradition and its role within the sacred landscape. With attention concentrated on the *Kashikhand*, the idea of Vishweshwur became the object of fierce veneration. In the absence of a temple, histories of contention as well as regenerated traditions were focused on the Gyan Vapi mosque and its precinct. Aurangzeb's order to dismantle the Mughal Vishweshwur temple reverberated in unexpected ways. As they set their sights on the entire subcontinent, Maratha chiefs were vocal about religious injustice at the hands of Muslim rulers. Several Maratha generals highlighted and recalled instances of temple destruction.[34] In 1742 the Maratha chief of Malwa, Malharrao Holkar (1693–1766), proposed to destroy the Gyan Vapi mosque and to rebuild the Vishweshwur temple at the same site.[35] In a significant gesture, Holkar wished to replace the mosque rather than choose the option of a new site, a departure from the strategy adopted by the Kacchawahas a half-century earlier. His plan was unsuccessful, partly due to intervention by his political and military rivals, the Nawabs of Awadh.[36] The Holkar regime remained persistent in its efforts to erect a new Vishweshwur temple, although the proposal was not without its political risks and controversies. Subsequent events suggest that the Holkars may have been at least partially successful, once they were willing to move the proposed site to an adjacent plot of land, rather than replacing the mosque.

In 1755 the *qazi* (judge) of Banaras (who held court in the *adalat* located on a principal street that connected the Vishweshwur temple to the Aurangabad *saray*) rallied a crowd to destroy the temple, resulting in widespread protests in the city.[37] Dragged into the conflict, Balwant Singh, then the Raja of Banaras, was a reluctant referee in a climate of exacerbated tensions. The occasion was an opportunity for Brahmin activism, and

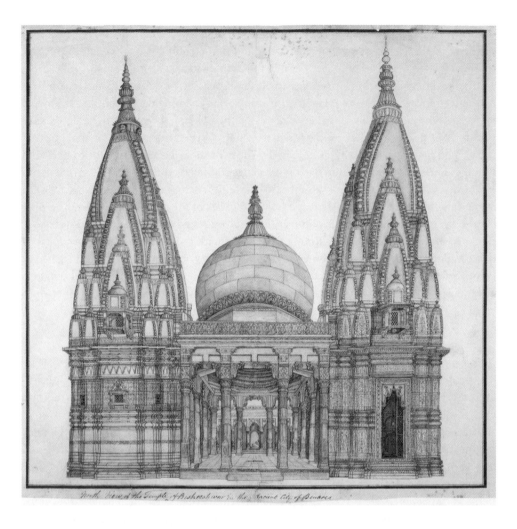

FIG. 3.1   Elevation of Ahilyabai's Vishweshwur temple, ca. 1810, by anonymous artist.
British Library Board.

Narayan Dikshit Patankar undertook a fast to protest the act.[38] Balwant Singh was compelled to deviate from his neutral stance in order to convince Patankar to abandon his fast. Together, the *qazi*'s actions and Patankar's public penance drew further attention to Vishweshwur. This meant that the enclosure of the Gyan Vapi mosque retained its attraction as sacred site and pilgrimage destination. The platform of the mosque was worshipped and the act further sustained the memory of the temple. Priests frequently led pilgrims into the precinct. Describing one such visit, Vijayaram Sen listed the various pilgrimage sites that Ghoshal and his entourage visited ca. 1768. He enumerated visits to the Vishweshwur and Annapurna temples as well as to the *panchatirtha*—that is, the site of the Gyan Vapi well and the shrines of Dandapani, Mahakaleshwur, Nandikesh, and Tarakesh.[39] In other words, he spent a good deal of his time and attention in and around

FIG. 3.2   Rooftop view, Ahilyabai's Vishweshwur temple, 1905. Photo by Madho Prasad.
British Library Board.

the precinct of the Gyan Vapi mosque. From his descriptions, Sen's pilgrimages are quite distinct from the ones popular in the nineteenth century. Most significant, the Panchkro-shi and Antargriha pilgrimages do not feature in his accounts, which suggests that at this time it was a ritual landscape still in the making.

A new version of the Vishweshwur temple was erected around 1781 by Malharrao's daughter-in-law and successor, Ahilyabai Holkar (1725–1795), at a site to the immediate south of the Gyan Vapi mosque.[40] Her act provided the Antargriha pilgrimage zone with a new and invigorated focus (Fig. 3.1 and Fig. 3.2). Designed with twin *garbha-griha* dedi-cated to Vishweshwur and Dandapani, Ahilyabai's temple was ritually inconsistent with the spatial descriptions in the *Kashikhand*. The temple did not include the shrines of Nandikesh and Mahakaleshwur. And there were no concentrated efforts at replicating the archaic *purana*-based scheme. Rani Bhawani had built a new shrine for Tarakeshwur (also known as Bhawaneshwur) a couple of decades earlier, but it was located in relation to the Gyan Vapi precinct and bore little connection to Ahilyabai's temple.[41] In short, a spatial configuration of multiple "*mandapas*" was replaced with a focus on Vishweshwur. Despite these changes (or perhaps shortcomings), the new Vishweshwur temple initially remained in competition with the Gyan Vapi precinct and was only gradually incorporated into reconfigured pilgrimage routes. James Prinsep, who wrote his account of the city four decades after the temple's construction, observed this shift and the increasing popularity of the new temple.[42]

Since the older precinct was never completely relinquished either by pilgrims or priests, it remained at the center of debates regarding its antiquity and provenance. Prinsep's conjectural reconstruction (1822) of the temple is based on an analysis of the site that he most likely derived from the spatial interpretations of Brahmins in the city, who based their accounts on the *Kashikhand*.[43] His drawing is based on a cruciform plan with nine individual spaces, with the central space dedicated to Vishweshwur.[44] Although Prinsep created a plan based on the ideas of individual, interconnected *mandapas*, his labels for the remaining deities were only loosely based in the *Kashikhand* (Fig. 5.3). In subsequent decades, however, this conjectural plan would often be referred to as the actual plan of the Mughal Vishweshwur temple. As the Mughal history of the Vishweshwur temple faded away, its memory gained an ancient legacy, reflected in early colonial opinion.

RE-CREATING THE ANTARGRIHA ZONE

The early decades of the eighteenth century saw vigorous investment within the city's sacred zones, and universal focus on an inclusive text such as the *Kashikhand* provided multiple avenues for patronage. Patrons could enhance the ritual landscape at a variety of physical and ritual scales, and their actions created a text-based consensus about its extents as well as its constituent deities and sites. Patrons and their designers drew on revivalist as well as contemporary concerns and located temples at a number of sites within the Antargriha zone. Temples were often built to resurrect pilgrimage sites mentioned in religious texts.[45] They were also frequently built to cement or even augment older ritual spaces and routes. Patankar succeeded in promoting the early eighteenth-century (ca. 1720) temple of Annapurna in the vicinity of Vishweshwur. He persuaded his patron, the Peshwa, to support its charitable activities by providing free meals to all visitors.[46] Patankar also capitalized on the temple's proximity to the Gyan Vapi precinct. Its role as a charitable institution ensured a steady stream of visitors to the plinth of the dismantled Mughal Vishweshwur temple.[47] A century later, Sherring described Annapurna's public role: "under the express orders of Bisheswar, she is supposed to feed all its inhabitants, and to take care that none suffer from hunger."[48] Annapurna (the provider of food) was a symbol and "persons that can afford it," distributed food in her name.[49] Although the deity was not mentioned in the *Kashikhand*, the Annapurna temple was incorporated within several pilgrimage routes including the Antargriha circuit.

FIG. 3.3   Gyan Vapi and Baizabai's colonnade, 1880, by anonymous photographer.
British Library Board.

The attentions lavished on the Vishweshwur shrine and the adjacent Gyan Vapi precinct were persistent examples of the socioreligious sphere at work. Following the growing popularity of Annapurna, Ahilyabai's new Vishweshwur temple continued to attract
donors well into the nineteenth century. The Bhonslas of Nagpur donated a "silver Howge"
to the temple in 1841.[50] In yet another instance, "Maharaja Runjeet Sinh of Lahore" paid
for the gilding of the "dome" and "tower" with gold leaf.[51] The Gyan Vapi precinct received
the attentions of Baizabai Shindhia, the exiled dowager Maratha regent of Gwalior and
widow of its former ruler, Daulatrao Shindhia.[52] In 1828 she sponsored a "handsome low-
roofed colonnade, the stone pillars of which are in four rows, and are upwards of forty in
number" that could support a sheltering roof for the well.[53] Supported on Mughal baluster
columns, the design for the pavilion was simultaneously a reference to the *Jnan Mandap*
of the *Kashikhand*, while being reminiscent of a late Mughal *baradari* (Fig. 3.3). Older
established elites such as the Rajas of Jaipur retained their properties and maintained
establishments for dispensing charity.[54]

Renewed interest in the Antargriha zone is reflected in Prinsep's 1822 map in which he delineated precise coordinates for some of the shrines on the route.[55] Although Prinsep marked the complete circuit, in his list of "Chief Shiwalas," he included merely fourteen specific sites and shrines. His number was smaller than the twenty-two that were listed by Narayan Bhatt or the twenty-five that were noted by Bishan Singh's and Sawai Jai Singh II's surveyors. However, Prinsep marked a path that corresponds closely to the contemporary pilgrimage route, and the temples that he singled out correspond to the ones listed by Bhatt as well as the Kacchawaha surveyors.[56] Prinsep surveyed an evolved pilgrimage that included several of the sites and deities described by the authors of the *Kashikhand.* Over a century of interest, the city was transformed in the image of a text.

Comparisons between early eighteenth-century *tarahs* and Prinsep's map from a century later can elicit some significant changes in the urban character of the Antargriha zone. The pattern of *havelis* as controlling points for large sections of urban land was gradually replaced by a *muhalla* structure of smaller houses of equivalent size, grouped around a cul-de-sac or restricted square. The *muhalla* was the generic urban unit of the eighteenth-century North Indian urban settlement. It was based on a close-knit grid of courtyard houses constructed with shared walls. This new urban pattern usually indicated a more uniform social origin for its inhabitants. The construction of *brahmapuris* (housing clusters for Brahmins) lent this pattern a fresh twist.

Brahmin neighborhoods were certainly not unknown in Banaras before the eighteenth century. As mentioned earlier, Maratha Brahmin enclaves at the Durga and Brahma ghats could be dated to the sixteenth and seventeenth centuries, but these were limited urban developments subsumed by the overall framework of a Mughal city. The Brahmin of the Girvan texts, for instance, had expressed anxieties over caste and ritual purity in a context of changing social roles and identities. In the absence of an overarching central political and cultural impetus, other forms of social organization such as caste and region began to merge as more significant. This shift toward a more uniform social profile within neighborhoods was neither abrupt nor absolute. Caste and group identities that had become somewhat fluid, at least within urban settlement patterns, were reasserted and even realigned in the absence of powerful political affiliations. Moreover, the concept of the *brahmapuri* was in of itself a revivalist notion, a throwback to an archaic and largely theoretical model of urbanism and social order within idealized notions of Hindu kingship.

Building a *brahmapuri* could satisfy ritual concerns as well as notions of public charity. It was an effective way to intervene in the city's socioreligious sphere. The concept of a settlement intended exclusively for Brahmins can be traced to treatises on building such as the eleventh-century *Mayamata.* In more recent times, *brahmapuris* were created in cities such as Jaipur, a trend that was consistent with Sawai Jai Singh's II's interest in certain archaic planning practices and social models. However, it would be a mistake to trace a direct line between an idea found in an eleventh-century treatise and building practices in eighteenth-century Banaras.[57] The authors of treatises tended to describe plans for *brahmapuris* that were based in the application of orthogonal planning principles. In practice, *brahmapuri* designs in eighteenth-century Banaras reflected trends in contemporary building and spatial practices.

The Marathas (Peshwas) made the earliest investments of this kind. In the 1730s they began to build *brahmapuris* near the river at Ugneshwar ghat. For Narayan Dikshit Patankar, the campaign to enhance the city's Brahmin life included organizing and sponsoring ritual feasts for priests as well as support for *brahmapuris*. Since 1735, the Marathas had visibly espoused the cause of reproducing the Brahminical tradition in Banaras. In a letter to the Peshwa, his agent, Sadashiv Naik Joshi, referred to projects that he undertook to provide financial and institutional support for the city's Brahmins. The Peshwas built eleven *brahmapuris* and renovated a garden near the temple of Vriddhakaleshwur where ritual feasts could be held.[58] Other established and emergent elites followed with similar investments. Rani Bhawani built a *brahmapuri* on Dashashwamedha ghat in the vicinity of the Man Mandir and donated it to a group of Bengali Brahmins, a fact that was noted by the surveyors of the Man Mandir, who labeled it as a neighborhood of Bengali Brahmins.[59] Later in the eighteenth century, Ahilyabai Holkar sponsored a *brahmapuri* (ca. 1781) on a site adjacent to her mansion, also on Dashashwamedha ghat.

The former Mughal center within the Antargriha zone was a coveted location among emergent elite in the eighteenth century. Several prominent actors, including Rani Bhawani and Beniram Pandit, acquired large sections of urban property in the vicinity of the Gyan Vapi/Vishweshwur precinct.[60] Beyond the immediate Antargriha zone, older urban patterns were also altered. The dispersed nature of capital in the eighteenth century meant that multiple agents and their investments could impact urbanization. By the late eighteenth century, 133 *muhallas* and the numbers of houses in each as well as their mode of construction were noted and tabulated by the East India Company's government.[61] *Muhallas* were also defined through property ownership and could consist of smaller houses clustered around a mansion owned by a member of the city's administrative or landowning elite. In such cases, the mansion, often built around multiple courtyards, functioned as the physical and symbolic center of its *muhalla*. The difference between these mansions and earlier Mughal examples lay in that these were often developed more as speculative ventures rather than as instruments of administrative control. Where older Mughal patronage structures did survive, they were often remnants of an earlier age, sustained by artificial means. The pattern of elites living in sections of the city surrounded by their retinue persisted, for instance, at Sonarpura, where the Mughal prince Jahandar Shah and his entourage were settled in the palace on Shivala ghat. This was, however, an aging and fading Mughal prince, living on a pension provided by the East India Company.[62]

New *muhallas* in the eighteenth century were planned more often for reasons of profit as well as prestige. In several instances, *muhallas* were defined through homogenous residential patterns where members of a particular religious, caste, or ethnic group would form a neighborhood. A number of Bengali families who moved to Banaras in the eighteenth century settled in the new neighborhood known as the "Bengali Tola." Its development and growth effectively extended the city's edge once defined by the Jangambadi *muth* and its land holdings. This "Tola" held the attention of visiting Bengalis who recounted such visits in travelogues intended for an audience in Bengal. Shrines such as the one dedicated to Tilbhandeshwur acquired new patrons and pilgrims.[63]

Affiliations based on caste and region were equally compelling social bonds among mercantile groups. Oral narratives survive about a *nai patti* (literally "new strip of land") populated by the celebrated *naupatti mahajans* (bankers) in the Thateri bazaar north of the Gyan Vapi precinct. Several of these families were followers of the Vaishnava Pushtimarg, and many of them traced family origins to the western regions of the Indian subcontinent. Many prominent banking conglomerates, such as the family of Fateh Chand (active ca. 1722–1744), built mansions in Banaras. Several of them transferred business interests from a Mughal world to more dispersed agents and partners and eventually in support of the entrepreneurial endeavors of the East India Company.[64] Built to the north of the *chowk*, the *nai patti* (a *muhalla* of large mansions) emerged around the equally new Gopal Mandir (ca. late 1800s–1829). Despite the community's dispersed business interests, they formed a cohesive social group, and many religious and social events and charities were organized and managed through this temple. The community also gathered for collective ceremonies and celebrations at this temple that functioned simultaneously as a place of worship and a social institution. The Gopal Mandir represented an established Vaishnava tradition from beyond Kashi that was newly introduced to the city. Its inclusion, however, strengthened the idea of Kashikshetra even though the temple lay beyond the concerns of its *purana* literature.

Vestiges of Mughal investment such as the Aurangabad *saray* survived into the eighteenth and nineteenth centuries. The *saray* remained a magnet for trade and commerce. In keeping with contemporary trends, however, it became the nucleus of the new *muhalla* of Aurangabad. *Muths*, whether established or newly instituted, owned and managed rental properties and continued in their roles as significant landowning entities.[65] The Jangambadi and Kumarswamy *muths* arrived at satisfactory arrangements with new regimes and retained their large land holdings and added *muhallas* and other rental properties to their urban possessions. In sum, urban patterns within the Antargriha zone were based on the formal and legal attributes of a transformed Mughal urbanism. Although created by a fragmented group of elites with diverse motivations, their shared vision for Banaras ensured its regulation.

CONCEPTUALIZING AND REALIZING THE PANCHKROSHI

The collective attention paid to various pilgrimage traditions associated with Kashi escalated with the increasing prominence of Ahilyabai's Vishweshwur temple. The Panchkroshi became an indelible part of its sacred landscape by the turn of the eighteenth century. Narayan Bhatt had mentioned isolated sites along the route, and Sawai Jai Singh II's surveyors had created a list of sites. Neither list corresponds with the complete criteria and details laid down for the Panchkroshi in the *Kashirahasya*. As mentioned earlier, it was cited in a piecemeal manner in texts written before the eighteenth century. By the turn of the nineteenth century, the pilgrimage was considered mandatory for any visitor or pilgrim. The *Kashirahasya* was considered the last word on the subject. Visitors frequently discussed and defined the city's sacred limits and identified the Panchkroshi route as a more tangible boundary.[66]

Patrons began to pay sustained attention to the infrastructure of the Panchkroshi pilgrimage route. Rani Bhawani sponsored the renovation of tanks in the villages of Bhimchandi, Kapildhara, and Kandwa, as each of them was a halt along the route.[67] According to nineteenth-century oral memory, she repaired the route as well.[68] Where temples along the route were concerned, she first turned to refurbishing an existing temple at Kardameshwur. She also reserved substantial investment for the Durga temple and its adjoining water tank as well as its charitable endowment (ca. 1760).[69] The site was an overnight halt and ritual site along the Panchkroshi circuit. By selecting a shrine dedicated to a female deity, the Rani could reinforce her own identity as a widowed authority figure. At the same time, she could make a connection between the Durga temple at Banaras and the Durga *puja* tradition of Bengal—an idea that resonated with the city's Bengali diaspora. Ahilyabai Holkar renovated the tank at Sheopur, another halt on the Panchkroshi.[70] Chet Singh, who succeeded Balwant Singh as the Raja of Banaras, conspicuously performed the Panchkroshi pilgrimage, an event showcased in his hagiography, the *Chet Sinha Vilas*.[71] Several elites also sponsored the production of texts, maps, and paintings to represent this sacred landscape.

Among the Bengali compradors who pursued similar channels of power, influence, and patronage, three generations of the Ghoshal family were successful at cultivating an aristocratic and beneficent image. Having amassed considerable wealth through their connection to the East India Company and its expansionist activities, the Ghoshals maintained an active interest in and connection to the city. One of their members, Jaynarayan Ghoshal (Krishnachandra Ghoshal's nephew), sustained this interest by sponsoring a Bengali translation of the *Kashikhand*. He added a text of his own composition in Bengali verse that he titled the *Kashiparikrama* (ca. 1792) as an epilogue to this effort. Ghoshal wrote his ballad in praise of the Panchkroshi tradition, encouraging his readers to undertake the pilgrimage. He presented them with brief glimpses of the five major halts along the route, through catchy couplets and appealing verse.[72] This author's own survey along the Panchkroshi revealed that most of the temples along the route can be dated back between 250 and 500 years. The greater numbers, however, were built since ca. 1700, and at each of the halts along the route, major fresh investments in new tanks and temples were undertaken.[73]

As the Rajas of Banaras continued to patronize a "self-consciously Hindu" court culture over the course of the nineteenth century, they aligned their interests with the rejuvenation of the city's ritual life.[74] Their court poet and spiritual mentor in the mid-nineteenth century, Kashthajivhaswami, described and praised the Panchkroshi pilgrimage route in his poem, the *Panchkroshsudha*. Although Kashthajivhaswami's text included references to particular shrines and deities and was filled with greater detail than Jaynarayan Ghoshal's poem, he was more concerned with the circuit as a whole, rather than in conducting meticulous inventories of sites or connecting them to texts.[75]

Gradually, expectations of a geometrically uniform, comprehensive, and ancient route were shared by patrons, pilgrims, and Brahmin priests. In this spirit a Brahmin named Mahadev Bhatt collected funds to renovate the path in the early nineteenth century, and he succeeded in building a few bridges across streams and roads to circumvent heavily wooded areas.[76] However, the continuing tensions between conceptualizations of a perfect geometry for Kashikshetra and the realities of a meandering Panchkroshi route that skirted the city's edges resulted in debates on its authenticity. Subsequently, when Brahmin activists such as Ketkar swami and his student, Pathak swami, began to assess the Panchkroshi route, they found that its alignment (especially the stretch between Bhimcandi and Rameshwur) was far from perfect.[77] Since the route was increasingly identified with the edge of Banaras, it became desirable to align the Panchkroshi route with a perfectly circular Kashikshetra, thereby conflating two distinct ideas and practices.

WITHIN THE PANCHKROSHI: THE GARDEN AND THE *GUNJ*

The diverse patrons who paid attention to the sacred landscape of Kashi were certainly influenced by the idea of Kashikshetra. Though the concept itself was several centuries old by this time, its conflation with the Panchkroshi route provided a definite boundary within which temples and mansions could be built and material vestiges from earlier times could be identified and renovated. A precise definition of the sacred zone was not determined and the location of its center and profile of its limits were enthusiastically debated. By the early decades of the nineteenth century, Kashikshetra had two ritual centers when the Madhyameshwur temple located in the city's northern area was renovated (ca. 1822). Unprepossessing by itself, the structure nevertheless marked the center of Kashikshetra as prescribed in several texts, including the *Krtyakalpataru*. An inscription with the relevant *shloka* (couplet) from the *Kashikhand* established its role as the center of Kashikshetra. In practice, however, Vishweshwur remained the ultimate ritual center of this sacred zone.

Several patrons built at resurrected ritual sites located beyond the city's eighteenth-century urban limits and nestled among the elite suburban estates that began to fill Kashikshetra. In the mid-eighteenth century, Rani Bhawani renovated and refurbished several tanks and ritual sites. Besides the tanks along the Panchkroshi route, such as the Durga *kund* and its accompanying temple, she renovated the Kurukshetra tank near Assi ghat as well as the Kapal Mochan tank in the city's northern portion.[78] In each case, projects were carefully chosen and linked to an established ritual geography with a basis in those of the city's textual traditions that were in vogue.[79] As Banaras was reconstructed, its sacred aquatic landscape was also altered and adjusted to the demands of contemporary patronage and the Mughal *chahar-bagh* (quadripartite Persian garden) provided an innovative means of intervention and reinterpretation that could fulfill religious and social desires. Enclosed *chahar-baghs* were carefully added to an existing web of pools, catchments, streams, and ritual tanks that formed the city's designated sacred waters.[80]

In its Mughal context the walled *chahar-bagh* had been an idealized enclave, evocative of paradise. It was also charged with more earthly memories of gardens in Samarkand and Kabul for the Persian and Central Asian elites who designed gardens as funerary settings and as sites for elite recreation and entertainment. The many *chahar-baghs* around imperial Mughal tombs, such as the garden setting of the tomb built for the emperor Humayun in Delhi (completed 1572), is an early example.[81] Like many other aspects of Mughal cultural and artistic life, the "tomb in the *chahar-baghs*" was widely imitated by aspiring late Mughal elites. The tomb built in Delhi for the second Nawab of Awadh in 1754 is an early example of this trend (Fig. 3.4 and Fig. 3.5).[82] In an archetypal model of the *chahar-bagh*, the tomb structure or pillared pavilion was placed in the center, at the intersection of four identical channels of water, each representing a stream in paradise.

FIG. 3.4   Safdarjung's tomb, Delhi.

Such gardens had become an integral part of privileged urban life in eighteenth-century northern India. In Banaras the tomb of Lal Khan, a minister in the court of the Rajas of Banaras, was designed on this classic idea and was completed in 1769.[83] The Rajas also added an enclosed *chahar-bagh*, the Rambagh (Fig. 3.6), near a sacred pool and temple north of Ramnagar, their settlement across the river from Banaras. As the *chahar-bagh* was adapted and integrated into the life of a Hindu pilgrimage city, it was reproduced with multiple variations and accommodated a variety of functions.

Besides its symbolic role as the appropriate setting for a tomb or temple, the *chahar-bagh* was incorporated within palaces, urban enclaves, and mansions in imperial cities such as seventeenth-century Shahjahanabad. It follows that designs for many large mansions within Banaras would include such gardens.[84] Temples and tanks were frequently accommodated within their plan (in place of a tomb) or placed in close proximity. Many such spaces were designed as essential components of the elite estates that ringed the city.[85] In domestic contexts, gardens were designed to perform dual roles as recreational as well as ritual spaces. Walled gardens gradually filled the urban periphery within Kashikshetra. They were represented in maps and views of the city, including pilgrimage maps, as an integral part of its sacred landscape. Madho Dass's garden on the banks of the Mandakini *talao* (pool or catchment) was one such *chahar-bagh*. Madho Dass chose a location within the flood plain of a well-identified sacred tank but created a private space that could reflect contemporary tastes. Such attention to the city's aquatic landscape was never uniform, however, and the Matsyodari lake was surrounded by dense urban settlements by this time. The once sacred lake had grown into a cesspool by the late eighteenth

FIG. 3.5 Safdarjung's tomb, Delhi, ca. 1820, by anonymous artist. British Library Board.

century, remarkable for its stench. The varying significance of many of these lakes and ponds was directly related to their place within changing practices.

As in the case of other architectural and spatial adaptations, the landscape culture of the Mughal world was also modified at Banaras as the *chahar-bagh* became a site of religious festivity and public charity. Designed originally as elite spaces, they were transformed into public spaces on festive occasions such as religious fairs and festivals. For instance, the "Durga Mela" associated with the Durga temple spilled over into several gardens in its vicinity.[86] These were fluid spaces and could be used as temporary residences, often being leased as overnight halts to pilgrims who could afford their rent.[87] They were also used as sites for ritual events and for organizing and dispensing charity. The enclosed *chahar-bagh* was an ideal site for elite self-fashioning, since it could become a manageable "public space" where access could be controlled and occasionally denied, based on a patron's wishes and whims.

Amrit Rao Peshwa owned a garden on the outskirts of the city, also described as a walled precinct with four doors, suggesting a *chahar-bagh* typology.[88] In one of several manifestations of his elite role within the city's socioreligious sphere and its spaces, he used the garden as a site to distribute alms. Access and dispensation were strictly controlled with three of the doors being used to monitor applicants of "three different classes."[89]

FIG. 3.6   Rambagh, Ramnagar (Banaras), 1905. Photo by Madho Prasad. British Library Board.

The fourth door was reserved for Amrut Rao and his servants. If an applicant received a *dakshina* (gift), he had to spend the rest of the day within the garden "lest he should apply twice."[90] This account is backed by family recollections of *brahmin-bhojans* (ritual feasts for Brahmin priests) that were served in this space.[91] By using the spatial orientation of the *chahar-bagh* to organize social hierarchies and control the distribution of charity, Amrut Rao reoriented the symbolic meaning of the walled garden, while retaining its formal attributes.[92] In other instances, such as in the case of the Gopal Mandir, its walled garden was turned into a vibrant public space on religious occasions. This temple was planned on the *haveli*-temple typology, which meant that it was built to mimic the design of an elite mansion, one that belonged to a presiding deity who was imagined in the guise of a feudal lord, Thakurji. The *chahar-bagh* of the Gopal Mandir became a site for religious festivities much in the manner of similar gatherings in the gardens and mansions of the city's elite.

The *chahar-bagh* was not the only means for emergent elite to claim Kashikshetra. As the idea of a sacred zone within the bounds of the Panchkroshi became widespread and consistent, the garden estate and speculative building, and often even a combination of the two, became an ideal vehicle for an elite intent on associating their rising fortunes to the city's regeneration. The planned *gunj* (residential or commercial settlement, also market town), in keeping with the by now well-entrenched relationship between late Mughal urbanism and the ritual landscape of the city, was an adaptable unit of urban growth. A speculative development that could incorporate commercial and residential land uses, the *gunj* was a tool for developing cities as well as generating urban income.[93] On occasion, the *gunj* would be combined with a *haveli*. The *gunj* would usually consist of a marketplace, workshops, and residential areas for artisans. No *gunj* in Banaras is quite like another, and each was an example of the variations that could be prevalent within a broad concept.

A number of new *gunjes* (market towns) and *qasbas* (provincial administrative towns) were built in the eighteenth century in the Gangetic plains.[94] A drawing of a model city, probably created ca. 1810 in or around Delhi, is a window into contemporary urban imagination and organization.[95] A regular, rectangular *chowk* (town square) marks the center defined by intersecting and perfectly aligned, colonnaded bazaars. The *chowk* was also adjacent to the palace of a fictitious petty ruler, "Sher Singh," which was built around an enclosed courtyard (Fig. 3.7). On the ground a new *gunj* rarely followed such an idealized spatial pattern, yet this drawing is a clue to the fragmented nature of urban form and institutional relationships. These were piecemeal, smaller-scale investments, in sharp contrast to the citywide restructuring projects undertaken by the Mughal state. They were controlled and managed by enterprising and adventurous newcomers as suggested by the tongue-in-cheek moniker "Sher Singh." Several emergent elites with aspirations to a Rajput lineage adopted the suffix "Singh" in the eighteenth century. The artist suggests that "Sher Singh" is in truth a bold but nevertheless upstart pretender with a borrowed name, who has acquired or even built a *gunj* of his own. New *gunjes* were usually initiated and developed on the outskirts of an existing city, sometimes at a larger scale, as in the case of Ramnagar, seat of the Rajas of Banaras located across the river.

Nearer Banaras, several new *gunjes*, albeit at a smaller scale, were built by aspiring elites who were cognizant of the city's sacred geography. For instance, James Prinsep, in his early nineteenth-century map, depicts a number of *gunjes* on the edge of the city.[96] The location of Aussangunj (late eighteenth century) as well as that of Jagatgunj (1794) was determined through very similar considerations. Both founders, Aussan Singh and Jagat Singh, were connected to the family of the Rajas of Banaras and were newly established Bhumihar aristocrats.[97] Although they remained in attendance at the court in Ramnagar, they also considered it prudent to create their own spheres of influence within Kashikshetra. In the case of Aussangunj, this development included a principal *haveli*, a bazaar, and a private temple. Similarly, Jagatgunj included a principal *haveli* surrounded by commercial development.

Gunjes were also built as commercial ventures, in direct relation to the enhanced ritual landscape of Kashikshetra with the intention of profiting from its burgeoning ritual life. Nawabgunj—established by a member of the city's Muslim elite, Nawab Shumsuddaulah, and built in a symbiotic relationship to Rani Bhawani's Durga temple—is a case in point. Urban developments such as these anchored social and economic interests

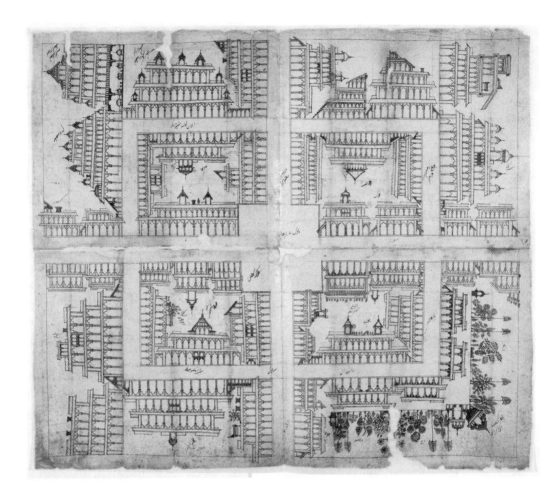

FIG. 3.7 *Plan of a City*, ca. 1810, by anonymous artist. British Library Board.

to religious motivations. Nawabgunj was specifically built to capitalize on the ritual activity connected with the refurbished Durga temple, including its location on the Panch-kro-shi route.[98] However, the architectural language used to build the various *chahar-baghs*, *havelis*, and *gunjes* within an ever popular Kashikshetra was based on Mughal precedents that remained invested with elite symbolism and prestige.

KASHIKSHETRA REIMAGINED

Fresh attention to the concept of Kashikshetra changed the ritual cartography of the city, as is evident from a pilgrimage map created ca. 1820 (Plate 2). The Varuna and the Assi streams defined the map's northern and southern edges. The Panchkroshi pilgrimage path circled the city, with its eastern boundary aligned with the river's edge. Its authors depicted the five distinct halts along the route without any details of deities, shrines, or ritual spaces at each place. Rather, their attention to the route emphasized its role as a physical boundary. Within it, artists delineated the nested sacred zones of Kashi, Varanasi, Avimukta, and Antargriha. This innermost zone was rendered as petal-shaped layers around a prominent Vishweshwur shrine. Taken together, this ensemble formed the Chaturvidhkshetra of Kashi.[99] Prominent and specific ritual sites were depicted alongside more general representations of Kashi as a sacred forest filled with temples. The map's authors addressed a significant change in the ritual imagination of the city. Besides the focus on the Vishweshwur temple, its refurbished pilgrimage routes were treated as equally significant.

The intense urbanization that Kashikshetra experienced during the eighteenth century was largely sidelined. In the contemporary city the areas of Adampura, Jaitpura, and Madanpura were predominantly Muslim residential areas.[100] The spaces that correspond to these areas in the map are replaced with Shaiva sites and temples. A vision of Kashikshetra as Anandakanan (the forest of bliss) prevailed and was realized on the ground through a patchwork of *chahar-baghs*. The protagonist of this map is a pilgrim. Whether on the Panchkroshi pilgrimage path, or bathing in the river, or praying at shrines and ritual tanks, it is the figure of the pilgrim that defines Kashi as a pilgrimage destination. The creators of the map captured a moment when the *Kashikhand* and *Kashirahasya* were considered mutually complementary and equally definitive texts for a Shaiva Kashi with well-defined sacred zones and routes.

MUGHAL LEGACIES AND THE ELITE PRECINCT

The authors and artists who created the pilgrimage map of ca. 1820 depicted a row of buildings along the riverfront that included the Dharhara mosque and Lal Khan's tomb as well as a few East India Company soldiers in bright-red coats, sole acknowledgments of the city's contemporary context or recent history. Yet, as its ritual life thrived, the city expanded within its revised sacred boundaries and several elites built within Kashikshetra. Besides the acquisition of swathes of property around the Vishweshwur temple (and by extension, the older Mughal center), patrons invested in new estates and *gunjes* on the periphery of the Mughal city. Alongside such developments, numerous ritual sites were enhanced and augmented, and yet other sites were newly identified. The skills of masons and master-builders who had once worked for Mughal patrons became available to a new group of patrons. They transformed and transmitted established forms and aesthetics and tailored them to individual tastes and preferences. Architectural patronage remained a tested conduit for channeling social and political ambitions, and spatial and formal innovations allowed patrons to incorporate spaces for display and reception within conventional designs.

A climate of transitioning tastes were noticed by the traveling British artist Ozias Humphry, who pointedly sketched (indeed documented) elite residences from the reign of Aurangzeb.[101] Many of Humphry's Indian hosts were keen to adapt Mughal precedents to frame their rising status as aristocrats and landowners. Eager to impress parochial as well as cosmopolitan audiences, they oversaw the reworking of Mughal forms and symbols in a variety of unique ways, combining them with revivalist inclinations as well as experiments in strategic Occidentalism.[102] Mughal architectural elements provided an aspirational palette accessible to subcontinental elite, regardless of their religious affiliation.[103] William Hodges, in an account of his travels across North India in the 1780s, described the buildings he saw as being constructed in "the more modern style of Moorish Architecture, in which all the great monuments are constructed."[104] Hodges distinguished this architecture from that of the "original inhabitants" of the subcontinent.[105] At the same time, he also declared that in the late eighteenth century there was no distinction between architecture commissioned by "Moorish or Hindoo" patrons.

Four elite residential enclaves in Banaras, built between the last quarter of the eighteenth century and the first quarter of the nineteenth century, provide examples of the ways in which a diverse set of elites utilized and adapted established precedents. Prominent, flamboyant façades and ornate reception spaces suggest the social and political potential of architectural experimentation in a period of change. But conformity with older models remained a way to establish legitimacy and lineage. Besides external characteristics, associated public rituals were recognizable markers for the building and, by extension, its patrons. The five examples discussed here were each located in new neighborhoods within Kashikshetra. Temples that were located within such estates were often created with the dual intention of anchoring ritual sites drawn from texts as well as supporting newly invented traditions. They were suitable anchors for patrons who wished to play a role within the city's burgeoning socioreligious sphere, though individual aims, compulsions, and benefits could greatly vary.

Aussan Singh built his *haveli* in the late eighteenth century as part of the speculative development appropriately called Aussangunj. A Bhumihar Brahmin with familial connections to the Rajas of Banaras, he had a history of contentious relationships with both Balwant Singh's widow, Rani Gulab Kunwar, and Chet Singh.[106] By commissioning a *haveli* and *gunj*, he struck a balance between enhancing personal status and maintaining careful distance from the Rajas of Banaras and their court at Ramnagar. Begun in the late eighteenth century, the original *haveli* was built around a single courtyard supported on simple columns and brackets (Fig. 3.8). The structure included a rooftop *tibari* (colonnade with three bays) that was supported on Mughal columns and used as a space for elite gatherings and entertainment.[107] A diminutive temple with a small *mandapa* and *garbhagriha*, covered with shallow domes, stood beside the *haveli*. The temple was intended as a family shrine, and its builders made no overt effort to forge a significant relationship with either the city's sacred landscape or its socioreligious sphere. The *haveli* conformed to a traditional mold and had several features in common with Ozias Humphry's aforementioned illustration (Fig. 3.9).[108]

As a member of a *zamindar* (landowning) family with a role in an upstart Raja's regime, Aussan Singh visibly associated himself with traditional forms and practices even as his *haveli* anchored a speculative and commercial urban formation, a *gunj*. Aussan Singh treaded on narrow and occasionally uncertain ground, maintaining hierarchical relationships with the Rajas as well as their overlords, the Nawabs of Awadh. All the same, he refrained from making any visible effort to upstage the Rajas. This conservative approach in design stands in clear contrast with the designs for two other *havelis* that can also be dated to the late eighteenth century. As the East India Company gradually became the

FIG. 3.8   *Haveli* in Aussangunj.

FIG. 3.9   *Malla Dosi's Garden House*, 1786, by Ozias Humphry. British Library Board.

dominant power in Bengal and the Gangetic plains, another group of newly minted aristocrats benefited greatly from this connection. They fashioned themselves as lingering Mughal aristocrats in a nascent colonial environment.

The Mitra Kothi (also commonly known as the Bengali Deohri) in the city's Chaukhamba area was built toward the late eighteenth century by a Bengali *zamindar* family that had close links to the East India Company. A sprawling complex of interconnected courtyards and rooms, the *haveli* was built to occupy an entire section along the Thatheri bazaar.[109] Several levels were added over its hundred-year history, with numerous individual patrons dictating the location, size, and architectural style of individual apartments. Styles range from late Mughal to colonial neoclassical to colonial gothic revival. The *haveli*, though, was more than just an opulent residence. It was a means for the family to position themselves as loyal supporters of the British, while simultaneously claiming a role within more established elite circles. This was a strategy employed by several prominent *zamindar* and *amil* (revenue collector) families in eighteenth- and nineteenth-century Banaras. Their mansions, by necessity, bridged the ground between convention and innovation.

FIG. 3.10

Grecian pediment on exterior of Mitra *kothi*.

With its European neoclassical references, particularly its whitewashed Grecian pediments, the façade of the *haveli* played a dual role.[110] On the one hand, the Mitra family could proclaim their Bengali and, more significantly, colonial associations to a local audience (Fig. 3.10). On the other hand, colonial officials could read affirmations of loyalty toward the East India Company's regime in these details even if they criticized and derided what they saw as crude and ill-proportioned translations of neoclassical elements on the *haveli* facade.[111] Prinsep, for instance, thought it was "in Bengali taste, with a barbarous admixture of European architecture."[112] Although he clearly disapproved of such choices, it is significant that he both noticed and remarked upon them. Colonial visitors on tour "up the country" occasionally traversed the streets of Banaras and would have provided a ready audience for the Mitra family.

The principal courtyard in the *haveli* was designed as a venue for a Durga *puja*. The Mitras initiated an annual Durga *puja* celebration in Banaras and designed it as a public event that included daily *puja* rituals centered on a silver image of the Goddess Durga, ensconced within a silver pavilion (Fig. 3.11). In addition, a larger clay image of the goddess was taken in procession around the neighborhood and was ritually immersed in

FIG. 3.11 Durga *puja* pavilion, Mitra *kothi*.

FIG. 3.12 Outer courtyard of Mitra *kothi*.

the Ganges at the end of a celebration that lasted several days. In terms of spatial design, its designers selectively drew on conventions followed in elite residential architecture with multiple courtyards partitioned loosely on the basis of gender and function. Within such buildings, select visitors would generally move from areas that were designated as public and entertainment spaces to the more private areas reserved for intimate friends and female members of the household. The large oblong courtyard that was the site of the Durga *puja* was put to intensive use since this space was created for the event (Fig. 3.12).[113] During the days of the *puja*, the courtyard became part of the city's public spaces. The use of the Mughal baluster column in the inner court was intended to project a refined and aristocratic image.

The Mitras also staked a claim to the city's socioreligious sphere through their patronage of temple architecture. Their *haveli* included two temples and, as the circumstances of their building reveal, the family carefully aligned themselves with distinct and divergent trends. The first was an association with the traditions of Banaras. The family recalls that when the building foundations were excavated, a Shivalinga was found at the site. Subsequently, the *linga* was consecrated and a temple built at the spot in a local idiom. This narrative of a "found" or *swayambhu linga* has currency across the country and is particularly potent in Banaras. Its incorporation within the *haveli* allowed the family to link themselves to the city's Shaiva traditions. The family's Vaishanava affiliation was cemented through a

FIG. 3.13 *Shikhara* of Shiva temple within Mitra *kothi*.

temple dedicated to Radha-Krishna and designed as a domestic shrine. Significantly, though, it is the Shiva temple built around the *swayambhu linga* that has a *shikhara* and a *mandapa*, thus aligning it with local architectural trends and allowing the family to proclaim their commitment to the city (Fig. 3.13).

The design for the Devkinandan *haveli* straddled convention and innovation through a different set of formal and spatial devices. The patron, Devkinandan, was an *amil* who had been in service to several revenue collectors, including officials of the East India Company.[114] He was a member of an elite that straddled the late Mughal world as well as an age where the East India Company became increasingly dominant across the Gangetic plains. The *haveli* form, its embellishments, and furnishings reflect this transition. Devkinandan began to build the mansion in the late eighteenth century (ca. 1790) in the newly settled Ramanpura neighborhood. It was designed as a double-storied structure around a court-yard with a Shiva temple in an adjoining courtyard that was completed by 1805.[115] The *haveli* also occupied a prominent location in its *pura* or neighborhood, and a number of the city's elite were beginning to build spacious estates and gardens in this part of town at the turn of the nineteenth century.

The complex is best understood in terms of three distinct components: the temple precinct, the gateway, and the enclosed courtyard (Fig. 3.14). The first floor of the gateway was designed to accommodate an enclosed *baradari* accessed by a narrow staircase. In the early nineteenth century, this functioned as the principal reception room (Fig. 3.15).

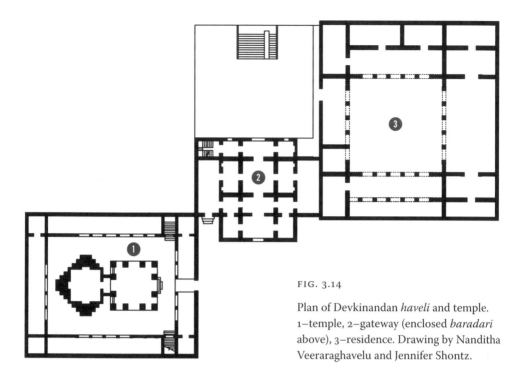

FIG. 3.14

Plan of Devkinandan *haveli* and temple.
1–temple, 2–gateway (enclosed *baradari*
above), 3–residence. Drawing by Nanditha
Veeraraghavelu and Jennifer Shontz.

FIG. 3.15 Interior of enclosed *baradari* above gateway, Devkinandan *haveli*.

Another view of the Temple of Mohadeo and suburbs of Benares to the west

FIG. 3.16 *Another view of the Temple of Mahadeo and suburbs of Benares to the west*
(Devkinandan *haveli*), 1814, by Sita Ram. British Library Board.

Generally, *baradaris* were located on rooftop terraces, placed there to attract cool evening breezes, and used as spaces for formal reception and entertaining. Devkinandan's designers modified the idea to place a *baradari* at the center of an enclosed space, suggesting a salon. Spectacular waterworks were included to release welcoming sprays around a central, arcaded platform, and a collection of European and Company-style paintings and prints, showcasing Devkinandan's anglicized affiliations and tastes, were displayed on the enclosing walls.

Mughal references were retained through extensive use of the baluster column that were designed to be more ostentatious than in any other part of the *haveli*. Devkinandan's mansion was a stop on the "up the country" tour that British visitors undertook and was illustrated by the Indian artist Sita Ram who accompanied the Marquess of Hastings on such a tour in 1814–1815 (Fig. 3.16).[116] The flamboyant waterworks as well as the carefully placed paintings did not fail to leave an impression on the visiting Bishop Reginald Heber.[117] The eclectic display included English prints, works by the "Company artist" Lalljee of Patna, as well as portraits (in oils) of Devkinandan, his patrons and employers, as well as a "daub" of the Mughal emperor Akbar Shah II.[118] Heber noted the large plat-form and open square before the *haveli* gateway that allowed visitors to step back and admire its architecture. He waxed eloquent, comparing its appearance to "some of the palaces of Venice, as represented in Canaletti's views."[119] If visitors such as Heber sought and responded to familiar sights and symbols, Devkinandan and his contemporaries took care to make such identification easier.

Heber described the family temple, a ubiquitous feature of mansions, as being small but also "as rich as carving, painting, and gilding could make it," with "a large silver bell, suspended from the roof like a chandelier."[120] It was constructed on an archaic scheme of the *garbha-griha* and *mandapa*.[121] The temple precinct stood at right angles to the *haveli*, facing the *chowk*. Although privately owned and managed, limited public access was always permitted. The dedication in Sanskrit over the door of the temple marked a gesture toward the city's resurgent religious life. Although the tiered *shikhara* over the sanctum is a dominant feature (Fig. 3.17), the Mughal baluster column is conspicuously absent in the *mandapa*. Instead, the temple designers added archaic columns, brackets, and a corbeled ceiling (Fig. 3.18).

FIG. 3.17 Shiva temple in Devkinandan *haveli*.

FIG. 3.18 *Mandapa* of Shiva temple, Devkinandan *haveli.*

Patrons embellished private estates with temples to express and enable personal beliefs and convictions. Jaynarayan Ghoshal's Gurudham temple is both a noteworthy example and exception.[122] When he built the temple in the late eighteenth century, Ghoshal made a statement of personal piety, but one that referenced contemporary building trends and fashions in Bengal, thereby emphasizing his family's connection to the rising power of the East India Company. At the same time, the temple was connected to the city and its religious traditions by virtue of its location on his estate within the bounds of the Panchkroshi pilgrimage route. Visitors pass through a gateway into an octagonal precinct. Single-storied colonnades radiate from a double-storied octagonal structure at a central node. This precinct is connected to a second, enclosed rectangular space to the rear. A pavilion was placed on a platform at the opposite end of this space. Seven smaller circular chambers on each of the other two sides of the rectangle complete the complex (Fig. 3.19a and Fig. 3.19b). Each of the circular chambers contained an iron shaft, interpretations of the ubiquitous Shivalinga. Its designers and patron drew on two well-known precedents and clothed them in a "Bengali" neoclassical vocabulary.

Like his contemporaries, Jayanarayan's preferences were based on multiple legacies and addressed multiple audiences. He drew on the familiar seventeenth-century legacy

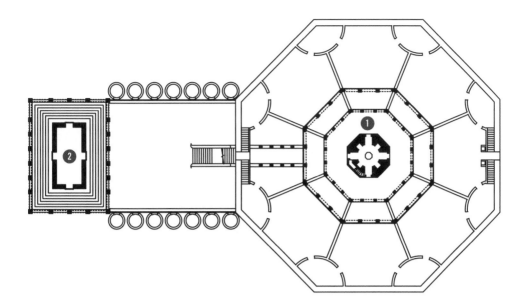

FIG. 3.19A Plan of Gurudham temple. 1–two-storied temple, 2–pavilion. Drawing by Nanditha Veeraraghavelu and Jennifer Shontz.

FIG. 3.19B Section through Gurudham temple. Drawing by Nanditha Veeraraghavelu and Jennifer Shontz.

of the *ratna* temple form, a model for Gaudiya Vaishnav shrines in parts of Bengal.[123] At the same time, he drew on a colonial trend that had taken root in Bengal and that was transferred through pattern books to Indian masons building for colonial as well as Indian elites (Fig. 3.20). The temple form could simultaneously address Jayanarayan's private religious beliefs and inclinations as well as bolster a vision of modernity.[124] The elaborate octagonal plan of the main structure with its radiating walls could signify a mandala, an idealized worldview within early modern Vaishnava practices. The rectangular pavilion follows the model of a *chandi mandap* that was an integral part of a number of elite homes in Bengal. It was intended as a strong statement of a radical personal philosophy, and Jaynarayan refrained from including overt architectural symbols that could reference conservative local trends. Ironically, this absence, as well as the typological association with the *ratna* temple form, allowed his son Kalishankar to alter it into a traditional Vaishnava (Radha-Krishna) temple quite easily.[125]

FIG. 3.20 Gurudham temple.

A fairly different set of political and cultural motives lay behind the design of the Kali Bari complex, built by the Rajas of Cooch Behar. The kingdom of Cooch Behar had been incorporated into the Mughal world in the seventeenth century.[126] More recently, their territories and allegiance were commandeered by the East India Company. It was necessary for the Rajas to acknowledge new alliances, while maintaining their position as an older, more established aristocracy. To this end, the Cooch Behar family acquired the Lolark *kund* from the Kacchawahas of Jaipur in the late nineteenth century.[127] By so doing, they supported a textually based and popular tradition in the city. Yet it was no longer enough to merely be "Mughal" elites. Begun in 1818 and in keeping with established Bengali precedent, the temple dedicated to the Goddess Kali was also based on the typology of a Bengali *chandi mandap*. Built as a rectangular hall, its elevation was embellished with elements and details forged in a colonial milieu (Fig. 3.21 and Fig. 3.22). At the same time, its location in the new context of Banaras was acknowledged with the inclusion of three almost identical Shiva temples within the precinct. Each was designed in the local idiom of a single-cell *garbha-griha* with a *shikhara*. Neighborhood residents and visitors were allowed access to the Shiva temples and by extension into the courtyard of the *chandi mandap*. If the Shiva temples represented a venerated religious tradition that was synonymous with Kashi, the *chandi mandap* addressed the goddess tradition that was popular among the city's Bengali diaspora.

The designs for each of these precincts suggest that the central role once enjoyed by symbols of Mughal authority had given way to multifaceted cultural and religious symbols. In each case, emerging or aspirational elites engaged and managed shifting and

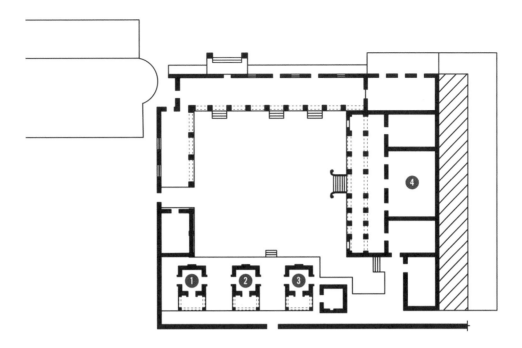

FIG. 3.21 Plan of Kali Bari precinct. 1, 2, and 3–Shiva temples, 4–*chandi mandap*. Drawing by
Nanditha Veeraraghavelu and Jennifer Shontz.

FIG. 3.22 Courtyard of Kali Bari precinct.

often contradictory allegiances through patronage for temple construction. Religious traditions were invented with a rich palette of architectural and ritual expression. Such careful choices also enabled emerging elites to address and appease multiple constituencies within the socioreligious sphere. New deities could be placed within the overarching framework of Kashikshetra and housed in temples of archaic design. A critical survey and close reading of temples with firmer connections to the ritual landscape of Kashikshetra provided rich answers about the role of revivalism and invention over a century of prolific patronage for temple building.

REVIVALISM AND TEMPLE ARCHITECTURE

The skyline of eighteenth-century Banaras was punctuated by numerous *shikhara* forms, simultaneous statements of piety and revivalism. In its general profile this new *shikhara* was certainly similar to eleventh-, twelfth-, and even fourteenth-century predecessors found across northern India, and yet it was no replica. Easily identified by its silhouette, it was distinguishable from earlier examples by its smaller size and minimal amounts of figural sculpture on its exterior. The *shikhara* form had never quite disappeared from the built landscape of South Asia, but its preponderance was considerably diminished as patrons and masons experimented with domical and even horizontal or flat roof forms.

As all revivalisms, this instance in eighteenth-century Banaras said more about their immediate environment and cultural climate than the hoary past that its proponents invoked. Experiments in form as a means of self-fashioning were a persistent feature of temple building at this time as new types such as *haveli* temples and *ratna* temple forms were connected to specific traditions and were usually intended for limited though specific audiences. For instance, patrons from Bengal often re-created the *chandi mandap* as they re-created the forms and rituals of goddess worship. In Banaras these patrons were careful to engage local interests and attention and also built temples with more conventional plans and archaic *shikharas*. As the Mughal state waned in power and influence, temple designers began to abandon radical experiments or at least to combine them with archaic forms, especially the *shikhara*. Yet, as was true for the elite mansion, a memory of Mughal architecture was alive and well. Elements and building types including baluster columns, pavilions, and domes could be extensively replicated and incorporated into temple designs. The religious and political incentives behind such selective revivalism said a lot about perspectives on the past.

The idea of "revival" was integral to the vision of Kashikshetra. With the goal of providing the sacred zone with an anchor, the Peshwas and their mentor Patankar enhanced the role of the deity Annapurna and sponsored the construction of a new temple, ca. 1720, at a site near the Gyan Vapi precinct. Built two decades after the Adi-Vishweshwur temple, the Annapurna temple was based on an archaic design, with distinct and carefully separated *mandapa* and *garbha-griha*. Surmounted by a *shikhara* over the sanctum, its designers eschewed the explicit Persian-inspired forms of the Mughal temple.[128] Yet Mughal columns were used, albeit sparingly, in the vestibule directly before the temple sanctum. In a deliberate departure from the visible integration of forms and spaces in Mughal shrines, including in the Mughal Vishweshwur temple, designers in the eighteenth-century main-

FIG. 3.23

Kardameshwur
temple, Kandwa.

tained clear and deliberate separation between individual ritual spaces. The appeal and
necessity for selective rather than sweeping revivalist gestures were based in politics.
As they replaced the Mughals, the need to imprint the landscape of conquered territories with distinct identities and symbols of legitimacy was urgent. In the cultural space
vacated by diminishing Mughal power, many regional Hindu rulers began to take notice
of the pre-Islamic temples within their territories.[129]

Several such rulers restored older temples and endowed them with land grants and
ritual infrastructure. The ca. 1760 refurbishment of the fifteenth-century Kardameshwur temple by Rani Bhawani signified similar interests (Fig. 3.23). Her actions established a precedent for the emulation of archaic architectural forms locally.[130] The decision

FIG. 3.24 Durga temple and Durga *kund*.

certainly held appeal for some of her contemporaries and admirers. In his 1792 description of Kashi, Jaynarayan Ghoshal applauded the design for Rani Bhawani's Durga temple, its stone sculptures, its *shikhara*, and the as yet unbuilt *mandapa* (Fig. 3.24, Fig. 3.25, and Fig. 3.26). Ghoshal used archaic tropes and terms to describe the Durga temple, and he praised similar forms that he noticed on Ahilyabai's Vishweshwur temple. Yet, despite the emergence of an antiquarian discourse within which an ideal Hindu temple was to be defined, the practice of selective revivalism was to persist well into the early decades of the twentieth century. Temples constituted some of the city's most significant public spaces and were significant charitable institutions.[131] The Durga temple stood sans a *mandapa* until the mid-nineteenth century. Rani Bhawani may indeed have planned a *mandapa* to be raised on ornate Mughal baluster columns, in a manner similar to the temples she built and endowed in the Bengali Tola neighborhood.

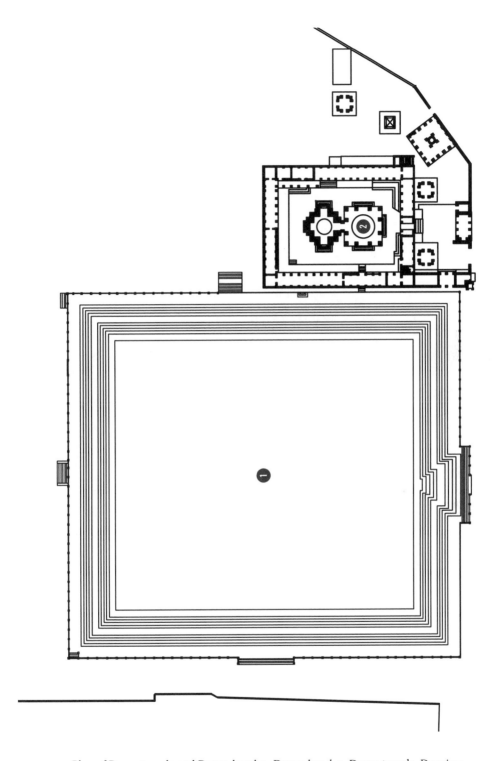

FIG. 3.25 Plan of Durga temple and Durga *kund*. 1–Durga *kund*, 2–Durga temple. Drawing by Nanditha Veeraraghavelu and Jennifer Shontz.

FIG. 3.26 *Shikhara* of Durga temple.

Ahilyabai Holkar supported religious activity through temple restoration and patronage for ritual at several venerated sites across the subcontinent. Her actions consolidated personal as well as familial power. Her political experience was clearly at play as she sponsored the construction of a new temple dedicated to the Vishweshwur tradition. Built on a site adjacent to the Gyan Vapi precinct, the temple form reflected a deliberate reference to an archaic language by placing twin *shikharas* over identical *garbha-griha* that faced each other across a shared *mandapa* (Fig. 3.27). This shared central space was, however,

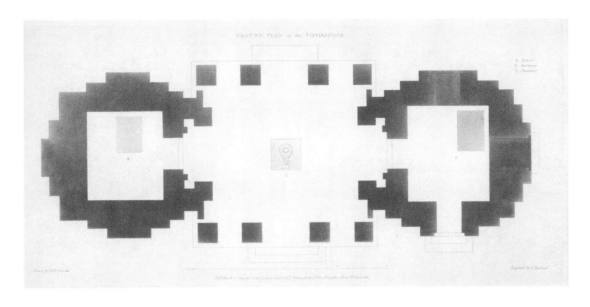

FIG. 3.27 Plan of Ahilyabai's Vishweshwur temple, 1781, by Garstin. British Library Board.

covered with a dome. Such juxtapositions can be explained in light of the Maratha quest for power and legitimacy. Several Maratha rulers (including Janoji Bhonsle and Ahilyabai's own father-in-law, Malharrao Holkar) articulated dissatisfaction with Mughal rule and supported the reestablishment of Hindu ritual sites. At the same time, they depended on the cultural capital that could be derived through Mughal references. Furthermore, with a decline in Mughal power, large pools of artisans were available and willing to work for new patrons. Masons in present-day Banaras relate family histories that include stories of migration to the city from Delhi and Rajasthan.[132] Masons modified Mughal fashion as well as transformed Hindu precedents, appropriated Mughal columns and arches, and experimented with archaic forms, particularly temple *shikharas*. This transmutation was noticed by Prinsep, who observed contemporary masons merging templates for "mouldings, scrolls, lattice work &c" with archaic plans and forms.[133]

These new temples were enthusiastically received by pilgrims and residents. Archaic *shikharas* invited references to the *shastras*. When Lieutenant Colonel Garstin presented his report on Ahilyabai's temple, he insisted that the new shrine had been designed on the basis of the "shaster."[134] While this was not a surprising remark for a colonial surveyor (with Orientalist inclinations) to make, it is pertinent that his Indian informants appeared to agree with his assessment. Although Ghoshal did not make any explicit reference to "shastras" when he praised the Durga temple, his archaic metaphors were certainly intended to invoke a valued past. The astute Veeraswamy distinguished temples built in the eighteenth and nineteenth centuries from those built earlier, in the fifth century of the Common Era.[135] He referred to the *shastras* in connection with examples from pre-Islamic times. Similarly, when Garstin's informants referred to "shastras," they may have signaled their recognition of an archaic form rather than indicated approval for accurate interpre-

FIG. 3.28 *Elevation of a Hindoo Temple*, 1831–1833, by James Prinsep. British Library Board.

tations of architectural treatises.

Discussions regarding an ideal Hindu temple may indeed have occurred at Banaras. Prinsep published an "elevation of a Hindoo temple" in his *Benares Illustrated* (Fig. 3.28).[136] He depicted an example with distinct *mandapa* and *garbha-griha*, each surmounted by *shikharas*. No such temple exists in the city, if it indeed exists anywhere at all. It was a utopian idea, however—the perfect, unadulterated "Hindu" shrine, freed of Indo-Islamic elements, an idealized rather than a documented case study. Prinsep indulged in wishful thinking as he deleted references to the city's Indo-Islamic context. However, the "Benares temple" is a useful term to classify and group together similarities in *shikhara* types first built during the eighteenth century. Several elite patrons adopted this temple type. It was the form of choice for more "public" shrines including the Vishweshwur and Durga temples. The Mitras, Devkinandan, the maharaja of Cooch Behar, and others adopted this form for temples within their *havelis* as well as the ones they sponsored beyond their precincts within Kashikshetra. Regional or sectarian identities were occasionally expressed through unique religious architecture, but patrons almost always balanced such choices with a Shiva temple in the "Banaras style."

The authors of the *Kashikhand* and *Kashirahasya* had envisioned a Kashi with its symbolic center in a Vishweshwur shrine that was surrounded by the Antargriha and Panchkroshi pilgrimage routes. Over the course of the eighteenth century, Kashikshetra—an abstract idea for most of its history—was created as a tangible space through the elaboration of pilgrimage routes and sacred sites. The emergent elites who channeled piety, politics, and financial wherewithal into its creation conducted these transactions within a shared socioreligious sphere that was shaped through competition as well as cooperation. Conspicuous patronage eased the path of social mobility and helped them in acquiring political and economic clout. Archaic spatial concepts and forms were recovered, and Mughal elements and embellishments released from imperial and political hierarchies were reworked by a diverse group of aspirational patrons who arrived at a common consensus regarding the nature of the ritual landscape. As they consolidated the sacred landscape of Kashikshetra, the city's riverfront provided them with an ideal arena for architectural and ritual spectacle.

SPECTACLE AND RITUAL

A N essential element of its sacred landscape and visual identity, the riverfront at Banaras emphatically establishes its connection to the Ganges River. Clusters of ritual bathers against a backdrop of magnificent riverfront fortress-palaces and temples have frequently featured within visual representations of the riverfront, at least since the late eighteenth century (Fig. 4.1). Along with the spectacle of cremations at Manikarnika and Harishchandra ghats, they continue to constitute a quintessential image for Banaras. In popular perceptions it is often supposed that the built environment of the riverfront naturally represents the fabric of an ancient Hindu city. The archaic appearance of numerous temple *shikharas* that tower over the riverbank can deceptively belie the recent origins of the edifices that line the Ganges. More informed observers, however, notice the relatively late construction of these buildings as well as their stylistic connections with Mughal architectural trends. As with the pilgrimage landscape of Kashi, patrons who built these temples and riverfront palaces added new ritual and spatial practices to deep-seated religious and topographical meanings and mythologies. Their architectural and typological preferences reflected attempts at self-fashioning even as their buildings modified notions of sanctity and significance for specific sites.

A sacred riverfront along the Ganges has been a significant feature of the topography of Kashikshetra since at least the twelfth century. Successive authors of several religious texts and pilgrimage maps enumerated a series of discrete spaces and *tirthas* along its length, as it flowed between its junctions with the Assi stream to the south and the Varuna stream to the north. Among them, authors of several *purana* and *nibandha* texts provided detailed lists of *tirthas* along the stretch, although as may be expected, the exact numbers, orders, and particulars always differed between any two texts. Lakshmidhara's list of sites is predictably different from the order that Narayan Bhatt considered significant. Both authors were principally concerned with the religious significance of sites. Authors of more secular texts treated the riverfront as a backdrop for their narratives, often including more popular references and place-names. The authors of the Girvan texts enumerated a list of "ghatta" that was more extensive than the list of *tirthas* composed by Bhatt. Varadaraja as well as Dhundiraja included many sites that were referenced within religious texts but also added place-names that had more everyday associations. Each of these authors, whether they wrote within religious or secular contexts, addressed contemporary

FIG. 4.1   Fortress-palaces along the riverfront at Banaras.

concerns and preoccupations. All authors also agreed in a more general way that the stretch of riverbank between the Assi and Varuna was sacred.

Architectural interventions by Mughal patrons in the late sixteenth and early seventeenth centuries had already established the riverfront as a social and political canvas. The architectural vocabulary that patrons and designers used was a honed reflection of political relationships. It was also intended to capitalize on ritual meanings associated with particular locations. Built interventions resulted in a shift in ritual and symbolic meanings that was vividly captured in texts and visual representations. The riverfront buildings discussed here were added between the early eighteenth and early nineteenth centuries during a period of political fragmentation and shifting allegiances. Inevitably, their creation further altered the role and significance of individual sites.

Given the potential of the riverfront as a site for architectural spectacle, the façades of riverfront edifices (also known as ghats) played a critical role in reflecting a patron's pious intentions and refined tastes. To this end, building activity was often accompanied either by religious spectacle or instances of conspicuous patronage for one of the city's significant ritual sites. In several cases a combination of architectural intervention and invented ritual allowed patrons to claim a role in the city's socioreligious sphere. As elsewhere in the city, altered and adapted Mughal typologies and styles were combined with visible markers of a resurgent Hindu identity to fashion social roles and lineages.

FIG. 4.2   Riverfront terrace of the Red Fort at Agra.

Contemporary descriptions of riverfront edifices elicit details of their formal characteristics as well as reception among visitors and pilgrims. William Hodges, who accompanied Warren Hastings in 1781, provides some insights into spatial models used for these buildings as well as the social roles that they were meant to play. Hodges's visit coincided with a period of active construction on the riverfront. He noticed a number of stone embankment walls (*pushtas*) with numerous variations. These could be enclosures for mansions and temples. Several of them also included *baradaris* (pavilions) placed within *chahar-baghs* and were usually accessed ceremonially, through monumental riverfront gateways.

Hodges was particularly impressed by Gelsi Ghat (Jalsai ghat) and its "splendour and elegance." Enticed to explore further by a view of its impressive riverfront gateway and exterior, he was disappointed to find that the massive stone walls contained only an enclosed garden rather than (one might guess) an imposing set of rooms.[1] Hodges also observed that these structures were built for the benefit of a "public."[2] Edifices were built with private funds, and they largely remained under private ownership. The rituals and festivals associated with these buildings, not to mention the availability of partial or even complete public access to their spaces, smoothed their patrons' way to a presiding role in the city's socioreligious sphere. By 1822 riverfront mansions, monasteries, and temples extended intermittently between the Varuna and the Assi.[3] Most representations of the city were from the river, and patrons were keenly conscious of their theatrical potential. To acquire a riverfront site, though highly desirable, could turn into an expensive proposition. The visiting Veeraswamy noticed several regional rulers vying to build here, despite escalating land prices in the city and especially along its riverbank.[4] The ability to overcome such obstacles and to sponsor a building in stone was itself a marker of wealth and status.

The forms and spaces that Hodges described indicate an adaptation of a Mughal fortress-palace, albeit at a more modest scale. Yet again, a Mughal model, once reserved for the imperial family and select courtiers, became available to emergent elite, not just at Banaras but across northern India. The Mughal emperor Shahjahan had refurbished and built two imperial fortress-palaces along the Jamuna River, first at Agra (Fig. 4.2) and subsequently for the new capital at Shahjahanabad (Delhi). Within each fortress, private palaces were designed around enclosed gardens, with several freestanding pavilions connected by a shared riverfront terrace and channels of flowing water. The design for the iconic Taj Mahal at Agra is a modification of the riverfront garden as well (Fig. 4.3).[5] This celebrated Mughal mausoleum was the crowning object placed on a riverfront terrace at the end of a quadripartite garden. This enclosed *chahar-bagh* was strung along the river, a spectacular vision among the gardens and enclaves of courtiers and aristocrats.

A Mughal fortress-palace was to be observed and approached from a boat that glided along the river. Such precedents of building and use became widely accessible through their visual representations. By the eighteenth century, illustrated folios from the *Amal-i-Salih* were copied and circulated beyond the Mughal court (Plate 3 and Plate 4), and

FIG. 4.3   Riverfront terrace of the Taj Mahal at Agra.

FIG. 4.4 *A View of the Riverbank at Benares*, ca. 1790, by anonymous artist. British
Library Board.

emergent elites could hitch their rising star to architectural patronage by following well-
established imperial trends.[6] As it was adapted into the late Mughal fortress-palace,
it underwent spatial as well as stylistic transformations. Besides being smaller in size,
eighteenth-century examples were usually more modest in scale. A high, solid embankment wall of dressed sandstone was surmounted by one or two built levels, usually embellished with Mughal columns, foliated arches, and *chattris* (pavilions).[7] Private apartments
were placed at intermediate levels, and the ubiquitous *baradaris* associated with pleasure
and entertainment were placed on rooftop terraces.[8] Although many sites were identified
as ritually significant within *purana* and *nibandha* texts, the creation of a built environment fixed locations and provided amorphous sites with a definite architectural and
visual identity. By the late eighteenth century, fortress-palaces were also designed to act as
foundations for towering temple spires at the Banaras riverfront. Many of these projects
were featured in riverfront panoramas and pilgrimage maps, often along with the names
and titles of their patrons (Fig. 4.4).[9]

The artists who created the *Amal-i-Salih* (ca. 1815) copied folios from the seventeenth-
century *Padshahnama*, as a way of establishing a direct connection between architectural
patronage and royal authority.[10] The manuscript was sent as a diplomatic gift from the
Mughal emperors to officials of the East India Company.[11] More pertinently, the gift was
offered in a climate where such images (and the services of the artists who created them)
became available to a wider group of patrons. Their representational value was certainly

not lost on the emerging elites of Banaras. Emergent patrons could be identified through their architectural creations much in the same manner that the emperor Shahjahan had been associated with his architectural creations. Substantial parts of the city's riverfront were depicted, for instance, in the ca. 1820 pilgrimage map. A continuous façade of mansions lines the riverfront on this map and marks the city's southern boundary. Several of the buildings are labeled with attention to ownership and patronage. At Banaras the ubiquitous *qila* of the enterprising petty ruler was transformed and consecrated into the religious ghat on the riverfront.

EARLY EXPERIMENTS

In the early eighteenth century, the riverfront was a site of struggles over elite authority. Although quite steadfast in his defense of the Gyan Vapi mosque, Meer Rustam Ali (in common with his political overlords, the Nawabs of Awadh) promoted a syncretic culture, most conspicuously through support for the Hindu festival of Holi. He also built a fortress-palace in 1735 on Dasashwamedha ghat, the site of several such festivities.[12] When his father successfully sidelined Meer Rustam Ali and paved the way for him to become *zamindar* of Banaras, Balwant Singh built a new fortress-palace at Ramnagar across the river, established a court, and presided over ceremonies derived from Mughal precedence. He also appropriated several of Meer Rustam Ali's architectural symbols.

Balwant Singh dismantled his predecessor's riverfront mansion to build another fortress-palace to the south at Chet Singh ghat (now also known as Shivala ghat), effectively distancing himself from the urban sites and activities of Meer Rustam Ali. The act itself, combined with the possibility that the new structure was built from spolia, was an effective political ploy. Its memory is preserved as oral tradition in the city and is often retold as a triumphant story of usurpation crowned by the creation of a new lineage for the Kashi Naresh. Other evidence suggests, however, that the Rajas of Banaras purchased the mansion and ghat from Meer Rustam Ali and his descendants.[13] Nevertheless, the symbolic value of this act captured public imagination in Banaras and became an indelible part of the story of its regeneration.

The new Chet Singh ghat is an early instance of the fortress-palace type in Banaras. Entering through the riverfront gateway, a visitor had to move through a musician's gallery and up the steps to the level of the terrace (Fig. 4.5a and Fig. 4.5b). Its designers placed a *baradari* at the level of the terrace (Fig. 4.6). Visible from the river as a delicate structure perched on solid embankment walls, it was a canopy for politics as well as pleasure.[14] The *baradari* was often covered by a temporary pavilion that is visible in a painting by William Daniell from 1802.[15] Beyond the gateway and the *baradari* lay the more public and formal areas of the court.

Chet Singh ghat had a dual ceremonial relationship, with access to the city as well as to the river. A visitor who approached the precinct from the city instead of the river would encounter a second pavilion placed a little way away from the riverfront, set at right angles. This *diwan* (reception room) was placed at the end of a *chahar-bagh*. Also referred to as "Chet Singh's *mahal*," it included a central audience hall, smaller chambers to the side, and a viewing gallery (possibly a *zenana* gallery), all supported liberally on Mughal

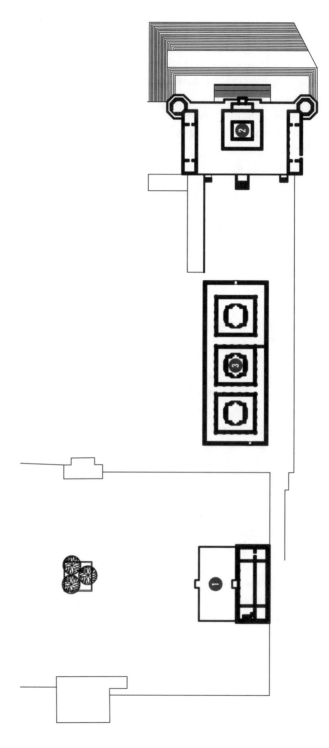

FIG. 4.5A Schematic plan of Chet Singh ghat. 1–*diwan*, 2–*baradari*, 3–temples. Drawing by
Nanditha Veeraraghavelu and Jennifer Shontz.

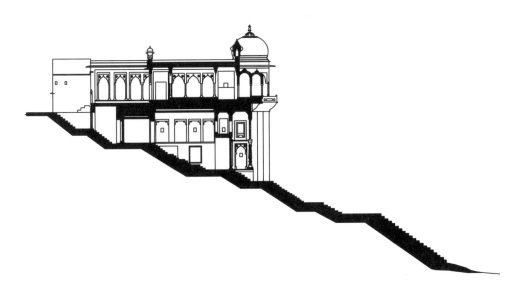

FIG. 4.5B Section through *baradari*, Chet Singh ghat. Drawing by Nanditha Veeraraghavelu and Jennifer Shontz.

FIG. 4.6 *Baradari* over gateway, Chet Singh ghat.

FIG. 4.7 *Diwan* in Chet Singh ghat.

baluster columns (Fig. 4.7, Fig. 4.8, and Fig. 4.9). Taking their cue from the audience pavilions of Mughal fortress-palaces, its patron and designers combined these with residential elements drawn from urban mansions. Twin *baradaris* on the roof were probably used for musical performances and poetry recitations. Its design was consistent with examples at contemporary regional courts across northern India.[16] Conceivably, Meer Rustam Ali's mansion was built on a similar pattern.

As the Maratha Peshwas expanded their territories northward from their base in the Deccan and continued to maintain an interest in acquiring the *Tristhali*, the riverfront at Banaras merited their special attention. Peshwa preoccupations with promoting Brahminical ritual meant that they were, at least initially, less interested in replicating the fortress-palace. Peshwa investment in the city in the early eighteenth century was geared toward achieving a connection between religious texts and the sacred geography of Kashi as was manifest through Brahminical practices in the city. Their choice of riverfront sites was dependent to a large extent on the traditions current among the Brahmins then residing in the city.[17] The Peshwas encouraged rituals and rites at Manikarnika, Dashashwamedha, and Panchganga *tirthas*, through the promotion of existing activities—namely *snan-puja* (ritual bathing and worship).[18] Peshwa efforts in the 1730s were undertaken against a sparsely built riverfront, and they concentrated on strengthening the Brahmin presence in the city. To this end, they also sponsored construction at Brahma and Durga ghats, building on existing Maratha Brahmin networks and connections in the city.[19] The sacred stretch and its two ends, the Assi *sangam* and the Varuna *sangam*, were marked by new temples by the mid-eighteenth century.[20] The *shikhara* of the Adi Keshav temple

FIG. 4.8 Interior of *diwan* looking down from gallery, Chet Singh ghat.

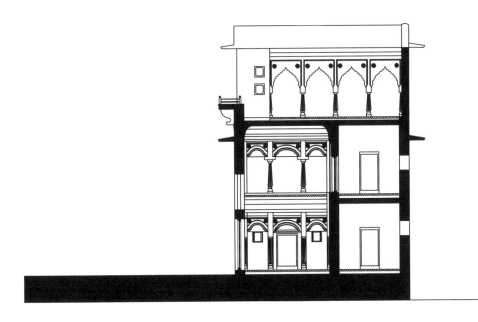

FIG. 4.9 Section through *diwan*, Chet Singh ghat. Drawing by Nanditha Veeraraghavelu and Jennifer Shontz.

marked the Varuna *sangam*, and its patron, Bajirao Peshwa I, built a modest mansion on the riverfront near this site.[21]

At the other end of this riverfront stretch, the patrons of the Jagannath temple at the Assi *sangam* established a connection with the principal Vaishnava deities of the pilgrimage town of Puri. Its location on Assi ghat provided an avenue for participation in the city's socioreligious sphere while maintaining a connection with one of its significant ritual nodes. This temple was established through the patronage of "a rich and powerful fuqueer of this sect . . . [who] at his death left it to Bishumbur Pandit."[22] As mentioned earlier, Bishambar and his brother Beni Ram were members of a Nagar Brahmin family of service elites. They had worked for a number of powerful employers in turn. Beni Ram Pandit had been *vakil* (agent) to the Maratha Bhonslas of Nagpur, but by 1781 he switched employers and became an agent for Warren Hastings of the East India Company. His brother Bishambar continued in service, in sequence, to several Maratha chiefs, and these social connections allowed them the access and means to build and support a significant public temple.

Built ca. 1760 and initially with the support of the Maharaja of Cuttack, the temple was passed on to Bishambar Pandit (at that time Dewan of the principality of Cuttack) after 1781.[23] Family tradition holds that the Maratha governor of Chattisgarh also provided funds for the maintenance of this temple.[24] For its design, patrons largely drew on a local idiom. Keeping alive the idea of a precinct, three axially connected enclosures accommodated a garden with a tank, two temples, and a smaller shrine dedicated to Garuda, Vishnu's companion "vehicle." The principal temple was dedicated to the deities Jagannath, Balram, and Subhadra and the second was dedicated to the deity Narasinh, in keeping with the precinct's Vaishnava affiliation. Other notable features included elements of the *chahar-bagh* within the first court as well as temple vestibules supported on Mughal baluster columns. In keeping with local trends, a "Banaras" *shikhara* surmounted each shrine.

The Pandit family derived considerable social recognition through their connection to the temple and its public festivities that were designed to re-create the annual ritual procession at Puri. During the festival ("on the 2nd, 3rd and 4th days of Asarh"), replica idols of the three presiding deities (Jagannath, Balram, and Subhadra), almost identical to the ones at Puri, were carried around the city in a *rath* (temple chariot).[25] The procession was first held ca. 1780, and three chariots began their ceremonial journey at the temple precinct, traveled through city streets that ended in the "garden of Beni Ram."[26] The route imitated a ritual geography at Puri where the procession also begins at the Jagannath temple and ends with the ritual immersion of the idols in the sea. Festivities culminated in a *mela* (carnival) in the family's garden.[27] The Pandit brothers established a connection to a religious site that was less prominent than Kashi but nevertheless boasted an older, well-established, and robust tradition of a temple procession. Large numbers of the elite and nonelite (thirty thousand, according to a contemporary observer) of Banaras attended this celebration. By inventing a tradition that they could control, yet one that drew on a deep-seated legacy, the brothers forged an association with the socioreligious sphere.[28] Through simultaneous patronage of architecture and formalized ritual, they became part of the city's elite culture of patronage.

FIG. 4.10 *A Prospect View of the City of Benares*, ca. 1765, by anonymous artist.
British Library Board.

The history of the changing use and role of Manikarnika ghat into a site for cremation is an example of the continual reinterpretations that have characterized and shaped
Banaras. Its transformation is suggested by the adjacency between ritual cremation and
ritual bathing at this ghat. By itself, this juxtaposition underlines a contradiction between
ritual uncleanliness and ritual purity, anathema to observant Hindus. As a site for ritual
bathing, Manikarnika is prominently mentioned in several texts including the *Kashikhand*
and the *Tristhalisetu* and is conspicuously featured within several visual representations.
The ghat was marked on Maratha maps from the early nineteenth century as the symbolic
center of the world. More important, the focus of the map was on the site of Manikarnika
rather than Kashi.[29]

The transformation of a part of Manikarnika ghat from an occasional site for cremations into the city's premier funeral ghat was closely connected to Maratha efforts. Manikarnika featured prominently among the objectives of Narayan Dikshit Patankar, who
was intent on promoting pilgrimage to Banaras. Other Brahmin scholars, such as Nagesh
Bhatt, who could claim an established and illustrious scholarly lineage, promoted the idea
of the city as an ideal site for cremation.[30] It is Patankar, however, who is credited with
promoting this ghat as a cremation site.[31] Oral tradition in Banaras also holds that the

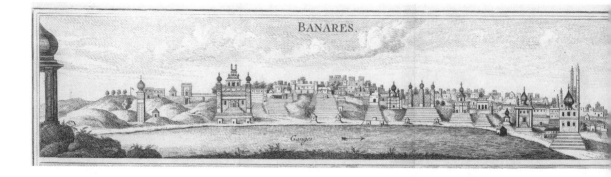

FIG. 4.11 Riverfront panorama, plate VII.1 in Tieffenthaler, 1785. Bancroft Library, University of California–Berkeley.

ghat has been a funeral site only since the eighteenth century.[32] To be more precise, the funeral ghat is the Jalsai ghat, to the immediate south of Manikarnika. Neither the artists of the Vaishnava pilgrimage panorama nor those of the pilgrimage *pata* from Mewar ever emphasized the site's connection to funerary activities. Funerals at this site are also absent in visual representations of the riverfront from the mid- and late-eighteenth century (Fig. 4.10). Among foreign visitors, neither the Jesuit priest Tieffenthaler in his illustration from 1785 (Fig. 4.11) nor the British officer Charles Forrest in his illustration (drawn during a visit in 1807) chose to depict funeral activity on this ghat.[33] Given his active public role in promoting pilgrimage and supporting charities, such activism is consistent with Patankar's general agenda.

Numerous other sources indicate the enhanced popularity of cremation at Manikarnika ghat. Jaynarayan Ghoshal provides a clue when he refers to the funeral ghat as "Rajvallabh Mashan," a term that can be translated as "Royal Cremation Ground."[34] Yet by the early decades of the nineteenth century, this was a thriving "public" funeral ghat, and in his 1822 map of the city Prinsep clearly labeled it as such. Gradually, buildings around Manikarnika ghat began to cater to the business of cremation. The adjacent *pushta* of Jalsai ghat (that enclosed the garden that Hodges admired) was also taken over by *dom* (specialist priests) in the cremation business.[35]

Given its popularity and dual significance, several elites sponsored building projects at Manikarnika. Rani Bhawani built a temple there, and although it was unconnected to specifications in the *Kashikhand*, it was built with the intention to enhance the ritual significance of the site. The visiting Veeraswamy described bathing at Manikarnika ghat and using the services of Brahmins at the riverfront.[36] The site remained fairly significant for Maratha sensibilities. Ahilyabai Holkar substantially renovated the ghat and consecrated two significant shrines at the site, the Tarakeshwur and Ratneshwur temples (ca. 1789–1791).[37] Although these were new structures, in keeping with the theme of resurrecting ritual sites and referencing the *Kashikhand*, Ahilyabai also sponsored the renovation of the Chakrapushkarni *kund*. This bathing tank was a prominent halt on several pilgrimages, including the Antargriha and Panchkroshi.

Fortress-palaces built in the previous century acquired new meanings in this altered political and cultural climate. Some of these, such as the Man Mandir, were modified. As the Mughal Empire receded in terms of its power and territorial control, several subordinates, even those with deep familial ties to the imperial family such as the Kacchawahas, began to assert a degree of autonomy, while continuing to acknowledge the emperor's titular authority. Sawai Jai Singh II ventured beyond the boundaries observed by his predecessors and oversaw the planning and construction of a new capital city, Jaipur. He also pursued his interest in astronomy and sponsored the construction of five observatories at various locations across northern India. The list included one at Banaras, built sometime between 1710 and 1734. Since the Man Mandir was already located on the ritually significant Dashashwamedha ghat, its terrace served as an ideal location for the new observatory.[38]

Three decades later, the Kacchawahas initiated a shift in the use as well as symbolism of the riverfront fortress-palace. Plans to add a temple to the Man Mandir were sketched ca. 1760. Although the project did not materialize in quite the form that it was originally envisaged, the addition of a temple to a riverfront mansion was a novel idea.[39] The sketch on the Man Mandir *tarah* indicates that the temple was located to be visible from the river and was designed on an archaic plan with separate *garbha-griha* and *mandapa*, which suggests the possibility that a *shikhara* over the sanctum was also visualized.[40] These plans may have inspired the numerous Maratha patrons who began to incorporate temples in the revivalist "Benares style" into their riverfront fortress-palaces. One of the first initiatives came from Ahilyabai Holkar, who added a mansion connected to a *brahmapuri* and a temple at the southern limits of Dashashwamedha ghat.

The design for Ahilyabai's mansion, or *wada* in Maratha parlance (ca. 1789–1791), both reinforced and altered the symbolism of this site. Like Man Singh before her, Ahilyabai chose this site because of its place within the limits of the venerated Dashashwamedha ghat. Once these buildings were built, they acquired independent identities and were no longer considered part of the older ghat. Dashashwamedha was divided into three parts that now included the Ahilya, Dashashwamedha, and Man Mandir ghats in sequence, moving northward. Ahilyabai Holkar, however, was a different kind of patron than her Mughal predecessor, Man Singh Kacchawaha. Groomed by her father-in-law, Malharrao Holkar, to act as regent of Malwa after his death, she combined and successfully projected the twin attributes of a powerful ruler and pious widow. These contradictory qualities and therefore complex motivations are reflected in the design of the Ahilyabai mansion. Although visible as an imposing building from the riverfront, the building has an appearance of studied austerity (Fig. 4.12). It was planned as a two-storied structure around a single, sparsely embellished courtyard. Unlike other buildings of similar size that had patrons of a similar stature, the *wada* did not have designated spaces of elite pleasure such as a *baradari* on its terrace.

In late Mughal circles elite men could use a *baradari* (literally, a pavilion with twelve doors) with its carved arches and columns as a social space for evening soirees. They would be entertained among ornate pillars by poets, (usually) female dancers, and musicians.

FIG. 4.12 Ahilyabai *wada* and *brahmapuri*.

Its associations were therefore pleasurable as well as slightly risqué. While courtesans accompanied by entourages would make their way to a *baradari* by invitation, elite women were usually confined to the more private and restricted areas of a mansion, usually the apartments around the *zenana* courtyard. In keeping with their social status and public image of respectability, elite women usually avoided the rooftop soirees presided over by their male relatives.

A widow who led an army and frequented circles of power could find herself in a difficult and contradictory position. She was required to simultaneously project an image of authority while maintaining the aura of a "well-bred" and modest "lady" who, but for adverse circumstances, could have remained sheltered within the female quarters of her mansion. Ahilyabai bridged this difficulty by cultivating an image of sober respectability, consistent with cultural expectations of a pious widow. At the same time, she projected a public persona of generous piety and patronage. Her religious building program extended across the subcontinent, and she was concerned primarily with reviving places of Hindu and particularly Shaiva pilgrimage. Within Banaras, the Vishweshwur temple was prominently and visibly associated with her munificence. Significantly, the Ahilyabai *wada* is not divided into *mardana* (male) and *zenana* (female) courts, in deference to the presiding role of its female patron (Fig. 4.13). The sole courtyard is also, by implication, the principal courtyard of the mansion with no ambiguity about who might be in charge. At the same time, its spaces are conspicuously plain and austere, with a careful avoidance of suggestive ornamentation or decorative details that could be read as indicators of a dissipated or even luxurious lifestyle.

Ahilyabai sponsored construction of a *brahmapuri* to the immediate south of her mansion, and it was designed to house sixty Brahmin priests and their families.[41] The adjacent

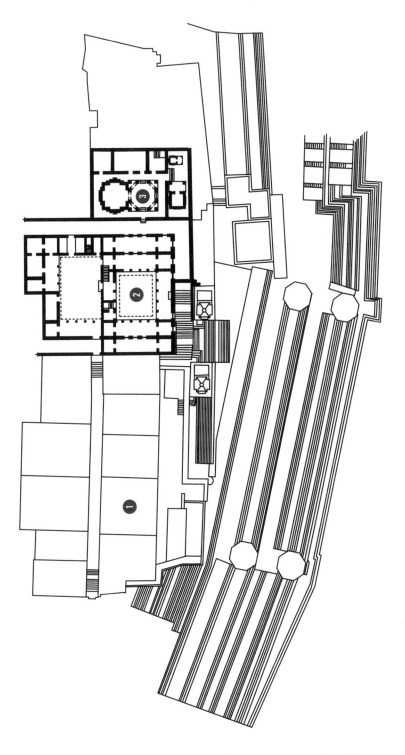

FIG. 4.13 Plan of Ahilyabai *wada* and *brahmapuri*. 1–*brahmapuri*, 2–*wada*, 3–temple.
Drawing by Nanditha Veeraraghavelu and Jennifer Shontz.

FIG. 4.14 Bhonsla ghat from river.

location of the *brahmapuri* and its connection to the mansion was enhanced through architectural details that unite the façades of the two buildings. When viewed from a boat, they read as a single, plain but imposing structure adjoining a significant ghat. Besides the charitable act of constructing and endowing a *brahmapuri* that enhanced her reputation as a pious patron, the combination of imposing façade and minimal architectural detailing underlined an image of simplicity and frugality that she carefully cultivated. In both the *brahmapuri* and the *wada*, a generic typology was adapted to the specific requirements of an individual agenda of self-fashioning. In the design for the temple attached to the ghat, however, Ahilyabai's designers created a more ornate building. Since temples had divine associations, their ornate exteriors did not adversely affect the image their patron might carefully cultivate. Indeed, their embellished exteriors and expensive building materials could favorably proclaim their patron's piety and devotion.

Another Maratha project, the complex on Bhonsla ghat was a space where private religious observance was successfully combined with public visibility (Fig. 4.14). The fortress-palace was built by Raghuji Bhonsle II (1788–1816) at a time when the Bhonslas were losing their hold on their kingdom in central India.[42] In common with other Maratha chiefs, the Bhonslas positioned themselves as custodians of Hindu traditions, even as they selectively adopted Mughal social mores, etiquette, and material culture. However, they

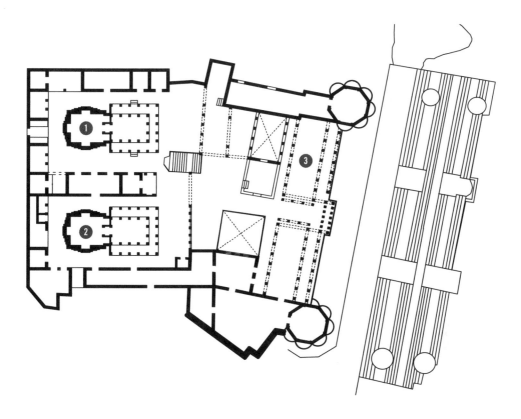

FIG. 4.15A Plan of Bhonsla ghat. 1 and 2–temples, 3–*baradari*. Drawing by Nanditha
Veeraraghavelu and Jennifer Shontz.

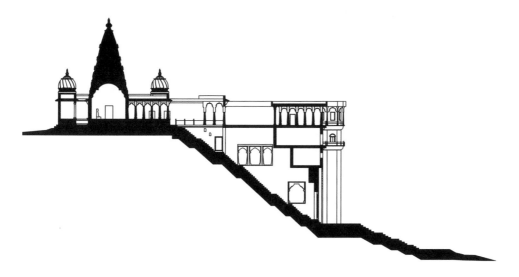

FIG. 4.15B Section through Bhonsla ghat. Drawing by Nanditha Veeraraghavelu and
Jennifer Shontz.

FIG. 4.16 *Shikhara* of Laxmi Narayan temple, Bhonsla ghat.

espoused an identity that was distinct from their Peshwa Brahmin competition. Their official title within the Maratha federation was that of "sena-sahib subah," a reference to their original governorship of the province of Berar in present-day central India. With the acquisition of Nagpur, however, the Bhonslas began to espouse an overt royal identity and image. The Bhonsla fortress-palace at Banaras was built ca. 1800, a complex design in which several architectural and spatial precedents were reconfigured (Fig. 4.15a and Fig. 4.15b). A monumental gateway in an embankment wall supported a twin courtyard *haveli* and a terraced, second level with temples and a *baradari*. Additional spaces at lower levels were used for storage. Two temples, both visible from a boat in the river, were added to the precinct over a span of four decades.

The first of these, the Laxmi Narayan temple, was built and endowed at the same time as the fortress-palace (Fig. 4.16). In 1840, and with the intention to commemorate Raghuji Bhonsle II, the family built and consecrated a second shrine, the Raghurajeshwur temple.[43] In general typological terms the two temples are similar to each other as well as to temples in the religious complex that the Bhonslas built ca. 1728, in Nagpur, where they built a new capital. No strangers to appropriating a late Mughal architectural language, the royal Rukmini complex, as it is known (which included the Rukmini and Mahadev temples), was located within the Bhonsla palace precinct in Nagpur; it was designed after a careful selection and combination of Mughal as well as revivalist elements.

Similar to the shrines in Nagpur, each temple within the fortress-palace at Banaras is also designed with *garbha-griha* and *mandapa*. The *garbha-griha* is surmounted with a *shikhara*. Although the exteriors of each *shikhara* are extensively carved and also include some figural sculpture, the *mandapa* of each shrine is modeled on a Mughal *baradari* with a flat roof supported on baluster columns. Public access to the precinct was always permitted, and together with the temples, the *baradari* over the riverfront terrace provided a communal space for religious gatherings (Fig. 4.17).[44] As previously noted, several patrons provided similar, partially accessible yet privately controlled spaces as a means of exercising influence over the socioreligious sphere. The Bhonslas merely extended this idea to the riverfront. The complex included private spaces for elite living. A small mansion organized around a courtyard was carefully ensconced within the second level of the structure. The principal chambers of this mansion were placed within the *burjes* (towers)

FIG. 4.17 *Baradari* in Bhonsla ghat.

of the fortress-palace. Each *burj* chamber was organized around octagonal platforms surrounded and supported by baluster columns and foliated arches. Wall panels were once covered with paintings. The living spaces within the mansion, however, were designed as secondary to the religious spaces on the terrace level. Directly accessible through city streets, they were integrated into the city's socioreligious sphere.

Visible patronage remained crucial to the acquisition of cultural capital. Patronage remained a critical way to fashion an elite persona, where issues of power, status, caste, and visible piety could be negotiated and represented. The example of Amrut Rao Peshwa demonstrates the delicate balancing act between a Brahmin identity and piety in light of his having been deposed as the Peshwa in 1803, after a tenure that lasted less than six months. He had been installed as Peshwa by Holkar but had to step down for Bajirao II, who had the support of the British after the Treaty of Bassein in 1802–1803.[45] Unsuccessful in his attempts to have his son Vinayakrao adopted and designated as the heir by the Peshwa Madhavrao II's widow, Amrut Rao moved to Banaras in 1804. Once settled in the city, he adopted and actively celebrated two symbols of Peshwa patronage: the deities Ganesh and Annapurna. His patronage of religious architecture and ritual can be viewed in light of real political loss as Amrut Rao tried to reattain some of his former place in the world and reinforced visible links to a family heritage that he was unable to legally inherit.

FIG. 4.18   Ganesh ghat.

CHAPTER 4

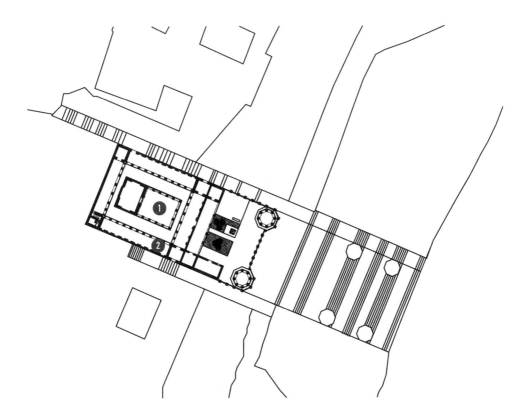

FIG. 4.19A Plan of Ganesh ghat. 1–Amrutvinayak temple, 2–residence. Drawing by
Nanditha Veeraraghavelu and Jennifer Shontz.

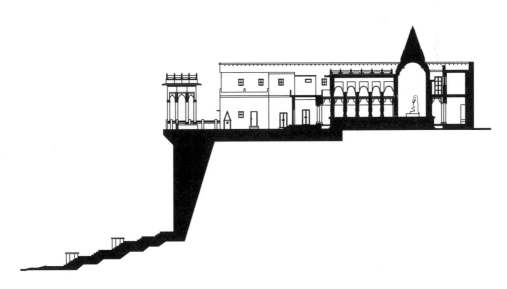

FIG. 4.19B Section through Ganesh ghat. Drawing by Nanditha Veeraraghavelu
and Jennifer Shontz.

Consistent with this strategy, the Annapurna *chattra*, a refectory where lavish meals were served to Brahmin priests, was added on Raja ghat.[46] This refectory and temples were built between 1807 (based on family tradition) and 1817 (according to endowment information in Benares Archives).[47] Amrut Rao also sponsored construction of the Amrutvinayak temple on Ganesh ghat in 1807. The temple and the refectory complex were endowed together as a charitable trust in 1817.[48] The Amrutvinayak temple complex was designed to occupy a prominent place along the riverfront, and its designers created optimum visibility for the structure that was located in proximity to the ritually significant site of Panchganga ghat (Fig. 4.18). The temple and its ancillary spaces were accommodated within a rectangular precinct within a stone embankment wall (Fig. 4.19a and Fig. 4.19b). Within, the temple was designed with a *garbha-griha* and a *mandapa*—a traditional spatial scheme that reflected similar trends in several regions of the Maratha country.

In contrast to the opulent private spaces of the Bhonsla mansion next door, ostensible austerity remained a measured statement of self-denial. Mughal columns are reserved for the temple *mandapa* (Fig. 4.20). Living spaces within the precinct were sparse. Amrut Rao exercised direct control over the temple's activities, management, and publicity. His relations with the colonial government and willingness to work within a colonial administrative framework suggest a personality very distinct from that of Raghuji Bhonsle II. Amrut Rao was an active supporter of Ganesh worship and supported several temples

FIG. 4.20 *Mandapa* of Amrutvinayak temple.

FEAST OF GANESA, BENARES.

FIG. 4.21 *Feast of Ganesh*, 1876, in Rousselet, *India and Its Native Princes*.

in Banaras that were dedicated to the deity. A Ganesh float was included among others plying the river during the annual Burhvamangal celebrations (Fig. 4.21).[49]

The second complex is relatively diminutive in terms of height, but the solid mass of its well-dressed chunar stone walls assures a prominent presence for the Annapurna *chattra* (Fig. 4.22 and Fig. 4.23). The designers of the Annapurna *chattra* merged two typologies. As an architectural type, the *chattra* (literally a "shelter" or refectory) was often part of temple complexes. *Chattras* were associated with pilgrimage sites and used as residential facilities for pilgrims. They could also be used as dining halls where charitable feasts were held, usually for Brahmin priests. At the Annapurna *chattra*, Amrut Rao merged this typology with that of the riverfront mansion. Designed as two interlinked precincts that were divided by a set of stairs, the *chattra* occupied the northern portion and was encased within stone embankment walls. The southern precinct encloses three freestanding temples on an enclosed terrace. The largest temple, dedicated to Shiva, was named Amruteshwur, after its patron (Fig. 4.24).

The three temples appear to be placed at random locations within the precinct, suggesting that these may have been built to mark "found" *lingas* that already existed at the

FIG. 4.22 Annapurna *chattra* and temples.

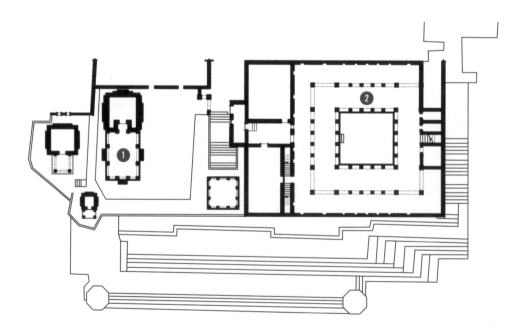

FIG. 4.23 Plan of Annapurna *chattra* and temples. 1–Amruteshwur temple, 2–refectory. Drawing by Nanditha Veeraraghavelu and Jennifer Shontz.

FIG. 4.24 Amruteshwur temple in Annapurna *chattra* precinct.

site. The interior columns of the *chattra* are designed with rectangular shafts and ornamented only with brackets, a studied departure from the much-used baluster column. Living quarters are minimally embellished and created as appendages to the principal complex. Mughal columns were reserved for the *mandapas* of the temples. There is no ornate *baradari* on the terrace, since the inclusion of one could suggest that its patron was given to aristocratic indulgences and a lavish lifestyle. A simple pillared pavilion stood in its place and was used as a ritual altar (for *hom-havan*) rather than dance performances and poetry recitals. Family members recall that Amrut Rao confined his spending to sponsoring lavish and conspicuous feasts for Brahmins in this refectory.

The Amrutvinayak temple and the Annapurna *chattra* should therefore be analyzed and understood together. The designs for both complexes combine visible grandeur on the riverfront with austere interiors. As the designs for the Bhonslas as well as Amrut Rao reveal, Mughal forms could be adapted and modified to accommodate individual aims and preferences. The temple and *chattra* were also projected as institutions for the public dispensation of charity, and Amrut Rao studiously avoided any suggestion of their being royal precincts. A comparison between his buildings and the Bhonsla ghat suggests that the socioreligious sphere and, by extension, religious public space could be highly variable and fractured.

Subtle differences between the Bhonsla ghat and the Munshi *wada*, built by the Bhonsla agent and manager, Sreedhur Munshi, further illustrate the careful choices made by patrons. The Munshi *wada*, built between 1812 and 1822, was placed on Dashashwamedha ghat, and its design remained in tension with the mansion on Bhonsla ghat.[50] Sreedhur Munshi built his mansion using a courtyard typology supported by an embankment wall. A monumental gateway or a terrace space with a *baradari* that might have indicated regal aspirations were avoided. At the same time, certain elements of its design share aspects with the Bhonsla ghat. *Burj* rooms in the two front corners as well as a covered gallery on the first level are derived from the design for the Bhonsla mansion.[51] The relative restraint in its design allowed its patrons to indulge a desire for a conspicuous building without overshadowing the Bhonsla mansion.

Chet Singh ghat became a site of shifting meanings in the nineteenth century. It is since remembered as the site of a celebrated altercation between Chet Singh and Warren Hastings that ended with Chet Singh's eventual escape. Following this incident, the fortress passed into the possession of the East India Company. In 1788 the Mughal prince Jahandar Shah was moved there with his entourage by the company. Large sections of the ghat were given over to him, and his descendants lived there till 1920, when the Rajas of Banaras completed their purchase of the property. The Rajas of Banaras, however, continued to maintain their association with the site. In the 1820s, with the British firmly in control of the city and the region, the Rajas turned anew to religious patronage and spectacle, conspicuously styling themselves as "Kashi Naresh." Riverside festivals were ideal occasions for garnering social recognition. The Burhvamangal festival that the Rajas sponsored is commonly believed to be a nineteenth-century adaptation of Meer Rustam Ali's Holi celebrations. The Rajas maintained their principal seat at Ramnagar across the river, from where they presided over an annual Ramlila performance that mapped the entire city as the narration of Ram's story unfolded.

As "Kashi Naresh" it followed that the Rajas should have a place within the city's prescribed sacred limits, staking a claim to spiritual and political kingship. James Prinsep responded to the theatrical qualities of the Burhvamangal festival, describing the river as "covered with boats of all descriptions, fitted out with platforms and canopies, covered with white cloth, and lighted with variegated lamps, torches, and blue-lights."[52] The festival was also supported by wealthy merchants, who hired "parties of singing and *nach* girls, or male buffoons, and dancing boys, to exhibit before the guests invited to pass the night upon their boats."[53] Celebrations began at the Chet Singh ghat, which is the scene of action in Prinsep's illustration of the event (Fig. 4.25).[54] Several generations of Rajas supported the Burhvamangal festival, and the theatrical potential of edifices such as the gateway of Chet Singh ghat was fully exploited. Besides the Burhvamangal, a sense of theater extended to other occasions including during regular boat rides up and down the river, with its fortress-palaces as scenic backdrop to its ritual life. Vessels such as the Raja of Banaras's "peacock boat" were both spectator and spectacle in these scenes and were captured in various representations of the riverfront as a vibrant social theater.[55]

A number of visitors to the city noticed and described many of the impressive edifices along the riverfront. Vijayaram Sen visited the Dharhara mosque and described the climb up its minaret as well as the view from its pinnacle. In his *Kashiparikrama*, Jaynarayan

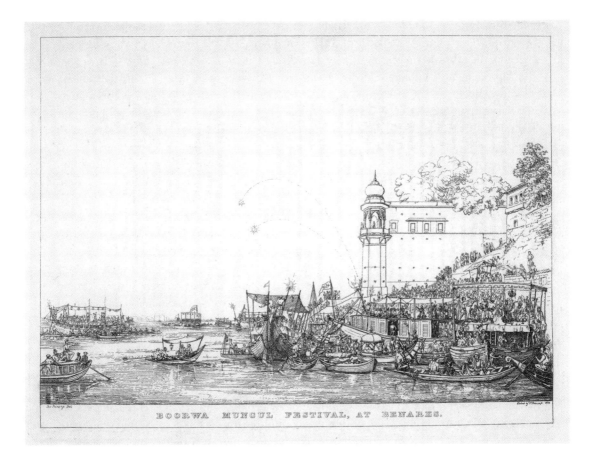

FIG. 4.25 *Boorwa Mungul Festival, at Benares* (Burhvamangal), 1831–1833, by James Prinsep. British Library Board.

Ghoshal provided an extensive list of riverfront sites, punctuating his enumeration with remarks on their aesthetic appeal. Although he remained preoccupied with the details of ritual and pilgrimage, Veeraswamy also enjoyed traveling along the riverfront, either admiring or critiquing the ghats.[56] The emergence of this critical but appreciative audience provided additional opportunities for a self-conscious emergent elite to garner social status and influence.

This phase of construction on the riverfront—that is, a preference for the fortress-palace with a monumental façade, well-defined precinct, and adaptations of Mughal precedents—lasted into the early decades of the nineteenth century. By the mid-nineteenth century, however, Maratha elites scaled back their patronage for such edifices and also lost interest in inventing and supporting new traditions. The explanation for this development is rooted in the politics of the early nineteenth century and the rising subcontinental hegemony of the East India Company. Maratha power, considerably diminished after the Second Anglo–Maratha war of 1805, dissipated further over the subsequent decade. In

1817 the Maratha confederacy and their nominal leader, the Peshwa Bajirao II, lost to the East India Company at the Battle of Khadki (Kirkee). As a result, the East India Company became the most dominant power in South Asia by 1820.

Although the company had direct control of the city since 1781, its officials always acknowledged the authority and sensibilities of Maratha patrons. Their representative, Nawab Ali Ibrahim Khan, wrote letters to several elites, assuring continued support for building activity and ritual life in Banaras.[57] All the same, patrons gradually began to lose interest in building elaborate complexes that could function as loci for spectacular festivities. The city remained a significant pilgrimage destination, with enhanced attention being paid to its ritual landscape and place within Hinduism. The patrons who supported its religious life, however, gradually changed. The 1820s and 1830s were characterized by construction projects at a smaller scale, accompanied by a general reluctance to invent new traditions on a grandiose scale. Patrons either built smaller, independent temples or relatively modest riverfront mansions. Patronage for religious events and donations for charities were channeled toward prominent temples such as the ones dedicated to Vishweshwur and Annapurna. As a complex social network, where a number of patrons could carve separate yet connected spheres and spaces of influence, the socioreligious sphere had a diminishing role.

Some examples of patronage in the second and third decades of the nineteenth century illustrate this shift in power. Nawab Ali Ibrahim Khan had proceeded in a gingerly fashion, sending formally composed letters of assurance and appeasement. By 1823, however, the East India Company's government created a Committee for Local Improvement (1823–1829) to manage and adjudicate new projects and any related disputes. Elite patrons were now required to petition this committee for permission to build temples or mansions or even to repair a stretch of riverfront paving. In 1825, for instance, another Maratha patron, Gahunabai Gaekwad, wished to build a temple on a riverfront site.[58] She also wished to sponsor construction on Ugneshwur ghat with the intention of adding stone pavements and steps that could provide easy access to the river, and she petitioned the committee through her *mukhtiar* (agent).[59] Though permission was promptly granted and the temple and adjoining ghat successfully constructed, a shift in the city's power structure is evident.

The shift is clearly apparent in the circumstances surrounding the construction of a ghat by the deposed Maratha Peshwa Bajirao II.[60] Having surrendered to the British in 1817, he was exiled by them to the town of Bithor (near present-day Kanpur) in northern India, far from his capital and power base in Pune. Bajirao II directed his attention and resources to supporting building activity and Brahminical ritual in Banaras. The details of his patronage underline the significant shift in power that the Peshwas experienced. A mere decade earlier, his adopted (and disinherited) brother Amrut Rao had successfully overseen the construction of two edifices on the riverfront and had also instituted public rituals and celebrations.

Bajirao II, however, had a different experience, as he selected a site that was highly venerated in Maratha circles (Fig. 4.26). His mansion was to be located near Manikarnika, where Ahilyabai had previously constructed a ghat, tank, and several temples. By the early decades of the nineteenth century, Manikarnika had become a popular pilgrimage

Bajiraogbat

FIG. 4.26   Bajirao ghat, 1905. Photo by Madho Prasad. British Library Board.

destination. As a result, the location of the proposed mansion was dense with temples and *madhis* (chambers where the sick could lie and watch the Ganges River). Bajirao proposed to rebuild the adjoining embankment with steps that could lead down to the river. Accordingly, he petitioned the Committee for Local Improvement. Inevitably he heard complaints about his plans from neighbors as well as members of the committee.

Other actors such as "Bada Krishn, the agent of Munee Lal" complained that this new construction had placed his employer's temple below grade, and access to it was almost impossible.[61] Another petitioner, Jyram Gir Ghoosyn (Jairam Gir Gosain), the leader of a powerful sect of Naga *sadhus* (ascetics), complained in turn about access to his temple, the "Dusnam Shivala."[62] It was left to the committee to intervene and suggest the addition of a "sunken passage" between this temple and the new ghat as well as to mediate all disputes. Despite significant amounts of investment, Bajirao II could not directly influence or intimidate less prominent but increasingly vocal neighbors and competitors. The mansion and *ghat* were built, but Prinsep, also the secretary of the committee, complained about shoddy construction and a lack of attention to detail. Recognizing his diminished status in an altered political climate, Bajirao II scaled back his patronage for religious festivities. He continued his family's long-standing support for the Annapurna temple and its charitable activities but refrained from constructing a new temple or installing a deity that would be celebrated through invented ceremonies and novel rituals.

The case of another Maratha widow, Baizabai Shindhia of the family of Gwalior, illustrates the realities of a diminishing socioreligious sphere commanded by South Asia's ruling elite at this time. Her late husband, Daulatrao Shindhia, along with the heads of the other Maratha ruling houses, had surrendered his sovereignty to the East India Company in 1818. He remained the nominal ruler of his "princely state," under British hegemony, until his death in 1827. He was briefly succeeded by Baizabai as regent, but she was shortly replaced by an adopted son and heir. The two had a contentious relationship, and the son had her exiled to Banaras. Once settled in the city, Baizabai decided to sponsor the construction of a riverfront mansion and its adjoining ghat. She arranged for funds to be transferred to the city to pay for the structure. Baizabai established a *kothi* (banking establishment) in Banaras where *hundis* (checks) could be cleared and funds made available for construction. The *kothi* was also intended as a conduit for channeling funds earmarked for charity.

The site of the proposed Shindhia ghat was adjacent to the ritually significant Manikarnika ghat. The edifice was designed to face the river with a prominent façade (Fig. 4.27). It was also designed to accommodate public ritual space along the riverfront, enhanced by paved steps as well as the *madhis* incorporated within its design.[63] Although the ghat has not survived the ravages of time, records indicate that construction began in 1835, but the project ran into a number of hurdles.[64] A mason's drawing of the ghat survived into the twentieth century and was published in 1931 and suggests a scheme for an ornate design for the façade.[65] Based on this sketch and a photograph taken in 1905, this was an ensemble of foliated arches and Mughal baluster columns without a supporting embankment wall.

A mere three decades before Baizabai, the Bhonslas had successfully demonstrated that building a ghat could simultaneously enhance elite authority as well as an image of piety. Sponsoring the building of a ghat should have provided Baizabai with ample opportunities to enhance her political role. Times, however, had changed and similar actions did not necessarily yield identical results. Baizabai did not spare expense, and unlike another though more powerful widow, Ahilyabai Holkar, she may have been seen as failing to exercise restraint in her aesthetic choices. Baizabai projected a more complex persona. She indulged a taste for expensive equestrian pursuits but fashioned her lifestyle along norms considered acceptable for a pious widow: eating simple food and sleeping on a mat placed directly on a bare floor. Such visible self-denial was intended to work together with her patronage for opulent building. As her correspondence with Charles Metcalfe, then governor-general, revealed, Baizabai sought "reward in a future state and of a good name in this world" by building the ghat.[66]

Baizabai, however, was less than consistent in maintaining this persona. A contemporary British visitor, Fanny Parks, observed the ghat under construction and described it as the "handsomest" she had seen as its "scale is so grand, so beautiful, so light, and it is on so regular a plan."[67] Parks claimed to be privy to financial information, revealing

Manikarnikaghat

FIG. 4.27   Photo of Shindhia ghat (adjacent to Manikarnika ghat), 1905. Photo by Madho Prasad. British Library Board.

that Baizabai had spent 1.5 million rupees on its construction and that it would probably take another 2 million rupees to complete it.[68] By 1834, Baizabai transferred 3.7 million rupees to the banking house. The enterprise ran into controversies when she was accused of diverting funds for her personal use rather than for charitable activities. Her *kothi*'s "reputation" in her words was "injured" and she sought Metcalf's intervention for its restoration and also for better regulation of funds designated for "sacred purposes."[69] With the stated intention of settling the dispute between Baizabai and her adopted son, the East India Company seized the *kothi*'s assets (including funds provided for feeding Brahmins to the tune of 200 rupees a day). The mansion (on what would become the Shindhia ghat) remained unfinished.[70]

Like several of her predecessors, Baizabai's motives for building the ghat were never exclusively religious. In a climate of shifting political fortunes, a dispossessed yet elite subject such as Baizabai could use charitable activities including patronage for architecture as a means to consolidate social authority. However, the continued success of such proj-

FIG. 4.28   Tarakeshwur temple on Manikarnika ghat.

CHAPTER 4

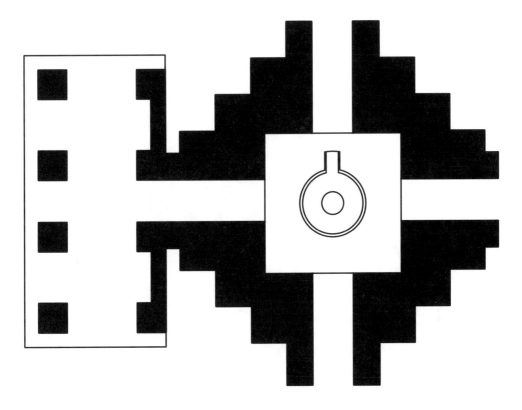

FIG. 4.29 Plan of Tarakeshwur temple, Manikarnika ghat. Drawing by Nanditha Veeraraghavelu and Jennifer Shontz.

ects as reflections of their patron's authority became increasingly doubtful. As has been noted, her plans for erecting a pavilion within the Gyan Vapi precinct to cover the Gyan Vapi well in 1828 were more successful, since the project was associated with a sacred space that was firmly located within a shared pilgrimage landscape. Baizabai's ghat, however, was to be built with a more quasi-public role in mind. In an uncertain political climate and circumstances of diminished authority, her motives were more easily cast as suspect and by extension the success of her project was inevitably jeopardized.

TEMPLES ON THE RIVERFRONT

The numerous temple spires that mark the riverfront almost universally display the "Banaras profile." Many patrons paid careful attention to South Asia's pre-Islamic landscape and renovated, built, and consecrated temple sites across the subcontinent to participate in a demanding world of religious revival. They also jockeyed for a place in the courtly culture of eighteenth-century northern India armed with Mughal symbols and forms. The complex relationship between aspirational identity, patronage, and architecture is visible in the choice of form and style for the Tarakeshwur (Fig. 4.28 and Fig. 4.29) and

FIG. 4.30   Ratneshwur temple on Manikarnika ghat.

Ratneshwur (Fig. 4.30 and Fig. 4.31) temples on Ahilyabai Holkar's Manikarnika ghat. The Tarakeshwur temple is designed with a *shikhara* and late Mughal *mandapa*, whereas the Ratneshwur temple is designed with a heavily carved *shikhara* and *mandapa* with pyramidal roof. Indeed, this latter temple is completely unique in Banaras. Built on a smaller scale than the contemporary Vishweshwur temple, the *shikhara* of the Tarakeshwur temple is similar to that of the Ahilyeshwur temple on Ahilya ghat. In contrast, the design for the Ratneshwur temple was a direct repudiation of a late Mughal architectural lan-

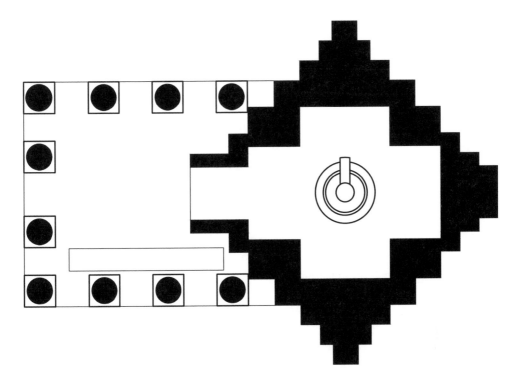

FIG. 4.31 Plan of Ratneshwur temple, Manikarnika ghat. Drawing by Nanditha Veeraraghavelu and Jennifer Shontz.

guage. Its consistent and deliberate trabeated construction and ornate exterior make an explicit reference to a pre-Islamic past.

In a remarkable twist in trends, the fading desirability of the fortress-palace or ghat as a medium for channeling patronage was accompanied by its widespread representation as a stereotypical feature of the city. As the English East India Company gained control of the city, institutions, spaces, and buildings in Banaras underwent a transformation. Such changes inevitably also had consequences for the ways in which the ritual landscape of the city would be experienced and represented. The experience of colonial rule further altered the ways that Indians experienced and expressed religious and social identities.

CHAPTER FIVE

ORDER AND ANTIQUITY

B Y the early decades of the twentieth century, Banaras presented a significantly different picture than the one that either Vijayaram Sen or Enugula Veeraswamy might have experienced. Besides a general outward expansion of the city, its skyline was dotted with many more temple *shikharas*, placed along denser, modified pilgrimage routes. The city also boasted a town hall, colleges, hospitals, and urban parks—the collective trappings of a modern city. The elite continued established patterns of patronage through a new group, with enhanced links to the colonial regime, and were keen to restructure social, political, and material relationships. Colonial knowledge, as Bernard Cohn has defined it, certainly influenced the workings of the colonial government.[1] At the same time, its selective adoption by Indian elites altered their expectations from the city.[2] Newer survey techniques, archaeological methods, and a burgeoning print culture played a key role in reshaping the city both materially and imaginatively.[3]

Beginning in 1781, the East India Company took direct control of the Banaras region and Warren Hastings's appointee, Ali Ibrahim Khan, was established as city magistrate and judge in the courthouse on Dal Mandi.[4] Viewing themselves as stepping into Mughal shoes, the company's British officials and their Indian partners tried to fulfill some of the roles of their predecessors.[5] Company officials rented homes and garden houses from the city's elite, to some degree continuing their lifestyles and investments.[6] The city's late Mughal-built landscape simultaneously became home as well as exotic picture, as the sketches and notes of the artist Ozias Humphry reveal.[7] Ali Ibrahim Khan avowed a personal commitment to the city's socioreligious sphere and its elite participants, which included several Indian compradors with connections to the company. Khan intended to incorporate the city's elites into the company's governance structure by offering a semblance of institutional continuity against tumultuous change.[8] As Ghulam Husain "Tabatabai," one of the company's Indian critics, observed, Hastings and his officials ostensibly promoted Mughal forms but actively altered the nature of control and management.[9]

The East India Company's policies shifted visibly toward the last decade of the eighteenth century under Jonathan Duncan. Appointed in 1787, Duncan initiated a departure from established company policies, particularly in light of Hastings's infamous impeachment trial.[10] Duncan was unhappy with Khan's older administrative methods, particularly what he derided as excessive reliance on delegation and conciliation rather than decisive resolution.[11] Duncan began to institute centralized control predicated on ideas of a general "public good" for a city of responsible and uniformly governed citizens. A universal and legally regulated civic consciousness, he hoped, would include the entire city and transcend immediate *muhalla* environments and social affinities. His administration began to levy citywide taxation, beginning with a tax on every new idol installed in a temple.[12]

Many of Duncan's concerns were about the lack of urban cleanliness, sanitation, and by extension public morality.[13] Company administrators and surveyors repeatedly expressed concern regarding the general filthy state of the city. In his 1789–1790 survey of the state of sewage and drainage in Banaras, F. Wilford was astounded to find that a principal tank in the city had degenerated into a common site for defecation.[14] To ameliorate what they saw as an endemic problem, the administrators introduced public toilets in 1790.[15] The measure did not go down well with residents, and Duncan remained unhappy about "a vast multitude of lower classes of the natives" assembled on the outskirts to protest against the regulations for keeping the town clean by having "public necessaries." A *hurtal*, or protest, where many shopkeepers closed their shops, was followed with a petition to the effect that although women had been excused from going within the "jetties," it was unacceptable and objectionable to the men as well.[16]

Besides orchestrating attempts to cleanse the city, Duncan began to establish institutional and administrative mechanisms that would lie beyond the purview of established networks of patronage and power.[17] He began to distance himself from the courthouse on Dal Mandi, and by 1788 the East India Company was considering sites at Secrole (to the north of the city) to develop a cantonment, carefully avoiding the villages of Rameshwur and Kapildhara that were located along the Panchkroshi pilgrimage route.[18] Plans for a *dewany adalat* (courthouse) and *fouzdaree* (jail) at Secrole were also drawn up.[19] Before civic order could be instituted, the city had to be understood, enumerated, and mapped. Company administrators commissioned several surveys of the urban areas and *muhallas* of Banaras.[20] This information became the basis for a novel system of taxation and surveillance that quickly also became a source of tensions between administrators and residents. Taxation systems and security measures had been organized at the level of the *muhalla* for much of the eighteenth century. In the face of such rooted systems of urban management, instituting uniform taxation to fund various citywide "improvements" for a universal "public good" elicited vigorous objections.

Phatuckbandi, an existing system by which *phatucks* (gates) of *muhallas* could be controlled and watched at night, was modified in 1795 when Duncan connected universal urban taxation to a fund for the "improvement" of the city. Following rapid urban growth, the colonial government conducted another survey of *muhallas* in 1809, which was accompanied by a push for a centrally controlled system of *phatuckbandi* to be applied across several *muhallas*.[21] Watchmen were appointed by the *kotwal* (chief of police), and residents feared that they would in fact act as surveillance agents for the East India Company. They were uncomfortable with the company's appointees over whom they had little or no control.[22] Taking the idea of uniform governance further, the company tried to institute a citywide House tax in 1811.[23] Each of these measures was controversial and met with varied degrees and displays of collective resistance.

In yet another attempt at centralized control, Duncan intervened in the city's academic institutions. Hitherto, Brahmin scholars had taught students who became a part of their households, resulting in strong bonds of patronage, familial ties, and individual mentorship that had perpetuated the city's academic legacy. Duncan's intention was to shift patronage for Sanskrit learning away from "native princes" and to the East India Company, for which he initiated establishment of the Sanskrit *pathshala* in 1791. The institution was intended as a training ground for Indian experts in "Hindu Law" who would eventually assist "European judges" in dispensing authentic and impartial justice.[24] Taken together, Duncan's actions had wide-reaching implications for civic identity, the economy of patronage, and the city's ritual landscape.

HISTORIES AND MYTHS

Despite extensive differences in their policies, both Duncan and Hastings believed in the antiquity and cultural significance of Banaras and in their divergent ways, each was interested in co-opting its legacy to legitimate and bolster the East India Company's rule. Early colonial histories of South Asia included Alexander Dow's *History of Hindostan* (1772) followed by James Mill's *The History of British India* (1817).[25] Although published four decades apart and with vastly different motivations, both histories were compiled as linear progressions of events premised on a clear distinction between South Asia's Hindu and Islamic pasts. Company officials, including Hastings, Duncan, their successors as well as subordinates, eagerly embraced Orientalist notions about Banaras. They viewed it as an authentic Hindu artifact, a subject for intellectual investigation that was to be preserved and enhanced, much in the same way that antique objects were being collected, displayed, and preserved throughout the company's expanding dominions. Positivist historical perspectives were promoted through the Asiatic Society (established in 1784, an association of amateur colonial historians and dilettantes based in Calcutta). The Asiatic Society's activities and publications triggered a discourse through which Indians began to imagine their past in new ways.

The discovery of the Buddhist site of Sarnath to the north of Kashikshetra (beyond the Panchkroshi circuit) in 1794 altered the city's history as well as its imagined geography (Fig. 5.1).[26] Sarnath became pivotal to the story of Banaras. Conscious of its significance, Jaynarayan Ghoshal pointedly referred to a deity near the edge of the Panchkroshi that he named Sangheshwur, implicitly incorporating a vaguely understood Buddhist past within the city's burgeoning pilgrimage routes.[27] As the colonial apparatus continued to produce a historical timeline for the subcontinent, the *puranas* were consigned to a "medieval" age and were no longer sufficient sources for authenticating its antiquity. Indian (Hindu) visitors, in particular, endeavored to close this gap between a rooted view of the past and the demands of new historical perspectives.

Another Bengali visitor (also a member of the Asiatic Society), Bholanauth Chunder, commented on the absence of visible signs of antiquity, such as "architectural vestiges of the time of Judishththira or Vicramaditya," that could provide tangible evidence that a *purana*-based mythology was evidence of a hoary past.[28] Even careful queries always resulted in the unsatisfactory conclusion that archaeological or historic remains that

FIG. 5.1   Dhamek stupa, 1905. Photo by Madho Prasad. British Library Board.

could sustain such a narrative were minimal. As Chunder observed, "the oldest building dates only from the age of Akbar."[29] If historical accounts had to be supported by physical vestiges as substantive proof that Banaras was indeed an ancient city, instances of Islamic iconoclasm could also explain the glaring lack of ancient (pre-Islamic) remains that could be linked to accounts in *purana* texts. Another dilemma introduced through historical perspectives was that the *puranas* could no longer be considered "ancient," since they were consigned to a medieval age. The solution, as Jaynarayan had previously demonstrated, was to incorporate the city's Buddhist past within its Hindu identity.

Chunder numbered among the many Indians who espoused historical perspectives, and the existence of Sarnath allowed them to project the city's antiquity beyond the now medieval age of the *puranas*. For such an argument to be convincing, the location as well as religious antecedents of Sarnath had to be reconciled with the city's *purana*-based ritual geography. To accomplish this successfully, Chunder, along with many of his contemporaries, accepted Buddhism as integral to a monolithic Hindu faith and merged the city's *purana* tradition with the history of "the Gupta and Pal periods." Using Sarnath as an anchor, he imagined an ancient city that extended well beyond its mid-nineteenth-century limits.[30] Chunder then proceeded to connect every major event in South Asia's newly established historical timeline to the material environment of nineteenth-century Banaras. He suggested that the name Sarnath was derived from one of the names for Shiva and that its origins lay in "a small Brahminical temple of Shiva, on the spot." Chunder may merely have repeated a narrative then current in the city, although even he was not entirely convinced. He conceded that "most probably, the appellation is Buddhistic, and has a reference to Buddha under the name of Saranganath, or the 'Lord of Deer.'"[31]

Antiquarian interests and historical perspectives that began to accompany mythical and religious associations resulted in altered expectations from the city's built environment. Chunder speculated about the possibility that "the temple of Ad-Biseswara may be detected to have been raised upon the ruins of Buddhist monastery."[32] Elites such as Chunder who had close associations with colonial institutions and networks tended to espouse antiquarian interests and nascent nationalist sensibilities that could readily conflate the city's Buddhist and Hindu pasts. They were less interested in the city's religious life. If he ever took a dip in the Ganges, or prayed at the Vishweshwur temple, Chunder was silent on the subject. This schism was apparent when the city's Brahmins remained reluctant to ascribe Buddhist origins to Shaiva practices, and Chunder roundly accused them of a sly attitude and of holding on to narrow beliefs and concerns.

Other observers, such as the missionary Matthew Atmore Sherring, searched for multiple layers among sparse antique remains. While conceding that the contemporary city had been recently erected, Sherring believed that "architectural remains of various stages of antiquity" were to be found in the city's northern sections.[33] He was convinced that most of these "remains" were Buddhist in origin.[34] Also linking the city to every age in Indian history, Sherring berated Hindu writers for their "distaste for noting and recording historical facts in a simple and consecutive manner."[35] He also blamed this propensity of the Hindus for robbing the city of Banaras of its "glory."[36] Sherring further observed that contemporary Hinduism was "puranic" in character and that "temples which stud the streets, the idols worshipped in them, the religious observances practiced by the people, in short, the materialistic and sensuous characteristics of the Hindu faith, as exhibited there, are, to a very great extent, Puranic in their origin."[37] Sherring made a case for the city's antiquity by pointing to various instances of spolia being used in relatively new buildings in the "northern and north-western quarters of the city," an area he concluded was the ancient site of a Buddhist Banaras.[38]

Following Sherring, the missionary James Kennedy described the city and its various pasts in very similar terms.[39] By the early decades of the twentieth century, a number of Indians widely accepted and promulgated the idea that an Indic cultural legacy was based in an amalgam of Buddhist and Hindu beliefs and material cultures.[40] Such a view was supported by positing the assimilative qualities of Indian civilization and its uninterrupted continuity through the ages. Bengali lawyer Rajani Ranjan Sen, who visited the city in 1909, was quick to remark on the lack of visible antiquity within the city's built fabric. The explanation, he felt, lay in acts of violent destruction perpetrated by invading

Muslims. Sen went a step further in his explications. Since there was little to reconcile a city of "prehistoric ages" and "the actual paucity of such remains," the blame lay with agents who wished to supplant Hinduism both with a violent Islam and, even earlier, with the "simplicity" of Buddhism.[41] Like his contemporaries, Sen expressed affinity for Buddhism even as he wished to find material remains that could confirm antiquity and, by extension, a Hindu identity for Banaras. The *puranas* lived on as an alternate view on the city. Since in its current *puranic* form Hinduism was a successor to Buddhism and a Vedic religion, Banaras could also be viewed as playing a central role in each distinct faith. In Sen's account the effects of Islam were ultimately construed as being equally devastating to both Buddhism and Hinduism.

These debates were included in the city's official colonial gazetteer written by H. R. Neville and published in 1905.[42] Neville's account was based on material gathered from the annual reports of the Archaeological Survey of Northern India as well as issues of the *Journal of the Royal Asiatic Society* and the *Journal of the Bengal Asiatic Society.* He also depended on Henry Miers Elliot's *The History of India as Told by Its Own Historians.*[43] He began by recounting myths related to the city's creation, even as he discounted their veracity as legitimate history. For Neville, these narratives were "uncertain and fragmentary," and he emphasized that accounts in "epics" and from "works of the later Puranic period" could not be taken seriously. Instead, Neville declared that the first "historical" age was connected with the life of the Buddha, confirmed by the excavations at Sarnath. The next stage in the city's history was connected with the fifth-century travels of Chinese Buddhist monk and traveler Fa-Hian. This was followed by the seventh-century descriptions by Chinese traveler and monk "Hiuen Thsiang" (Yuan Chwang). Neville continued to enumerate the reigns of several Muslim dynasties and emphasized the repeated destruction of the Vishweshwur temple, beginning with a first instance in 1194 by Qutbud-din Aibak and the latest instance by Aurangzeb in 1669. He concluded his account with the establishment of a Hindu ruling house in Banaras and the building of their fort in 1752, at Ramnagar across the river.[44] In sum, Neville framed this past within a historical timeline, beginning with a Buddhist Banaras, continuing into a Hindu age, followed by Islamic iconoclasm from which the city always seemed to bounce back. He concluded with the ameliorating effects of British rule.

Authors of popular guidebooks, whether British or Indian, tended to accept and reiterate a fluid relationship between history and myth. Major Hebert Newell, an officer in the colonial army, produced a guidebook for Banaras in 1915, in which he described a city "of narrow tortuous streets, its myriad shrines and saints, its wide, wonder-working Ganges, its unparalleled wealth of tradition, and vast accumulation of legendary lore." He also claimed that he had "given the history of Siva's city in a form so condensed as to be capable of immediate digestion."[45] Newell presented the legends as well as histories of Banaras, accompanied by a tour that started with its principal shrines close to and including the Vishweshwur temple. He then continued to the riverfront, and concluded with a visit to Sarnath. He was careful to include living legends (usually from a *purana* source) associated with the tangible built environment that visitors would encounter. In the construction of a popular (as opposed to an academic) discourse for the city, the mythical viewpoint lost neither its appeal nor its adherents.

The author of another guidebook, *All About Benares* (1917), combined *purana* references within a historical outline. Styling himself as an "Old Resident," this author relied on the specter of Islamic destruction to account for the lack of "any great antiquity" to the city's "modern buildings."[46] Instead, the contemporary city became a replacement for an ancient original. The sixteenth- and seventeenth-century origins of much of the built environment of contemporary Banaras were easily sidelined. The city's eternal character was supported by the purported antiquity of its contemporary built environment. Although the dilemma around questions of antiquity was partially resolved, Indian elites continued to confront the reality of a decaying city that they felt lacked suitable institutions, spaces, and buildings. An ideal Banaras would be both ancient and modern, a suitable emblem of the past and an impressive city that would showcase a vibrant and contemporary Hindu identity. In its current state, as several discontented elites observed, it failed to satisfy either desire.

URBAN DISCONTENTS AND DESIRES

The rapid urbanization and increasingly cosmopolitan culture of colonial Calcutta left Banaras with a provincial identity, a fact that visitors and residents alike noted with disappointment. Bholanauth Chunder, for instance, presented his readers with a city that was "thoroughly Hindoo—from its Hindoo *muts* and *mundeers*, its Hindoo idols and emblems of worship, . . . a bona fide Hindoo town, distinguished by its peculiarities from all other towns upon the earth."[47] Besides the dearth of visible signs of antiquity, Chunder's dissatisfaction was compounded by the absence of such institutions and spaces as art galleries, museums, and public libraries. He bemoaned the lack of a modern built environment as well as the absence of public institutions that could embody a collective history, complaining that "there is no such scene as a Hindoo Westminster Abbey, in which repose the most remarkable men of Hindoo history."[48] Celebrations and spectacles that were initiated mere decades earlier left Chunder unimpressed and even disgusted.[49] The influence of religion on "public opinion and social institutions" as well as on "arts and learning" and "festivals and amusements" was, in his view, highly undesirable.[50] Chunder conceded that the riverfront was admirable, but only when viewed from the comfort and distance of a steamship moored along the riverbank. In other words, the socioreligious sphere with its deep connections to older forms of patronage had lost its potency as well as some of its relevance.

A new building for the Sanskrit *pathshala*, now the Queen's College, marked a major escalation in scale and set a new register of expectations among the city's Hindu elite.[51] Designed by Major Markham Kittoe and completed in 1852, this building marked a departure from the ones erected previously by the East India Company (Fig. 5.2). The Mint designed by Prinsep, the Nadesar *kothi* (mansion), and several churches in the city and in the cantonment all paled when compared to Kittoe's edifice built in a "severe style of perpendicular Gothic." The building was constructed through a combination of government and private—that is, elite Hindu as well as British—subscription.[52] It catered to an idealized vision of Indian scholastic tradition (with students and teachers seated cross-legged on carpets) ensconced within a building and setting that recalled "the gardens of Oxford

FIG. 5.2   Queen's College (Sanskrit University), 1905. Photo by Madho Prasad. British
Library Board.

and Cambridge."[53] Chunder hoped the building would "enlighten and form the native
population into a new Hindoo nation, with new ideas in their heads, and new institutions distinguishing their national character."[54] For other Indian elite, Calcutta was an
urban ideal, its "elegance" derived from its impressive public buildings and open spaces.[55]
Banaras was to be transformed but simultaneously retain its ritual significance and its
antiquity. In this regard, Kittoe's design established a new scale and standard for civic
architecture in Banaras. If a socioreligious sphere was directly connected to patronage,
the city's civic sphere was forged as elites in the city began to imagine a modern urban
future that could be shaped through a unifying Hindu identity and through institutions
of shared urban governance. Architectural and urban forms played a key role in their
imagination.

    Between 1823 and 1867 substantial areas of the city were drained and reclaimed as
part of an urban sanitization scheme followed by designs for a citywide sewage plan in
1879–1880. Frank Fitzjames, the architect/engineer, drew attention to the filthy state and

stench of streets and spaces in Banaras as a justification for draining several catchments that were designated as sacred pools.[56] Looking back at these efforts in 1909, the missionary Edwin Greaves remarked favorably upon the "vast improvements" effected by the colonial government, although it was agreed that Banaras could never be as clean as a European city.[57] Similar unfavorable comparisons to metropolitan environment remained a consistent theme across travel accounts, especially those written by European visitors.

For Indian elites, visions for the city often took on complex forms. Sustaining its sacred geography and ritual life were abiding concerns, as was the desire for spaces and buildings that could compare favorably with the edifices, esplanades, and parks of Calcutta and Bombay. Bharatendu Harishchandra articulated such concerns in his play *Premjogini*, which was first serialized in his journal *Harishchandra Chandrika* in 1874.[58] The third act is set in a railway station in another town, and one of the characters, a Brahmin, describes Banaras to a fellow traveler.[59] The Brahmin dwells on the city's role as a pilgrimage destination where devotion and public charity enliven its vibrant mythology.[60] He is equally concerned with the city's religious identity as with its modern institutions, including colleges, libraries, and hospitals. He enumerates deities mentioned in the *puranas*, colonial officials, and the city's contemporary elite in almost the same breath. Harishchandra's protagonist takes his readers on a tour that includes the observatory at Man Mandir, the stupas at Sarnath, the impressive Queen's College, as well as the "golden dome of the Vishweshwur temple." Taken together, these sites merely strengthen the city's description in the *puranas* as "unique in three worlds."[61] By the turn of the twentieth century, the intersection of colonial regulation, antiquarian sensibilities, and Indian desires reshaped the urban spaces, ritual landscapes, and cartographies of Banaras.

VISHWESHWUR

Pilgrimage to the city was on the rise since the British took over Banaras and as Ahilyabai's Vishweshwur temple (ca. 1781) gradually became a principal destination.[62] Cognizant of the role of religion and religious patronage, Warren Hastings (along with Ali Ibrahim Khan and Bishambar Pandit) ordered repairs to the Dharhara mosque and also ordered the construction of a *naubat khana* (gateway) for Ahilyabai's Vishweshwur temple.[63] Critics such as "Tabatabai" complained about the East India Company's lack of attention to infrastructure in its conquered territories, and Hastings may have chosen projects of high visibility to safeguard his regime's reputation.[64] Given their predilection for antiquarian perspectives, colonial officials were understandably fascinated with the idea of an older Vishweshwur temple subsumed by the Gyan Vapi mosque. James Prinsep drew a conjectural plan of this "ancient" temple, based on his observations of its lone standing wall as well as the precinct.[65] He depicted nine interconnected chambers, a reference to the multiple *mandapas* described in the *Kashikhand*. He assigned individual deities to each chamber with "Mahadeo" at the center. "Tarakeshwur," "Dundpaun," and "Mankeswur" occupied the three northern chambers, and "Ganesh," "Dwarpal," and "Bhyro," the three southern ones (Fig. 5.3). In the central row a "Siwa Mundip" flanked "Mahadeo" or Vishweshwur on either side. Prinsep's depiction is far from being realistic and differs quite significantly from Vijayaram Sen's account of the precinct and its immediate vicinity.[66]

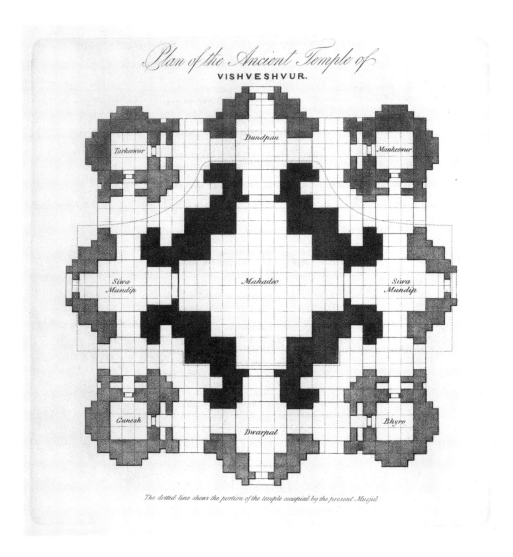

Plan of the Ancient Temple of
VISHVESHVUR.

Tarkeswur — *Dundpan* — *Mankeswur*

Siwa Mundip — *Mahadeo* — *Siwa Mundip*

Gunesh — *Dwarpal* — *Bhyro*

The dotted line shews the portion of the temple occupied by the present Musjid.

FIG. 5.3 *Plan of the Ancient Temple of Vishveshvur*, 1831–1833, by James Prinsep.
British Library Board.

Prinsep traced the outline of the Gyan Vapi mosque with a dotted line. Like many of his contemporaries, whether British or Indian, he was preoccupied by the perceived antiquity of the site as well as its devastation and occupation by an Islamic regime. The colonial administration tended to simplify events and gloss over nuances of opinion, viewing them as confrontations between monolithic groups of Hindus and Muslims.[67] As a result, the Mughal legacy of Narayan Bhatt's Vishweshwur temple was sidelined in favor of an exclusionary identity. Similarly, the Gyan Vapi mosque was dissociated from the policies of a single emperor and placed within the grand narrative of inevitable Islamic destruction and iconoclasm.

Similar sentiments were expressed by several other Indian visitors as well as residents. For Jadunath Sarvadhikari, a Bengali visitor to the city ca. 1854 and the author of the *Tirthabhramana*, the precinct of the Gyan Vapi mosque was a sacred space to be claimed by either bribing or hoodwinking "Muslim" guards.[68] His account of the 1809 Lat Bhairo incident was deeply colored by sectarian sentiments. In his version the colonial government had allowed the Hindus to take revenge on the Muslims for destroying the Lat and presented them with a new one as compensation.[69] Writing in his *Itihas Timirnashak* (1873), Raja Shivprasad Sitarehind, another influential figure among Banaras elites, emphasized the common roots of Hindu and Buddhist beliefs.[70] He acknowledged a debt, among others, to the British archaeologist Alexander Cunningham, for providing his ideas with a foundational logic. He emphasized their scientific basis while reiterating the distinction between "history" and beliefs rooted in faith.[71]

As Sitarehind stated in the preface to the *Itihas Timirnashak*, the historian's task was a "thankless business," since the true historian could not please or flatter any faction or opinion and could merely deal with facts.[72] At the same time, Sitarehind believed that in writing a scientific history of the subcontinent, he was restoring the glories of its pre-Islamic past. While discounting the mythological accounts that constituted the principal interpretations of the subcontinent's Hindu legacy, he emphasized historical methods as the only means of uncovering the past.[73] To this end, physical vestiges such as the lone standing wall of the Mughal Vishweshwur temple, now also the *qibla* wall of the Gyan Vapi mosque, were treated as evidence of its destruction. This was seen as yet another instance of the violence on "Hindu" society that was supposedly perpetrated by successive Islamic regimes.[74] At the same time, Sitarehind emphatically discounted popular religious narratives (as opposed to narratives based in historical reasoning) as grounds for belief in the continued validity and potency of Hindu religious and cultural ideas and symbols. He stated that "for Vishweshwur to have appeared to his Priest in a dream and to have jumped into the Gyan Vapi (well) is solely a matter of belief among the Hindus. Such an account would not be appropriate for a History."[75] If the *puranas* could not be taken seriously, memories of Mughal investment and patronage were also largely forgotten and sidelined.[76]

In a continued effort to assign "Hindus" and "Muslims" to their respective spaces, the colonial government handed the Gyan Vapi mosque to a local community of weavers in Banaras. An imperial mosque was aggressively reshaped as a public place of worship. Notwithstanding these efforts, the weekly Friday congregation in the mosque remained skeletal.[77] Although the mosque was sparsely used, its plinth remained at the heart of rival claims well into the twentieth century. A peepul tree within the mosque precinct was an object of veneration as well as contention. As Sherring observed, "the Hindus will not allow the Mohammedans to pluck a single leaf from it."[78] Rivalries flared up once again in 1924 as Hindus refused to cut down tree branches (a source of bird droppings) that overhung a ritual ablution tank. In addition, the Brahmins who claimed priestly rights over the dismantled Vishweshwur temple had built a plinth around the tree and other worshippers had placed an idol underneath its branches. Hindus also complained about Muslims bringing coffins onto the platform to the west of the mosque.[79]

A precinct once at the receiving end of Mughal imperial politics and (often) whimsical priorities was placed at the center of rivalries between "Hindus" and "Muslims." The colonial government tried to maintain the status quo through minute control of objects and spaces within the precinct. All objects were to be enumerated and although repair was permitted, no "innovations" were to be allowed. The standoff continued until a member of the city's Hindu mercantile elite and chairman of the Municipal Board, Babu Motichand (he eventually acquired the title Raja Sir Motichand), stepped in with "unobtrusive public spirit" and suggested that a tin shed be constructed over the water tank.[80] Similar conversations and confrontations regarding antiquity and improvement resulted in transformations to the city's pilgrimage routes and built environment.

THE ANTARGRIHA AND WITHIN

The twin guiding hands of Orientalism and the impulse for improvement resulted in East India Company officials advocating the preservation of traditional building practices even as they radically altered systems of administrative control. Prinsep viewed the city as a living artifact and produced his map of Banaras in a spirit of Orientalist inquiry and hubris.[81] As the energetic secretary of the Committee for Local Improvement (1823–1829), he promoted traditional practices of building and repair that would mask any tangible signs of the colonial presence or of colonial modernization.[82] Despite the transfer of its administrative role to the cantonment in Secrole, the commercial and religious core around the Vishweshwur temple retained its significance for Banaras residents, as did most of the residential *muhallas*. Anxious to establish visible symbols of authority, the colonial government intervened to reshape a signature space: the *chowk* (town square). This was also the center of the principal bazaar, located in close proximity to the city's late Mughal administrative center.[83]

This "improvement," overseen by acting magistrate D. Morrison in 1808, was a continuation of the East India Company's practices across several towns located within their territories in the Gangetic plains.[84] Since the central urban square and bazaar were a significant node within urban imaginations in late Mughal northern India, the act of enlarging and refurbishing the principal square was also viewed as an effective way to claim urban authority.[85] The enlarged *chowk*, it was hoped, would continue to accommodate the office of the *kotwal* (chief of police) as well as provide rental income to the colonial administration.[86] To this end, officials appropriated buildings alongside the existing town square in 1805.[87] The space and adjoining buildings were reorganized so that the lower levels would be occupied by twenty-four shops, and the upper level would be used for the *kotwali* (police station). Its designers felt that although it still appeared confined in their view, the enlarged space would provide a more spacious experience.[88] The government was interested in creating a clear, geometrically regulated, rectangular space, and such practices as encroachments onto the street by shopkeepers and extending verandas out into the *chowk* remained abiding concerns. Owners of existing shops were to be accommodated, although as tenants rather than owners.[89]

The end result was a space based on established late Mughal spatial and architectural forms and models, even as its place within the city's administrative systems and power structure had shifted. In sum, the colonial government intervened in the material and institutional environment of nineteenth-century Banaras and established procedures for the centralized control of the city, while perpetuating the appearance of what they saw as "indigenous" forms. An emphasis on space and spaciousness became a universal preoccupation throughout the nineteenth century as Indian elites, by employing various strategies of cooperation, resistance, or appropriation, altered public and ritual spaces and architecture.

A new generation of aspiring patrons in the city included well-established elites as well as newly sprung aristocrats and prosperous traders.[90] A number of them requested permission from the Committee for Local Improvement to build temples, tanks, and wells. Many of them adopted notions of urban order and universal regulation but steered projects toward also incorporating aspects of the city's ritual life. For instance, the committee received a petition from "Jewan Ram and parties" who wished to build a temple in the Dharam Kup enclosure on the Antargriha route.[91] This trend continued even after the committee was formally dissolved. Patrons remained enthusiastic about refurbishing existing temples and building new ones. A donor identified by Sherring as one Ganpat "extensively repaired" the Adi-Vishweshwur temple and "embellished its interior with paintings traced on the walls, making them look fresh and modern."[92] Other patrons resurrected sites on pilgrimage routes, such as the Sankata Devi temple that was mentioned in the *Kashikhand*. This temple was also integrated into the city's goddess traditions and pilgrimages through popular (as opposed to Brahminical and textual) practice.

Such identification became urgent in light of the intrusive urban planning and infrastructure projects initiated by the colonial government. Tensions were exacerbated between residents and the colonial government when the latter planned to demolish a temple in the city's Bhadaini *muhalla*, to clear land for a piped water supply scheme in 1891. Residents and the maharaja of Banaras were aligned against the colonial government. They were also aligned against a group of elites (including Raja Shiva Prasad and Babu Brashear Miter) whom the editors of regional newspapers accused of acting as stooges for the British collector and of participating in "high-handed proceedings."[93] One regional newspaper, the *Hindustani*, accused the Collector of Banaras of being insensitive to the sensibilities of the city's Hindus, and also accused the municipality's Hindu members of abrogating their roles as custodians of a socioreligious sphere. In the end, the colonial government left the temple intact, although the *Nasim-I-Agra* declared that the situation was reminiscent of "the days of Aurangzeb, and is highly dangerous on political grounds."[94]

Tensions flared when the colonial government acquired land for the construction of a pumping station along the banks of the river near the sacred Lolark *kund*. The *kund* was mentioned in the *Kashikhand* and was a prescribed halt on many pilgrimage routes. It had been successively purchased and maintained by a number of princely families interested in strengthening their ties to the city.[95] The agent of the maharaja of Cooch Behar, the owner in 1892, resisted the government's plan on the grounds that the acquisition of land along one side of the *kund* would disrupt its integrity, and by extension, the integrity of the city's ritual geography. Instead, the agent insisted that the colonial government had promised to enhance the well and that "a series of steps might be built at the cost of the municipality inside the northern part of the *kund* to enable people to go around it."[96] The maharaja and his agent refused to part with the land, resenting the administration's assumption that they might consider negotiating a transfer for monetary compensation.[97]

PLATE 1   Pilgrimage *pata*, ca. 1700. National Museum, New Delhi.

PLATE 2   *Pilgrimage Map of Banaras*, ca. 1820. National Museum, New Delhi.

PLATE 3   *The Palace of Shahjahan at Delhi*, from the *Amal-i-Salih*, 1815. British Library Board.

PLATE 4   *Divan-i-Am*, from the *Amal-i-Salih*, 1815. British Library Board.

PLATE 5   *The City of Bunarus*, 1822, by James Prinsep. British Library Board.

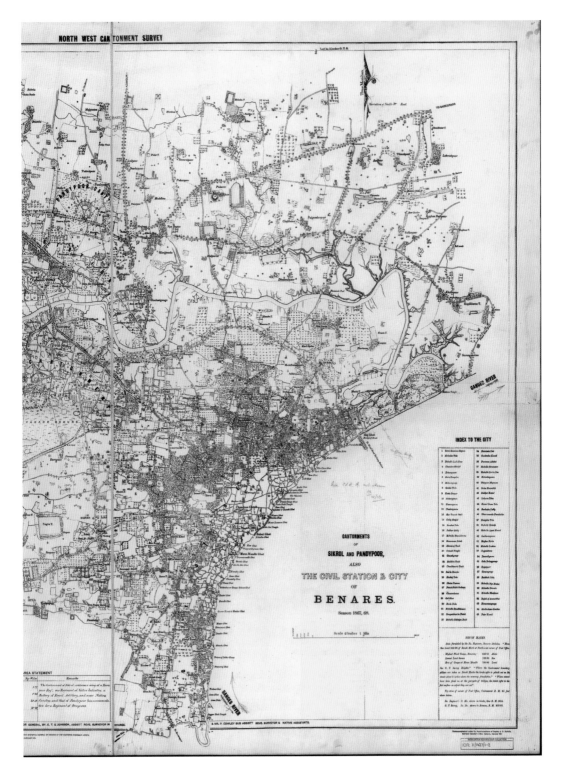

CANTONMENTS
OF
SIKROL AND PANDYPOOR,
ALSO
THE CIVIL STATION & CITY
OF
BENARES.
Season 1867, 68.

PLATE 6   *Cantonments of Sikrol and Pandypoor, also The Civil Station and
City of Benares, 1867–68.* British Library Board.

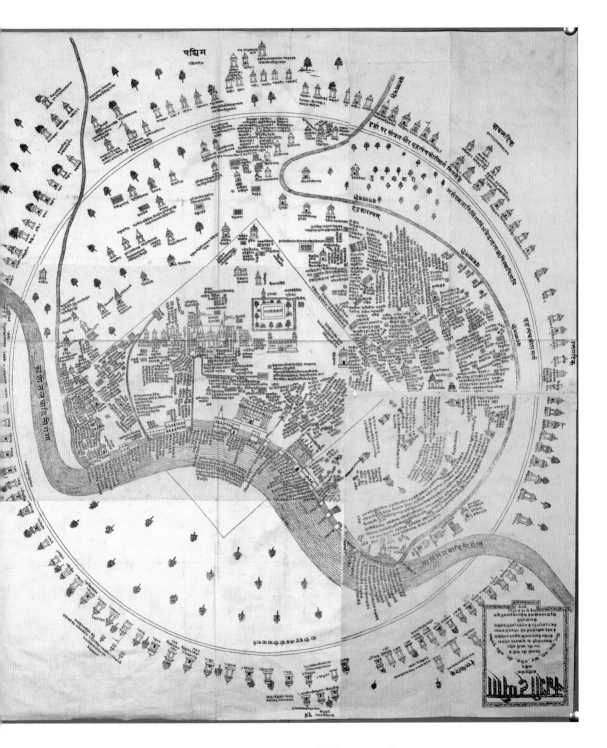

PLATE 7   *Kashidarpana*, 1876, by Kailasnath Sukul. British Library Board.

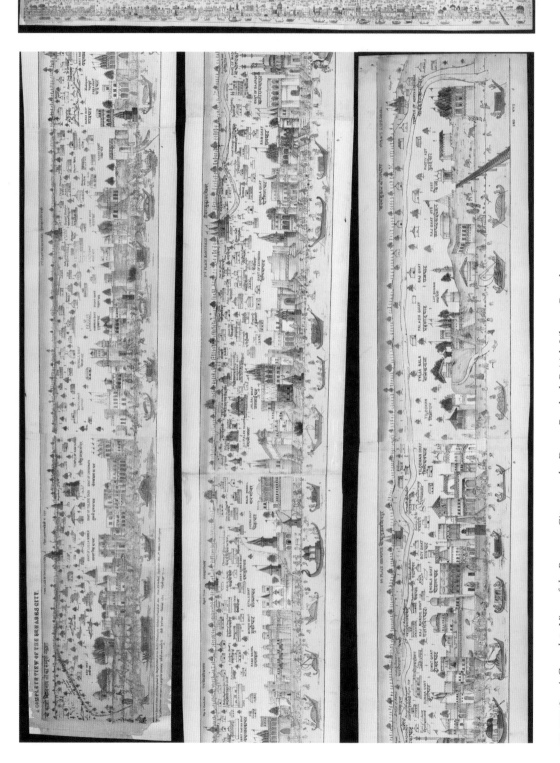

PLATE 8   *A Complete View of the Benares City*, 1901, by Durga Pershad. British Library Board.

Toward the latter half of the nineteenth century, Indian elites began to play a greater role in the direct administration of the city, through institutions such as the Municipality (established 1867).[98] Motichand, chairman of the Municipal Board in 1904, remained committed to the *Sanatan Dharma* that asserted the significance of deities and rituals in perpetuating an authentic Hinduism. Along with many of his elite associates, Motichand valued urban order and the idea of universal regulation and was interested in sustaining the city's role as a *tirtha*, albeit as a modernized pilgrimage destination. To this end, he formed the Kashi Tirtha Sudhar Trust (1926) to promote and implement this vision for the city.[99] Although the trust membership was concerned with preserving and enhancing the city's religious landscape and its ritual traditions, urban modernization was an objective that they also doggedly pursued. For instance, Motichand used a government agency, the Co-operative Credit Society, to ensure a consistent supply of "pure" milk, deemed necessary for religious rituals. Suppliers from the rural hinterland would gather with their cows, and milking proceeded under the society's watchful eye. The milk was then sold at controlled prices in government-regulated shops.[100]

The Kashi Tirtha Sudhar Trust also worked to create spatial and ritual order within the Antargriha zone. In 1929 the trust decided to widen the lane leading to the Vishweshwur temple and initiated discussions with "the learned Pandits of Benares."[101] Unable to acquire land through "private negotiations," the trust resorted to the colonial tactic of "Land Acquisition," with plans for the municipality to pay requisite compensation. In 1927 the Municipal Board, under Babu Baij Nath, proposed that the *chowk* gain some ornamental attributes including a "park" and "a fountain in the center for public use"—features that could enhance the new *thana* (police station) for which land had been acquired in 1902.[102] An Indian magistrate, V. N. Mehta, countered the proposal with the desire to leave the *chowk* wide open to control a potential "stampede."[103] The desire for spaciousness and order was fairly widespread and freely expressed by this time. In a similar vein, Motichand proposed a scheme for opening up "congested" areas on grounds of concern for public health.[104] One such commercial development proposal in Bisheshurgunj included setbacks and height restrictions for the safe passage of light aircraft.[105] Whether or not an airplane was ever likely to fly over Bisheshurgunj, modern urban development and building standards were to be emulated and maintained. The creation of urban order and the pursuit and preservation of tangible antiquity were pivotal in shaping the city's built environment as well as its ritual landscape.

PANCHKROSHI

Since its earliest days in Banaras, the colonial administration was involved in cataloging and managing the city's ritual life and related physical environment. Warren Hastings commissioned a map of the city, with specific instructions to include the Panchkroshi pilgrimage route as well as the new settlement of Ramnagar across the river in the survey.[106] Hastings may have done so in recognition of the increasing popularity of the route. Half a century after Hastings's cartographic initiative, the Committee for Local Improvement played a role in adjusting and realigning parts of the route. Established to oversee "improvements" in the city, the committee had the entire region of Kashikshetra under its jurisdiction. Residents brought several niggling complaints to their attention, including one concerning the "cutting of a mudwall on the side of the Juanpoor road near Sheopoor" on the Panchkroshi.[107] Among other roads within Kashikshetra, the committee proposed repairs to the Panchkroshi road toward the Kapildhara *talao* (pond or lake).[108]

Further alterations to the route were overseen by a colonial government determined to fix a "correct" profile for the pilgrimage.[109] Expectations of precision and accuracy engendered through colonial surveys meant that the Panchkroshi route was expected to align with the perfect geometry of Kashikshetra. It was a conversation driven by antiquarian sensibilities as well as the empowering potential of colonial survey techniques. Bharatendu Harishchandra who took an active interest in the city's antecedents, described the changes that were made to the Panchkroshi route in an essay that he published in the *Kavivachanasudha*. The elite committee of bankers and landowners that the British city magistrate Gubbins convened (ca. 1842–1872) was charged with addressing the "purity" and accuracy of the route between the two overnight halts of Bhimchandi and Rameshwur. Its members were also charged with devising ways to enhance and develop infrastructure for pilgrims. The committee depended on Brahmin scholars at the Sanskrit College as well as colonial surveyors and cartographers.[110] Pandit Bapudev Shastri's research (based, as he emphasized, in the *shastras*) strengthened the committee's imperative to realign the Panchkroshi route as a perfect circle or, failing that, at least a perfect arc. A survey was commissioned and following its conclusion and subsequent evaluation, the committee suggested alterations to the route and to fulfill these recommendations, land was donated by the Raja of Banaras.[111]

Interest in "correcting" aspects of the city's ritual landscape on the part of multiple agents was driven by a desire for accuracy and textual probity. The city's burgeoning print culture provided an avenue for the dissemination of this information. A new generation of Brahmin activists embarked on a quest to identify and list the various deities and sites described in both the *Kashikhand* as well as the *Kashirahasya*. They began to interpret the city's *purana* literature as a universal and timeless discourse on the city, rather than as a collection of diverse and often fragmented opinions. In light of such efforts, the Panchkroshi route of the nineteenth century, it was felt, must correspond to the descriptions in the *Kashirahasya*. By the late nineteenth century, Gorji Dikshit had identified a ritual landscape based on specifications from the *Kashirahasya* in a guidebook that he titled the *Kashiyatraprakash* (ca. 1890) and related them to precise locations in the city. Assisted by his students, Dikshit initiated a project of turning the descriptions in texts into physical realities. In 1891 one of his students, Dwarkanath Dubey, facilitated the construction of several shrines. Based on Dikshit's interpretation of the *Kashirahasya*, Dubey oversaw construction of the Neelkantheswur Mahadev, Virupakshagana, and Somnatheswur temples at Kardameswur.[112] Dikshit himself placed a new image of Parvatyeswari that was promptly incorporated into the route.[113] The city's bankers also patronized the Panchkroshi, and in 1905, Babu Motichand sponsored the construction of a *dharamshala* (rest house for pilgrims) at the overnight halt at Sheopur.[114]

The emergence of colonial archaeology as a robust field of knowledge-making meant that for Kashikshetra to hold its own, its proponents had to produce architectural and sculptural remains as proof of its antiquity. If a realigned Panchkroshi could encircle Sarnath as well as Banaras, the city's Buddhist past could be conflated with a more recent Hindu identity. The Panchkroshi pilgrimage circuit, as Bholanauth Chunder had noted, included the site of Sarnath as well as the shrine of Vishweshwur.[115] Since Chunder described the site of Sarnath as falling within the Panchkroshi circuit, he viewed it as an integral part of the city. In a similar vein, Bharatendu Harishchandra ascribed both Buddhist and Jain origins to the Panchkroshi pilgrimage. He also cited the "reign of the Muslims" as a way to explain away a lack of antique remains that could legitimately be associated with the route.[116] Traditional texts and a new archaeology were creatively combined, and the city's religious landscape was reconceptualized to reflect this latest reality. When the Hindus began to rule Kashi, Harishchandra further suggested, the Panchkroshi became popular again. It now only remained to reestablish its antiquity and perfect geometry.

Skeptics, however, remained vocal. Sherring remarked on the recent date of most of the construction along the Panchkroshi route. He commented on the general paucity of antiquities as material evidence. Besides the Kardameshwur temple and a few sculptural remains, Sherring pointed out, most of the shrines and tanks along the route had been constructed since the late eighteenth century.[117] He expected Hindus to direct gratitude to the colonial administration for repairing and maintaining the Panchkroshi, in contrast to the "destructive and prohibitive" Muslim rulers they had replaced.[118] All through the nineteenth century, shrines, temples, and several *dharamshala* were added along the route with the intention of completing the ritual prescriptions in the *Kashirahasya*, making the city's textually based ritual landscape a tangible reality.

WITHIN THE PANCHKROSHI

The *chahar-bagh* had been a means to provide urban infrastructure, since it could simultaneously function as recreational landscape and religious space. As mentioned earlier, many of these gardens had been located within the boundaries of the Panchkroshi route, often within the catchments of sacred pools and tanks, and played a role in sustaining the socioreligious sphere. The Committee for Local Improvement had begun draining the city's catchment areas in 1823.[119] Over the following century, the colonial administration continued to drain the Benia, Mandakini, and Matsyodari lakes. A "picturesque" park was to replace Beniram Pandit's garden as well as twenty acres of the freshly drained Benia catchment. The park would provide a civic amenity and compensate all residents for their everyday existence among confined streets and urban squalor.[120] Yet the elite Indians who were touched for subscriptions insisted on a memorial to the British sovereign Victoria as the centerpiece of the park, rather than contributing toward a space intended for a nebulous "public." Although they were as keen as the colonial government to provide the city with modern infrastructure, ownership over this emerging civic sphere was actively contested.

Over the last two decades of the nineteenth century, Hindu elites created a new center of civic life in the city's northern regions, around the drained catchment of Maidagin. In the early eighteenth century, *chahar-baghs* had clustered its edges, and Brahmins in the city continued to label it as the Mandakini *tirtha* within pilgrimage routes and maps,

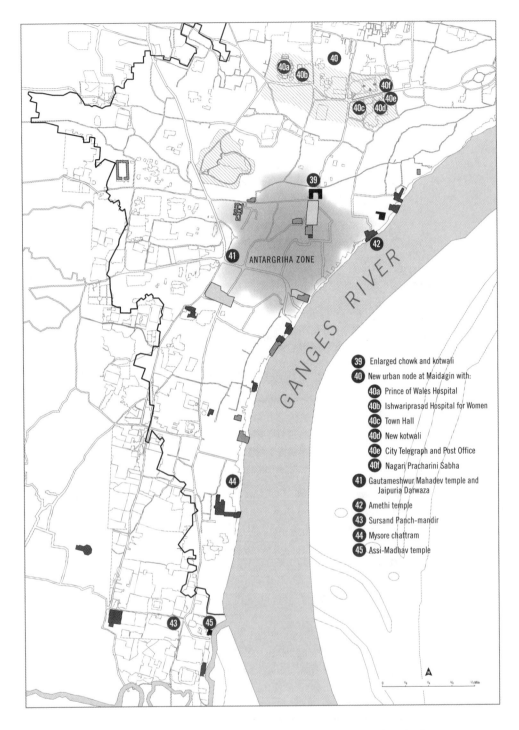

GANGES RIVER

ANTARGRIHA ZONE

39 Enlarged chowk and kotwali
40 New urban node at Maidagin with:
40a Prince of Wales Hospital
40b Ishwariprasad Hospital for Women
40c Town Hall
40d New kotwali
40e City Telegraph and Post Office
40f Nagari Pracharini Sabha
41 Gautameshwur Mahadev temple and
        Jaipuria Darwaza
42 Amethi temple
43 Sursand Panch-mandir
44 Mysore chattram
45 Assi-Madhav temple

MAP 5.1 Map of Banaras City, ca. 1900, based on *Benares City, 1928–29*. Drawing by
Gretta Tritch Roman, Jennifer Shontz, Nanditha Veeraraghavelu, and Rohan Haksar.

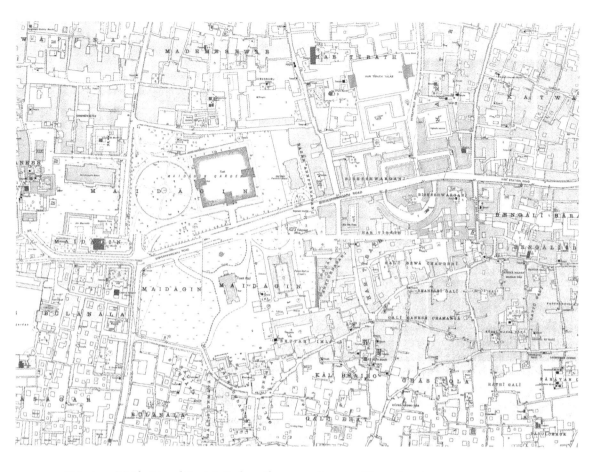

FIG. 5.4   Maidagin and its vicinity from the survey *Benares City, 1928–29.*

as was also noted by Prinsep in his map (Plate 5).[121] As the catchment was restructured, it was divided into individual parcels between 1883 and 1905 that became sites for new institutional buildings (Map 5.1, Fig. 5.4).[122] The construction of institutional and administrative buildings was undertaken and encouraged by the colonial government as well as sponsored by native elites in such cities as Bombay and Calcutta. Most such buildings were constructed in an architectural style devised by colonial architects. Hospitals, colleges, and office buildings were based on imported plan types that were subject to a degree of modification appropriate for local climatic and cultural conditions. The buildings were clothed in what British administrators called "Indo-saracenic" architectural details. Although the term was originally used by colonial observers and antiquarians to describe the architectural preferences of Indian elites in the eighteenth and early nineteenth centuries, both term and style were applied to newer buildings.

This trend was also followed at Maidagin, albeit on a lesser scale. The Prince of Wales hospital (also known as the King Edward VII hospital) was established in 1865 in a large, octagonal structure with rectangular wards arranged around a partially enclosed space

FIG. 5.5   Prince of Wales Hospital, 1905. Photo by Madho Prasad. British Library Board.

(Fig. 5.5). The buildings of the Ishwari hospital for women were based on a series of rect-angular footprints and completed by 1893 on an adjacent site (Fig. 5.6).[123] Construction of a Town Hall was sponsored by the maharaja of Vizianagaram (1845–1879) in a local interpretation of the Indo-saracenic idiom (Fig. 5.7). The building was ostensibly built to commemorate the visit of Prince Alfred to the city in 1870. Named the "Alfred Hall," con-struction was begun in 1873, and the building "was presented as a free gift to the citizens of Benares" by the Prince of Wales in 1876.[124]

This symbolic gesture was meant to emphasize the building's civic role even as its spaces accommodated new forms of rituals. The interior was planned with galleries over-looking a central double-height space that were articulated on the façade with pointed "saracenic" arches and minarets. The exterior of the Town Hall referenced a colonial architectural vocabulary that was seen as appropriate for an Indian population. Yet, to its patrons, the architecture of the Town Hall signified modernity much in the same way that modified Indian dress could signal a modern persona. Indeed, in each of these three public buildings the Indo-saracenic idiom was used only after careful modifications, and

FIG. 5.6   Ishwari Memorial Hospital, 1905. Photo by Madho Prasad. British Library Board.

in each case a historicist architecture was used to project an image of urban modernity for a Hindu pilgrimage city.

The colonial government initiated plans for a new *kotwali* (police headquarters) in this area in 1891, and the building was designed in the official version of the Indo-saracenic idiom, this time by the local Public Works Department.[125] A plan was proposed in 1902 to enhance the site with the aim of carrying out "improvements of the site of the New Kotwali; Town Hall and the City Telegraph Office."[126] A post and telegraph office was built to the east of the new *kotwali*, ca. 1909.[127] In a departure from convention, this building was embellished with neoclassical tone. It was also at this time, and as part of the same civic scheme, that the Nagari Pracharini Sabha acquired land for its building in 1902.[128] A number of regional rulers contributed financially toward the Sabha's activities as well as to this construction project.[129] It was in the architecture of the Sabha building that the city's

FIG. 5.7 Town Hall, 1905. Photo by Madho Prasad. British Library Board.

modern religious identity was expressed simultaneously through Grecian pediments and miniature replicas of the Hindu temple *shikhara*. In each of the buildings around the node, new spatial norms were adopted to fulfill their roles as modern institutions. Once the historicism inherent to the "Indo-saracenic" was appropriated by Indian elites, it could be rendered in a variety of forms to express shifting ideas of modernity.

Urban "improvement" implied wider roads, open spaces to interrupt a dense urban fabric, and the application and enforcement of uniform building standards. Temples that came in the way of such schemes were a different matter. They could not be easily acquired and disposed. In the case of the new *kotwali*, and especially with the circumstances surrounding the Lolark *kund* fresh in the city's memory, a temple dedicated to the Hindu deity Hanuman had to be excluded from the government's plan.[130] By 1917 the new public node included, besides the Town Hall, the Nagari Pracharini Sabha library, the police station, the post office, and also the Maidagin park.

Ancestral *havelis* in the *pucca maholl* were retained as family legacies, but many of the trust's members began to build mansions in the city's expanding suburbs, designed with spacious reception rooms and grounds for lavish entertainments.[131] Motichand's mansion,

FIG. 5.8   Azmatgarh palace.

also known as the Azmatgarh palace, built in 1904, was resplendent in its grounds, surrounded by tennis courts and extensive lawns (Fig. 5.8). Its ornamental exterior and decorative details were created, according to family accounts, by craftsmen brought in especially
from Jaipur. The mansion was the scene of fashionable events such as Motichand's garden
parties, where select elites mingled with local officials of the colonial administration.[132]
Yet spaces were also created and discreetly set aside to follow more traditional practices
such as the serving of ritual meals and the practice of purdah (the physical and visual segregation of women from visitors). Other elites, including the maharaja of Vizianagaram
and the descendants of Aussan Singh, added extensions and reception spaces to their
mansions, where they would preside over similar and equally select gatherings.

TEMPLES AND COLONIAL KNOWLEDGE

By the turn of the twentieth century, the Banaras skyline was dense with temple *shikharas*.
The city's image as the quintessential Hindu pilgrimage destination was firmly fixed. The
extent of temple construction even by the late nineteenth century can be gleaned from

258.   Temple of Vishveshwar.   (From Prinsep's ' Views in Benares.')   No scale.

FIG. 5.9   Ahilyabai's Vishweshwur temple, published in 1891 by James Fergusson
(after Prinsep).

the writings of James Kennedy, who noted that much of the city was being resurrected in accordance with a geography prescribed through *purana* texts. In 1872, Kennedy declared that the total number of temples in the city was 1,454, although he added that this number did not account for "smaller shrines in niches in the walls, which may be reckoned by thousands."[133] Sherring expressed a similar view and stated that temples in the city had "multiplied at a prodigious rate . . . against the new doctrines of European civilization and religion.[134]

In formal terms, these nineteenth-century temples differed significantly from their eighteenth-century predecessors. Mughal elements were minimally used and in many cases abandoned altogether. Archaic plan types were resurrected. The cause for this shift lay at the intersection of Hindu religious and cultural practices and colonial knowledge and politics. James Fergusson undertook the first comprehensive survey and classification

FIG. 5.10 Lingaraja temple, 1865. Photo by Henry Dixon. British Library Board.

of the subcontinent's architecture. Like William Hodges before him, Fergusson based his survey on a division between the categories of Hindu and Islamic.[135] This meant that for a building to be "Hindu," it had to conform to a pre-Islamic vocabulary of post and lintel construction with a strict avoidance of arches or domes. Understandably, in *The History of Indian and Eastern Architecture*, Fergusson described the Vishweshwur temple at Banaras (Ahilyabai's temple), built as it was with "a dome borrowed from the Mahomedan style," as a building burdened with mismatched "details" (Fig. 5.9).[136]

Fergusson's work laid the ground for a basic grid of comprehension that informed the work of an entire generation of British and Indian scholars. For Indian scholars this division also became the basis for defining authenticity and Indian roots. Although the prominent Indian antiquarian Rajendralal Mitra disagreed with Fergusson on the age of the Ajanta caves in 1880, many of Mitra's fundamental premises were not very different from those held by his rival.[137] Mitra's quest for authenticity in temple architecture took him to Orissa in eastern India. For Mitra, Orissa was a site "comparatively little exposed to the tide of foreign invasion" and therefore had been able to retain its "original character."[138] It had escaped "the iconoclastic zeal of Moslem fanatics."[139] In the winter of 1868–1869, the colonial government commissioned a team of modelers and molders to make casts of "some of the more important sculptures of India."[140] Mitra suggested the temple city of Bhuvaneshwur (Fig. 5.10), and he accompanied the team as archaeologist. As part of his comprehensive investigations, Mitra examined existing buildings and contemporary building traditions.[141]

Mitra's quest for living authenticity brought him to Banaras, an active site of contemporary temple construction. He depended, in particular, on the specialized knowledge of the master-mason employed by the Maharaja of Vizianagaram. Mitra concluded that the Vishweshwur and Kedar temples provided models for smaller temples in the city. His goal was to establish continuity between the Orissa temples that he was studying and the norms of temple building in nineteenth-century Banaras. He highlighted indigenous innovation as well as greater refinement in the "Visvesvara" and "Kedara" temples, emphasizing its "slender steeple" (as opposed to the "heavy tower" of the Orissan temple), "delicate pilasters," and "elegant plinth."[142] He was careful to mention only the sanctum and tower of the Vishweshwur temple, while ignoring the dome over the *mandapa*.[143] His inclusion of Kedar is also interesting, given that it was built more than a hundred years earlier in a decidedly Mughal idiom.[144]

More generally, Mitra felt compelled to trace a continuous lineage between archaic examples and current building practices. Nonetheless, he never really deviated from Fergusson's categories of a trabeated "Hindu" versus an arcuated "Islamic" architecture. Mitra also created a historical category for temples that he termed "Indo-saracenic," in which he placed the Adi-Vishweshwur temple at Banaras, in which "the body of a pure Hindu edifice" was marred with "foiled arches" that were derived from the "true Saracenic style" (Fig. 5.11). With increased pilgrimage attention to Ahilyabai's Vishweshwur temple, and in the absence of an anchoring *purana*-based provenance for it, Adi-Vishweshwur was easily sidelined.

Mitra also worked with masons to arrive at a normative definition for a "Benares temple," an idea initiated by James Prinsep a few decades earlier. Mitra's "Benares temple" bears a close resemblance to the Prayageshwur temple on Dashashwamedha ghat, one of the few examples on the riverfront that did not include "Saracenic" elements. Viewed alternately, Mitra's "Benares temple" could have functioned as a partial model for many contemporary examples in the city. As he sketched his prototype, he highlighted its sanctum and *shikhara* and quietly put aside the *mandapa* with its ubiquitous Mughal arches, columns, and occasional domes.[145]

Mitra provided a tangible link between an academic discourse and elite Hindu opinion-makers in Banaras. Although the Hindu temple at Banaras largely remained beyond the purview of colonial authority and administration, intersections with the antiquarian discourse of the Asiatic Society were not entirely unknown. The designs of many nineteenth-century temples were inflected with colonial conceptual categories. Mitra's formulation of an ideal and uncorrupted "Benares temple" may have circulated within elite

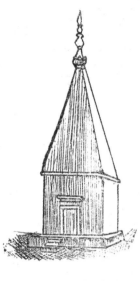

Fig. 9 Primitive Benares
Temple

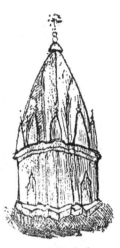

Fig. 10 Typical
Benares Temple

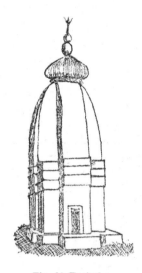

Fig. 11 Typical
Orissa Temple

Fig. 12 Indo-Saracenic Temple.

Fig. 13 Bengali Temple

FIG. 5.11 Classification of temple types including "Typical Benares Temple," 1875,
by Rajendralal Mitra.

FIG. 5.12

Gautameshwur
Mahadev temple.

circles in Banaras, and the colonial antiquarian discourse could, at least tangentially, have
influenced patronage and design decisions. All the same, the nature of the architectural
revival at Banaras cannot be completely conflated with the discursive environment of
colonial institutions such as the Asiatic Society and the Archaeological Survey of India.
Despite a lively academic conversation centered on determining a pristine Hindu language for temple architecture, most patrons in Banaras shaped their designs through a
range of choices, often resulting in buildings that British and Indian antiquarians dispar-
agingly characterized as "Indo-saracenic."

Built between 1883 and 1905 by Raja Prabhunarain Singh, the Gautameshwur Mahadev
temple was designed and constructed by local masons and a group of artisans invited

FIG. 5.13 Jaipuria Darwaza.

from Jaipur (Fig. 5.12). The *mandapa* is designed with a flat roof, and domes are conspicuous by their absence. Mughal columns are also absent, although pointed arches are incorporated, as are miniature *jharokhas*, reminiscent of the sixteenth-century Govind Dev temple at Brindavan. It is significant that the gateway to the temple precinct was popularly referred to as the "Jaipuria Darwaza," a direct reference to the source of inspiration for its design (Fig. 5.13). Its designers freely accommodated *chattris* and *jharokhas* with *bangla* roof forms and Mughal columns, signaling a connection to a Rajput heritage that was still relevant to an elite Hindu identity. Subsequently, this temple precinct was placed within the ritual geography of the city and identified as the specific shrine of the same name that is mentioned in the *Kashikhand*.

By the late nineteenth century, elite circles in Banaras were actively conscious of the nature of an appropriate "Hindu" architecture, even as some among them continued to fashion themselves on residual Mughal mores.[146] Select patrons, however, were indeed influenced by the conversation about an ideal form for a temple. For instance, the design for the pillars of the *mandapa* that was added to the Durga temple (ca. 1875) by a "superior native commissioned officer" was possibly derived through exposure to a colonial discourse.[147] Its ornamental columns are derived from their counterparts in the Annapurna temple and are a studied departure from the ubiquitous Mughal baluster column that Rani Bhawani had preferred for several of her commissions.

Another patron active in the city at the turn of the twentieth century, the Rani of Sursand, supported construction of the Sursand "Panch-mandir" (ca. 1909), which was located near the Kurukshetra ritual tank in the Assi *muhalla*. This temple was designed on the idea of the *panchayatana* (cluster of five temples) with a central *garbha-griha* surrounded by secondary shrines located at the four corners of a shared platform (Fig. 5.14).[148] Although the arch was selectively used, the principal elements of the composition were the towering "Benares" *shikharas*. The Rani was in search of an innovative plan that could evoke memories of archaic temples, and her descendants recall that the *panchayatana* scheme was jointly planned by the Rani and her master-mason.[149] By the early decades of the twentieth century, the city was filled with numerous temples with archaic *shikharas*, and their provenance was established by a new generation of religious cartographers.

KASHIKSHETRA REVISITED

Urban development and attention to urban surveys resulted in an expectation of precision in representations of the ritual landscape. The preferred medium for specifying precise routes and locations in Banaras was the pilgrimage guidebook. This was a practical tool that contained information regarding the precise location of sites in a changing and growing city. Authors of guidebooks could distill vague and esoteric information from Sanskrit texts and connect them to actual sites, listing specific *muhalla* (neighborhoods) and street names. A burgeoning print culture made it possible for Brahmin priests to not only identify a greater number of sites but also to disseminate that knowledge among a larger number of pilgrims. In this climate the *Kashirahasya* and the *Kashikhand* were presented as parts of a single continuous tradition.[150]

It is within these broader trends that Nandapandita Dharmadhikari published a guidebook in 1876, which he titled *Kashidarpanam*, "the mirror of Kashi."[151] Dharmadhikari prescribed thirty-eight pilgrimages, including the Panchkroshi and the Antargriha. This guidebook was translated by his student, Krishnachandra, and with wide dissemination in mind he cited relevant *puranas* alongside their Hindi translations in connection with several sites. Krishnachandra also retained his mentor's quotations in Sanskrit, since authenticity was consistently derived from a scholarly reference to the *puranas*.

FIG. 5.14 Sursand Panch-mandir.

Gorji Dikshit listed several pilgrimages, including the individual sites and deities along each route, in his *Kashiyatraprakash* and actively worked to popularize his findings.[152] By the mid-nineteenth century, Dikshit succeeded in reinstalling several shrines that were mentioned in the *Kashikhand* but did not exist on the ground in the contemporary city. Fearing the city's degeneration and decay, he concentrated on "discovering" unknown and neglected deities and ritual sites. Sherring described the methods that Dikshit employed.[153] He would inscribe relevant Sanskrit quotations from the *Kashikhand* on plaques and place them at specific locations, particularly at newly unearthed sites. The quotations were relevant lines from the *Kashikhand* that concerned a particular deity's place within a pilgrimage tradition as well as on a specific pilgrimage route.[154] Besides referring to a past based in *purana* texts, Dikshit provided his readers with unambiguous and specific contemporary addresses.

Dikshit went a step further and enhanced this pilgrimage landscape through additions such as a Nityayatra in which he recommended a daily visit to the Annapurna shrine.[155] In 1908, Narayanpati Tripathi Sharma published a version of the *Kashikhand* in print, along with a supplemental guide to various religious sites in the city.[156] He included details of multiple pilgrimages prescribed in the *Kashikhand* alongside their corresponding verses from this text. He also included the Panchkroshi and mentioned its link to the *Kashira-hasya*. Sharma cited the various locations in the contemporary city along with the actual names of *muhallas* (neighborhoods) where these shrines were to be found. This publication was printed by the Khemka press in Bombay and was designed to replicate the appearance and orientation of a manuscript. Information that had been available through the mediation of *tirtha purohits* (Brahmins specializing in pilgrimage) was now standardized through print and became accessible to a wider audience.

Popular access to print technology altered the cartographic imagination and representations of Kashikshetra. The city was successively and officially surveyed by the colonial government in 1867–1868, 1879–1880, 1883, and 1928–1929.[157] These surveys continually emphasized the desire for greater degrees of accuracy in mapping techniques (Plate 6). Their production either preceded or accompanied large-scale and intrusive urban planning measures, transportation projects, or infrastructure initiatives. By incorporating colonial surveys, or at least by making references to them, Brahmin priests could claim greater precision in their own mapping exercises.[158] By the late nineteenth century, lithographic prints were available for several pilgrimage maps, and these were sold at major bookshops as well as the railway station, linking them to the increased pilgrimage traffic to the city. The desire for precision was accompanied by an urgent need to establish an objective but *purana*-based antiquity for the ritual landscape of Kashikshetra.

The basic idea anchoring another map, the *Saptapuriyatradiprakashapatram* (1873), was that of the Saptapuri or the seven sacred cities (*tirthas*) that are manifest within the physical space of Kashi. Support for this publication endeavor was provided by two other personalities, Ramkrishna (Gorji) Dikshit and Govind Raghunath Thatte, a publisher associated with the city's thriving print culture. Kailasnath Sukul also produced a lithographed map (1876) that he titled the *Kashidarpana* (mirror of Kashi) in which he combined ideas about a perfectly delineated circular Panchkroshi and a perfectly square Antargriha sacred zone and marked precise locations for religious sites (Plate 7).[159] He depicted a sacred zone but did not mark out a pilgrimage route for the *Antargriha*. The map's authenticity was emphasized through a dual invocation of *puranas* as sources of religious information and colonial survey techniques as guarantors of spatial accuracy and precision. The *Linga, Shiv, Nandi, Skanda, Ganesh* and *Agni Puranas*, and the *Kashikhand* were the principal *purana* texts used in representing the city's mythological connections.[160] For Sukul, such specific *purana* references could successfully assert the city's Shaiva antecedents.

The Ganges marked the western edge of the city, and the Varuna and Assi streams its eastern and western boundaries respectively. Sukul depicted contemporary Banaras only selectively with very few buildings on the riverfront acting as landmarks. Similarly, in the *Srikashichitra* (1897), the publisher Bengali Sahu depicted a Banaras based in the *puranas*, where a sacred landscape displaced most of the material environment of the contemporary city. Following Sukul's map, Krishnachandra Dharmadhikari produced an addendum for it that he titled the *Kashidarpanpurti* (completion of the *Kashidarpana*) in 1877.[161] Besides additional sites, he included delineations of several other sacred zones nested within Kashikshetra. He added that his map was based on *purana* sources but that it had also been verified against contemporary British surveys of the city. Jung Bahadur, the force behind the *Srikashichitra*, followed a similar practice. Sukul, Jung Bahadur, and others were preoccupied with the locations of specific shrines, and they were careful not to let the idea of a generalized sacred zone blur an impression of precision and specificity.

The *Saptapuriyatradiprakashapatram* set a precedent for depicting a perfectly circular Panchkroshi route in several pilgrimage maps, including the *Kashidarpana* and the *Srikashichitra*.[162] The route was imagined as a perfect circle in the form of a ring of shrines around the city at sites that their authors claimed had been accurately surveyed and located. In the *Kashidarpana*, Sukul labeled this circle of temples as the Brihadpanchkroshi (Greater Panchkroshi), a route that circled the entire city and spanned either side of the Ganges River. Its center was located in the shrine of Madhyameshwur (in the *muhalla* of the same name), the time-honored center of Kashikshetra. In practice, however, the older route remained the preferred one, except for the limited changes effected by Shastri and the Gubbins committee.

Given its proven Buddhist antecedents, how could Banaras remain relevant for a modern Hindu society? As mentioned earlier, in a two-part essay titled "Buddhism Is India's Ancient Civilization," Rameshwar Prasad Varma extolled the assimilative qualities of Hinduism while folding Buddhism within a nationalist religious sentiment.[163] Yet none of the authors of these three maps made any overt references to the city's Buddhist or Jain pasts or any of the sites connected with these two religions. Unlike writers such as Chunder or Harishchandra, creators of pilgrimage maps (including Sukul, Dharmadhikari, Jung Bahadur, and Bengali Sahu) did not depict Sarnath on their maps. Their vision, instead, was strictly based on interpretations of the *puranas* and, by extension, an orthodox Hinduism. Whereas the greater preoccupation with detail in these maps can be attributed to the authors' anxieties about the rapidly changing urban landscape of Banaras, their preoccupation with a perfectly circular Panchkroshi is less easily attributed to the same causes.

It is pertinent that the outer extent of the newly circular route in each map could encompass the location of Sarnath, without any acknowledgment of the site. This new alignment affected the geography of sites and the configuration of an existing route. The authors of each map developed unique solutions to this dilemma. For the authors of the *Srikashichitra* as well as the *Saptapuri*, the five halts on the Panchkroshi and their associated shrines were moved outward and aligned along the edges of the new, circular route. The authors of the *Srikashichitra* included sites of general interest such as the fortress-palace at Ramnagar, tanks, and temples built by the Rajas of Banaras in "Vyas Kashi," but avoided any direct acknowledgment of the Buddhist site or its monuments. This Brahmin-oriented *purana* perspective was at odds with the new vision of an all-encompassing Hinduism connected to shared cultural sensibilities and a national identity. Appropriation was also apparent as temples and traditions connected to particular instances of patronage were dissociated from their specific histories and placed within a purely textual and, by extension, timeless realm of religious authenticity (see Map 2.3). The creators of the three pilgrimage maps found a way to selectively appropriate the tangible antiquity of Sarnath, without making any references to its Buddhist associations.

If colonial ideologies and interventions initiated changes to institutions and urban spaces, an identifiable civic sphere became notable only when Indian elites took control of its legal as well as discursive frameworks. A new group of patrons transformed religious identities through the interplay of antiquarianism, religion, and nationalism. The shared subcontinental roots of Hinduism and Buddhism became the basis of a national identity. It was also part of the founding principles of a new institution, the Banaras Hindu University—an idea presented to the Sanatan Dharma Mahasabha (congress of orthodox Hindu religion) in 1906 as a means to promote "the Hindu shastras and of Sanskrit literature generally," widely believed to be in "decline."[164] Unlike the Sanskrit University (now known as the Queen's College), the new university would preserve and promote the interests of culture and religion in the service of the nation.[165] For its elite Indian patrons, urban regulation and civic provision in Banaras were meaningless without accommodating its vibrant ritual life. This exchange between colonial knowledge and Indian expectations found renewed expression along the riverfront.

CHAPTER SIX

VISIONS AND EMBELLISHMENTS

I N Banaras, wrote Bharatendu Harishchandra, Brahmins engage in *sandhya* (ritual) and *shastrartha* (religious debate) on the riverfront, and they are as important to the city as its elite patrons.[1] Along with the towering minarets of the Dharhara mosque that Harishchandra described as "the two hands of Madhoray," Brahmins and their ritual activities were critical to the experience, image, and identity of the riverfront and the city. Harishchandra's notions about Banaras stemmed from an idealized vision in which the riverfront anchored narratives of antiquity and nostalgia. Although elites made efforts to introduce modern institutions as well as an architecture that could represent their ideals, it was the riverfront that stood for a quintessential Kashi.

The visiting Rajani Ranjan Sen was nostalgic for an authentic experience, free from "notions and ideals of foreign infusion."[2] He lamented that the "treasured wisdom of hoary sages" had been set aside elsewhere by "our own ignorance, apathy and consequent want of aptitude to grasp the real underlying the visible."[3] At Banaras, however, one could be in touch with all that was most significant in ancient Hindu religion and culture. Sen wrote about his experiences at a time when the riverfront, as it stands today, had largely been built. The more prominent fortress-palaces had been constructed, as had most of the riverfront temples. Sen also wrote at a time when this built environment had been treated as the ancient face of a city with a deep association with its religious past for more than a century. Historical perspectives were gaining currency as the most common interpretations of this past. Since historical perspectives required a logical temporal progression that had to be anchored in material evidence, the riverfront was simultaneously represented as historically rooted and ageless. In an improbable juxtaposition of ideas, colonial administrators and Indian elites imposed a chronological timeline on the city even as they coded all edifices along the riverfront (including ones then under construction) as ancient.

Such a perspective was promoted by James Prinsep when he presented the riverfront as a space dedicated to an authentic and timeless Hinduism. He featured the riverfront as an antique environment even as he monitored, illustrated, and wrote about the temples and ghats that were being constructed during his stay in the city. He concentrated in particular on a stretch between the Dashashwamedha and Panchganga ghats, where much building activity had taken place over the previous century. Prinsep tacitly assumed that the riverfront had always existed in a similar guise, and he seamlessly merged his own descriptions with those by the seventeenth-century French traveler Jean-Baptiste Tavernier. For Prinsep, Tavernier's account depicted "a lively picture of Benares in 1668, before the prostration of its temples by Aurangzebe, and while there yet remained some vestiges of the splendor of its idolatries."[4]

Prinsep was not alone in representing this contemporary face of the riverfront as though it represented the material fabric of an ancient city. By the early decades of the twentieth century, the riverfront was widely photographed and placed within guidebooks and albums as material evidence for an antique city. By the late nineteenth century, the connections between individual buildings and patrons were mediated through colonial knowledge and urban regulation, and the riverfront was coded as a public space, built in the service of a unified Hinduism. When juxtaposed against historical and mythical narratives, the picturesque illustrations, panoramic depictions, and photographs of the riverfront all became metonymic representations of the city.

MYTHOLOGIES AND PICTURESQUE VISIONS

In 1796 the British landscape artist Thomas Daniell published an illustration of the newly built Dashashwamedha ghat that faced the river (Fig. 6.1). In Daniell's image a monumental stone mansion is approached by a flight of equally monumental stone steps. The scene is dotted with boats, cows, and figures of natives. His buildings are imbued with a nostalgic grandeur and monumentality. In his *A Picturesque Voyage to India*, the artist found that Indian buildings were "often elucidated by the manners of the present inhabitants, who with unexampled fidelity have preserved their primitive customs unimpaired by time or conquest; and in their domestic institutions still present the image of a remote and almost obsolete antiquity."[5] Daniell's illustration effectively consigned a contemporary landscape to the past.

Fleeting descriptions and illustrations by colonial travelers and artists often focused on Dashashwamedha and Manikarnika ghats.[6] Anchored in a practice in which built environments were represented as antique and decaying within natural backgrounds that were given to mild disorder, the riverfront with its temples, ghats, and palaces provided ample material for picturesque representation. Illustration in this mode also allowed artists to selectively re-create a landscape based on their own biases.[7] The picturesque in Britain had been used to aestheticize real economic inequities sharpened by agricultural capitalism and the implementation of enclosures.[8] In particular, unpleasant sights, smells, and sounds could be filtered out, and the viewer could take pleasure in a framed scene from an aesthetic distance. As William Gilpin, a theorist of this aesthetic, insisted, the picturesque eye was to merely wander over nature in a broad sweep. While "parts" could be examined, the eye was not to descend to "particles."[9] Thus the eye could sweep over any elements that disturbed the composition or the aesthetics of picturesque form, such as "utilitarian traces of industry, improvement, or modernity."[10] In addition, the picturesque landscape always depicted the past rather than the present. Ruins predominated and a sense of stasis pervaded such depictions. In Britain the picturesque was often used to depict ruined castles and abbeys, landscapes from a remote past that could be contemplated "in the spirit of nostalgic detachment."[11]

FIG. 6.1   *Dusasamade Gaut, at Benares on the Ganges* (Dashashwamedha ghat), 1796,
by Thomas Daniell. Royal Academy of Arts, London.

In colonial South Asia the picturesque intersected with an Orientalist viewpoint and allowed artists to treat contemporary indigenous subjects as well as their environments and histories as decrepit but exotic objects in an equally strange landscape that had already been conceived of as belonging in the past. Indeed, the Indian subcontinent as a whole "seemed always already picturesque, redolent with exotic examples of robed figures adding color to dramatic natural locales . . . Indians in all their Oriental splendor themselves seemed picturesque."[12] The riverfront at Banaras, with its monumental architecture and its masses of people, was just such an ideal subject.

Visiting British artists such as William Hodges (active years in India, 1780–1783) and Thomas Daniell (active 1786–1793) portrayed vestiges of the Mughal past as decaying and antique, while being sympathetic to the subcontinent's pre-Islamic pasts. Early years of rule by the East India Company saw the active production of Orientalist knowledge on the laws, customs, literature, and visual culture of South Asia. The pre-Islamic linguistic, literary, and cultural traditions of South Asia were valued as authentic and indigenous as opposed to Islamic traditions and culture that were viewed as foreign interlopers. Hodges saw his own role as part of this Orientalist mission no less significant than the efforts of scholars who were admired for their explanations and theories on "the Laws and the Religion of the Hindu tribes; as well as for correct and well-digested details of the transactions of the Mogul government."[13] To this end, he illustrated and described scenes in Banaras, viewing it as the epitome of an authentic, "pure," and unspoiled Hindu city, "undepraved by any intermixture with Mahomedans."[14] Hodges accepted the city's *puranic* representation as indicative of a reluctance to incorporate "innovations from foreigners" at a site that was "perhaps the oldest in the world."[15] At Banaras the relatively recent origins of its built environment were merged with narratives of its antiquity that circulated alike within colonial and Indian circles.

The inherently manufactured nature of this picturesque riverfront as well as its association with Hindu antiquity was adroitly adapted and enhanced by the Indian artist Sita Ram.[16] A protégé of the Marquess of Hastings (governor-general of Bengal between 1813 and 1823), Sita Ram traveled with his patron on a trip up the Ganges from Calcutta and on to Agra and Delhi, in 1814 and 1815. He produced a number of watercolors that are

FIG. 6.2 *The Temple of Raja Dusserath with the House He Lived in to the Left* (Dashashvamedh ghat), 1814, by Sita Ram. British Library Board.

preserved in a set of albums (the *Hastings Albums*) commissioned as mementos for the governor-general's children. Building on the premises of the colonial picturesque, Sita Ram went a step further. Whereas Hodges and the Daniells had merely implied the antiquity of the riverfront through visual and narrative strategies, Sita Ram directly portrayed a decaying Mughal world that could be contrasted with the living mythology of Hindu sites, whether real or invented.[17] When he created a view of the riverfront at Banaras, he combined architectural elements from various buildings along the stretch along the Manikarnika and Jalsai ghats to create a pair of fictitious buildings that he titled "the temple of Raja Dusserath with the house he lived in to the left" (Fig. 6.2). In representing Dusserath, a character from the Hindu epic the *Ramayana*, Sita Ram directly constructed a landscape that maintained concrete visual connections to an actual built environment but was associated with a mythical yet relevant character from a story that was performed every year in Banaras during the annual Ramlila celebrations.

MADHORAY GHAT & THE MINARETS AT BENARES.

Drawn on Stone by I. Haghe, from a Drawing by James Prinsep, Esq.ʳ
Printed by W.Day 17 Gate St.ᵗ London.

FIG. 6.3

Madhoray Ghat and the Minarets at Benares, 1831–1833, by James Prinsep. British Library Board.

FIG. 6.4 *Benares, A Brahmin Placing a Garland on the Holiest Spot in the Sacred City*,
1831–1833, by James Prinsep. British Library Board.

Despite the existence of the Dharhara mosque on Panchganga ghat that several artists
including Sita Ram and Prinsep captured (Fig. 6.3), the picturesque mode persisted as a
powerful instrument to reinforce an antique Hindu identity for Banaras. Most traveling
visitors and artists wrote about and depicted the riverfront from the comfort of a boat
anchored midstream.[18] They tended to privilege the "first impression" of a general view.[19]
In contrast, Prinsep—the empathetic Orientalist and self-styled *Banaras*—preferred to
linger over details. Understandably, then, he was unhappy with the Daniells' representations, finding them "detached" and failing to "satisfy curiosity regarding a place which
exhibits a larger remnant of the external characteristics of Hindoo taste and habits, than
is to be met with in any other Eastern city within the pale of British dominion."[20] Prinsep's
drawings (like his map) were saturated with details of the city's built elements as well as
social and religious life (Fig. 6.4). His depictions were akin to an exercise in the "ethnographic picturesque," yet this remained an equally selective and filtered process.[21] Prinsep

FIG. 6.5 *The City of Benares*, 1857. Published by Read. British Library Board.

paid equal attention to sites and buildings as well as the patrons who commissioned them, many of whom he knew in a professional and often personal capacity. Yet he was consistent in underlining a pervasive and unchanging Hindu antiquity as the prime motivation in elite support for religious buildings and rituals.

Picturesque illustrations were often accompanied by descriptions within travel narratives that reinforced a timeless quality for the subcontinent's landscapes. Banaras with its connotations of authenticity remained a favored subject. Often its practitioners were committed to ideas of naturalism and verisimilitude even as they manufactured a reality for the riverfront. In her 1835 publication, Emma Roberts placed herself within a lineage of picturesque authority beginning with the Daniells.[22] The nature of illustration and description was often defined by the conventions and approved itineraries of colonial travel. For instance, when Fanny Parks traveled to Banaras in 1844, her view of the riverfront was mediated by a guidebook that she referred to as the "Directory."[23] Parks claimed that her opinion differed from that sanctioned by the "Directory," since it took more than a "distant view" to gain a true idea of the "beautiful ghats and temples," and that a "small boat with an awning" was the best conveyance to gain a view that was close enough to provide sufficient detail yet not be completely immersed in the city.[24] This arrangement could provide the viewer with a theater of Hinduism that could provide the right combination of detail and distance.

Colonial narratives created a generic view of the riverfront, one filled with temples and crowds of natives. The specificity of individual ghats, their histories and purposes, were usually lost in such representations. For instance, in a lithograph of the riverfront at Banaras produced in 1857, and published by Read, the Shivala ghat was depicted next to the Dharhara mosque, several ghats away from its actual location (Fig. 6.5).[25] This drawing was published as part of a series produced after the rebellion of 1857, to give consumers in England an idea about the Indian landscape. Despite the competition posed by photography and increasingly precise survey techniques, picturesque conventions of selective representation lingered well into the mid-nineteenth century. As they consolidated power and territories, colonial administrators began to place emphasis on survey techniques of greater accuracy and on enumeration.[26] All the same, an affinity for the picturesque persisted in depictions and descriptions of the riverfront as a colorful yet benign vision. The sole exceptions were the towering minarets of the Dharhara mosque, indispensable in picturesque views but a thorny contradiction in narratives of antiquity.

THE MINARETS

The minarets were favored subjects for artists illustrating the riverfront and Hodges, Sita Ram, and Prinsep each devoted attention to them. Designed to visually dominate the landscape, the Dharhara mosque and its minarets were simultaneously depicted as a valued landmark as well as a marker of violence. For Prinsep the minarets could be objects of admiration, and he devoted his energies to sketching them as well as making plans for enhancing their structural stability and integrity. At the same time, he identified them as evidence of Islamic iconoclasm and derided their intrusive role in the lives of Hindus since they "overlook the privacy of their houses, the upper apartments and terraced roofs of which are always tenanted by the females of the family."[27] Prinsep's reactions to the minarets were shared by several Hindu visitors to the city. Veeraswamy recognized the Dharhara mosque as a symbol of Islamic iconoclasm, even as he admired the edifice. In his account of the city, he referred directly to the Islamic presence as well as the mosque.[28]

Similarly, Bholanauth Chunder described the Dharhara mosque as "a blot upon the snow-white purity of Hindooism. It cannot fail to be regarded by the Hindoos as a grim ogre which obtrudes its mitered head high above everything else, and looks down with scorn—gloating in a triumphant exultation. To drop the metaphor, the altitude of the minars is 225 feet from the bed of the river. The view from their height is exceedingly picturesque."[29] Like Chunder, many visitors climbed to the top of the minarets, admired their height and the view from the top, and derided the mosque to which they were attached. Prinsep's accounts indicate that the mosque had a more complex role in the city's religious life. Perched on rising ground above Panchganga ghat, it was usually in the midst of every public celebration. As Prinsep observed, during the festival of the eclipse of the moon in 1831, the "khadim of the Minaret-mosque does not scruple, for a *consideration* of about 200 rupees, to throw open the suhun or floor of the Musjid for the accommodation of the children of the superstition."[30]

Given its unique site and architecture, the mosque retained its ambivalent place in the minds of visitors and pilgrims well into the early decades of the twentieth century, when one of the minarets was damaged in an earthquake, following which both were dismantled. The changing role of the riverfront as a space for a universal rather than fragmented Hindu identity was the result of more than mere aesthetics. Always a backdrop for spectacle, it became a site of protest following the Lat Bhairo incident of 1809. Contentions over religious differences in the city came to a head over a *lat* (pillar) that Hindu groups worshipped as a symbol of Shiva. The pillar was located right outside a mosque, close to the Kapal Mochun tank, one of the ritual sites renovated by Rani Bhawani in the previous century.[31] Subsequent violent events in the city reportedly included the destruction of a mosque, the pouring of a cow's blood into a well held sacred by Hindus, and the mixing of a cow's blood into the Ganges. Brahmins in the city, led by Bishambar Pandit, staged a protest on the riverbank. The incident remained in the memories of residents and colonial administrators well into the next century, and several visitors heard versions of the incident. Bird, the acting magistrate related details to Bishop Heber, emphasizing the role of the riverfront as a dramatic and symbolically charged site for a protest led by one of the East India Company's prominent Brahmin allies. As Heber related the incident, the riverfront presented a "spectacle of woe such as few cities but Benares could supply."[32]

Rajani Ranjan Sen, who visited the city nearly a century after Heber, drew a similar though significantly more partisan picture. For Sen the "Hindus" were clearly the injured party, "disconsolate at the desecration and defilement of the sacred stream," and were only consoled when assured "that the desecration of the Ganges was not possible" and after "expiatory" rituals were conducted to ensure penance.[33] Increasingly perceived as a space dedicated to the practices of a universal Hindu religion, the riverfront lost its place within the elite patronage structure of the eighteenth century. As it was established as a synecdoche of the city, its regulation became equally urgent in the views of the colonial administration and a new group of Hindu elites.

EMBELLISHMENT AND IMPROVEMENT

Urban "improvement" had been a goal for the East India Company's administration since the early nineteenth century. "Embellishments" to the city's riverfront that were also "picturesque" were of particular interest to governing bodies and their members who intervened to encourage and shape material alterations.[34] The Committee for Local Improvement became an active agency in the regulation and "embellishment" of signature spaces in Banaras.[35] Prinsep served as the committee's secretary, and he was an active initiator and executor of various projects geared to achieving this goal. The committee's interventions often involved the acquisition of private property and its transfer into a public domain. For instance, when repairs were begun on the minaret, the embankment was acquired from its owner, one Jewan Ram, by overriding a decree of ownership signed by the Mughal emperor Shah Alam. Some of the city's newly established elite, such as Bishambar Pandit, owner and patron of the Jagannath temple and sometime company loyalist, were preoccupied with control of ownership and access.[36] Yet others colluded with the committee to facilitate schemes that would preserve and even create the sacred landscape that they desired.[37]

The Committee for Local Improvement also remained concerned with religious rivalries among supposedly monolithic communities of "Hindus" and "Muslims." In its first meeting the members resolved to repair the minarets of the Dharhara mosque because they were an "ornament of the town."[38] Although religious buildings were beyond the committee's usual purview, such an action could satisfy its aesthetic concerns.[39] With a memory of the Lat Bhairo incident of 1809, however, the committee resolved that the Nag Kuan, a sacred well in the vicinity of which an annual quasi-religious fair was held, could provide the committee with a project that could potentially pacify the city's Hindus.[40]

In 1826 the committee read a representation by another member of the city's new elite, Baboo Kalee Shunkur (Kalishankar, Jaynarayan Ghoshal's son), who complained that "nuisances were allowed to exist in the neighborhood of Manikarnika ghat."[41] "Nuisances" were a delicate way of saying that people were urinating and defecating on the ghat. Asking for the committee's assistance, Kalishankar requested permission to station a peon at the ghat and offered to incur the cost of the service.[42] The practice of mixed bathing at the riverfront offended the sensibilities of colonial administrators and, increasingly, the sensibilities of "respectable natives." Although women bathed fully clothed, the practice was eroticized and folded within picturesque illustration and in written descriptions produced by British and elite Indian observers alike.[43]

The interest that the sight generated also led to expressions of outraged public morality. Indians who were swayed by Victorian mores, such as Baboo Ishuree Dass ("a native Christian"), hastened to explain the practice on the grounds that "men and women all bathe at the same places in promiscuous crowds—only that women pay so much regard to decency as that each one of them keeps at the distance of a few yards from men."[44] Ishuree Dass further described the custom of purdah among Hindus of northern India as a custom adopted "at the time of the Mohomedan government on account of the violence and irregularity of the conduct of the Moslems."[45] By bathing without a "screen," Hindu women, it was supposed, merely reverted to their authentic customs. Nevertheless, in 1855 the colonial administration tried to pressure the Holkars into constructing a separate bathing ghat for women, to be known as the *zenana* ghat within Manikarnika ghat.[46] Although the Holkars agreed in principle and undoubtedly under pressure, the project was first held up due to the uprising of 1857–1858 and dragged on until 1885.[47] The colonial administration made repeated appeals on the grounds that the project would have the support of "respectable" Hindus and would also be in the "public" interest.[48]

Where an opportunity to carve a sphere of influence was more fragile, Indian elites were reluctant to intervene or invest. For instance, between 1855 and 1863 the government repeatedly appealed to the Shindhias of Gwalior to repair their ghat since it was "dangerous to parties who bathe there," and "pilgrims have to pass over it daily in the journey of the Punchkrosee."[49] By 1864, and after continued pressure from the British, the Shindhias declared that they were willing to leave the details of the job to the government's Public Works Department and merely asked for an estimate of the cost.[50] The Public Works Department recommended that the repairs be carried out by "professional contractors" from Calcutta.[51] In the meantime, the Shindhias intimated that they were not going to concern themselves with either the details of the repairs or any transactions connected with it and would restrict their contribution to a maximum of three thousand rupees.[52]

An irate president of the municipal committee, one W. Kaye, gave up any expectations from the Shindhias, declaring that "unless they like to go to very considerable expense in repairing their ghat, it must remain an eyesore and an obstruction on the sacred road."[53] He decided that the committee would only repair the Panchkroshi road that passed over the ghat and leave the remainder as an "eyesore."

This exchange sheds some interesting light on the making of the riverfront as a public space in the 1860s. Members of the general population were now taking their complaints to the municipal committee and no longer looked to former patrons such as the Shindhias to manage these spaces. However, the colonial administration persisted in seeing a specific though limited role for elites and expected them to maintain the ghats in the "public interest." For the Shindhia family, repairing a ghat—let alone building one in the years after the uprising of 1857–1858—no longer held the same cache and public notice that it had done for Baizabai a mere three decades earlier.

Certain elites such as the Kacchawahas added an enclosed reception hall on the first floor of their mansion. Others, including the Rajas of Banaras, Rewa, and Darbhanga, continued to invest in the riverfront either by purchasing mansions or even building on a smaller scale. Despite such investments in private property, most regional rulers from around the subcontinent stalled patronage for fortress-palaces and the comprehensive maintenance of their ghats. A few, such as the maharaja of Mysore, acknowledged the emergence of a new civic sphere and sponsored the construction of a *chattram* (rest house) for pilgrims from his regions who wished to visit Banaras. Although the Mysore *chattram* had been established in the city in 1822, it was moved to the riverfront to a site then part of Hanuman ghat, in 1919.[54] The new structure was designed to reflect a regional identity with historicist details derived from the medieval temple architecture of the Carnatic region of southern India. A religious public space was converted into a civic space by a maharaja who elected to build a charitable institution for his pilgrim-subjects rather than a mansion for his personal use.

For other elites with modernizing sensibilities, such as Rajani Ranjan Sen, the ghats framed a single space where pilgrims and priests mingled together as "Hindus" and circumvented distinctions of caste, sect, and class. In Sen's view, people came together, without distrust, divisions, or tensions, to forge a unified identity, at an ancient and quintessentially "Hindu" destination.[55] He did not express concerns about filth or even the greed and aggression of Brahmin priests that had so upset Veeraswamy in 1831. Sen and his contemporaries romanticized the city's religious life and focused on the aesthetic qualities of the riverfront. Through such representations the riverfront came to be viewed as built heritage worthy of systematic urban preservation efforts.

A QUESTION OF ANTIQUITY

The language of "improvement" once initiated by the Committee for Local Improvement became the purview of urban organizations such as the Kashi Tirtha Sudhar Trust and the Municipality that were controlled and managed by the city's elite. As in the city, Indian elite began to project their own ideas regarding a "public" onto the riverfront. For instance, by 1927 the aims of the trust included "prevention of the pollution of the water of the Ganges and other sacred tanks as far as possible representing to the Municipal and District Boards, the necessity for taking steps for the stopping of public drains or sewers from running into them and for the efficient disposal of sewage."[56] Along with concern for the ritual purity of the riverfront, members of the trust were preoccupied with its aesthetic merits. Informed by colonial sensibilities as well as concern for the ritual authenticity of this space, they devised a novel strategy for its preservation.

The central role of material remains in establishing the antiquity of a site was widely accepted by the late nineteenth century. The Kashi Tirtha Sudhar Trust directed its efforts toward preserving buildings along the riverfront and enhancing this space. To this end, the trust published a report titled *Benares and Its Ghats* in 1931. Its authors relied equally on "hard" facts such as the dates of construction and ownership of various ghats, but also favored the sensibilities of a transformed colonial picturesque. In this spirit they quoted from the writings of Orientalist and art historian Ernest Binfield Havell. His lyrical description of sunrise on the riverfront could dispel "miasmatic mists . . . lighting up the recesses of the cave-like shrines, flashing on the brass and copper vessels of the bathers and on the gilded metal flags and crescents which surmount the temples of Shiva."[57]

The choice of this quotation was motivated as much by Havell's empathy with Hindu mythology as his reputation as an Indologist. Inspired by romantic inclinations, he could seamlessly blend mythological references with descriptions of the material environment of the riverfront. In 1905, Havell created a past for the city framed by a now well-established subcontinental history and merged this account with the city's *purana* traditions.[58] Havell chose to follow a timeline for the city that was endorsed by his contemporaries among the Indian elite. It was a chronology that was concerned with the spiritual history of South Asia rather than being merely based in dates and dynasties. By extension, it could be implied that Kashi was at the center of each of these historic developments.

Havell began with the Kashi of "Vedic hymns" and the "Upanishads," continuing to the age of Hindu epics such as the Mahabharata and the Ramayana, on to the age of the Buddha, concluding with Sankaracharya and the rise of "modern" Hinduism.[59] Thus the "Aryans" and their Vedic culture were followed by the age of the Sanskrit epics, followed by the age of Buddhism, and on to a period of "Medieval" Hinduism, concluding with the respective periods of Muslim and British rule. Like his elite Indian contemporaries, Havell sustained a belief in an original Brahminical or Hindu civilization. He wished to present the city's built environment, particularly its riverfront, as evidence for its antiquity. He dismissed the skepticism of his predecessors and contemporaries, including Sherring, who attributed Buddhist origins to any physical vestiges of antiquity in the city.[60] All the same, Havell and his admirers among the trust's membership could not entirely ignore the widely accepted historical timeline. Neither could they deny the value of artifacts and material environments as historical evidence. Havell merged perspectives, citing the unique topography of the riverfront as a logical theater for its spiritual history. Havell saw this "magnificent natural amphitheatre" as the first home of "the Aryan tribes" and conjectured that it may have been "a great center of primitive sun worship" for their "Turanian predecessors."[61]

The sheer aesthetic value of the riverfront could then be positioned as evidence for antiquity, much in the traditions of the colonial picturesque. Following this precedent, the

Dharhara mosque and its minarets could seamlessly blend into a scene. When confronted with the mosque, the authors of *Benares and Its Ghats* retreated into another description, this time by Edwin Greaves, describing the scene as "the quaint buildings tumbled together in indescribable confusion, and crowning the whole, the Mosque and Minarets of Aurangzeb."[62] In the case of more persistent inquisition, the presence of the mosque could be used to explain the absence of true antiquity, the result of conquest by successive Islamic regimes that instigated "a general loot and plunder" in Banaras.[63] As the authors added, the consequence of these actions was the "destruction of its glorious buildings and temples, not through the familiar ravages of time but directly through human agency."[64]

The picturesque idiom facilitated an erasure of harsh historical realties and the simultaneous celebration of myth and sensation as antiquity. Where historical facts (such as the existence of mosques) had to be confronted and explained, repeated instances of destruction by Muslim-led armies could be cited. As a historical narrative was constructed for the city over the course of the nineteenth century, Indian elites absorbed this past and produced a composite narrative. Their accounts incorporated a mythical past immured in faith as well as a historical past based in "scientific" knowledge. The two pasts became inextricably entwined and produced a discourse for the city that asserted its role as the material and cultural basis for creating a modern Hindu identity.[65]

The Kashi Tirtha Sudhar Trust remained at the helm of such efforts. In a petition presented to the British viceroy, Lord Irwin, in 1927, Babu Motichand, in his capacity as president, welcomed Irwin to the "historic" city of Banaras that was also an ideal *tirtha* defined through the *purana* texts that were the foundation of a Hindu *sanatan dharma*.[66] Favorable opinions among a colonial audience were critical to the success of this project. In his simultaneous roles as pious Hindu patron and loyal British subject, Motichand provided European visitors to the city with free rides along the riverfront on his boat, flamboyantly named the "pearl boat."

For many of the city's Hindu elites, aesthetic pleasures were intricately entwined with ritual participation. They could bathe ritually in the Ganges as well as enjoy boat rides to view the riverfront and take satisfaction in its supposed antiquity and undiluted Hindu character. Patrons continued to channel financial resources and efforts to build temples on the riverfront well into the early decades of the twentieth century. In contrast to the fortress-palaces of the eighteenth century, their projects were modest in scale and appearance and were designed to express a public purpose as well as an uncorrupted Hindu identity. Informed by colonial antiquarian efforts, these patrons and their masons reinvented the "Benares temple."

RECASTING THE TEMPLE ON THE RIVERFRONT

Since widespread faith in the antiquity of Banaras had been enhanced by the discoveries at Sarnath, visitors and pilgrims alike transferred these expectations to the riverfront. Pilgrimage maps aided patrons and priests as they undertook projects of religious archaeology and "discovered" or identified many of the sites listed in the *Kashikhand* within the contemporary city. Since interpretations of a *purana*-based landscape were frequently published and widely circulated, many new temples and their deities were assigned names and identities derived from *purana* texts. Temples on the riverfront were no exception. The Raghurajeshwur temple that was added to their fortress-palace by the Bhonslas in the 1840s became associated with the deity of Nageshwur, identified as such by Gorji Dikshit in his *Kashiyatraprakash*.[67] Over the course of the nineteenth century, several temples that were added to the riverfront, including the Prayageshwur temple (ca. 1822) on Dashashvamedha ghat, were assigned names and identities based in *purana* texts.

In most cases these shrines were built by a new group of patrons, landowners, and *zamindars* from the city's hinterland in the northwest provinces. Many of them worked with the city's Brahmin priests to enhance the authenticity of the religious landscape. For instance, in the mid-nineteenth century the Raja of Amethi worked with Gorji Dikshit to resurrect and embellish shrines in the city.[68] The raja wished to construct a new temple on Manikarnika ghat, and Dikshit convinced him to find a permanent home for the Siddhivinayak shrine. The Amethi temple was first constructed in 1840, but this structure was destroyed in a fire. It was subsequently rebuilt in 1854. Siddhivinayak, a significant deity on the Antargriha route, lay in the way of its reconstruction. This shrine was listed by the authors of several guidebooks and pilgrimage maps, including by Dikshit in his *Kashiyatraprakash*.[69] Siddhivinayak was placed in a niche within the lower level of the new multilevel temple and was easily approached by pilgrims on the Antargriha route.

The new structure for the Amethi temple was designed on two levels and on an archaic *panchayatana* plan (Fig. 6.6). It was embellished with innovative motifs and ornamental details.[70] The five shrines of the Amethi temple were each surmounted with a "Benares temple" *shikhara* (Fig. 6.7). As discussed earlier, this *shikhara* form had been carefully honed by masons and their apprentices since the mid-eighteenth century. With the construction of the Amethi temple the form was incorporated within a new plan type. The application of the *panchayatana* plan, the incorporation of figural imagery in the form of "flying *gandharvas*" as bracket figures, and the absence of dominant Mughal elements all indicate a new sensibility toward religion as well as the spatial and decorative aspects of temple design (Fig. 6.8). Although unconnected to the ritual landscape described in the *Kashikhand*, the new Amethi temple enhanced the general religious identity and aesthetic value of the riverfront.

The image of a riverfront crowded with temple spires caught the imagination of a number of patrons. Temples were added to older fortress-palaces and were often assigned new ritual roles. The temples within Chet Singh ghat were added ca. 1880, during the reign of Prabhunarain Singh, in memory of his predecessor, Ishwariprasadnarain Singh, and were named the Ishwareshwur temples.[71] The temples were incorporated within the Burhvamangal festivities and before the formal festivities began, the Rajas of Banaras always worshipped the Ishwareshwur *linga*. The temples were built as a complex of three shrines, each occupying the center of an interlinked courtyard and each with an articulated single-cell plan and a tiered "Benares" *shikhara* (Fig. 6.9; see Fig. 4.5a). The three shrines are equal in height, but the one in the center is more elaborately embellished with a larger numbers of offsets. The attached *chattra* (refectory) was designed for dispensing public charity to Brahmins. The temples were carefully placed opposite the approach from the riverfront gateway. From the river the monumental gateway of Chet Singh ghat remained visually dominant, tempered by a triad of rising temple towers in its backdrop.

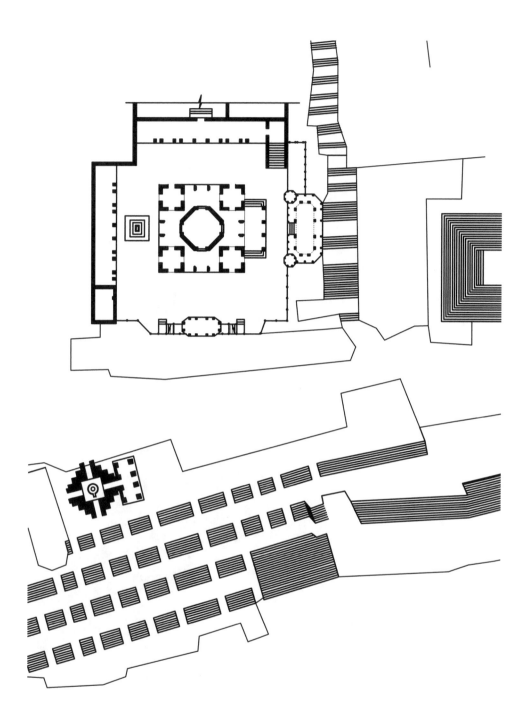

FIG. 6.6 Plan of Amethi temple on Manikarnika ghat. Drawing by Nanditha Veeraraghavelu and Jennifer Shontz.

FIG. 6.7 Amethi temple on Manikarnika ghat.

FIG. 6.8 Bracket with "flying *gandharva*" on Amethi temple.

FIG. 6.9   Ishwareshwur temples on Chet Singh ghat.

A second shrine built by the Rani of Sursand and dedicated to Radha-Krishna (ca. 1905) was located on Assi ghat along the riverfront. The Rani was interested in resurrecting the Vaishnava "Assi Madhav" tradition associated with the site and also used the archaic *panchayatana* plan for this temple (Fig. 6.10).[72] Increasingly influenced by colonial classifications and definitions of authentic Hindu forms, a new group of patrons altered their definitions of appropriate religious architecture, selectively incorporating colonial definitions and categories. However, for many of these elite, Mughal precedents continued to have purchase and the occasional Bangla roof, baluster column, or foliated arch often played a minor albeit visible role. Replete with temple spires crowding fortress-palaces and coded as antique, the riverfront defined the city's image and its visible Hindu identity.

THE PANORAMA, THE PILGRIMAGE MAP, AND THE PHOTOGRAPH

Toward the latter half of the nineteenth century, novel forms of visual representation were used to circulate images of the entire length of the sacred riverfront between the Assi and Varuna junctions. Created by Indian artists and their Brahmin collaborators, panoramic representations of the riverfront were placed within lithographed pilgrimage maps. As these illustrations included elements from the city's tangible built environment, they allowed pilgrims to more readily experience its religious cartography. As discussed earlier, panoramic representations of the riverfront were by no means a new phenomenon, but nearly a century later the discourse around the city's ritual landscape had shifted, as had expectations from its built environment and ritual spaces. Since the riverfront was a metaphor for the city and was increasingly treated as tangible material evidence for its

FIG. 6.10 Assi Madhav temple on Assi ghat.

antiquity, panoramic representations were also strategically placed within a generation of lithographed and printed pilgrimage maps as evidentiary support for updated interpretations of its ritual landscape. Since these pilgrimage maps were modestly priced, they could be easily purchased from vendors and were widely circulated among pilgrims and visitors alike.

Despite its venerable roots in the painting tradition of South Asia, the panorama in its nineteenth-century guise can also be linked to contemporary trends in a global visual culture. Panoramas on display in imperial London were integral to the project of imperialism and its cultures of display.[73] A technology of visualizing the world, the spectacular panorama allowed a viewer to encapsulate a space within a single sweeping glance. Several such panoramas depicting battle scenes, landscapes, and cityscapes were aimed at a general population curious about the sights and sounds of far-flung outposts of the empire. Since it was already popular as a stock image of Britain's dominions in South Asia, a panorama devoted exclusively to the Banaras riverfront was created in 1840 and put on display in Leicester Square.[74] Visitors could view panels that covered a full 360 degrees of the display space and exhibited images of either sides of the Ganges River.

The accompanying guidebook contained a schematic sketch of the entire display with a key explaining the various buildings and figures in the panorama (Fig. 6.11). Usually sites and their names were correctly identified, including Dusamere (Dashashwamedha) Ghaut or Munkanka (Manikarnika) Ghaut. Descriptive labels explained images of the

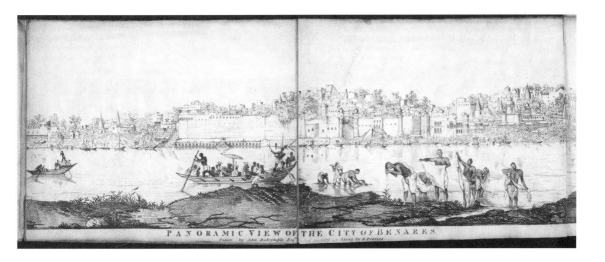

FIG. 6.11   Page from printed guide accompanying *Royal Panorama of the Holy City of Benares and the Sacred River*, 1840, by R. Burford. British Library Board.

city, its buildings, its inhabitants, and its religious life. "A Native of Rank," "Dead Bodies," "A Palace," and "Native Smoking a Hubble Bubble" could satisfy visitors curious about Britain's Indian empire as well as substantiate descriptions that circulated through magazines, newspapers, journals, and travel accounts. Other images and labels for the "Great pagoda of the Hindoo Trinity," "Marriage Procession," and "Elephants bathing" also supported popular notions. Within the discursive and visual spaces of imperial culture, this panorama functioned simultaneously as a particular view of Banaras as well as a general spectacle of "native" life.

Brahmin authors of pilgrimage maps, however, were more interested in the riverfront as a metaphor for an antique and authentically Hindu city. Panoramic depictions of the riverfront, even if selective, could suggest the tangible materiality of an antique environment. In this vein Kailasnath Sukul combined *tirtha* sites with elements from the urban environment in the *Kashidarpana* (Plate 7). He selected the Town Hall that was completed the same year that his map was published. He also included the riverfront, which he depicted as a continuous stretch of built steps. Sukul highlighted selected buildings and sites that were either ritually significant or visually spectacular. The two ends of the riverfront, the junctions of the Ganges with the Assi and Varuna streams, were clearly indicated. The Kedareshwur temple was added close to the Assi *sangam* and the Adikeshav (Sangameshwur) temple near the Varuna *sangam*. Besides these anchoring *tirthas*, the Bhonsla ghat labeled as "Bhonsla Mandir/Ghat" and the Dharhara mosque, labeled as "Aurangzeb ki Masjid," were prominently featured. A partial yet critical depiction allowed Sukul to incorporate the city's positivist histories and selected scenic elements that were folded into such accounts. He could also imply antiquity for the city by combining ritual sites that had a textual provenance with the oldest extant Hindu building, the Kedar temple, as well as the monumental Bhonsla ghat.

In keeping with the increasing rigidity of religious boundaries, the authors of pilgrimage maps continued to retain an ambivalent attitude to the city's mosques. Although smaller mosques and tombs were usually filtered out, the Dharhara and Gyan Vapi mosques were often selectively appropriated and captioned with the names of the Hindu shrines that they had replaced. The Dharhara mosque and its minarets were more popular and were almost always depicted in maps, panoramas, and views of the riverfront, even as they were often erased in textual narratives. The Gyan Vapi mosque, however, presented a more complex problem. Lacking the picturesque qualities of the Dharhara mosque, its presence was an inescapable reminder of Aurangzeb's dismantling of the Mughal Vishweshwur temple. Although the Dharhara mosque had replaced a temple as well, the Bindu Madhav deity and shrine did not have an equally prominent role in the city's nineteenth-century ritual landscape, and Dharhara could be more easily appropriated for its dramatic physical presence.

In the 1897 *Srikashichitra* the riverfront is depicted as a continuous stretch of riverfront buildings, many of them with temple spires. The only building with any semblance to its real counterpart is the Dharhara mosque, although it is labeled as "Madhoray ka Dharhara." A diminutive Bindu Madhav shrine (rebuilt ca. 1822) is depicted next to the dominant mosque. The *Srikashichitra*, more than the *Kashidarpana*, was aimed at a burgeoning pilgrim and tourist market and included many sites, such as the "Ramnagar ka Killa" (the fortress-palace at Ramnagar) and "Raja sahib ka talab" (the Raja *talab* [lake or pond]) that lay outside formal ritual destinations and boundaries.

A lithographed panorama titled *A Complete View of the Benares City* (1901), produced by the Allahabad-based artist Durga Pershad, encapsulated similar concerns (Plate 8). Designed as a scroll, Pershad's map was aimed at the pilgrim-tourist, and the artist effectively combined features from the city's Mughal and late Mughal architecture with its ritual landscape as well as recent additions to its civic infrastructure. The riverfront was portrayed in great detail, although major attractions such as the Kedar temple and the Man Mandir were embellished with exaggerated domes. Both the Dharhara and the Gyan Vapi mosques were represented but without any captions that might establish a connection with Islam. Although the physical structure of each mosque was appropriated as a landmark, the religious function of either building was sidelined. The Dharhara mosque was labeled "Madhoray ka ghat" and the Gyan Vapi mosque was merely labeled as "Gyan-vapi," accompanied by the label "Vishweshwarnathji ka purana mandir," or the "Old temple of Vishweshwurnathji." The artist added prominent landmarks such as the mansion of the Raja of Vizianagaram as well as the Town Hall.[75]

A stylized depiction of the Panchkroshi pilgrimage route as well as its principal halts was included, as were the prominent temples Vishweshwur and the Gopal Mandir. Durga Pershad and his associates produced a number of such panoramas for tourists. By combining the most significant elements of the city's ritual landscape with prominent landmarks and the riverfront panorama, the artist presented a selection of sites that were meaningful to pilgrims who were increasingly also interested in tourism. This combination of sites and activities meant that the antiquarian discourse on Banaras could be loosely applied to its religious identity. Images of the riverfront in particular could represent a ritually significant space and satisfy a visitor's antiquarian expectations.

FIG. 6.12 Manikarnika ghat, 1865. Photo by Samuel Bourne. British Library Board.

By the early nineteenth century, the riverfront was depicted within multiple representations and was widely read as tangible evidence for the antiquity of Banaras. With the rising popularity of photography by midcentury, this conflation was realized through a medium that could effectively resolve a knotty problem of geography. Banaras was a foregone halt on the photographer's route, and early examples include photographs of the riverfront taken by Samuel Bourne in 1865. The city could certainly be cast as an object for the Orientalist photographer in much the same manner as it had been for the artist of the picturesque. With the emergence of scientific archaeology in the nineteenth century, photographs of Banaras became necessary items in collections of architectural images. Photographers such as Bourne played to both expectations. Several photographs by Bourne, currently in the collections of the British Library, provide an example of this strategy. Bourne concentrated on the ghats, particularly Manikarnika ghat, of which he produced several images, often with the minarets of the Dharhara mosque in the distance (Fig. 6.12). In the MacNabb Collection these images are combined with a generic image of a ghat from 1885 and labeled as "women and children washing and collecting water."[76] Other photographs by Bourne found their way into various collections of architectural images on sites in South Asia.

FIG. 6.13   Man Mandir, 1869. Photo by Brojo Gopal Bromochary. British Library Board.

The Bellew Collection, a set of one-hundred-and-eighty images by several photographers, is a collection of architectural "views" that includes eight images of Banaras. Of these, four images, by an unknown photographer, are of the riverfront (Manikarnika and Tulsi ghats). The set includes two images of the Sumeri temple at Ramnagar, including one by Bourne taken in 1865. Also included is an image of a "modern temple" at Sarnath, photographed with the ancient stupa in its background.[77] The collection includes images of the tenth- and eleventh-century temples at Khajuraho, the seventeenth-century Taj Mahal at Agra, as well as buildings built more recently, during the eighteenth and nineteenth centuries. The riverfront was included as an iconic image, comfortably nestled in a collection of notable architectural sites awaiting its eventual designation as "heritage."

By the late nineteenth century, photography gained a following among Indians and was put to innovative uses beyond its original purpose as an instrument to create knowledge for and by the colonial state.[78] Indian photographers such as Brojo Gopal Bromochary addressed a different set of concerns. Some of Bromochary's images certainly follow the precedent established by Bourne. Indeed, some of his photographs were commissioned as part of the antiquarian and ethnographic projects of the colonial regime. For instance, Bromochary produced a set of photographs as part of a project to document material antiquities as well as living traditions for the Archaeological Survey of India. Included in this group is an image of Pandit Bapudev Shastri of the Queen's College in Banaras. Bromochary depicted Shastri seated on the floor in the transept of this gothic revival building, teaching an astronomy class to a group of students who are seated around him in a similar fashion. A colonial institution and a colonial employee were carefully cast as living examples of a traditional activity in progress in the most celebrated institution of the holiest city in India. At another level, this image of Shastri and his students was placed alongside similar images of artisans and craftsmen in the city as all of them were supposedly engaged in performing timeless tasks in an ancient environment.[79]

Bromochary simultaneously catered to the city's Indian elite, who were well aware of this new medium and its potential as a vehicle of self-representation. He produced an album of twenty-three "Views of Benares, from the River Side" in 1869 for Iswariprasadnarain Singh, Raja of Banaras, as a frame for the preservation and projection of his image as "Kashi Naresh." Bromochary presented the riverfront as the inevitable end result of sustained Hindu patronage and devotion that was intermittently interrupted by instances of Islamic iconoclasm. Of this group (image 13) a photograph of the Man Mandir ghat is labeled as the location of an observatory built by "Raja Jay Singh," a descendant of the "ancient Rajas of Ambheri" (Fig. 6.13). Although a historical date of "1693" is provided for Sawai Jai Singh II's ascension, he is presented as a torchbearer for an ancient Hindu ruling house. Similarly, a photograph (image 6) of "The Minarets" includes a note on the "Madhav" temple that once occupied the site of the Dharhara mosque. Aurangzeb, Bromochary noted, was interested in the "propagation of his own faith in a part entirely inhabited by the Hindus."[80]

In succeeding decades, Prabhunarain Singh, maharaja of Banaras, espoused a renewed Hindu identity and sponsored the construction of several edifices to achieve that end. This included a riverfront mansion called the Ganga Mahal at a location just north of the Assi *sangam*. Prabhunarain Singh ensured that edifices that could represent a civic realm were combined with more established images. An album of forty-one prints, presented to prominent British visitors by the maharaja (in this case, to Lord Reading in 1921) includes prints of the ghats but also contains images of civic buildings such as the Town Hall and public hospitals, the maharaja's symbolic seat at Ramnagar, and the new excavations at Sarnath that were conducted in 1905.[81] Included in the set is the temple at Godaulia with the "Jaipur gateway" that would later be identified as the "Gautameshwur Mahadev" temple from the *Kashikhand*. Many of these photographs were taken by Madho Prasad in 1905, although a few were by Babu Jageswar Prasad from 1885.

The two albums, created under the patronage of two different maharajas, make for an interesting comparison and reveal the nature of the shifting discourse on the city and its spaces. Ishwariprasadnarain Singh's album by Bromochary is a catalog of an ancient Hindu city built by a number of patrons and by implication associated with their venerable lineages. The notes that accompany the photographs are replete with overt references to religious traditions in the city and the patrons who sustain them. Prabhunarain Singh's album presents an ancient city, but its antiquity and continued value as "tradition" is simultaneously established through scientific archaeology and new buildings. These two faces of the city are seamlessly linked to the rajas and their patronage. They are presented as the faces of an ancient city with a robust contemporary built environment.

FIG. 6.14   Antiquities excavated at Sarnath, 1905. Photo by Madho Prasad. British Library Board.

Authors of guidebooks from the early twentieth century began to incorporate photographs and employ some of the strategies used by Prabhunarain Singh. The more recent excavations at Sarnath featured prominently in many publications from this time (Fig. 6.14). Photo albums and guidebooks could bypass the constraints of precise locations that were less easily avoided in a map. The question of whether Sarnath lay within or beyond the Panchkroshi circuit could be bypassed. Geographically disparate and often contextually unrelated images could be combined within shared covers and tied together through narrative. The city could be viewed as both ancient and modern, its many layers contradictorily representing a timeless quality. For this new generation of patrons and photographers, the city's antiquity could be asserted only through an ancient and visible material environment.

Through multiple representational strategies the riverfront was placed within the representational legacy of the mythically charged panorama. It was captured through photography and indexed as objective evidence of the city's antiquity. The grids of universal cartography and global history that were laid on the city modified narratives based in sectarian beliefs and timeless mythologies. This new history became the basis for defining a universal Hindu identity.

BANARAS REVISITED

CONTEMPORARY visitors to Banaras, tourists and pilgrims alike, often linger on the riverfront in the evening, waiting for the Ganga Arati to begin. First established in 1999, the event has grown into a widely publicized spectacle and is included in the itineraries of most visiting dignitaries and celebrities. The Ganga Arati is indeed a remarkable sight. Priests in identical crimson and cream robes stand in a row on ghat steps, holding multitiered brass trays with flickering flames to perform an *arati*—a Hindu ritual in which either a priest or lay devotees hold up and wave votive lamps aloft in a slow circular motion as a symbolic offering of light to either a deity or a venerated person or persons. By implication, the ritual is an auspicious act, intended to dispel darkness and ignorance and usher in good fortune. *Aratis* are usually also accompanied by hymns that devotees sing in praise of the deity, and the one held at Banaras is no exception. Prerecorded hymns in praise of the Ganges are played on a public address system as the priests go through the motions of the ritual with deliberate, synchronized movements. Aimed at domestic as well as foreign pilgrims and tourists, and initially performed at Dashashwamedha ghat, the ritual has expanded since its inception and has grown into a major spectacle that is held simultaneously at multiple ghats. Its scale in any given year is usually affected by the vicissitudes of the global tourism industry.

Religious traditions and their continued invention have a thriving legacy in Banaras. The notion is that a spectacle can be designed to accommodate piety, pleasure, and politics while remaining tethered to the city's enduring religious identity and ritual life. This pervasive simultaneity combined with a widespread expectation of permanence led observers like the visiting Mark Twain to exclaim that this city was "older than history, older than tradition, older even than legend, and looks twice as old as all of them put together."[1] Along with most of his contemporaries, Twain assumed that the physical environment that he saw represented an ancient stage for unchanging practices with roots in a mythical past. It is equally understandable that no informant or acquaintance ever disabused him of this notion. Twain's rather ascerbic remarks have become an oft-quoted truism for the city. If historical perspectives were ever wielded to unpack or demystify Banaras, these were quickly overwhelmed by the more hoary claims of "tradition" and "legend." In more recent times, such spectacles as the Ganga Arati thrive on a premise shared by most visitors, pilgrims, and residents that although it may have been initiated quite recently, the ritual is a fitting and even timeless tribute to the sacred river and the ancient city that rises on its banks. Banaras is a creation of the imagination, and its representations are as critical to shaping the city's image and identity as its material reality.

The connected histories of texts, religious practices, politics, and the built environment that have been explored in this book strongly suggest that imagination and negotiation usually preceded the creation of its physical environment. Both the *Kashikhand* and the *Kashirahasya* were cited as sources of universal knowledge and authenticity only once the routes, shrines, and deities that their authors listed had gained wide acceptance. In addition, the authors of these texts were concerned with the configuration of routes and their relationship to both deities and ideas about sacred spaces. Without the benefit that accrued from the consolidation of diverse belief systems that were often also the result of intense political and social negotiation, neither text would have held the stature that it currently enjoys. In this equation the temple as a centering entity emerges as a mere afterthought. The intertwined histories and tortured proximity of the Vishweshwur temple/Gyan Vapi mosque that have shaped the city's identity through alternating instances of conciliation and competition were in fact marginal to the essential concerns of pilgrimage texts. Thus pilgrimage routes emerged through a focus on particular deities and sacred geographies rather than as accessories to temples and religious monuments.

The individuals who created and shaped this city and its monuments did so for a range of motivations from political consolidation to self-fashioning. The roles of diverse patrons in rearranging social identities as well as built form can be analyzed as a negotiation between individual ambition and the recurrently assertive social structures of caste, class, and gender. Aspiring patrons included men and women from varied social backgrounds, and they promoted their built creations as contemporary statements of authority as well as preexisting ritual anchors in an ancient city. The roles of initiative and innovation were as critical as "tradition" in advancing their ambitions. The case of elite women patrons is illustrative of this trend. The most successful among them used markers of tradition such as archaic temple forms in association with social norms of austerity considered suitable for maintaining a state of pious widowhood. At the same time, visible symbols of authority associated with the Mughal (and later, the colonial) regime were equally critical to the consolidation of political and social authority. In other words, these women patrons pursued individual and familial goals rather than enhancing the role of their gender or realizing an ideal of social justice. Other groups of aspiring elites such as newly minted aristocrats and Brahmin aspirants to political authority also followed similar strategies.

As this book understands Kashi or Banaras, the implications for other pilgrimage centers in South Asia are equally rich and revealing. Several of the region's significant pilgrimage sites—including, for instance, the temple city of Madurai dedicated to the goddess Meenakshi, the Vaishnava site of Brindavan, and the Shaiva destination of Omkareshwur—underwent similar processes of revival and rejuvenation through injections of fresh interest and investment. Madurai was expanded under seventeenth-century Nayaka rulers, and Brindavan enjoyed support from Mughal courtly circles. One of the Jyotirlingas (the twelve significant Shaiva sites), the pilgrimage center at Omkareshwur flourished as the Marathas (under Ahilyabai Holkar) built riverfront ghats and temples.

It is also significant that in each of these cases patrons lived in a wider Indo-Islamic environment of cosmopolitan Persianate cultures, and each possessed a penchant for selectively promoting archaic architecture. Whereas the unsullied "Hindu" character of many of these sites is a figment of desire, their built environments and narratives are the combined result of the transformative energies of cultural and religious encounters. Such mediation is a suitable lens through which "public" spheres and spaces in South Asia can be understood. A completely unmediated and secular public sphere has proven to be as imaginary a construct elsewhere, as it is in South Asia. Moreover, the interconnected roles of religion, politics, patronage, and opinion-making across social divisions provide a rich perspective on the nature of this sphere and its related spaces.

The implications for understanding Mughal urbanism and architecture are equally significant. Beyond the capital cities of Shahjahanabad and Agra, Mughal urbanism reshaped several Hindu religious centers. Therefore, not only did Mughal cities exist beyond the artificially constructed frame of so-called "Islamic" urbanism, their spatial and formal structures reshaped the nature of the early modern South Asian city. The consequences for understanding urbanism and architecture in the eighteenth century are equally far-reaching. Beyond major urban centers such as Calcutta and Mumbai, colonial forms, knowledge, and power structures reshaped the spaces and rituals of Hinduism.

The many imaginative and material layers of contemporary Banaras were created through shifting ideas of sanctity and urban order, and some of their inherent tensions persist in the form of robust domestic and international tourism as well as heightened communal tensions and sharply etched religious boundaries. Tourists, scholars, and pilgrims undertake the Panchkroshi pilgrimage and enjoy the spectacle of the Ganga Arati even as the Vishweshwur temple as well as the Gyan Vapi and Dharhara mosques are guarded around the clock by Indian national security personnel. At the same time, multistoried apartment blocks are being built within the Antargriha zone by speculative builders and enterprising masons, adept at erecting concrete structures on reinforced eighteenth-century foundations. Their clients are a new generation of affluent retirees in search of the purifying benefits of Kashibas as well as the material comforts of a modern lifestyle. Banaras is an ancient idea and site, but it holds its place in our imaginations as an eternal city only because it was created and re-created through the reinvention of its conceptual structures and its material details. As the religious and cultural identities of its patrons and pilgrims shift, its sacred zones, built environment, and symbolic meanings will undoubtedly be transformed yet again.

NOTES

1   Motichandra, *Kashi Ka Itihas* (1962; reprint, Varanasi: Vishwavidyalaya Prakashan, 2003), 149. In his comprehensive history of Banaras, Motichandra establishes a historical basis for the military conquest of Banaras as well as instances of iconoclasm practiced by early Indo-Islamic regimes during the twelfth and thirteenth centuries. Although some disruption is undeniable, there is no conclusive picture of what exactly might have been destroyed in Banaras. Several scholars of Banaras—including Kubernath Sukul in *Varanasi Vaibhav* (Patna: Bihar Rashtrabhasha Parishad, 1977), 30–31, and Diana L. Eck in *Banaras: City of Light* (1982; reprint, New York: Columbia University Press, 1999), 83–89—suggest that these were times of trouble and conflict, while revealing that Hinduism remained largely unchanged although its institutions and rituals may have flourished in some instances.

2   "Introduction" in *Krtyakalpataru of Bhatta Lakshmidhara*, ed. K. V. Rangaswami Aiyangar (Baroda: Oriental Institute, 1942), lxxiv. Aiyangar concludes that since the *Kashikhand* was translated into Telugu in 1440, the text was compiled sometime earlier, most likely in the fourteenth century.

3   Jagdish Narayan Dubey, ed., *Kashirahasyam* (Varanasi: Adarsh Prakashan Mandir, 1984), 87–98.

4   Wendy Doniger, "Introduction," in *Purana Perennis: Reciprocity and Transformation in Hindu and Jaina Texts*, ed. Wendy Doniger (Albany: State University of New York Press, 1993), vii–xii. Also see Velcheru Narayana Rao, "Purana as Brahminic Ideology," in *Purana Perennis*, ed. Doniger, 85–100.

5   Rao, "Purana as Brahminic Ideology," 85–92.

6   Catherine B. Asher, "The Architecture of Raja Man Singh: A Study of Sub-Imperial Patronage," in *Architecture in Medieval India*, ed. Monica Juneja (New Delhi: Permanent Black, 2001), 370–397. Also see Catherine B. Asher, "Sub-Imperial Palaces: Power and Authority in Mughal India," *Ars Orientalis* 23 (1993): 281–302.

7   For details on Aurangzeb's early years on the Mughal throne as depicted in painting, see Laura Parodi, "Darbars in Transition: The Many Facets of the Mughal Imperial Image after Shah Jahan as Seen in the ex-Binney Collection in the San Diego Museum of Art," in *Indo-Islamic Cultures in Transition*, ed. Alka Patel and Karen Leonard (Leiden: Brill, 2012), 89–90.

8   Hermann Kulke and Dietmar Rothermund, *A History of India* (1986; reprint, London: Routledge, 2006), 139.

9   John F. Richards, *The Mughal Empire* (1993; reprint, Cambridge: Cambridge University Press, 2008), 33.

10   For an overview of Rajput-Mughal relations, see Norman P. Ziegler, "Some Notes on Rajput Loyalties during the Mughal Period," in *The Mughal State, 1526–1750*, ed. Muzaffar Alam and Sanjay Subrahmanyam (New Delhi: Oxford University Press, 1998), 168–210.

11   For an extensive survey of Mughal architecture, see Catherine B. Asher, *Architecture of Mughal India* (Cambridge: Cambridge University Press, 1992).

12   P. J. Marshall, "Introduction," in *The Eighteenth Century in Indian History: Evolution or Revolution?* (New Delhi: Oxford University Press, 2003), 1–49. A number of states, collectively known as the "post-Mughal" states, emerged in eighteenth-century India. See, for instance, Irfan Habib, ed. *Confronting Colonialism: Resistance and Modernization under Haidar Ali and Tipu Sultan* (London: Anthem Press, 2002), and Muzaffar Alam, *The Crisis of Empire in Mughal North India: Awadh and the Punjab* (Delhi: Oxford University Press, 1986). Alam contends that rather than viewing the eighteenth century as a period of imperial unraveling, it should be understood as a period of dynamic change and various regional political centers.

13   Marshall, *Eighteenth Century in Indian History*, 5.

14   Peter Van der Veer, "'God Must Be Liberated!' A Hindu Liberation Movement in Ayodhya," *Modern Asian Studies* 21, no. 2 (1987): 289. Van der Veer suggests that the rise of Ayodhya as a pilgrimage center in the eighteenth century was partly due to the rule of the Awadh Nawabs, who needed the support of Hindu groups.

15   Marshall, *Eighteenth Century in Indian History*, 3.

16   Ibid., 5–6. Marshall also suggests that these cultural forms may have gained greater influence in the eighteenth century through emulation as well as the more inclusive attitudes toward Shiite and Hindu groups by later Mughal emperors. For instance, Muhammad Shah (Aurangzeb's grandson) reintroduced some of the policies of cultural and religious tolerance that had been pursued by his forebears. During Muhammad Shah's thirty-year reign, artists produced paintings depicting diverse religious themes. See J. P. Losty and Malini Roy, *Mughal India: Art, Culture, and Empire* (London: British Library, 2012), 151–153.

17   Motichandra, *Kashi Ka Itihas*, 194–205.

18   State-based support for Hindu institutions such as temples and *muthas* (monasteries) has been documented in the case of the "Islamic" Mughal successor state of Hyderabad. See Karen Leonard, "Indo-Muslim Culture in Hyderabad: Old City Neighborhoods in the Nineteenth Century," in *Indo-Islamic Cultures in Transition*, ed. Alka Patel and Karen Leonard (Leiden: Brill, 2012), 181–184.

19   The Nawabs of Lucknow were among early initiators of this trend that was reflected in various artistic practices and multiple media. See Stephen Markel and Tushara Bindu Gude, eds., *India's Fabled City: The Art of Courtly Lucknow* (Munich: Prestel Verlag, 2011).

20   C. A. Bayly, *Rulers, Townsmen, and Bazaars: North Indian Society in the Age of British Expansion, 1770–1870* (1983; reprint, New Delhi: Oxford University Press, 1992); Anand A. Yang, *Bazaar India: Markets, Society, and the Colonial State in Bihar* (Berkeley: University of California Press, 1998); and Kumkum Chatterjee, *Merchants, Politics, and Society in Early Modern India, Bihar: 1733–1820* (Leiden: E. J. Brill, 1996).

21   Vasudha Dalmia, *The Nationalization of Hindu Traditions: Bharatendu Harishchandra and Nineteenth Century Banaras* (1997; reprint, New Delhi: Oxford University Press, 1999), 6. Dalmia cautions against use of the term "revival" when applied to religious movements because such usage overtly rejects the idea of transformation and change. In the context of this book, however, the term "revivalism" implies a conscious engagement with the past as a way of actively considering and negotiating contemporary culture and politics.

22   Motichandra, *Kashi Ka Itihas*, 226.

23   Bernard S. Cohn, *Colonialism and Its Forms of Knowledge* (Princeton: Princeton University Press, 1996), 3–8. Cohn explains the circumstances under which Warren Hastings in 1772 had decided that Indians were to be ruled through their own laws and customs.

24   Romila Thapar, *Somanatha: The Many Voices of a History* (New Delhi: Penguin Books India, 2004), 170–171. In her nuanced examination of the historiography of the eleventh-century raid on the temple of Somanatha by Mahmud of Ghazni, Thapar demonstrates the ways in which this event has been historically constructed to the present. In the nineteenth century the incident was retold in colonial histories as part of a larger narrative representing iconoclasm as the premium instrument of conquest and subjugation used by the Muslim invaders of South Asia.

25   Cigdem Kafescioglu, *Constantinopolis/Istanbul: Cultural Encounter, Imperial Vision, and the Construction of the Ottoman Capital* (University Park: Pennsylvania State University Press, 2009). Kafescioglu explores the theme of "encounter," in her study of Constantinople/Istanbul, as the Byzantine city was reshaped into the Ottoman imperial capital in the mid-fifteenth century. As an example of in-depth urban analysis across various scales, see the classic by John Summerson, *Georgian London* (New York: C. Scribner, 1945). For a recent study that explores the relationship between aspiration, discourse, and urban form, see Maurie D. McInnis, *The Politics of Taste in Antebellum Charleston* (Chapel Hill: University of North Carolina Press, 2005).

26   Michel Foucault, *The Archaeology of Knowledge and the Discourse on Language* (1972; reprint, New York: Pantheon, 1982), 31–39.

27   Finbarr Barry Flood, *Objects of Translation: Material Culture and Medieval "Hindu-Muslim" Encounter* (Princeton: Princeton University Press, 2009). In his study of Hindu-Muslim interactions in medieval South Asia, Flood examines this exchange in terms of a "translation" that encompassed confluences as well as tensions between two largely disparate cultures.

28   Richard M. Eaton and Phillip B. Wagoner, *Power, Memory, Architecture: Contested Sites on India's Deccan Plateau, 1300–1600* (New Delhi: Oxford University Press, 2014). Also see Philip B. Wagoner, "'Sultan among Hindu Kings': Dress, Titles, and Islamicization of Hindu Culture at Vijaynagara," *Journal of Asian Studies* 55, no. 4 (November 1996): 851–880. Wagoner discusses exchanges across Hindu-Muslim boundaries in the context of the Vijayanagara Empire in southern India as an expression of a "shared language" in which self-consciously Hindu elite adopted many aspects of the dress and lifestyle of their Islamic counterparts from adjacent and competing kingdoms.

29   Molly Emma Aitken, *The Intelligence of Tradition in Rajput Court Painting* (New Haven: Yale University Press, 2010).

30   Tony K. Stewart, "In Search of Equivalence: Conceiving Hindu-Muslim Encounter through Translation Theory," *History of Religions* (2001): 269–274. Also see Tony K. Stewart, "Alternate Structures of Authority: Satya Pir on the Frontiers of Bengal," in

Beyond Turk and Hindu: Rethinking Religious Identities in Islamicate South Asia, ed. David Gilmartin and Bruce B. Lawrence (Gainesville: University Press of Florida, 2000), 21–54.

31   Alka Patel and Karen Leonard, eds., "Introduction" in *Indo-Muslim Cultures in Transition* (Leiden: Brill, 2012), 6–7.

32   Crispin Branfoot, "Imperial Frontiers: Building Sacred Space in Sixteenth-Century South India," *Art Bulletin* 90, no. 2 (2008): 171–194.

33   Allison Busch, "Hidden in Plain View: Brajbhasha Poets at the Mughal Court," *Modern Asian Studies* 44, no. 2 (2010): 267–309.

34   Patel and Leonard, *Indo-Muslim Cultures in Transition*, 2–7.

35   In *Banaras: City of Light*, first published in 1982, Eck considers the city's religious geography and produces a narrative in which a material environment that was largely created in the eighteenth and nineteenth centuries merges with descriptions in Sanskrit texts including the *Kashikhand*. Eck's account runs parallel to Orientalist descriptions produced in the nineteenth century, in which assertions of the city's mythical antiquity were combined with descriptions of a contemporary city. Also see Jonathan P. Parry, *Death in Banaras* (Cambridge: Cambridge University Press, 1994). Parry's monograph is a valuable study of contemporary funerary practices in the city, although he ignores the historical developments that shaped them.

36   See, for instance, Ronald B. Inden, *Imagining India* (1990; reprint, Bloomington: Indiana University Press, 2000).

37   Eck, *Banaras: City of Light*; and Parry, *Death in Banaras*. See also Norbert Peabody, "Review of *Death in Banaras* by Jonathan P. Parry," *Modern Asian Studies* 30, no. 3 (1996): 698–701. Peabody cautions against depictions of an "ethnographic present" even as he lauds Parry for a "sympathetic" critique of Louis Dumont that he finds refreshing when contrasted against the "hostile" stances taken by many scholars of South Asian history and culture against Orientalizing positions.

38   For examples of the former, see Anthony D. King, *Colonial Urban Development* (London: Routledge and Kegan Paul, 1976). Also see Robert Grant Irving, *Indian Summer: Lutyens, Baker, and Imperial Delhi* (New Haven: Yale University Press, 1981). Irving describes the making of a new British capital in India without much attention to the opinions and reactions of the Indians who built, lived, worked in, and paid for the new capital.

39   Swati Chattopadhyay, *Representing Calcutta: Modernity, Nationalism, and the Colonial Uncanny* (London: Routledge, 2006); William J. Glover, *Making Lahore Modern* (Minneapolis: University of Minnesota Press, 2008); Preeti Chopra, *A Joint Enterprise: Indian Elites and the Making of British Bombay* (Minneapolis: University of Minnesota Press, 2011); and Jyoti Hosagrahar, *Indigenous Modernities: Negotiating Architecture and Urbanism* (London: Routledge, 2005). These scholars have analyzed colonial cities as products of the human agency of the colonizer as well as the colonized.

40   See Sandria B. Freitag, *Collective Action and Community: Public Arenas and the Emergence of Communalism in North India* (Berkeley: University of California Press, 1989), 6. Also see Sandria B. Freitag, ed., *Culture and Power in Banaras: Community, Performance, and Environment, 1800–1980* (Berkeley: University of California Press, 1989), 27–33.

41   Michael S. Dodson, ed., *Banaras: Urban Forms and Cultural Histories* (New Delhi: Routledge, 2011). Contributors to this edited volume explore a range of interventions in colonial Banaras. Also see Michael S. Dodson, *Orientalism, Empire, and National Culture: India, 1770–1880* (New York: Palgrave Macmillan, 2007).

42 James Fergusson, *History of Indian and Eastern Architecture* (London: John Murray, 1876); and Rajendralal Mitra, *Indo-Aryans: Contributions Towards the Elucidation of Their Ancient and Medieval History*, vols. 1 and 2 (London: Edward Stanford, 1881).

43 Pika Ghosh, *Temple to Love: Architecture and Devotion in Seventeenth-Century Bengal* (Bloomington: Indiana University Press, 2005). Ghosh examines the development of the *ratna* temple form in seventeenth-century Bengal as a response to the ritual demands of the new sect of Gaudiya Vaishnavism in a wider context in which Hindu and Muslim patrons coexisted and worked together in the political and economic realms. Also see Alka Patel, *Building Communities in Gujarat: Architecture and Society during the Twelfth through Fourteenth Centuries* (Leiden: Brill, 2004). Patel analyzes the simultaneous evolution of temple and mosque architecture in northwestern India during the twelfth, thirteenth, and fourteenth centuries, as the result of innovation and expansion through the new social and ritual demands made by Islam.

44 Richard M. Eaton, *A Social History of the Deccan, 1300–1761: Eight Indian Lives* (Cambridge: Cambridge University Press, 2005).

45 Postcolonial perspectives have built on the work of several historians of note, including Partha Chatterjee, *The Nation and Its Fragments* (Princeton: Princeton University Press, 1993); and Dipesh Chakrabarty, *Provincializing Europe: Postcolonial Thought and Historical Difference* (Princeton: Princeton University Press, 2000). Also see Sheldon Pollock, "Introduction," in *Forms of Knowledge in Early Modern Asia* (Durham: Duke University Press, 2011), 1. Pollock urges a scholarly focus on South Asia's precolonial histories.

46 Exceptions include Cynthia Talbot, "Inscribing the Other: Inscribing the Self: Hindu-Muslim Identities in Pre-colonial India," *Comparative Studies in Society and History* 37, no. 4 (October 1995): 692–722; and Romila Thapar, "Imagined Religious Communities? Ancient History and the Modern Search for a Hindu Identity," *Modern Asian Studies* 23, no. 2 (1989): 209–231.

47 Richard M. Eaton, *The Rise of Islam and the Bengal Frontier, 1204–1760* (1993; reprint, Berkeley: University of California Press, 1996), xxvi. Eaton's broader point is about the impossibility of compartmentalizing the subcontinent's past into distinct periods.

1. AUTHENTICITY AND PILGRIMAGE

1 T. K. Biswas, "Vestiges of the Past," in *Banaras: The City Revealed*, ed. George Michell and Rana P. B. Singh (Mumbai: Marg Publications, 2005), 46.

2 Thomas Watters, *On Yuan Chwang's Travels in India*, vol. 1 (1904; reprint, New York: AMS Press, 1971), 10–16.

3 Thomas Watters, *On Yuan Chwang's Travels in India*, vol. 2 (1905; reprint, New York: AMS Press, 1971), 46–47.

4 The ever-changing nature of Hindu belief between the twelfth and sixteenth centuries has most recently been explored by Andrew J. Nicholson, *Unifying Hinduism: Philosophy and Identity in Indian Intellectual History* (New York: Columbia University Press, 2010).

5 Diana Eck largely maintains this perspective on the *Kashikhand* in her work *Banaras: City of Light* (1982; reprint, New York: Columbia University Press, 1999), 22–23 and 85.

6 Kubernath Sukul, *Varanasi Vaibhav* (Patna: Bihar Rashtrabhasha Parishad, 1977), 278–280.

7   Sculptures from this period are on display in the galleries of the Bharat Kala Bhawan in Banaras as well as in the National Museum in New Delhi. Many of these are associated with distinct deities and belief systems, including Buddhism.

8   See Anne Feldhaus, *Connected Places: Religion, Pilgrimage, and Geographical Imagination in India* (New York: Palgrave Macmillan, 2003), 5–8. Feldhaus suggests that particularly in the context of pilgrimage and religious associations, the sacred region is an entity that is distinct from an administrative area or unit.

9   Currently these remain widely accepted explanations for Shiva's connection to the city.

10 K. V. Rangaswami Aiyangar, ed., *Krtyakalpataru of Bhatta Laksmidhara* (Baroda: Oriental Institute, 1942), lxxiv.

11 Jagdish Narayan Dubey, ed., *Kashirahasyam* (Varanasi: Adarsh Prakashan Mandir, 1984), 87–93.

12 Aiyangar, "Introduction," in *Krtyakalpataru*, xli and notes.

13 Ibid. Also see Hans T. Bakker and Harunaga Isaacson, eds., *Skandapurana: The Varanasi Cycle* (Groningen: Egbert Forsten, 2004), 48–54.

14 Bakker and Isaacson, *Skandapurana*, 48–54.

15 Ibid. Given these definitions, the *Krtyakalpataru* is simultaneously a *tirtha* text as well as a *nibandha*.

16 Bakker and Isaacson, *Skandapurana*, 70–79; also see Hermann Kulke and Dietman Rothermund, *A History of India* (1986; reprint, London: Routledge, 2006), 138–139.

17 Nicholson, *Unifying Hinduism*.

18 Motichandra, *Kashi Ka Itihas* (1962; reprint, Varanasi: Vishwavidyalaya Prakashan, 2003), 149. Motichandra presents his readers with a contradiction during Tughlaq rule, where he declares that despite "general atrocities" committed by Tughlaq rulers, the religious life of Banaras flourished in the thirteenth through the fifteenth centuries. He also describes sultanate-period mosques in Banaras that were built with spolia. The tombs at Bakariya *kund* in the contemporary city represent Sharqi interest in the city.

19 Klaus Rotzer, "Mosques and Tombs," in *Banaras: The City Revealed*, ed. George Michell and Rana P. B. Singh (Mumbai: Marg Publications, 2005), 51–55.

20 Bakker and Isaacson, *Skandapurana*, 81–82. In the *Ain-i-Akbari*, Abul Fazl Allami declared that Mahmud Ghazni's invasion of "Baranasi" in A.H. 410, disrupted the "old faith." See Abul Fazl Allami, *Ain-i-Akbari*, vol. 2, trans. H. S. Jarrett (1891; reprint, Calcutta: The Asiatic Society, 1993), 169–170.

21 Aiyangar, *Krtyakalpataru*, lxxi–lxxiii.

22 Ibid., lv, notes. In particular, Aiyangar surmises that authors of *nibandha* texts in the sixteenth century incorporated several new or "local" divinities in keeping with this practice.

23 Richard M. Eaton, "Temple Desecration and Indo-Muslim States," in *Beyond Turk and Hindu: Rethinking Religious Identities in Islamicate South Asia*, ed. David Gilmartin and Bruce B. Lawrence (Gainesville: University Press of Florida, 2000), 267.

24 Aiyangar, *Krtyakalpataru*, 37.

25 Ibid., 93.

26 Ibid., "Appendix B, Classified Index of Tirthas: *Varanasikshetrakundani*," 268–272.

27 Sukul, *Varanasi Vaibhav*, 130–148; and Eck, *Banaras: City of Light*, 131 and 347.

28 See Michael W. Meister and M. A. Dhaky, eds. *Encyclopedia of Indian Temple Architecture*, vol. 2 (parts 1 and 2), *North India* (Princeton: Princeton University Press,

1986). Also see Susan L. Huntington, *The Art of Ancient India: Buddhist, Hindu, Jain* (1985; reprint, Boston: Weatherhill, 2001). In this extensive and geographically comprehensive survey, Huntington does not mention Banaras or its vicinity as a site for monumental temple construction.

29 Pandit Damodar, *Uktivyaktiprakarana*, ed. Jinvijaya (Bombay: Singhi Jain Shastra Shikshapith, 1953).

30 Ibid., 21.

31 Ibid., 11, 29.

32 Alexander Cunningham, *Report of Tours in the Gangetic Provinces from Badaon to Bihar in 1875–76 and 1877–78* (Calcutta: Archaeological Survey of India, 1880), 118; and A. Fuhrer, *The Sharqi Architecture of Jaunpur: With Notes on Zafarabad, Sahet-Mahet, and Other Places in the North-Western Provinces and Oudh* (London: Trubner and Company, 1889), 51. Also see Motichandra, *Kashi Ka Itihas*, 149–150. Motichandra suggests that the destruction of the Padmeshwur temple by the Sharqi sultans of Jaunpur may have also accompanied the destruction of an earlier fifteenth-century Vishweshwur temple.

33 For dates and circumstances of Raziyyat's reign, see Kulke and Rothermund, *History of India*, 168–169. Local narratives ascribe the mosque to a prominent but lay (in some accounts, Sharqi royal or noble) female patron in the city.

34 Abul Fazl Allami, *Ain-i-Akbari*, vol. 2, 169–170. Abul Fazl does mention a major temple at Banaras, although he does not mention either Vishweshwur or Padmeshwur by name.

35 Vacaspati Misra, *Tirthacintamani*, ed. Kamalakrishna Smrititirtha (1912; reprint, Calcutta: The Asiatic Society, 1992), 360.

36 Ramkrishna Gorji Dikshit, *Kashiyatraprakash* (Banaras: Bengali Shah, ca. 1890), 9–10.

37 This tradition developed sometime after the *Kashikhand* was compiled since its authors do not mention this pilgrimage. Aiyangar, *Krtyakalpataru*, xlii and notes. Aiyangar also notes that although the tradition was incorporated into some later recessions of the *Skandapurana*, it certainly developed after Lakshmidhara had completed the *Krtyakalpataru*.

38 The *Gurucharitra* is a ca. fifteenth- and sixteenth-century text originally composed in Marathi and Kannada as part of a regional religious tradition. It was translated into Sanskrit by Vasudevananda Saraswati (1854–1914). This text includes one of the earliest references to the Panchkroshi pilgrimage at Banaras. See *Gurucharitra*, trans. K. V. R. Rao (Bombay: Samartha Vishwa Kalyan Kendra, 1995), 186–187.

39 *Gurucharitra*, 187.

40 Jorg Gengnagel, *Visualized Texts: Sacred Spaces, Spatial Texts, and the Religious Cartography of Banaras* (Wiesbaden: Harrassowitz-Verlag, 2011), 43.

41 A number of nineteenth-century authors described the "great antiquity" of this temple. See, for instance, "Benares, Past and Present," *Calcutta Review* 80 (1865): 253–294, 291.

42 This remains an approximate number. Authors of various lists and guidebooks compiled during the nineteenth century mention between seventy-six and eighty-seven independent entities along the route.

43 This deity was not mentioned in the *Kashikhand* but was incorporated within later guidebooks for the Antargriha route. See Karunapati Tripathi, "Bhumika," in *Srikashikhandaha*, vol. 1 (Varanasi: Sampurnananda Sanskrit Vishwavidayalaya, 1991), 4.

1   Banarasidas, *Ardhakathanak (A Half Story)*, trans. Rohini Chowdhury (New Delhi: Penguin India, 2009), 99–101.

2   For the Mughal relationship with Sufism and the Chishtis, as well as Akbar's inclusive policies, see Muzaffar Alam, "The Mughals, the Sufi Shaikhs, and the Formation of the Akbari Dispensation," *Modern Asian Studies* 43, no. 1, *Expanding Frontiers in South Asian and World History: Essays in Honour of John F. Richards* (January 2009): 157–166. For more on Akbar's beliefs and the resulting controversy among the Islamic clerical establishment, see A. Azfar Moin, *The Millennial Sovereign: Sacred Kingship and Sainthood in Islam* (New York: Columbia University Press, 2012), 138–146.

3   For more on the nature of relationships between the imperial Mughal state and its diverse regional participants, see Kumkum Chatterjee, "Cultural Flows and Cosmopolitanism in Mughal India: The Bishnupur Kingdom," *Indian Economic Social History Review* 46 (2009): 147–182.

4   State support for Sanskrit learning, particularly in the sixteenth and seventeenth centuries, is apparent in the large number of texts produced under Mughal patronage, where names of Muslim patrons are directly mentioned. Jatindra Bimal Chaudhuri, *Muslim Patronage to Sanskritic Learning*, part 1 (Delhi: Idarah-i-Adabiyat-I Delli, 1954), 91. As Chaudhuri explains, this occurred through direct support for scholars working in the classical fields of poetry, astronomy, and philosophy. A number of Muslim patrons commissioned projects where Sanskrit works were translated into Persian, Arabic, and several vernacular languages. Several elite Muslims became Sanskrit scholars and composed Sanskrit poetry besides writing commentaries of Sanskrit scholarship in Arabic and Persian. For recent scholarship on the Sanskrit-Persian exchange as well as Indo-Persian interactions and the Mughal sociopolitical climate, see Audrey Truschke, *Culture of Encounters: Sanskrit at the Mughal Court* (New York: Columbia University Press, 2016), and Rajeev Kinra, *Writing Self, Writing Empire: Chandar Bhan Brahman and the Cultural World of the Indo-Persian State Secretary* (Oakland: University of California Press, 2015).

5   P. K. Gode, ed., "Bernier and Kavindracarya at the Mughal Court," in *Studies in Indian Literary History*, vol. 2 (Bombay: Singhi Jain Sastra Sikshapıth, 1954), 364–379. For more on Mughal politics and alliances across several generations, see Munis D. Faruqui, *The Princes of the Mughal Empire, 1504–1719* (Cambridge: Cambridge University Press, 2012).

6   Francois Bernier, *Travels in the Mogul Empire*, ed. Archibald Constable (1891; reprint, New Delhi: S. Chand and Company, 1968), 342–343. Also see Jean-Batiste Tavernier, *The Six Voyages of John Batista Tavernier (Book III)* (London: John Starkey, 1678), 175–176; and *Travels in India in Two Volumes*, vol. 2, ed. and trans. V. Ball (London: Macmillan and Company, 1889), 234.

7   Rosalind O'Hanlon, "Speaking from Siva's Temple: Banaras Scholar Households and the Brahman 'Ecumene' of Mughal India," *Religious Cultures in Early Modern India: New Perspectives*, ed. Rosalind O'Hanlon and David Washbrook (New York: Routledge, 2012), 133. For more on the Mughal state and the adaptation of its forms and rituals in response to its neighbors as well as its subjects, see Muzaffar Alam and Sanjay Subrahmanyam, *Writing the Mughal World: Studies on Culture and Politics* (New York: Columbia University Press, 2011).

8   Rosalind O'Hanlon and Christopher Minkowski, "What Makes People Who They Are? Pandit Networks and the Problem of Livelihoods in Early Modern Western India," *Indian Economic and Social History Review* 45, no. 3 (2008): 386–392. O'Hanlon and

Minkowski discuss the connections between the Panch-dravid (including Maharashtra) Brahmans in Banaras and the Deccan in the seventeenth century.

9   Christopher Minkowski, "Advaita Vedanta in Early Modern History," in *Religious Cultures in Early Modern India*, ed. Rosalind O'Hanlon and David Washbrook (London: Routledge, 2012), 85.

10 The *puranas* were accepted as a part of the *Dharmashastra* (treatises on Hindu jurisprudence) at this time. See Lawrence McCrea, "Hindu Jurisprudence and Scriptural Hermeneutics," in *Hinduism and Law: An Introduction*, ed. Timothy Lubin, Donald R. Davis, and Jayanth K. Krishnan (Cambridge: Cambridge University Press, 2010), 135–136. For a discussion on the flexible nature of the *puranas* that made them available for interpretation as well as confluences of opinion and scholarly authority among prominent Shaiva and Vaishnava intellectuals in Banaras, see Christopher Minkowski, "I'll Wash Your Mouth Out with My Boot: A Guide to Philological Argument in Early Modern Banaras," in *Epic and Argument in Sanskrit Literary History: Essays in Honor of Robert Goldman*, ed. Sheldon Pollock (Delhi: Manohar, 2010), 126–132.

11 K. V. Rangaswami Aiyangar, "Appendix F: Bibliography of Treatises on Tirtha," in *Krtyakalpataru of Bhatta Laksmidhara* (Baroda: Oriental Institute, 1942), 293–294. The shifting and changing nature of this landscape is apparent: several of the *tirthas* that the seventeenth-century scholar Mitra Misra mentioned in his *Tirtha Prakash* (1620) were not mentioned by Laxmidhara when he compiled the *Krtyakalpataru*. See Aiyangar, "Introduction," in *Krtyakalpataru*, lxx.

12 See Bhattoji's composition *Bhattojidikshitkruta Tristhalisetuh* in the compendium by Suryanarayan Shukla, ed., *Bhattojidikshitkruta Tristhalisetuh, Nageshbhattakrut Tirthendushekharaha, Sureshwaracharyakrut Kashimokshavicharaha* (Varanasi: Sampurnananda Sanskrit Vishwavidyalaya, 1997), 35.

13 Aiyangar, *Krtyakalpataru*, lxxiii.

14 Interestingly, as the intellectual force behind the Mughal Vishweshwur temple, Narayan Bhatt made no mention of either an Adi-Vishweshwur temple or its memory.

15 Vacaspati Misra, *Tirthacintamani*, ed. Kamalakrishna Smrititirtha (1912; reprint, Calcutta: The Asiatic Society, 1992), 360.

16 Narayan Bhatt, *Tristhalisetuh*, ed. R. Gokhale and H. N. Apte (Pune: Anandashram, 1915), 208; and Aiyangar, *Krtyakalpataru*, lxxiv–lxxv.

17 *Kamsavadha*, a play with Vaishnava sensibilities, was performed in the temple courtyard ca. 1589. See Julius Eggeling, ed., *Catalogue of the Sanskrit Manuscripts in Library of the India Office*, part 7 (London: Gilbert and Rivington, 1891), page no. 1591, especially manuscript no. 4175 (copied 1800). Also see Motichandra, *Kashi Ka Itihas* (1962; reprint, Varanasi: Vishwavidyalaya Prakashan, 2003), 162.

18 Bhatt, *Tristhalisetuh*, 103. Also see Hans T. Bakker and Harunaga Isaacson, *Skandapurana: The Varanasi Cycle* (Groningen: Egbert Forsten, 2004), 50.

19 Bhatt, *Tristhalisetuh*, 142–148.

20 Ibid., 153–169.

21 Ibid. Bhatt paid attention to an area that corresponds to the contemporary extents of the Antargriha zone. However, the bulk of sites that he listed were located in the Brahmanal and Siddheshwari areas. An additional cluster of sites was located in the urban areas adjoining Brahma ghat. Several sources indicate that this was a neighborhood favored by Brahmins from the Maratha regions at least since the sixteenth century.

22 Ibid., 101.

23 Ibid., 102.

24 Ibid., 158 and 161.

25 Jorg Gengnagel, *Visualized Texts: Sacred Spaces, Spatial Texts, and the Religious Cartography of Banaras* (Wiesbaden: Harrassowitz Verlag, 2011), 43.

26 Bhatt, *Tristhalisetuh*, 142–148.

27 Ibid., 167–168.

28 Ibid., 133–138.

29 Ibid., 161–177.

30 For more on Sawai Jai Singh II's life and reign, see Jadunath Sarkar, *A History of Jaipur, 1503–1938* (Hyderabad: Orient Longman, 1984), 151–154 and 156–228.

31 *Tarah Kashijiki* (pilgrimage *tarah*), map no. 241, in Gopal Narayan Bahura and Chandramani Singh, *Catalogue of Historical Documents in Kapad-Dwara Jaipur: Maps and Plans* (Jaipur: Maharaja of Jaipur, 1990), 117–118. I refer to this map as the "pilgrimage *tarah*" to distinguish it from other maps also titled *Tarah Kashijiki* (Map of Kashi).

32 "Pilgrimage *tarah*," map no. 241, in Bahura and Singh, *Catalogue of Historical Documents in Kapad-Dwara Jaipur: Maps and Plans*, 117–118.

33 *Tarah Kashijiki* (survey *tarah* 191), map no. 191, in Bahura and Singh, *Catalogue of Historical Documents in Kapad-Dwara Jaipur: Maps and Plans*, 105–107.

34 This list is consistently more extensive in eighteenth-century manuscripts as well as in twentieth-century printed editions of this text. It is possible, however, that in a manner similar to the textual history of the Panchkroshi route in the *Kashirahasya*, the list of shrines was more limited in manuscripts from the sixteenth century and earlier.

35 James Prinsep, *The City of Bunarus*, 1822, British Library, London, Maps, Accession no. 53345. (6). Prinsep's mapping exercise included the extents of the Mughal city as well as the temples that comprised the Antargriha pilgrimage circuit.

36 *Tarah Kashijiki* (survey *tarah* 191), map no. 191, in Bahura and Singh, *Catalogue of Historical Documents in Kapad-Dwara Jaipur: Maps and Plans*, 105–107, and *Tarah Shrikashijiki* (survey *tarah* 183), map no. 183, 104.

37 *Tarah Kashijiki* (survey *tarah* 191), map no. 191, in Bahura and Singh, *Catalogue of Historical Documents in Kapad-Dwara Jaipur: Maps and Plans*, 105–107.

38 Ibid. and *pilgrimage panorama*, ca. 1700, map no. 138, Sawai Man Singh II Museum, Jaipur.

39 Prinsep, *The City of Bunarus*.

40 *Tarah Kashijiki* (survey *tarah* 191), map no. 191, in Bahura and Singh, *Catalogue of Historical Documents in Kapad-Dwara Jaipur: Maps and Plans*, 105–107; and *Man Mandir*, map no. 130,
Sawai Man Singh II Museum, Jaipur.

41 Stephen Blake, *Shahjahanabad: The Sovereign City in Mughal India, 1639–1739* (1991; reprint, Cambridge: Cambridge University Press, 2002), 44–51. Blake examines the seventeenth-century Mughal capital as a microcosm for the empire, where patronage defined urban form, the urban economy, and politics. This remains one of the few dedicated studies of the Mughal capital.

42 *Tarah Kashijiki* (survey *tarah* 191), map no. 191, in Bahura and Singh, *Catalogue of Historical Documents in Kapad Dwara*, 105–107.

43 H. Blochmann, trans., *The Ain-i-Akbari of Abul Fazl Allami*, vol. 1 (1873; reprint, Calcutta: The Asiatic Society of Bengal, 1993), 347–348. Abul Fazl describes the circumstances under which the alliance between the Mughals and Kacchawahas was formed as well as the foundations of familial and political ties that were sustained over

several generations.

44 The Amber court owned urban property in several Mughal cities, including a suburb of Shahjahanabad also called Jaisinghpura. See Blake, *Shahjahanabad*, 58.

45 *Man Mandir*, map no. 130, Sawai Man Singh II Museum, Jaipur (ca. 1760). The caption on this map merely reads as *pura*.

46 Blochmann, *Ain-i-Akbari of Abul Fazl Allami*, vol. 1, 449–450. Rao Surjan Hada was granted a *mansab* (troops) of two thousand and was made governor of Chunar (near Banaras) in the twentieth regnal year. Also see *pilgrimage panorama*, map no. 138, Sawai Man Singh II Museum, Jaipur. This urban pattern may also have been extended to the vicinity near Bundiparkota ghat on the riverfront, where Rao Surjan built a *haveli*. See also James Tod, *Annals and Antiquities of Rajasthan, in Three Volumes*, ed. William Crooke (London: Oxford University Press, 1920), vol. 3, 1482–1483. Tod recollects that the Mughal emperor Akbar granted the Hadas of Bundi "a residence at the sacred city of Kasi, possessing that privilege so dear to the Rajput, the right of sanctuary, which is maintained to this day."

47 Imperial *farmans* and other documents in possession of the Jangambadi *muth*. Also see First Appeal Number 58 of 1934, between Sri Mad Jagat Guru, Sri Mahanth Mallikarjun Swami Jangam alias Sri Mahanth Panch Akshar Shiva-Acharya Maha Swami Mahanth, and Nishikant Banerji and others, in the High Court of Judicature at Allahabad. Record of Proceedings.

48 Ibid.

49 *Tarah Kashijiki* (survey *tarah* 191), map no. 191, in Bahura and Singh, *Catalogue of Historical Documents in Kapad-Dwara Jaipur: Maps and Plans*, 105–107. For an account of Bir Singh Deo's association with Jahangir, see Blochmann, *Ain-i-Akbari of Abul Fazl Allami*, vol. 1, 509. For more on Bir Singh Deo's patronage for religious building, see Heidi Pauwels, "A Tale of Two Temples: Mathura's Kesavadeva and Orchha's Chaturbhujadeva," in *Religious Cultures in Early Modern India*, ed. Rosalind O'Hanlon and David Washbrook (London: Routledge), 146–167.

50 Muzaffar Alam and Sanjay Subrahmanyam, *Indo-Persian Travels in the Age of Discoveries, 1400–1800* (Cambridge: Cambridge University Press, 2007), 140.

51 Richard M. Eaton, *The Rise of Islam and the Bengal Frontier, 1204–1760* (1993; reprint, Berkeley: University of California Press, 1996), 228–267. Eaton describes the kinds of patronage that the Mughal state in Bengal provided to temples and shrines in the seventeenth and eighteenth centuries.

52 P. K. Gode, "Bernier and Kavindracarya Sarasvati at the Mughal Court," 364–379.

53 Francois Bernier, *Travels in the Mogul Empire*, second edition, ed. Archibald Constable and trans. Irving Brock (1891; reprint, New Delhi: S. Chand and Company, 1972), 342–343. Also see Gode, "Bernier and Kavindracarya Sarasvati at the Mughal Court."

54 Ibid. Bernier supposed that these views were being expressed to appease his Christian beliefs and sentiments. Since Kavindracharya had been a mentor to the Mughal prince Dara Shukoh, it is more likely that these views were formed through exchanges with Islamic, particularly Sufi philosophers and scholars.

55 Most foreign travel accounts describe journeys by boat along the Ganges River. They include accounts by Ralph Fitch, Francois Bernier (*Travels in the Mogul Empire*), and Jean-Baptiste Tavernier (*Six Voyages*), among others.

56 J. Horton Ryley, *Ralph Fitch, England's Pioneer to India* (London: T. Fisher Unwin, 1899), 103–109.

57   *Girvanpadamanjari* and *Girvanavanmanjari*, ed. Umakant Premanand Shah (Baroda: Oriental Institute, 1960), 2. I also observed this settlement pattern during my own survey of the city conducted in 2004 and 2005.

58   *Man Mandir*, map no. 130, Sawai Man Singh II Museum, Jaipur.

59   This was the case well into the last decades of the eighteenth century. For instance, one Jewan Ram owned part of the embankment of the Dharhara mosque on Panchganga ghat. Regional Archives, Allahabad, Duncan Records, Basta no. 96, Book no. 180, Proceedings of the Committee for the Local Improvement in the City of Varanasi, 1823–1829, Minutes for meeting held on May 29, 1824.

60   See Catherine B. Asher, *Architecture of Mughal India* (Cambridge: Cambridge University Press, 1992). Architectural historians agree that despite influences from multiple sources, Mughal art and architecture reflected a unique aesthetic.

61   The year 1600 as the date for the *haveli*'s construction is also accepted by the Archaeological Survey of India as stated on an official sign at the Man Mandir.

62   For more of Man Singh's efforts at self-fashioning, see Allison Busch, "Portrait of a Raja in a Badshah's World: Amrit Rai's Biography of Man Singh," *Journal of the Economic and Social History of the Orient* 55, no. 2–3 (2012): 287–328.

63   Catherine B. Asher, "Sub-Imperial Palaces: Power and Authority in Mughal India," *Ars Orientalis* 23 (1993): 286–287.

64   Kumkum Chatterjee, "Cultural Flows and Cosmopolitanism in Mughal India: The Bishnupur Kingdom," *Indian Economic Social History Review* 46, no. 2 (2009): 164–166. Chatterjee suggests that Vaishnavism, particularly the strand from Brindavan, provided a route into the cosmopolitan Mughal world for regional rulers such as the Mallas of Bishnupur, who were new entrants into the Mughal political and cultural sphere.

65   Jean-Baptiste Tavernier, *The Six Voyages of John Batista Tavernier (Book III)* (London: John Starkey, 1678), 176. Tavernier mentions the Kanganwali *haveli* as being adjacent to the Bindu Madhav temple.

66   Tavernier, *The Six Voyages of John Batista Tavernier*, 176. For more on the Mughal approach to European globes and cartographic techniques, see Ebba Koch, "The Symbolic Possession of the World: European Cartography in Mughal Allegory and History Painting," *Journal of the Economic and Social History of the Orient* 55 (2012): 547–580. Also see Sumathi Ramaswamy, "Conceit of the Globe in Mughal Visual Practice," *Comparative Studies in Society and History* 49, no. 4 (2007): 751–782.

67   Chandrashekhar, *Surjancharitamahakavyam*, ed. and trans. Chandradhar Sharma (Banaras: Banaras Hindu University, 1952).

68   Cynthia Talbot, "Justifying Defeat: A Rajput Perspective on the Age of Akbar," *Journal of the Economic and Social History of the Orient* 55 (2012): 354–360. Talbot discusses in some detail the simultaneously pious and kingly persona cultivated by Rao Surjan after his retirement from service as a Mughal subordinate.

69   Chandrashekhar, *Surjancharitamahakavyam*, 218.

70   *Panorama of Bundiparkota ghat*, ca. 1650, map no. 7, *Kapad Dwara*, Sawai Man Singh II Museum, Jaipur.

71   G. N. Sharma, *Mewar and the Mughal Emperors* (Agra: Shiv Lal Agarwala and Co. Ltd., 1954), 149–152. For early state formation in Mewar, see Nandini Sinha Kapur, *State Formation in Rajasthan: Mewar during the Seventh–Fifteenth Centuries* (New Delhi: Manohar Publishers, 2002).

72   Ebba Koch, "The Baluster Column: A European Motif in Mughal Architecture and Its Meaning," *Journal of the Warburg and Courtauld Institute* 45 (1982): 251–262. Koch

speculates on the origins of this column and mentions the changing circumstances and contexts for its use between the seventeenth and eighteenth centuries.

73 Giles H. R. Tillotson, *Rajput Palaces: The Development of an Architectural Style, 1450–1750* (New Haven: Yale University Press, 1987), 105–115.

74 Mewadi tradition maintains that the mansion was built in 1641, during the reign of Maharana Jagat Singh I (r. 1628–1652). For more on Jagat Singh I, see Shyamaldas, *Veer Vinod: Mewad ka Itihas, Volume II*, first edition (Udaipur: Rajyantralaya, 1886), 315–328. However, the Rana Mahal is not represented in pilgrimage maps from the seventeenth century. The earliest depictions include Joseph Tieffenthaler's panorama, published in 1785, and riverfront views from the mid and late eighteenth century. See Joseph Tieffenthaler, *Des Pater Joseph Tieffenthaler's Historische, Geographische Beschreibung von Hindustan* (Berlin: Bendem Berausgeber, 1785), plate VII.1.

75 *Farman* issued by the emperor Aurangzeb, dated 1658–1659, Bharat Kala Bhavan, Accession no., Banaras–1.

76 See Gopal Narayan Bahura and Chandramani Singh, *Catalogue of Historical Documents in Kapad Dwara, Jaipur* (Jaipur: Jaigarh Public Charitable Trust, 1988), document nos. 203 and 204, 30. Banaras is mentioned as "Muhammadabad" in these property transfer and sale deeds.

77 Saqi Mustad Khan, *Maasir-i-Alamgiri*, trans. Jadunath Sarkar (1947; reprint, Calcutta: Royal Asiatic Society of Bengal, 1986), 55. In this text, 1669 is mentioned as the year for the dismantling of the Vishweshwur temple, so it is possible that the Bindu Madhav temple may have been destroyed around the same time.

78 See documents in possession of Jangambadi *muth*.

79 See the inscription over the doorway of the refectory in the Kumarswamy *muth*. In some later interpretations of the legend, the land for the *muth* was granted by Dara Shukoh and others by Aurangzeb. The legend, however, merely mentions a "padushah."

80 Kumarsami Thambiran, *Saint Kumaraguruparar and the Two Great Mutts Associated with Him* (Tirupanandal: Sri Kasi Mutt, 1997), 8.

81 Austerity and monumentality have been features of Saiva *muth* architecture in South Asia since at least the ninth century of the Common Era. See Tamara I. Sears, *Worldly Gurus and Spiritual Kings: Architecture and Asceticism in Medieval India* (New Haven: Yale University Press, 2014).

82 Dara Shukoh, who is usually credited with supporting the *muth* and temple, was captured and executed by Aurangzeb in 1659, more than two decades before work on the building began in 1695.

83 Kacchawaha surveyors identified the temple as the "Mahadev of the Deccanis," suggesting that the Kedar temple lay outside of direct Mughal-Rajput patronage networks and religious ideas. *Tarah Kashijiki* (survey *tarah* 191), map no. 191, in Bahura and Singh, *Catalogue of Historical Documents in Kapad-Dwara Jaipur: Maps and Plans*, 105–107.

84 For more on Aurangzeb's political alliances as a prince, see Faruqui, *Princes of the Mughal Empire*, 168–178.

85 Motichandra, *Kashi Ka Itihas*, 152. Klaus Rotzer suggests that military mosques and barracks were located to the north of the Antargriha zone. See Klaus Rotzer, "Mosques and Tombs," in *Banaras: The City Revealed*, ed. George Michell and Rana P. B. Singh (Mumbai: Marg Publications, 2005), 51.

86 Shonaleeka Kaul, *Imagining the Urban: Sanskrit and the City in Early India* (New York: Seagull Books, 2011), 235.

87   *Gurucharitra*, trans. K. V. R. Rao (Bombay: Samartha Vishwa Kalyan Kendra, 1995), 103–106 and 220–226.

88   *Shrivenkatadhvaripraneetah Viswagunadarasachampuh*, trans. Surendranath Shastri (reprint, Varanasi: Chaukhamba Vidya Bhawan, 2011), 82–84. Also cited in Shah, *Girvanpadamanjari* and *Girvanavanmanjari*, 23.

89   Differences in customs, diet, spoken language, and other practices between the Gangaputra, Bengali, and Panch-dravid Brahmins were articulated well into the eighteenth and early nineteenth centuries. Their distinct patronage networks survive through the present day. This regional diversity is also suggested by the author of the *Shrivenkatadhvaripraneetah Viswagunadarasachampuh*, 86.

90   Shah, "Introduction," in *Girvanpadamanjari* and *Girvanavanmanjari*, 6 and notes. The reference is to the siege of Gingee (1691–1697) led by Zulfikar Khan for Aurangzeb. The *sanyasin* was supposed to fight in this battle for the Mughals.

91   Shah, "Girvanpadamanjari," in *Girvanpadamanjari* and *Girvanavanmanjari*, 1–2.

92   Ibid. For instance, the site known as Jarasandha ghat was renamed as Meer ghat after its acquisition by Meer Rustam Ali, the regional official of the Awadh Nawabs, who built his fortress-palace there.

93   Ibid.

94   *Tarah Kashijiki* (survey *tarah* 191), map no. 191, in Bahura and Singh, *Catalogue of Historical Documents in Kapad-Dwara Jaipur: Maps and Plans*, 105–107.

95   This practice continued well into the eighteenth century. See, for instance, Lieutenant Colonel Garstin, *An Account of the Hindoo Temple of Vissvisshoor or Bissinaut, at Benares* (London: T. Bensley, 1800). Garstin compiled his report in 1781, shortly after its successor, the "new" temple, had been built. Other accounts in the eighteenth and nineteenth centuries also suggest that the site of the dismantled Vishweshwur temple was consistently venerated. See Vijayaram Sen, *Tirthamangala*, ca. 1768–1769, manuscript (Calcutta: Bangiya Sahitya Parishad, 1905), 115. Also see Jadunath Sarvadhikari, *Tirthabhramana* (Calcutta, 1915), 441.

96   *Tarah Kashijiki* (survey *tarah* 191), map no. 191, in Bahura and Singh, *Catalogue of Historical Documents in Kapad-Dwara Jaipur: Maps and Plans*, 105–107.

97   The Amber rulers may indeed have commissioned the survey of the Antargriha zone with tacit imperial permission.

98   Hermann Kulke and Dietmar Rothermund, *A History of India* (London: Routledge, 2004), 127–146.

99   This designation is distinct from usages of the term as an architectural style preferred by colonial officials for institutional buildings as well as by rulers of "princely states" in the nineteenth century. For more on the subject, see Thomas R. Metcalf, *An Imperial Vision: Indian Architecture and Britain's Raj* (1982; reprint, New Delhi: Oxford University Press, 2002). Metcalf's book examines the creation of deliberately syncretic architectural styles by the colonizers that were meant to appeal to the colonized in South Asia.

100 The temples of Khajuraho that are now perceived as representative of the classic form of the Nagara (northern Indian) temple were largely sidelined and only "discovered" in 1838 by T. S. Burt who reported finding seven temples. See Editor's Report, "Notice of an Inscription on a slab discovered in February 1838, by Capt. T. S. Burt, Bengal Engineers, in Bundelkhund, near Chhatarpur," *Journal of the Asiatic Society*, no. 87 (March 1839): 163. Alexander Cunningham subsequently studied these temples in detail between 1852

and 1885. See Krishna Deva, "Key-note Address," in *Khajuraho in Perspective,* ed. Kalyan Kumar Chakravarty, Maruti Nandan Tiwari, and Kamal Giri (Bhopal: Commissioner Archaeology and Museums Madhya Pradesh, 1994), xxi.

101 The professional and scholarly reputation of the fifteenth-century master-mason Sutradhar Mandan was based in his success at just such a combination of talents. Mandan demonstrated a capacity to interpret a relevant past in the treatises he composed while creating innovative designs for contemporary religious and secular buildings. For building treatises attributed to Sutradhar Mandan, see *Rajavallabhamandanam*, trans. Shailaja Pandey (Varanasi: Chaukhamba Surbharati Prakashan, 2001). Also see Sutradhar Mandan, *Devtamurtiprakaranam*, trans. Bhagvandas Jain and Rima Hooja (Jaipur: Prakrit Bharati Academy, 1999).

102 Catherine B. Asher, "The Architecture of Raja Man Singh: A Study of Sub-imperial Patronage," in *Architecture in Medieval India*, ed. Monica Juneja (New Delhi: Permanent Black, 2001), 374–375. Also see Asher, *Architecture of Mughal India*, 68.

103 Catherine B. Asher and Cynthia Talbot, *India before Europe* (Cambridge: Cambridge University Press, 2006), 208.

104 Tavernier, *Six Voyages of John Batista Tavernier*, 178. Tavernier also describes figural sculpture on the exterior of this temple. Since the exterior of the Govind Dev temple is entirely aniconic, his descriptions are best taken with a pinch of salt

105 The deity "Bindumadhav" is included in the *Kashikhand*. However, it has a relatively insignificant role in this text. See Karunapati Tripathi, *Srikashikhandaha*, vol. 3 (Varanasi: Sampurnananda Sanskrit Vishwavidayalaya, 1991), 215–219.

106 Tavernier, *Six Voyages of John Batista Tavernier*, 175–177. In contrast to the public role of the Bindu Madhav temple, the Ram temple that was housed within the Kanganwali *haveli* had an institutional identity that would also explain its nonmonumental appearance. In the context of this discussion, see Catherine Asher, "Mapping Hindu-Muslim Identities through the Architecture of Shahjahanabad and Jaipur," in *Beyond Turk and Hindu: Rethinking Religious Identities in Islamicate South Asia*, ed. David Gilmartin and Bruce B. Lawrence (Gainesville: University of Florida, 2000), 121–148. Asher has raised important questions regarding the nonmonumental appearance of seventeenth-century Hindu temples in Western India and has questioned concealment from marauding Muslim armies as a motive.

107 Tavernier, *Six Voyages of John Batista Tavernier*, 175.

108 Bhatt, *Tristhalisetuh*, 188–190. Also see O'Hanlon, "Speaking from Siva's Temple," 133.

109 This was later marked by the Adi-Vishweshwur temple by the turn of the eighteenth century. Interestingly, there is no surviving tradition of *mandapas* around the Adi-Vishweshwur temple.

110 Mitra Misra, *Tirthaprakasha of Viramitrodaya*, ed. Pandit Vishnu Prasad (Benares: Chowkhamba Sanskrit series, 1917), 190–194.

111 See the inscription above the doorway of the refectory in this *muth*.

112 For more on the deeply held sanctity and history of Shiva Nataraja, see Padma Kaimal, "Shiva Nataraja: Multiple Meanings of an Icon," in *A Companion to Asian Art and Architecture*, ed. Rebecca M. Brown and Deborah S. Hutton (Chichester, UK: John Wiley and Sons, 2013), 471–485.

113 A street façade was added sometime during the late eighteenth century. For this the designers employed a late-Mughal architectural language then popular in the city.

114 *Tarah Kashijiki* (survey *tarah* 191), map no. 191, in Bahura and Singh, *Catalogue of Historical Documents in Kapad-Dwara Jaipur: Maps and Plans*, 105–107.

115 P. K. Gode, "The Asvamedha Performed by Sevai Jaysing of Amber (1699–1744 A.D.)," in *Studies in Indian Literary History*, vol. 2 (Bombay: Singhi Jain Sastra Sikshapith, 1954) 292–306. For more on Sawai Jai Singh II and his patronage of temple architecture, see Catherine B. Asher, "Amber and Jaipur: Temples in a Changing State," in *Stones in the Sand: The Architecture of Rajasthan*, ed. Giles Tillotson (Mumbai: Marg Publications, 2001), 68–77.

116 Susan Johnson-Roehr, "Centering the Chārbāgh: The Mughal Garden as Design Module for the Jaipur City Plan," *Journal for the Society of Architectural Historians* 72, no. 1 (2013): 28–47.

117 *Tarah Shrikashijiki* (survey *tarah* 183), map no. 183, in Bahura and Singh, *Catalogue of Historical Documents in Kapad-Dwara Jaipur: Maps and Plans*, 104. Since this map is basically an assessment of Todarmal's properties, the Kacchawaha rulers most likely intended to purchase land from his family. Its location, in all likelihood, was near the Adi-Vishweshwur temple.

118 Asher and Talbot, *India before Europe*, 231. Asher and Talbot suggest that Aurangzeb's motivations in ordering the destruction were largely political and his policies were actually intended as responses to acts of political dissension within his regime.

119 Such juxtaposition became common for several sites, including the Alamgiri mosque and the Krittivaseshwur temple. See Prinsep, *The City of Bunarus*. Prinsep depicts the rebuilt versions of the Bindu Madhav as well as the Krittivaseshwur temples on his map.

120 Members of the Peshwa family at Pune frequently undertook pilgrimages to Banaras. *Selections from the Peshwa Daftar 2: Letters and Dispatches Relating to the Battle of Panipat, 1747–1761* (Bombay: Government Central Press, 1930), 85–86. See letter no. 66, dated October 15, 1756, written to Sagunabai of the Peshwa family when she was visiting Banaras; *Selections from the Peshwa Daftar 9: Bajirao and His Family, 1720–1740* (Bombay: Government Central Press, 1931), 10–12. See letter no. 14, dated January 5, 1736, written by Vasudev Joshi while returning from a pilgrimage to Banaras. In the same volume, see also letter no. 16, dated April 1736, wherein Narayan Dikshit Patankar, the Peshwa's spiritual mentor, refers to Maratha Brahmins resident in Banaras.

121 Tripathi, "Bhumika," in *Srikashikhandaha*, vol. 1, 4. As Tripathi also remarks, this deity is not mentioned in the *Kashikhand*.

122 *Pilgrimage pata*, ca. 1700, National Museum, New Delhi, Accession no. 56.59/58. The vertical format of this painting from Mewar suggests Jain influences. For more on the tradition of the vertical Jain pilgrimage *pata*, see Sridhar Andhare, "Jain Monumental Painting," in *The Peaceful Liberators: Jain Art from India*, ed. Pratapaditya Pal (London: Thames and Hudson, 1995), 76–87. The vertical scheme predominates and allows us to place this map within a tradition of Jain pilgrimage *pata* conventions of monumental scale and geometric organization where the central focus of the map was also the ritual center of the city—in this case, the Vishweshwur temple.

123 *Tarah Kashijiki* (survey *tarah* 191), map no. 191, in Bahura and Singh, *Catalogue of Historical Documents in Kapad-Dwara Jaipur: Maps and Plans*, 105–107. The original location of the Vishweshwur *linga* at the Adi-Vishweshwur temple was formalized and commemorated ca. 1700 and marked on this map. Beginning in 1698, Sawai Jai Singh II of Amber began plans to acquire land around the precinct of the Gyan Vapi mosque. See Bahura and Singh, *Catalogue of Historical Documents in Kapad Dwara, Jaipur*, document nos. 200–254, 29–39.

124 Many of these depictions were created after the Mughal Vishweshwur temple was dismantled and may represent either a selective or a disrupted pilgrimage scene. However, evidence from oral histories compiled during an onsite survey in 2005 revealed that most of the temples along this route were built sometime between the fifteenth and eighteenth centuries, strongly countering any argument about disruption and broad "Islamic" intervention.

125 Vishweshwur is actually depicted twice on the scroll, once roughly accurately and the second time immediately behind the Man Mandir. In both cases it is treated as an ordinary shrine in the city, with pride of place reserved for the Vaishnava Dashavtar.

3. EXPANSION AND INVENTION

1   C. A. Bayly, *Rulers, Townsmen, and Bazaars: North Indian Society in the Age of British Expansion, 1770–1870* (Cambridge: Cambridge University Press, 1982), 177–178. Bayly describes the influence that the city's merchants had on its politics. See also Vasudha Dalmia, *The Nationalization of Hindu Traditions: Bharatendu Harishchandra and Nineteenth Century Banaras* (New Delhi: Oxford University Press, 1997), 82–90.

2   James Prinsep, *The City of Bunarus*, 1822, British Library, London, Maps, Accession no. 53345. (6). Also see P. Thankappan Nair, *James Prinsep: Life and Work* (Calcutta: Firma KLM Pvt. Ltd., 1999), vol. 1, 225–260.

3   Although most of these were identified as sacred within *tirtha* texts, by the late eighteenth century these were viewed, at least by company administrators, as cesspools that were potential health hazards.

4   Nagesh Bhatt, *Nageshbhattakrut Tirthendushekharaha* in *Bhattojidikshitkruta Tristhalisetuh, Nageshbhattakrut Tirthendushekharaha, Sureshwaracharyakrut Kashimokshavicharaha,* ed. Suryanarayan Shukla (Varanasi: Sampurnananda Sanskrit Vishwavidyalaya, 1997), 1–59.

5   Ibid., 49 and 32–33.

6   Examples of this include Jaynarayan Ghoshal's Bengali translation of the *Kashikhand*, 1792, manuscript (Calcutta: Bangiya Sahitya Parishad, 1905).

7   I view this sociopolitical sphere as distinct from the idealized Habermasian sphere where citizens, as bourgeois equals, assemble and encounter other citizens and share opinions and activities, including protest in universally accessible space. However, Habermas also describes this public sphere as having a corrective influence on the state. This latter characteristic is applicable to a sociopolitical sphere as well, since a culture of opinion formation is linked to religious patronage and has political consequences. Jurgen Habermas, *The Structural Transformation of the Public Sphere*, trans. Thomas Burger (1989; reprint, Cambridge, MA: MIT Press, 2000), 64–74.

8   Descendants of once prominent aristocratic families in contemporary Banaras frequently relate instances of such feasts hosted by their families in the late eighteenth and nineteenth centuries.

9   Eric Hobsbawm, "Introduction: Inventing Traditions," in *The Invention of Tradition*, ed. Eric Hobsbawm and Terence Ranger (1983; reprint, Cambridge: Cambridge University Press, 2015), 1–14.

10 Prinsep, *The City of Bunarus.* The Narayan Dicchit Muhalla in Prinsep's 1822 map and survey derives its name from Narayan Dikshit's mansion and the *brahmapuris* that he sponsored; *Benares City*, Survey Season 1928–1929, Sheet no. 10, Adampura, Chauk and Kotwali wards. It is labeled as "Narayan Dicchit" in this survey.

11 Prinsep, *The City of Bunarus.* Also see James Prinsep, *Plan of a Group of Buildings on Dal ki Mandi, Meer Roostum Ulee Ka Suraj, Dewan Shookr Oollah, Dal Kee Mundei,* 1822, British Library, London, Accession no. WD 4274.

12 Painting of Meer Rustam Ali playing Holi with courtesans (women) of his harem, Bharat Kala Bhavan, Banaras, Accession no. 1385.

13 Prachi Deshpande, *Creative Pasts: Historical Memory and Identity in Western India, 1700–1960* (New York: Columbia University Press, 2007), 9–10 and 48. As Deshpande clarifies, although being Rajput remained an aspiration, actual policies were more often based in a "kshatriya dharma" that was liberally laced with pragmatism. Also see Melia Belli, "Keeping Up with the Rajputs: Appropriation and the Articulation of Sacrality and Political Legitimacy in Scindia Funerary Art," *Archives of Asian Art* 61 (2011): 91–106.

14 *Collection of Treaties and Engagements with the Native Princes and States of Asia Concluded on Behalf of the East India Company* (London: United–East India Company, 1812), 308–309. The treaty between Amrut Rao Peshwa and the East India Company (represented by Wellesley) is dated August 14, 1803.

15 Krishnachandra Ghoshal's older brother, Gokulchandra Ghoshal, had been agent to Harry Verelst, governor-general of Bengal (1767–1769). Vijayram Sen was also Krishnachandra Ghoshal's physician. See Sudipta Sen, *Empire of Free Trade: The East India Company and the Making of the Colonial Marketplace* (Philadelphia: University of Pennsylvania Press, 1997), 33. Based on Vijayram Sen's account, Balwant Singh, then raja of Banaras, received and honored Ghoshal. See Vijayram Sen, *Tirthamangala* (ca. 1768–1769), manuscript (Calcutta: Bangiya Sahitya Parishad, 1905).

16 The Ghoshal estate subsequently passed to his nephew Jaynarayan (also *qanungo* of Sundwip) in 1779. See P. Thankappan Nair, *Tercentenary History of Calcutta,* vol. 2, *A History of Calcutta's Streets* (Calcutta: Firma KLM, 1987), 209.

17 Sen, *Tirthamangala*, 141.

18 Sandria B. Freitag, *Collective Action and Community: Public Arenas and the Emergence of Communalism in North India* (Berkeley: University of California Press, 1989), 19.

19 The Natore *zamindari* dated from the time of the Nawabs of Bengal. Rani Bhawani, therefore, represented an older, more established aristocracy. See A. K. Moitra, *A Short History of Natore Raj* (Natore: Rani Bhawani Printing Works, 1912), 2–4.

20 Sen, *Tirthamangala*, 152.

21 Ibid.

22 Matthew A. Sherring, *The Sacred City of the Hindus: An Account of Benares in Ancient and Modern Times* (London: Trubner and Company, 1868), 175.

23 Enugula Veeraswamy (Veeraswamiah), *Enugula Veeraswamy's Journal (Kasiyatra Charitra),* trans. P. Sitapati and V. Purushottam (Hyderabad: Andhra Pradesh Government Oriental Manuscripts Library and Research Institute, 1973), 103. By Veeraswamy's estimate, there were around twelve hundred Gangaputra Brahmins in Banaras at this time.

24 Ibid. Based on Veeraswamy's account in *Kasiyatra Charitra,* the "fees" could vary from four rupees for pilgrims who arrived on foot to twelve rupees for those who arrived on horseback and fifty rupees for those who traveled by carriage.

25 Ibid.

26 Sherring, *Sacred City of the Hindus,* 228.

27 Eighteenth- and early nineteenth-century texts on urban landscapes had a focus on personalities and institutions rather than a sole focus on monuments and buildings. This was a reflection of urban structure as well as the nature of patronage. See, for instance,

Dargah Quli Khan, *Muraqqa-e-Delhi: The Mughal Capital in Muhammad Shah's Time*, trans. Chander Shekher and Shama Mitra Chenoy (Delhi: Deputy Publication, 1989). Khan composed his account between 1739 and 1741.

28   Philip Lutgendorf, *The Life of a Text: Performing the Ramcaritmanas of Tulsidas* (Berkeley: University of California Press, 1991).

29   Sherring, *Sacred City of the Hindus*, 213–214.

30   Ibid., 220–221.

31   Ibid., 227–228.

32   For more details, see National Archives of India, Proceedings of the Foreign Department, between the years 1830–1839, including entries for Gwalior, Udaipur, Rewah, Nagpur, and Coorg. Also see National Archives of India, Proceedings of the Foreign Department, between the years 1860 and 1869, and entries for Rewah, Vizianagaram, and Tonk.

33   James Kennedy, *Life and Work in Benares and Kumaon, 1839–1877* (London: T. Fisher Unwin, 1884), 74.

34   In a letter addressed to Raghunathrao, Ramji Ballal described Janoji Bhonsle's anger at the devastation of temples by the Mughals and referred to the misfortunes of the "Hindu dharma." See *Selections from the Peshwa Daftar 20: The Bhonsles of Nagpur (1717–1774)*, ed. G. S. Sardesai (Bombay: Government Central Press, 1931), Letter no. 132, 125–126, dated November 18, 1762. For a general analysis of religion-based conflicts and their relation to political realignments during the long eighteenth century, see C. A. Bayly, "'The Pre-History of Communalism?' Religious Conflict in India, 1700–1860," *Modern Asian Studies* 19, no. 2 (1985): 177–203.

35   In a letter dated June 27, 1742, and received in the *daftar* (office) of Kaygavkar Dikshit, there is a reference to Malharrao Holkar's intentions with regard to the Gyan Vapi mosque. He intended that the Gyan Vapi mosque be destroyed and the Vishweshwur temple be erected on its site. See V. T. Gune, ed., *Sources of Maratha History from Marathyanchya Itihasachi Sadhane*, 22 vols., ed. Itihasacharya, V. K. Rajwade, part 1 (Dhule: Rajwade Itihas Samshodhan Mandal, 2010), 290.

36   Ibid. Fearful of the potential wrath of the Nawab's local administrators, "Dravid" Brahmins in the city petitioned against such an action.

37   Ashirbadi Lal Srivastava, *Shuja-ud-Daulah* (1939; reprint, Delhi: Shiva Lal Agarwala & Co., 1961), 27.

38   Ibid., 27–28.

39   Sen, *Tirthamangala*, 115–116.

40   Stewart Gordon, *The Marathas, 1600–1818* (1993; reprint, New Delhi: Foundation Books Pvt. Ltd., 1998), 160–162. Gordon discusses Malharrao Holkar's early mentorship of his daughter-in-law and future regent as well as Ahilyabai's carefully cultivated persona as a widowed but powerful female ruler. Many authors suggest 1777 as the date for Ahilyabai's temple. One can say with certainty that it was completed by 1781, when Warren Hastings, in a show of support for Hindu sentiments, commissioned a *naubatkhana* for the temple.

41   Based on observation, a newer version of the Tarakeshwur temple was under construction in late 2008 through early 2009, nearer to Ahilyabai's temple.

42   James Prinsep, *Benares Illustrated in a Series of Drawings* (Calcutta: Baptist Mission Press, 1831), description of plate titled "Old Temple of Vishveshvur." Also see Lieutenant Colonel Garstin, *An Account of the Hindoo Temple of Vissvisshoor or Bissinaut, at Benares* (London: T. Bensley, 1800), 4. This situation of juxtaposition became common

for the sites of other prominent mosques in the city. The Bindu Madhav temple was rebuilt adjacent to the Dharhara mosque before 1822, and the Krittivaseshwur temple was rebuilt, again before 1822, adjacent to the Alamgiri mosque.

43 Prinsep, *Benares Illustrated*, plate titled "Plan of the Ancient Temple of Vishveshvur."

44 Ibid.

45 Sherring, *Sacred City of the Hindus*, 97.

46 Umakant Premanand Shah, "Introduction," *Girvanpadamanjari* and *Girvanavanmanjari*, ed. Umakant Premanand Shah (Baroda: Oriental Institute, 1960), 12. The Annapurna temple can be traced back to at least the turn of the eighteenth century. Oral narratives collected in the mid-nineteenth century suggest that the present shrine was rebuilt in the early decades of the eighteenth century by a Maratha patron. See Sherring, *Sacred City of the Hindus*, 57.

47 Sherring, *Sacred City of the Hindus*, 58. Sherring declared: "The temple of Annapurna was erected, 150 years ago, by the Raja of Poona." The temple may have an older tradition in the city since it is depicted on the pilgrimage pata. See *pilgrimage pata*, ca. 1700, from the collection of the National Museum, New Delhi, Paintings Gallery, Accession no. 56.59/58.

48 Sherring, *Sacred City of the Hindus*, 57.

49 Ibid.

50 National Archives of India, Foreign Department, Proceedings for the years 1840–1849, India Political Despatch to Court of Directors, no. 1 of 1841, "Silver Howge presented by the Rajah of Nagpore to the Bisheshur temple at Benares."

51 Sherring, *Sacred City of the Hindus*, 50–51.

52 Amar Farooqui, "From Baiza Bai to Lakshmi Bai: The Sindia State in the Early Nineteenth Century and the Roots of 1857," in *Issues in Modern History: For Sumit Sarkar*, ed. Biswamoy Pati (Mumbai: Popular Prakashan, 2000), 47–58.

53 Sherring, *Sacred City of the Hindus*, 54. Sherring quotes from an inscription on a tablet at the site. The proposal had originally come from a member of the Peshwa family, Chimnajee Appa. See Regional Archives, Allahabad, Duncan Records, Basta no. 96, Book no. 180, "Proceedings of the Committee for the Local Improvement in the City of Varanasi," entry for April 7, 1828. Chimnajee Appa offered to contribute toward the road-widening scheme in the Assi Muhalla by purchasing and demolishing houses there.

54 National Archives of India, Foreign Political Department, Proceedings for the years 1830–1839; Proceedings for September 5, 1838, and November 21, 1838, "Jeypore's Charitable Endowment at Benares."

55 Based on the route for the Antargriha *yatra* demarcated by Prinsep in *The City of Bunarus*.

56 Ibid. In the list of ninety-two "Chief Shiwalas" or temples that Prinsep provided along with his map, only fourteen are also part of the Antargriha circuit. See Prinsep, *The City of Bunarus*.

57 Bruno Dagens, ed. and trans., *Mayamata: An Indian Treatise on Housing, Architecture, and Iconography* (New Delhi: Sitaram Bhartia Institute of Scientific Research, 1985), 29.

58 *Selections from the Peshwa Daftar 18: Private Life of Shahu and the Peshwas* (Bombay: Government Central Press, 1931), Letter no. 36, 20–22, no date.

59 See Regional Archives, Allahabad, Pre-mutiny Records, Benares Collectorate, File no. 121, "Ranee Bhawanee's Estate"; and Prinsep, *The City of Bunarus*. Prinsep labels an area adjacent to the Man Mandir ghat as "Brahmapuri Ranee Bhawanee"; *Man Mandir,*

map no. 130, Sawai Man Singh II Museum, Jaipur. This map of the Man Mandir ghat and vicinity depicts a neighborhood of Bengali Brahmins labeled as "Bangali Brahmanan ki Vasati" (settlement of Bengali Brahmins).

60 Prinsep, *The City of Bunarus*.

61 Regional Archives, Allahabad, Pre-mutiny Records, Benares Collectorate, vol. no. 8, Letters Issued and Received, Years 1800–1820, 152–153. Letter dated August 5, 1809, from E. Watson, magistrate, Benares, to William Fracroft.

62 Shayesta Khan, ed. and trans., *The Holy City of Benares: As Administered by a Muslim Noble: Social, Religious, Cultural, and Political Conditions, 1781–1793: Translations of Letters of Ali Ibrahim Khan Written to the Maratha Chiefs, the Trustees of Mandirs and Others* (Patna: Khuda Baksh Oriental Public Library, 1993), 1–2.

63 Jadunath Sarvadhikari, *Tirthabhramana* (Calcutta: Bangiya Sahitya Parishad, 1915), 439–459. Throughout his narrative description, Sarvadhikari refers to a Bengali urban and cultural landscape in Kashi, including the history of patronage by Rani Bhawani, the neighborhood of Bengali Tola and the temple of Tilbhandeshwur that was significant among Bengali pilgrims.

64 See *Tarah Kashijiki*, map no. 191, in Gopal Narayan Bahura and Chandramani Singh, *Catalogue of Historical Documents in Kapad-Dwara Jaipur: Maps and Plans* (Jaipur: Maharaja of Jaipur, 1990), 105–107. There is no mention of the Thatheri bazaar among the labels in this map, but the location of Fateh Chand's *haveli* in Banaras, ca. 1700, is noted. For more on banking networks in the eighteenth century, see Kumkum Chatterjee, *Merchants, Politics, and Society in Early Modern India, Bihar: 1733–1820* (Leiden: E. J. Brill, 1996). Also see Bayly, *Rulers, Townsmen, and Bazaars*, 177–183. Bayly notes that the *naupatti mahajans* are remembered for their political intrigues in favor of Balwant Singh and that this could explain the royal titles and honors that many of them received as well as the links between the rajas of Banaras and the Gopal Mandir.

65 Documents in possession of the Biharipuri *muth*.

66 Jaynarayan Ghoshal referred to the limits of Kashi and extoled the virtues associated with performing the Panchkroshi, suggesting a conflation of the two ideas. See Jaynarayan Ghoshal, *Kashiparikrama*, 23–42. Veeraswamy, writing in 1830–1831 (see Veeraswamy, *Kasiyatra Charitra*, 112), described a Kashikshetra and described the Panchkroshi as defining its limits.

67 Regional Archives, Allahabad, Pre-mutiny Records, Benares Collectorate, File no. 121, "Ranee Bhawanee's Estate." Rani Bhawani patronized the renovation of several pilgrimage sites including temples and tanks along the Panchkroshi.

68 Sherring, *Sacred City of the Hindus*, 180.

69 See Regional Archives, Allahabad, Pre-mutiny Records, Benares Collectorate, File no. 121, "Ranee Bhawanee's Estate." Rani Bhawani inherited the *zamindari* from her husband in 1748. Also see Moitra, *Short History of Natore Raj*, 7.

70 Duncani Bandobast of 1883–1884.

71 Devtirtha Kashthajivhaswami, *Panchkroshasudha* (Ramnagar, Varanasi: Sarvabharatiya Kashirajanyas, 1997). In his introduction (no page numbers) titled "Hari Iccha Balwana," the late Vibhutinarain Singh described the family tradition that the Panchkroshi had been reinvigorated by Balwant Singh and that Chet Singh went on the pilgrimage, as described in the *Chet Sinh Vilas*.

72 Ghoshal, *Kashiparikrama*, 23–42. This text accompanied a Bengali translation of the *Kashikhand*.

73 Onsite survey conducted during 2005.

74 Dalmia, *Nationalization of Hindu Traditions*, 79.

75 Kashthajivhaswami, *Panchkroshasudha*.

76 Bharatendu Harishchandra, "Bhumika," *Kavivachanasudha* 3, no. 19 (May 22, 1872): 152. The remaking of the Panchkroshi route in discussed in further detail in chapter 5.

77 Ibid.

78 Regional Archives, Allahabad, Pre-mutiny Records, Benares Collectorate, File no. 121, "Ranee Bhawanee's Estate." Rani Bhawani patronized the renovation of several pilgrimage sites, including the construction of temples and tanks along the Panchkroshi.

79 See unnumbered manuscript of *Kurukshetramahatmya*, Saraswati Bhandar (Library), Ramnagar. The manuscript was commissioned in the late eighteenth century.

80 See gardens in *pilgrimage pata*, ca. 1700. From the collection of the National Museum, New Delhi, Paintings Gallery, Accession no. 56.59/58. Also see the gardens depicted in *pilgrimage panorama*, map no. 138, Sawai Man Singh II Museum, Jaipur.

81 Sheila S. Blair and Jonathan M. Bloom, *The Art and Architecture of Islam, 1250–1800* (1994; reprint, New Haven: Yale University Press, 1995), 268.

82 Ibid., 286.

83 Catherine B. Asher, *Architecture of Mughal India* (1992; reprint, Cambridge: Cambridge University Press, 2003), 324.

84 Gwal Das Sahu's mansion, as well as the Gopal Mandir that was designed on a "domestic" *haveli*-temple typology, included gardens. See Survey of Banaras City, 1928–1929.

85 Prinsep, *The City of Bunarus*.

86 Sherring, *Sacred City of the Hindus*, 219.

87 See Ozias Humphry, *Sketch Book in India*, 1786, Additional MS.15962.37. Humphry added a note describing his sketch of "Malla Dosi's Garden House the Residence of James Grant Esq. at Benares."

88 For more on Amrit Rao's life and activities in Banaras, see chapter 4.

89 Reginald Heber, *Narrative of a Journey through the Upper Provinces of India, from Calcutta to Bombay, 1824–1825*, vols. 1 and 2 (London: John Murray, 1844), vol. 1, 163. Religious charities grew in numbers over the nineteenth century. The missionary Edwin Greaves remarked that "there are many well-endowed Chattras or Charity-funds, from which daily doles, in money or food, are distributed, largely to Brahmans, devotees, and widows. It has been calculated that through these charities provision is made for nearly 4,000 persons." See Edwin Greaves, *Kashi the City Illustrious or Benares* (Allahabad: Indian Press, 1909), 26–27.

90 Heber, *Narrative of a Journey*, vol. 1, 163.

91 The garden mentioned by Heber (in *Narrative of a Journey*) might be the one where the future Rani of Jhansi Laxmibai was born, a circumstance also preserved as a family recollection. A mansion located at the site is depicted by Prinsep (see *The City of Bunarus*).

92 The *chahar-bagh* was often reorganized and adapted to function as a space for dispensing charity in the Deccan regions of South Asia, and this idea may have been imported to the city. See Philip B. Wagoner, "In Amin Khan's Garden: Charitable Gardens in Qutb Shahi Andhra," in *Garden and Landscape Practices in Pre-colonial India: Histories from the Deccan*, ed. Daud Ali and Emma J. Flatt (New Delhi: Routledge, 2012), 98–119.

93 Chatterjee, *Merchants, Politics, and Society*, 58–60.

94 Ibid. Also see Bayly, *Rulers, Townsmen, and Bazaars*, 96–106.

95   *Plan of a City*, Add. Or. 3266, ca. 1810, British Library.

96   Oral narratives current in the city hold that Prinsep also went into business for himself and invested in a *gunj* of his own, called Bisheshurgunj.

97   Frederick Curwen, trans., *The Bulwuntnamah: Translated from the Tuhfa-i-taza of Fakir Khair-ud-din Khan* (Allahabad: North West Provinces Government Press, 1875), 120–121.

98   This *gunj* was destroyed by fire in 1826, and the Committee for Local Improvement, a colonial agency, deemed this as a good opportunity to widen the pilgrimage road while ignoring the Nawab's rights to manage and own his property and to perpetuate a vision for an unadulterated Hindu ritual landscape. See Regional Archives, Allahabad, Duncan Records, Basta no. 96, Book no. 180, "Proceedings of the Committee for the Local Improvement in the City of Varanasi," entry for April 8, 1826.

99   Each of these regions has been defined by Dharmadhikari. See Krishnachandra Dharmadhikari, *Kashidarpanam* (Calcutta: Kavyaprakash Namdheya Yantralaya, 1875), 16–18. In some interpretations, Avimukta is congruent with the Antargriha zone.

100 *Benares City*, Survey Season 1928–29: Sheet No. 1, Adampura & Jaitpura Wards. I draw this conclusion based on the high density of neighborhood mosques that is depicted on this map for these areas.

101 Humphry, *Sketch Book in India*, 37.

102 The relationship between Orientalism and power has been well researched. In a similar way the relationship between Occidentalism and the emerging role of the East India Company is equally noteworthy. In each case, emergent elites acquired or displayed access to knowledge and objects as a means of consolidating personal as well as political power.

103 Ebba Koch, *Mughal Architecture* (Munich: Prestel-Verlag, 1991), 132–133. Koch sees the "later Mughal style" as being prevalent across the entire Indian subcontinent by the eighteenth century. Asher, *Architecture of Mughal India*, 292–334. Asher examines the architecture patronized by Mughal successor states and discusses the diversity and experimentation present in these buildings, even as they were based on Mughal state architecture. The "later Mughal style" had many variations and was patronized by Muslim as well as Hindu patrons across the entire subcontinent.

104 William Hodges, *Travels in India during the Years 1780, 1781, 1782, and 1783* (London: J. Edwards, 1793), 63–64.

105 Ibid., 20.

106 Curwen, *Bulwuntnamah*, 63 and 168–169.

107 Mir Muhammad Taqi Mir, *Zikr-i-Mir*, trans. C. M. Naim (1999; reprint, New Delhi: Oxford University Press, 2005), 72. Mir described evening *mushairas* (poetry readings) held on the rooftops of similar *havelis*.

108 Humphry, *Sketch Book in India*, 37.

109 Prinsep, *The City of Bunarus*.

110 European "influences" and architectural elements can be seen in various locales and circumstances across northern India during the late eighteenth century. See Rosie Llewellyn-Jones, *A Fatal Friendship: The Nawabs, the British, and the City of Lucknow* (Delhi: Oxford University Press, 1992). Llewellyn-Jones discusses the roles of European entrepreneurs and mercenaries attached to the Nawab's court as they forged novel tastes and architectural forms in cosmopolitan Lucknow. For their part, the Nawabs selectively drew on European architectural and urban models and material culture. See Catherine B. Asher, "Lucknow's Architectural Heritage," in *India's Fabled City: The Art of Courtly*

Lucknow, ed. Stephen Markel and Tushara Bindu Gude (Munich: Prestel Verlag, 2011), 121–143.

111 See Prinsep, *Benares Illustrated*, description of plate titled "Thutheree Bazar."

112 Ibid.

113 The Shobhabazaar Rajbari in eighteenth-century Calcutta was designed with similar intentions. For more about this building, see Swati Chattopadhyay, *Representing Calcutta: Modernity, Nationalism, and the Colonial Uncanny* (London: Routledge, 2005), 150–167. For more on the Durga *puja* in Bengal, Rachel McDermott, *Revelry, Rivalry, and Longing for the Goddess of Bengal: The Fortunes of Hindu Festivals* (New York: Columbia University Press, 2011).

114 Heber, *Narrative of a Journey*, vol. 1, 163.

115 See inscription in Sanskrit above the gateway of the temple precinct.

116 The artist Sita Ram also depicted this mansion, suggesting its role as a stop along this route. See British Library, accession no. Add Or. 0004726. By the late eighteenth century, several Indian elites began to commission portraits in oils, often from visiting European artists. See Natasha Eaton, *Mimesis across Empires: Artworks and Networks in India, 1765–1860* (Durham: Duke University Press, 2013), 178–190.

117 Heber, *Narrative of a Journey*, vol. 1, 164.

118 Ibid.

119 Ibid.

120 Ibid., vol. 1, 164–165.

121 The temple is planned with separate *garbha-griha* and *mandapa* and is similar in this respect to the Durga and Annapurna temples.

122 Although he was a prominent public figure in the city, and a proponent of its religious life as well as its modern public institutions, Jaynarayan Ghoshal guarded his privacy where it concerned the Gurudham temple. For instance, the temple is not indicated on Prinsep's 1822 map of the city, suggesting limited access. See Prinsep, *The City of Bunarus*.

123 For more on the *ratna* temple form in Bengal, see Pika Ghosh, *Temple to Love: Architecture and Devotion in Seventeenth-century Bengal* (Bloomington: Indiana University Press, 2005).

124 Proceedings of the Committee for Local Improvement, see minutes of meeting held on Saturday, February 14, 1824. I am grateful to David Curley for sharing his insights and research on Jaynarayan Ghoshal's activities in Calcutta and Banaras. Curley suggests that in a search for status among Calcutta's prominent Brahmin families, Kalishankar carefully cultivated an orthodox (even regressive) image.

125 Currently, the temple is dedicated to a "Compassionate" deity.

126 Mirza Nathan, *Baharistan-i-Ghaybi: A History of the Mughal Wars in Assam, Cooch Behar, Bengal, Bihar, and Orissa during the Reigns of Jahangir and Shahjahan*, vol. 2, trans. M. I. Borah (Gauhati: Government of Assam, Department of Historical and Antiquarian Studies, 1936), 442–444. Also see details of "Map of Bengal," map no. 93, and "Map of Bengal, Bihar, Assam," map no. 279, in Bahura and Singh, *Catalogue of Historical Documents in Kapad-Dwara Jaipur: Maps and Plans*, 26 and 45. Such maps were often created to aid Mughal military campaigns in these regions.

127 The Lolark Kund was part of the properties of the Cooch Behar family by the late-nineteenth century. See Regional Archives, Banaras, List 3, Box 12, File 1, "Land Acquired for the unfiltered water pumping station M.W.W. Bhadaini," letter dated August 10, 1892, to the Collector, Banaras, from the Cooch Behar State Agent. The Cooch Behar family were owners of the Lolark *kund* by the late nineteenth century.

128 A revivalist temple form with a sanctum topped by a *shikhara* and preceded by a *mandapa* can also be observed in parts of Rajasthan in the seventeenth century, especially at Amber.

129 The classic Khajuraho temples were also restored in the nineteenth century by Maharaja Pratap Singh between 1843 and 1847, after their rediscovery and early scholarly exploration by the Asiatic Society. See Devangana Desai, *Khajuraho: Monumental Legacy* (New Delhi: Oxford University Press, 2000), 3–4.

130 Regional Archives, Allahabad, Pre-mutiny Records, Benares Collectorate, File no. 121, "Ranee Bhowanee's Trust." The temple may have been renovated by Rani Bhawani as part of a larger scheme to revive the Panchkrosi pilgrimage in the mid-eighteenth century. See also George Michell, "Temple Styles," in *Banaras: The City Revealed*, ed. George Michell and Rana P. B. Singh (Mumbai: Marg Publications, 2005), 79. To assume that the Kardameshwur temple provided sole inspiration would be to ignore the subcontinental extent of a revivalist trend.

131 Sherring, *Sacred City of the Hindus*, 42. Writing in the mid-nineteenth century, Sherring estimated the total number of temples at 1,454 and mosques at 272. He also noted the large numbers of images and deities in the city as its religious life thrived.

132 Author's conversations with master-masons Aftab Ali and Sadiq Ali in September and October 2005.

133 Prinsep, *Benares Illustrated*, description of plate titled "Elevation of a Hindoo Temple."

134 Garstin, *An Account of the Hindoo Temple of Vissvisshoor or Bissinaut*, 4.

135 Veeraswamy, *Kasiyatra Charitra*, 53.

136 Prinsep, *Benares Illustrated*, plate titled, "Elevation of a Hindoo Temple."

4. SPECTACLE AND RITUAL

1 William Hodges, *Travels in India during the Years 1780, 1781, 1782 and 1783* (London: J. Edwards, 1793), 60–61.

2 Ibid.

3 James Prinsep, *The City of Bunarus*, 1822, British Library, London, Maps, Accession no. 53345. (6); and illustrations in James Prinsep, *Benares Illustrated in a Series of Drawings*, parts 1–3 (Calcutta: Baptist Mission Press, 1831–1833).

4 Enugula Veeraswamy (Veeraswamiah), *Enugula Veeraswamy's Journal (Kasiyatra Charitra)*, trans. P. Sitapati and V. Purushottam (Hyderabad: Andhra Pradesh Government Oriental Manuscripts Library and Research Institute, 1973), 104.

5 Ebba Koch, *The Complete Taj Mahal and the Riverfront Gardens of Agra* (London: Thames and Hudson, 2006). Also see Ebba Koch, "Mughal Palace Gardens from Babur to Shah Jahan (1526–1648)," *Muqarnas* 14 (1997): 143–165.

6 J. P. Losty, "Depicting Delhi: Mazhar Ali Khan, Thomas Metcalfe, and the Topographical School of Delhi artists," in *Princes and Painters in Mughal Delhi, 1707–1857*, ed. William Dalrymple and Yuthika Sharma (New Haven: Yale University Press, 2012), 53–59. Losty discusses topographical views as vehicles in which buildings and patrons were strategically juxtaposed to depict authority. During the eighteenth century a large number of artists began to migrate from Delhi to smaller courts, offering their artistic skills to emergent elites eager to establish a social presence through valued and established modes of representation.

7 *Panorama of Bundiparkota ghat*, late seventeenth century, collection of the Sawai Man Singh II Museum, Jaipur, accession no. 7.

8   Mir Muhammad Taqi Mir, *Zikr-i-Mir*, trans. C. M. Naim (1999; reprint, New Delhi: Oxford University Press, 2005), 72.

9   See, for example, *A view of the city of Benares, represented on one lane, with the names of the owners of the Palaces inscribed in erosion, and shewing particularly the palace where the Rajah Cheyte Sing was arrested by order of Mr. Hastings, in 1781*, ca. 1770–1800, Egerton MS, 1062, British Library.

10 For more on the original *Padshahnama*, see Milo Cleveland Beach and Ebba Koch, *King of the World: The Padshahnamah, an Imperial Mughal Manuscript from the Royal Library, Windsor Castle* (London: Azimuth Editions and Sackler Gallery, 1997).

11 *Amal-i-Salih*, Add. MS.20735, ff. 367–371, British Library.

12 *Selections from the Peshwa Daftar, 30: Miscellaneous Papers of Shahu and his First Two Peshwas*, ed. G. S. Sardesai (Bombay: Government Central Press, 1933), Letter no. 131, 101–102, dated August 8, 1735. This is a note to the Peshwa from Sadashiv Naik Joshi, his agent/manager at Banaras. Joshi complained about the scarcity of building materials in the city since the local "*adhikhari*" or administrative head (presumably Meer Rustam Ali) was building a fortress-palace and had laid claims to all the supply in the city.

13 Regional Archives, Allahabad, Duncan Records, Basta no. 96, Book no. 180, Proceedings of the Committee for the Local Improvement in the City of Varanasi, 1823–1829, minutes for meeting held on November 19, 1827, p. 89. The committee mediated disputes related to construction and sale of property, especially along the riverfront. For instance, the raja of Banaras who purchased the Meer *pushta* was encouraged by the committee to complete the purchase speedily. It was also "ordered that the above should be communicated to the Raja, whose interest will behoove a speedy attention to the present very perilous state of the pooshta." The raja completed the purchase with the committee's mediation, and they transferred payment to the previous owner (Mohamed Khan) as well as to Rambhund, the holder of a mortgage on the property.

14 Contemporary masons in Banaras also work within a similar method. In this system of designing and building, permutations and combinations with a set of "modules" are easily executed.

15 William Daniell, *Shuwallah—Gaut, Bernares*, 1789, Shelfmark WD1295, British Library.

16 A similar structure was built at Farrukh Nagar (named after the Mughal emperor Farrukhsiyar) near Delhi. This was a new *qasba* built and administered by Faujdar Khan in the early eighteenth century.

17 *Selections from the Peshwa Daftar, 30: Miscellaneous Papers of Shahu and his First Two Peshwas*, ed. G. S. Sardesai (Bombay: Government Central Press, 1933), Letter No. 131, 101–102, dated August 8, 1735.

18 Ibid.

19 Prinsep, *Benares Illustrated*, description of plate titled "Bruhma Ghat."

20 Oral traditions and contemporary uses and affiliations suggest that the building of two prominent ghats, known as the Jain ghat and the Bacchraj ghat, were sponsored by the Jain banker Bacchraj sometime toward the late eighteenth century. Within Jain tradition, the city is known as the birthplace of the Tirthankara Parshwanath. Jaynarayan Ghoshal refers to a Parshwanath ghat in his description of the riverfront. See Jaynarayan Ghoshal, *Kashiparikrama*, 1792, manuscript (Calcutta: Bangiya Sahitya Parishad, 1905), 134.

21 Prinsep, *The City of Bunarus*.

22 James Prinsep, "Benares Directory," in *James Prinsep: Life and Work*, ed. P. Thankappan Nair, vol. 1 (Calcutta: Firma KLM Ltd., 1999), 258–259. Bishambar and Beni Ram Pandit were brothers. Oral narratives also credit the maharaja of Banaras with providing the

initial endowment. Interview with the family of the priest of the Jagannath temple conducted in January 2003.

23 Ibid.

24 Family tradition holds that the *mahant* (presiding priest) had an argument with the maharaja of Cuttack. Furthermore, the *mahant* only ate *prasad* (offerings) from the temple at Puri. The endowment from Chattisgarh was revoked when that principality was taken over by the British. Author's conversation with Deepak Shahpuri in December 2009.

25 Matthew A. Sherring, *The Sacred City of the Hindus: An Account of Benares in Ancient and Modern Times* (London: Trubner and Company, 1868), 218.

26 Ibid.

27 Ibid, 214–229.

28 Family tradition also maintains that the brothers were agents for the raja of Chattisgarh. Author interview with Deepak Shahpuri in December 2009.

29 See, for instance, *Prithvicha Naksha*, MssMar.G281, British Library.

30 Nagesh Bhatt, *Nageshbhattakrut Tirthendushekharaha* in *Bhattojidikshitkruta Tristhalisetuh, Nageshbhattakrut Tirthendushekharaha, Sureshwaracharyakrut Kashimokshavicharaha*, ed. Suryanarayan Shukla (Varanasi: Sampurnananda Sanskrit Vishwavidyalaya, 1997), 49.

31 According to one version, it was Narayan Dikshit Patankar who transformed Manikarnika into a funeral ghat. Yet another version credits the banker Kashmiri Mull with being the initiator of this tradition. On the basis of an oral tradition in Banaras, Kashmiri Mull wished to cremate his mother (in some versions, his mistress) at the Harishchandra ghat but could not agree on the amount for the fee that was to be paid to the *doms* (priests conducting the funeral). He then brought the corpse to Manikarnika ghat and completed the funeral there. The Khattri *chabutara* on Manikarnika ghat was installed as a platform that would be reserved for members of the Khattri community, and they could conduct funerals without having to pay a fee.

32 The Anwekar family claim to be *shraddha purohits* (priests who conduct last rites) near Manikarnika ghat for the past seven generations and have had their funeral hall at that site for that time. This would coincide roughly with the turn of the eighteenth century. Author interview with Sandeep Anwekar conducted in March, 2004.

33 British Library, London, Record no. 2814, Shelfmark WD 1409. This is a watercolor of the bank produced ca. 1765, based on Joseph Tieffenthaler's illustration of the riverfront; see Tieffenthaler, *Des Pater Joseph Tieffenthaler's Historische, Geographische Beschreibung von Hindustan* (Berlin: Bendem Berausgeber, 1785), plate VII.1. The illustration is a view across the Ganges River from its eastern bank, looking toward the city of Banaras. Across the tents in the camp of the Mughal emperor Shah Alam II, the artist had a view of the river, the opposite (western) bank of the Ganges, and the city. See also plate 14 in Charles Forrest, *A Picturesque Tour Along the Rivers Ganges and Jumna in India: Consisting of Twenty-four Highly Finished and Coloured Views, a Map, and Vignettes, from Original Drawings Made on the Spot; with Illustrations, Historical and Descriptive* (London: L. Harrison for R. Ackermann, 1824).

34 Ghoshal, *Kashiparikrama*, 143.

35 Hodges, *Travels in India*, 60–61. Hodges mentions a garden behind the gateway of Jalsai ghat. He makes no mention of a funeral ground on Manikarnika, adjacent to it.

36 Veeraswamy, *Kasiyatra Charitra*, 104.

37 See the inscription on the temple. The inscription was also recorded by Mukund W. Burway, *Devi Ahilyabai Holkar* (Bombay, 1920), 141.

38 There are two possibilities for the date of construction. The first date, 1710, is the date on an inscription at the site, and 1734 is the date determined by the Archaeological Survey of India. See also Robert Barker, *An Account of the Bramins Observatory at Benares* (London: W. Bowyer and J. Nichols, 1777). The observatory was renovated again in 1911, the year of the Delhi Durbar. See the inscription at the site.

39 Notation on *Man Mandir*, map no. 130, Sawai Man Singh II Museum, Jaipur.

40 A temple is part of the complex at present, but it is not built with a visible *shikhara*.

41 Burway, *Devi Ahilyabai Holkar*, 141. Ahilyabai was an active patron in Banaras at this time. Also see Prinsep, *Benares Illustrated*, description of plate titled "Dusaswumedh Ghat."

42 For an account of the Bhonslas of Nagpur, see Yadav Madhav Kale, *Nagpurkar Bhoslyancha Itihas* (Nagpur: Vidarbha Samshodhan Mandal, 1979).

43 National Archives of India, Proceedings for the Years 1840–1849, India Political Dispatch to Court of Directors, no. 68 of 1840, "Nagpore Rajah's buildings at Benares. Remission of duty on stone for the, Stones for buildings under construction at Benares for the Rajah of Nagpore. Remission of duties on," dated April 20, 1840.

44 The scale of their endowment suggests a lavish level of support for religious celebration and spectacle.

45 For details of the Treaty of Bassein, see *Collection of Treaties and Engagements with the Native Princes and States of Asia Concluded on Behalf of the East India Company* (London: United–East India Company, 1812), 233–245.

46 The ghat is also known as Narad ghat. As per family recollections, Amrut Rao sponsored many occasions of conspicuous feasting for Brahmins in this refectory.

47 Regional Archives, Banaras, List 1, Box 47, File no. 63, Department No. XV, Year (1904–1911), "Regarding Trusteeship of the Annapurna Chattra and Ganesh Mandir at Banaras," Letter no. 907/X-26 of 1916 from G. B. Lambert Esq. I.C.S., District Officer of Benares, to the Commissioner, Benares Division, Benares, dated December 12, 1916.

48 Ibid.

49 "Feast of Ganesa," from Louis Rousselet, *India and Its Native Princes* (New York: Scribner, Armstrong, and Co., 1876), 536.

50 Prinsep, *Benares Illustrated*, description of plate titled "Shreedhur Moonshee's Ghat and Rana Mahal."

51 An elevator was added to the front portion of the Munshi fortress-palace (now called the Darbhanga ghat) in the early twentieth century. Besides being a distinctive feature, the elevator shaft enhanced spectacle on the riverfront.

52 Prinsep, *Benares Illustrated*, section titled "Boorwa Mungul."

53 Ibid.

54 Ibid.

55 Debi Pershad, *All Benares Map*, ca. 1901, collection of Bharat Kala Bhawan, Banaras, paintings, Accession no. 86.405.

56 Veeraswamy, *Kasiyatra Charitra*, 104–105.

57 For more on Ali Ibrahim Khan's initial appointment under Warren Hastings and relationship to the Rajas of Banaras and their courtiers, see Frederick Curwen, trans., *The Bulwuntnamah: Translated from the Tuhfa-i-taza of Fakir Khair-ud-din Khan* (Allahabad: North West Provinces Government Press, 1875), 122–124. From this account the court was held on Dal Mandi, in the home of Raja Shitabrai, one of the prominent bankers and financiers of the East India Company.

58   Regional Archives, Allahabad, Duncan Records, Basta no. 96, Book no. 180, Proceedings of the Committee for Local Improvement in the City of Varanasi, 1823–1829, Minutes for meeting held on December 10, 1825.

59   Gahuna Bai Gaekwad was successful in sponsoring construction of the temple. See Prinsep, *Benares Illustrated*, description of plate titled "View Westward from Ghoosla Ghat."

60   Regional Archives, Allahabad, Duncan Records, Basta no. 96, Book no. 180, Proceedings of the Committee for Local Improvement in the City of Varanasi, 1823–1829, Minutes for meeting held on April 7, 1828.

61   Regional Archives, Allahabad, Duncan Records, Basta no. 96, Book no. 180, Proceedings of the Committee for Local Improvement in the City of Varanasi, 1823–1829, Minutes for meeting held on April 7, 1828 upon the Subject of the Ghat Building under Orders from Maharaja Bajee Rao Behadoor.

62   Ibid.

63   *Madhis* (chambers on ghat steps, built facing the river) were a feature of the riverfront at least since the sixteenth century.

64   Kashi Tirtha Sudhar Trust, *Benares and Its Ghats* (Banaras: Kashi Tirtha Sudhar Trust, 1931), 99.

65   Ibid. Based on the Kashi Tirtha Sudhar Trust's report, this drawing was included in the document almost a hundred years after its initial design.

66   National Archives of India, Foreign Department, Political, Letter no. 60–61, dated July 24, 1834, to Charles Metcalfe from Baeeza Baee.

67   Fanny Parks, *Wanderings of a Pilgrim in Search of the Picturesque, during Four-and-Twenty Years in the East; with Revelations of Life in the Zenana*, 2 vols. (1850; Reprint, Karachi: Oxford University Press, 1975), vol. 2, 61.

68   Ibid., 61–62.

69   National Archives of India, Foreign Department, Political, Letter no. 60–61, dated July 24, 1834, to Charles Metcalfe from Baeeza Baee.

70   Parks, *Wanderings of a Pilgrim in Search of the Picturesque*, vol. 2, 62.

5. ORDER AND ANTIQUITY

1   Bernard S. Cohn, *Colonialism and Its Forms of Knowledge: The British in India* (Princeton: Princeton University Press, 1996). Within this broad framework Cohn included a range of techniques employed by the colonial administration to acquire and organize information on South Asia.

2   Cohn (*Colonialism and Its Forms of Knowledge*) defined "colonial knowledge" largely as the creation of a colonial regime. Recent research has led to a modified view of this process in which Indians played a key role in the collection, translation, and interpretation of this knowledge. See, for instance, Nicholas B. Dirks, "Colin Mackenzie: Autobiography of an Archive," in *The Madras School of Orientalism: Producing Knowledge in Colonial South India*, ed. Thomas R. Trautmann (New Delhi: Oxford University Press, 2009), 29–47, as well as other essays published in the same anthology.

3   Vasudha Dalmia, *The Nationalization of Hindu Traditions: Bharatendu Harishchandra and Nineteenth Century Banaras* (New Delhi: Oxford University Press, 1997). Dalmia notes throughout her book that the Persianate culture once espoused by the city's elites was gradually and deliberately replaced by symbols of a self-conscious Hindu cultural sensibility.

4   James Prinsep, *The City of Bunarus*, 1822, British Library, London, Maps, Accession no. 53345. (6). By the late eighteenth century, part of this street was named Dal Mandi after a prominent merchant-banker named Dalchand, who became a resident of Banaras, ca. 1781. See Shayesta Khan, ed. and trans., *The Holy City of Benares: As Administered by a Muslim Noble: Social, Religious, Cultural, and Political Conditions, 1781–1793: Translations of Letters of Ali Ibrahim Khan Written to the Maratha Chiefs, the Trustees of Mandirs and Others* (Patna: Khuda Baksh Oriental Public Library, 1993), 9.

5   Cohn, *Colonialism and Its Forms of Knowledge*, 26. Cohn elaborates on the circumstances under which, beginning in 1772, Warren Hastings decided that Indians were to be ruled through their own laws and customs. Also see Eugene Irschick, *Dialogue and History: Constructing South India, 1795–1895* (Berkeley: University of California Press, 1994). Irschick examines the ways in which British administrators in South India adapted local customs to their advantage, even as they colluded with the population in imagining an ideal Tamil past.

6   Ozias Humphry, *Sketch Book in India*, 1786, Additional MS. 15962.

7   Ibid.

8   Khan, *Holy City of Benares*. Ali Ibrahim Khan was magistrate between 1781 and 1793. Khan had previously worked under the Nawabs of Bengal. Also see Bernard S. Cohn, *An Anthropologist among the Historians* (Oxford: Oxford University Press, 1987), 325.

9   Gholam Hossein Khan, *Seir Mutaqharin or View of Modern Times*, vols. 1–3, trans. Hadjee Mustapha (Calcutta: James White, 1789), vol. 2, 555.

10   V. A. Narain, *Jonathan Duncan and Varanasi* (Calcutta: Firma K. L. Mukhopadhyay, 1959), 20.

11   Regional Archives, Allahabad, Duncan Records, Basta no. 2, Serial no. 10, 75–77.

12   See National Archives of India, Home Public, March–April 1788, 3701–3774.

13   Duncan was particularly upset about women urinating in the streets. See Regional Archives, Allahabad, Resident Proceedings of Benares, Basta no. 29, August 1790, vol. no. 33, Part II, entry for August 24, 1790.

14   Cohn, *Anthropologist among the Historians*, 438.

15   Sanitation, or rather its lack, in the streets remained an abiding concern for the colonial government, but measures to enforce modes of public behavior were never completely implemented. It was only in the year 1853 that the first public latrines were constructed, and in 1856 only ten were in existence in the entire city. See H. R. Neville, *Gazetteer of Benares* (Allahabad: Government Press, 1908), 167. However, mandatory use of public toilets was never enforced, and their use remained marginal.

16   Regional Archives, Allahabad, Resident Proceedings of Benares, Basta no. 29, August 1790, vol. no. 33, Part II, entry for August 24, 1790.

17   Concerns over using a confined space that was to be shared across differences in caste and religion probably lay behind some of the protests, since collective action was connected to social organizations around caste. See Sandria B. Freitag, *Collective Action and Community: Public Arenas and the Emergence of Communalism in North India* (Berkeley: University of California Press, 1989), 41.

18   Regional Archives Banaras, Duncan Records 1788–1799, Register no. 1, Basta no. 1, List no. 9, entry for October 5, 1788.

19   See "A colored sketch of the ground at Secrole intended for the site of a Dewannee and Fouzdarree jail for the city of Benares, and shewing [*sic*] the highest known rise of the Burnah; drawn on a scale of 50 feet to an inch," British Library, Shelfmark Add. MS. 13, 907.

20 Regional Archives, Allahabad, Pre-mutiny Records, Benares Collectorate, vol. no. 8, Letters Issued and Received, Years 1800–1820, 152–153, letter dated August 5, 1809, from E. Watson, magistrate, Banaras, to William Fracroft, Registrar to the Court of Circuit, Banaras. Such surveys were a marked departure from the one commissioned by Warren Hastings, in which he asked his surveyors to focus equally on the city's ritual landscape as well as to mark its extents.

21 Regional Archives Allahabad, Pre-mutiny Records, Letters issued and received, Benares Collectorate, Register no. 8, Year 1800–1820, August 5, 1809, "Statement of the Assessment for local watchmen in the city of Benares."

22 Regional Archives Allahabad, Pre-mutiny Records, Benares Collectorate, vol. no. 8, Letters Issued and Received, Years 1800–1820, letter dated August 5, 1809, from E. Watson, magistrate, Banaras, to William Fracroft, Registrar to the Court of Circuit, Banaras.

23 Regional Archives, Allahabad, Pre-mutiny Records, Benares Collectorate, vol. no. 8, Letters Issued and Received, Years 1800–1820 (enclosures), copy of a letter to the court of appeal and circuit for the division of Benares dated January 21, 1811. In this instance, residents demanded exemption on the grounds that Banaras was a place of worship and hence could not be taxed.

24 George Nicholls, *Sketch of the Rise and Progress of the Benares Pathshala (with a Supplement Bringing the Story down to 1906)* (1906; reprint, Varanasi: Sampurnanand Sanskrit University, 2005), 1.

25 Alexander Dow, *The History of Hindostan, from the Death of Akbar to the Complete Settlement of the Empire under Aurangzebe* (London: T. Becket and P. A. de Hondt, 1772); and James Mill, *The History of British India*, vols. 1–3 (London: Baldwin, Cradock and Joy, 1817).

26 Jonathan Duncan, "An Account of the Discovery of Two Urns in the Vicinity of Benares," *Asiatic Researches* 5 (London: J. Sewell, 1799), 132. In 1794, very soon after the site at Sarnath was discovered, Duncan concluded that the bones found in one of the urns at the site must have belonged to "one of the worshipers of Buddha, a set of Indian heretics, who having no reverence for the Ganges, used to deposit their remains in the earth, instead of committing them to the river."

27 Jaynarayan Ghoshal, *Kashiparikrama*, 1792, manuscript (Calcutta: Bangiya Sahitya Parishad, 1905), 35. Ghoshal incorporated the city's visible Jain as well as newly discovered Buddhist pasts into his narrative.

28 Bholanauth Chunder, *The Travels of a Hindoo to Various Parts of Bengal and Upper India*, vols. 1 and 2 (London: N. Trubner, 1869), vol. 1, 240.

29 Ibid.

30 Ibid., 291.

31 Ibid., 292.

32 Ibid., 300.

33 Matthew A. Sherring, *The Sacred City of the Hindus: An Account of Benares in Ancient and Modern Times* (London: Trubner and Company, 1868), 26.

34 M. A. Sherring and C. Horne, "Description of the Buddhist Ruins at Bakariya Kund, Benares," *Journal of the Asiatic Society of Bengal* 34, part 1 (1864).

35 Sherring, *Sacred City of the Hindus*, 2.

36 Ibid., 4.

37 Ibid., 96.

38 Ibid., 290.

39 James Kennedy, *Life and Work in Benares and Kumaon, 1839–1877* (London: T. Fisher Unwin, 1884), 51–76.

40 Nationalist historians, including those based in the city, refuted the Orientalist idea that ancient Indian civilization was merely "a shadow" of ancient Rome or Greece. See Rameswar Prasad Varma, "Baudhha Bharat Ki Pracheen Sabhyata – 1," *Indu*, Kala 5, Khand 1, Kiran 1 (January 1914): 17–20; and Rameswar Prasad Varma, "Baudhha Bharat Ki Pracheen Sabhyata – 2," *Indu*, Kala 5, Khand 1, Kiran 1 (January 1914): 118–121.

41 Rajani Ranjan Sen, *The Holy City-Benares* (Chittagong: M. R. Sen, 1912), 69–70.

42 Neville, *Gazetteer of Benares*, i–ii.

43 Henry Miers Elliot, *The History of India, as Told by Its Own Historians: The Muhammadan Period*, ed. John Dawson (1867; reprint, New York: AMS Press, 1966).

44 Ibid., 183–200.

45 Herbert A. Newell, *Benares, The Hindus' Holy City: A Guide to Places of Interest with History and Map* (Madras, 1915), 1–2.

46 "An Old Resident," *All About Benares, Containing a Sketch from the Vedic Days to the Modern Times* (Benares City: K. S. Muthiah & Co, 1917), 11.

47 Chunder, *Travels of a Hindoo*, vol. 1, 239–240.

48 Ibid., 272.

49 Ibid., 272–273.

50 Ibid.

51 Ibid., 276.

52 Nicholls, *Sketch of the Rise and Progress of the Benares Pathshala*, 149.

53 Ibid., 149–150.

54 Chunder, *Travels of a Hindoo*, vol. 1, 276.

55 Enugula Veeraswamy (Veeraswamiah), *Enugula Veeraswamy's Journal (Kasiyatra Charitra)*, trans. P. Sitapati and V. Purushottam (Hyderabad: Andhra Pradesh Government Oriental Manuscripts Library and Research Institute, 1973), 173; and Chunder, *Travels of a Hindoo*, vol. 1, 2.

56 Frank Fitzjames, *Preliminary Report on the Sewage and Water Supply of the City of Benares* (Allahabad: North West Provinces and Oudh Government Press, 1880), 11.

57 Edwin Greaves, *Kashi the City Illustrious or Benares* (Allahabad: Indian Press, 1909), 29.

58 Bharatendu Harishchandra, *Premjogini*, in *Bharatendu Granthavali*, vol. 1, ed. Brajratnadas (Kashi: Nagari Pracharini Sabha, 1950), 319–354.

59 Neville, *Gazetteer of Benares*, 73–75. The railways were first brought into the district by the colonial administration in 1862 and grew rapidly by the turn of the century.

60 Harishchandra, *Premjogini*, 338.

61 Ibid., 340.

62 Lieutenant Colonel Garstin, *An Account of the Hindoo Temple of Vissvisshoor or Bissinaut at Benares* (London: T. Bensley, 1800), 4. Recall that though Garstin's report was published in 1800, it was prepared in 1781; Ghoshal, *Kashiparikrama*; Veeraswamy, *Kasiyatra Charitra*; and Jadunath Sarvadhikari, *Tirthabhramana* (Calcutta: Bangiya Sahitya Parishad, 1915). Several travel accounts by Indian visitors to the city include descriptions of the Vishweshwur temple.

63 See the inscription on the Dharhara mosque. The inscription in Persian states: "During the reign of Badshah Shah Alam, and with the help of Imaduddaulah Governor General Sir Hastings Bahadur Jaladat Jung, in the year 1198 Hijri, Nasiruddaulah Ali Ibrahim Bahadur the Hakim of Banaras built the mosque." Also see Ali Ibrahim Khan to Warren Hastings, February 20, 1785, and September 1786, BL, Hastings Papers, Add. MSS

NOTES TO CHAPTER 5

29202, folios 85–86. Also see the inscription on the temple's gateway, which reads: "This Naubatkhana of Vishweshwur was constructed by Nawab Ibrahim Khan on samvat 1842 (1785) by the order of Imaduddaulah, Governor-General Warren Hastings Jaladat Jung." For a Sanskrit version, see Surendranath Sen, *Sanskrit Documents: Being Sanskrit Letters and Other Documents Reserved in the Oriental Collection at the National Archives of India* (Allahabad: Ganganatha Jha Research Institute, 1951), 2–6.

64 Khan, *Seir Mutaqharin or View of Modern Times*, vol. 2, 577. "Tabatabai" and his contemporaries often complained that the East India Company had not dug wells, built *sarays*, or planted orchards.

65 James Prinsep, *Benares Illustrated in a Series of Drawings*, parts 1–3 (Calcutta: Baptist Mission Press, 1831–1833), description of plate titled "Plan of the Ancient Temple of Vishveshvur."

66 Following contemporary practices in the city, rather than texts, Vijayaram Sen mentioned a visit to Vishweshwur, Annapurna, and Gyan Vapi as well as visits to Dandapani, Mahakaleshwur, Nandikesh, and Tarakesh. He did not mention a *"mandap"* either. Also see chapter 3.

67 Gyanendra Pandey, *The Construction of Communalism in Colonial North India* (1990; reprint, Delhi: Oxford University Press, 1997).

68 Sarvadhikari, *Tirthabhramana*, 441.

69 Ibid., 439–459.

70 Raja Shivprasad Sitarehind, *Itihas Timirnashak: A History of India in Three Parts, Part III* (Allahabad: Government Press, 1873).

71 Ibid., i.

72 Ibid., ii.

73 Ibid., i.

74 Ibid., 9.

75 Ibid., 9–14. Sitarehind (*Itihas Timirnashak*) made a further case that since Hindus were descendants of Buddhists and Jains, these belief systems were precedents for medieval Hinduism. Sitarehind utilized and legitimized a Buddhist and Hindu genealogy and folded it into his notion of a national identity that was only selectively inclusive of Islam.

76 Ibid., 9.

77 It should be noted that the colonial government handed management of this mosque to the weavers' community of Banaras in the 1930s. Author's conversation in September 2005 with Abdul Batin, the chief administrator of the Gyan Vapi mosque.

78 Sherring, *Sacred City of the Hindus*, 53.

79 Regional Archives, Banaras, List 7, Box 8C, File 105, "Repair of Gyan Vapi Mosque," order issued on December 7, 1924, by L. Owen, Deputy Magistrate, Banaras.

80 Ibid., and also see Regional Archives, Banaras, List 7, Box 8A, File 212, "Note on the Satisfactory Solution of a Knotty Problem in the Sacred Precincts of the Vishwanath Temple and the Gyan Vapi Mosque," copy of the Resolution of the Municipal Board no. 267, dated July 25, 1926.

81 In his map (*The City of Bunarus*), Prinsep reinforced the city's religious character, meticulously depicting and labeling Hindu sites of pilgrimage besides documenting its built and open spaces. Unlike the utilitarian surveys conducted by the colonial government in the late nineteenth century, Prinsep's map was intended to furnish its viewer with information on the city's religious life.

82 Regional Archives Allahabad, Duncan Records, Basta no. 96, Book no. 180, "Proceedings of the Committee for Local Improvement in the City of Varanasi 1823–1829."

83 Regional Archives Allahabad, Pre-mutiny Records, Benares Collectorate, vol. no. 8, Letters Issued and Received, Years 1800–1820, letter dated June 15, 1808, to George Dowdeswell, secretary to the government in the judicial department, from D. Morrison, acting magistrate of Banaras.

84 Veeraswamy, *Kasiyatra Charitra*, 119. Veeraswamy noticed bazaars in Patna being widened by the company's administrators.

85 Indian observers such as Gholam Hossein Khan "Tabatabai" accused company officials of being unable to truly comprehend and appreciate Indian customs and practices. See Khan, *Seir Mutaqharin or View of Modern Times*, vol. 2, 554–555.

86 Regional Archives Allahabad, Pre-mutiny Records, Benares Collectorate, vol. no. 8, Letters Issued and Received, Years 1800–1820, letter dated June 15, 1808, from D. Morrison, acting magistrate of Banaras, to George Dowdeswell, secretary to the government in the judicial department, Fort William.

87 Ibid. The adjacent ground, 264 feet long and 112 feet wide, was acquired for enlarging the *chowk*.

88 Ibid. The total cost of demolition and rebuilding was estimated at 12,798 rupees.

89 Ibid. Rent was fixed at a yearly rate of 6 rupees, ensuring that the company's government was acknowledged as owner and manager.

90 Kennedy, *Life and Work in Benares and Kumaon*, 69–70. Kennedy noted the great rise in temple construction in the city by the late nineteenth century.

91 Regional Archives, Allahabad, Duncan Records, Basta no. 96, Book no. 180, "Proceedings of the Committee for the Local improvement in the City of Varanasi," entry for February 13, 1827.

92 Sherring, *Sacred City of the Hindus*, 55.

93 *The Hindustani* (Lucknow), May 27, 1891, as quoted in National Archives of India, *Selections from the Vernacular Newspapers Published in the North-Western Provinces, Oudh, Central Provinces and Rajputana, Received up to 4th June 1891*. The Hindustani also wrote scathingly about the colonial preoccupation with a "water-supply hobby" even as administrators ignored a general "scarcity of grain."

94 *Nasim-I-Agra*, May 30, 1891, as quoted in National Archives of India, *Selections from the Vernacular Newspapers Published in the North-Western Provinces, Oudh, Central Provinces and Rajputana, Received up to 4th June 1891*.

95 Neville, *Gazetteer of Benares*, 240. Neville claims that it was built by "Ahilya Bai of Indore, a Raja of Bihar and Amrit Rao."

96 Regional Archives, Banaras, List 3, Box 12, File 1, "Land Acquired for the unfiltered water pumping station M.W.W. Bhadaini," letter dated August 10, 1892, from the Cooch Behar State Agent, to the Collector, Banaras.

97 Ibid.

98 Neville, *Gazetteer of Benares*, 168.

99 Regional Archives, Banaras, List 7, Box 7, File 87, "Kashi Tirtha Sudhar Trust at Benares," letter dated October 21, 1926, from Collector, Banaras, to E. F. Oppenheim, Commissioner, Banaras Division.

100 Ravidutt Shukla, "Honorable Babu Motichandji," *Indu*, Kala 4, Khand 1, Kiran 4 (April 1913): 393.

101 Regional Archives, Banaras, List 1, Box 116, File 79, "Acquisition of Land and Houses in the lane of Bishwanathji temple, Benares city required by the Municipal Board for widening the lane," letter dated February 2, 1929, from B. E. Dreyfus, Collector, Banaras, to the Commissioner, Banaras Division.

102 Regional Archives, Banaras, List 7, Box 12A, File 189, "Construction of a Park in front of Police Station to Chowk," Copy of Board's Resolution no. 294, dated July 30, 1927, as well as Copy of Board's resolution no. 466, dated September 22, 1927, assuring the District Magistrate of the Municipality's commitment to "sanitary improvement." At this time the Municipal Board was largely staffed by Indians. Also see List 7, Box 12A, File no. 189, letter dated July 22, 1927, from Executive Officer, Municipal Board, to Magistrate, Banaras.

103 Regional Archives, Banaras, List 7, Box 12A, File 189, "Construction of a Park in front of Police Station to Chowk," letter dated September 6, 1927, to the Chairman, Municipal Board, Banaras, from V. N. Mehta, the District Magistrate.

104 The proposal was not approved for government funding by the Sanitary Board on the grounds that it smacked of speculation intended to enhance "municipal income," a strategy also followed by the company's government when it developed its *chowk* scheme at the turn of the nineteenth century. See Regional Archives, Banaras, List 1, Box 64, File 108, "Scheme for opening out a congested area lying to the south of Bishesharganj market at an estimated cost of Rs. 1,64,000/- in the Municipality," letter dated September 16, 1915, from P. Mason, Under-Secretary to Government, United Provinces, to the Commissioner, Banaras Division.

105 Regional Archives Banaras, List 1, Box 64, File 108, Years 1911–1915, "Scheme for opening out a congested area lying to the south of Bishesharganj market at an estimated cost of Rs.1,64,000/- in the Municipality," enclosed note.

106 National Archives of India, Home Department, Public Branch, "C" 28th February 1786, no. 12, letter addressed to the Governor General of the Supreme Council, from Captain Thomas Brown dated February 26, 1786. Thomas Brown was charged with preparing, "A Plan of the famous city of Benares, including part of Ramnaghur, on a large scale; and another Plan on a smaller scale of the City and its environs, including the Patchcoss a religious walk of 50 miles around Benares which every Hindoo upon his arrival performs in five days, all the people in the city go round it twice a year and all those who die within its pale are supposed to go to heaven."

107 Regional Archives, Allahabad, Duncan Records, Basta no. 96, Book no. 180, "Proceedings of the Committee for Local improvement in the City of Varanasi," entry for December 10, 1825.

108 Regional Archives, Allahabad, Duncan Records, Basta no. 96, Book no. 180, "Proceedings of the Committee for Local improvement in the City of Varanasi," entry for October 8, 1825.

109 Harishchandra, "Bhumika," 152–156. The committee met between 1842 and 1872; its members included landowners and prominent bankers such as Devnarain Singh Bahadur, Babu Fateh Narain Singh, Baboo Gurudas Misra, Rai Narayandas, and Baboo Vrajdas.

110 Baldev Upadhyay, *Kashi Ki Panditya Parampara* (1983; reprint, Varanasi: Vishwavidyalaya Prakashan, 1994), 187–199. Pandit Bapudev Shastri was appointed to the college in 1842. Harishchandra does not mention the exact date on which Shastri furnished his "proof."

111 Harishchandra, "Bhumika," 152–156.

112 See the inscription on the temples.

113 Sherring, *Sacred City of the Hindus*, 105.

114 See the documents in the possession of Shri Shah, Azmatgarh palace, Mahmurganj, Banaras.

115   Chunder, *Travels of a Hindoo*, vol. 1, 291.

116   Bharatendu Harishchandra, "Kashi," in *Bharatendu Granthavali*, vol. 3, ed. Brajratnadas (Kashi: Nagari Pracharini Sabha, 1953), 140.

117   Sherring, *Sacred City of the Hindus*, 179.

118   Ibid., 181.

119   Regional Archives Allahabad, Duncan Records, Basta no. 96, Book no. 180, "Proceedings of the Committee for Local Improvement in the City of Varanasi 1823–1829," entry for February 14, 1824.

120   Regional Archives, Banaras, List 1, Box 16, File 1, "Land Acquired for Benia Park, Benares," letter dated August 21, 1902, from G. R. Dampier, Joint Secretary to the Board of Revenue of the United Provinces of Agra and Oudh, to the Commissioner of the Banaras Division. Dampier mentions the Collector's desire to appoint a "European gardener" for the park. Also see letter dated January 13, 1902, from Collector H. V. Lovett, to the Commissioner of the Banaras Division.

121   Prinsep, *The City of Bunarus*.

122   See photographs by Madho Prasad in Kitchener of Khartoum Collection, British Library, London, photographs, Shelfmark photo 17/3(25) and Shelfmark photo 17/3/(26). Also see "An Old Resident," *All About Benares*, 142–143.

123   Regional Archives, Banaras, List 1, Box 27, File 158, "In the Matter of Babu Guru Das Sen's Endowment of Rs 1000 to the prince of Wales Hospital at Banaras," note regarding donation in the year 1865 from Babu Guru Das Sen of Madanpura. Also see List no. 2, Box 106, File no. 143, "Prince of Wales Hospital in Benaras," letter dated September 18 from G. Adams, Magistrate & Collector, Banaras to J. J. F. Lumsden, Commissioner, 5th Division Banaras. See also List 3, Box 11, File no. 16, Department no. VIII, "Land Required for the Construction of the Main Sewer," letter dated April 3, 1893, from the Collector of Banaras to the Commissioner, Banaras Division.

124   See the inscription on a plaque inside the building.

125   Regional Archives, Banaras, List 3, Box 11, File 8, "Kotwali Building," letter dated April 14, 1892, to the Magistrate, Banaras, from the Executive Engineer's Office, Banaras Division, Public Works.

126   Regional Archives, Banaras, List 3, Box 24, File 16, "Improvement to the Site of New Kotwali and Town Hall at Benares," letter dated February 24, 1902, to the Collector, Banaras, from B. B. Chakravarti, Executive Engineer.

127   Regional Archives, Banaras, List 4, Box 27, File 25, letter dated April 14, 1909, from District Engineer, Public Works Department, Banaras, to Land Acquisition Officer, Banaras District.

128   Regional Archives, Banaras, List 1, Box 103, File 207, "Sale of lot belonging to Benares Municipality to the Nagari Pracharini Sabha for Rs. 4000.00," copy of letter dated June 11, 1923, from the Secretary, Nagari Pracharini Sabha, Banaras, to the Chairman, Municipal Board, Banaras.

129   Regional Archives, Banaras, List 1, Box 103, File 207, Years 1921–1925, "Sale of lot belonging to Benares Municipality to the Nagari Pracharini Sabha for Rs. 4000.00," copy of English note showing the help received by the Nagari Pracharini Sabha from the government. Also see List 1, Box 103, File 207, copy of letter dated June 11, 1923, from the Secretary, Nagari Pracharini Sabha, Banaras, to the Chairman, Municipal Board, Banaras.

130   Regional Archives, Banaras, List 3, Box 24, File 16, "Improvement to the Site of New Kotwali and Town Hall at Benares," note dated April 1, 1902, signed by the Land

Acquisition Officer and the Collector, Banaras. Also see Regional Archives, Banaras, List 3, Box 24, File no. 16, "Improvement to the Site of New Kotwali and Town Hall at Benares," letter dated February 17, 1903, from B. B. Chakravarti, Executive Engineer, Banaras, to the Collector, Banaras. Based on this communication, land was acquired on December 26, 1902.

131 *Pucca maholl* is the term used for a cluster of *muhallas* around the *chowk* in Banaras, where buildings were constructed from more durable materials.

132 Ravidutt Shukla, "Honorable Babu Motichandji," 395.

133 Kennedy, *Life and Work in Benares and Kumaon*, 70.

134 Sherring, "Sacred City of the Hindus," 38: Also see Thomas R. Metcalf, *Land, Landlords, and the British Raj: Northern India in the Nineteenth Century* (Berkeley: University of California Press, 1979), 352–362. Metcalf traces this temple building boom in late-nineteenth-century Allahabad to the British creation of numerous landowners who used religious patronage as a means to consolidate their newly acquired status.

135 Thomas R. Metcalf, *An Imperial Vision: Indian Architecture and Britain's Raj* (Berkeley: University of California Press, 1989), 24–54.

136 James Fergusson, *History of Indian and Eastern Architecture* (London: John Murray, 1891), 461.

137 Rajendralala Mitra Rai Bahadur, "On the Age of the Ajanta Caves," *Journal of the Royal Asiatic Society of Great Britain and Ireland* (new series) 12 (1880): 126–139. Also see James Fergusson, "Notes on Babu Rajendralala Mitra's Paper on the Age of the Caves at Ajanta," *Journal of the Royal Asiatic Society of Great Britain and Ireland* (new series) 12 (January 1880): 139–151.

138 Rajendralal Mitra, *The Antiquities of Orissa*, vol. 1 (1875; reprint, Calcutta: Indian Studies, Past and Present, 1961), v. Also see Rajendralal Mitra, *Indo-Aryans: Contributions towards the Elucidation of Their Ancient and Medieval History*, vols. 1 and 2 (London: Edward Stanford, 1881).

139 Mitra, *Antiquities of Orissa*, vol. 1, iv.

140 Ibid., i.

141 Ibid., 30–32.

142 Ibid., 32.

143 Recall that Fergusson in his *History of Indian and Eastern Architecture*, 461, had remarked on the partial "Mahomedan" character of the Vishweshwur temple.

144 It is interesting that Mitra, *Antiquities of Orissa*, vol. 1, 32, compares the Kedar temple to temples at Bhuvaneshwar. It is, however, possible that he did not actually visit the Kedar temple in person but heard about its relative age as one of the oldest extant temples in the city, which became the basis of his assumptions.

145 Ibid., 31–32.

146 Cast as traditional, such mores were actively encouraged by the colonial state as an appropriate Oriental mode of behavior and comportment for natives. See "Archibald Gough's Journal," MssEur, Biography No. 2, D. "Residence in India 1869–71," entry for June 1870, D10. British Library, London.

147 "An Old Resident," *The Benares Guide-Book* (Benares: Medical Hall Press, 1875), 67–68. Also see "An Old Resident," *All About Benares*, 109.

148 Greaves, *Kashi, the City Illustrious or Benares*, 34–35. A similar design was employed in the Assi Madhav temple on Assi ghat. Author's conversation with Shri Shashank Singh, one of the Rani's descendants, in October 2005.

149 Ibid. The second *haveli* on the tract was built in the 1930s and was designed on the basis of a new plan type. Its fresh design also established a novel relationship to the riverfront. The monumental gateway was replaced by a "residential" façade, with emphasis on the corner rooms that overlook the river. The fortress-palace was no longer in vogue.

150 Among late nineteenth- and early twentieth-century authors, Narayanpati Sharma cites the *Kashirahasya* as the source of the Panchkroshi. See Narayanpati Sharma, *Athasrikashikhandam Bhashateekasahitam Prarabhyate* (Bombay: Khemka Press, 1908), 16. Another nineteenth-century scholar, Gorji Dikshit, also cites the *Kashirahasya* as the source for the Panchkroshi *yatra*. See Ramkrishna Gorji Dikshit, *Kashiyatraprakash* (Banaras: Bengali Shah, ca. 1890), 9. Dharmadhikari cites the *Brahmavaivartapurana* as the source for the Panchkroshi *yatra* and also draws a reference to the Panchkroshi *yatra* from the *Naradiyapurana*. See Krishnachandra Dharmadhikari, *Kashidarpanam* (Calcutta: Kavyaprakash Namdheya Yantralaya, 1875), 135.

151 Dharmadhikari, *Kashidarpanam*.

152 Dikshit, *Kashiyatraprakash*.

153 Sherring, *Sacred City of the Hindus*, 105–106.

154 Ibid., 106.

155 Dikshit, *Kashiyatraprakash*, 1.

156 Sharma, *Athasrikashikhandam Bhashateekasahitam Prarabhyate*.

157 *Cantonment of Sikrol and Pandypoor, also the Civil Station and the City of Benares 1867–68.* From the collection of the British Library, London, IOL Shelfmark X/1427/1-2; *Plan of Benares City, Cantonment and Civil Station, 1879–1880.* From the collection of the Bharat Kala Bhawan, Banaras, Paintings, accession no. 800; *Duncani Bandobast* (Land Records) of 1883–1884; *Benares City, 1928–1929*, Private Collection.

158 Indians had participated in colonial survey efforts as assistants since the early days of East India Company surveys. See Jennifer Howes, *Illustrating India: The Early Colonial Investigations of Colin MacKenzie (1784–1821)* (New Delhi: Oxford University Press, 2010).

159 Kailasnath Sukul, *Kashidarpana*, 1876, British Library, London, Maps, Shelfmark 53345. (2). Multiple copies of this map are part of collections worldwide.

160 Sukul, *Kashidarpana*, 1876. Sukul purportedly produced this map of the city's sacred geography on the basis of specific *puranas* that he also listed on the printed map.

161 Dharmadhikari, *Kashidarpanapurti*.

162 *Saptapuriyatradiprakashaptram*, 1873, Private Collection, Banaras.

163 Rameshwar Prasad Varma, "Bauddha Bharat Ki Pracheen Sabhyata-1," *Indu*, Kala 5, Khand 1, Kiran 1 (January 1914): 17–20; and Rameswar Prasad Varma, "Baudhha Bharat Ki Pracheen Sabhyata-2," *Indu*, Kala 5, Khand 1, Kiran 1 (January 1914): 118–121.

164 V. A. Sundaram, ed., *Benares Hindu University: 1905–1935* (Benares: Benares Hindu University, 1936), i.

165 Ibid., xlx, 7.

6. VISIONS AND EMBELLISHMENTS

1 Bharatendu Harishchandra, *Premjogini*, in *Bharatendu Granthavali*, vol. 1, ed. Brajratnadas (Kashi: Nagari Pracharini Sabha, 1950), 337.

2 Rajani Ranjan Sen, *The Holy City—Benares* (Chittagong: M. R. Sen, 1912), iii.

3 Ibid., ii.

4   James Prinsep, "Preface" in *Benares Illustrated in a Series of Drawings*, parts 1–3 (Calcutta: Baptist Mission Press, 1831–1833), 5.

5   Thomas Daniell and William Daniell, *A Picturesque Voyage to India by Way of China* (London: Longman, Hurst, Rees and Orme, Paternoster-Row; and William Daniell, No. 9, Cleveland Street, Fitzroy Square, 1810), ii.

6   Charles Forrest, *A Picturesque Tour along the Rivers Ganges and Jumna in India: Consisting of Twenty-four Highly Finished and Coloured Views, a Map, and Vignettes, from Original Drawings Made on the Spot; with Illustrations, Historical and Descriptive* (London: L. Harrison for R. Ackermann, 1824), 151. Forrest visited the riverfront in 1807 and wrote about and illustrated the scenes he encountered. He described the "face of the city towards the river" as an "ornament" besides being "commodious and useful in the facility for bathing which they present to its vast population." He added that "the immense crowds of all sexes, in their varied and graceful costumes, who constantly frequent these public resorts, is truly wonderful."

7   Kim Ian Michasiw, "Nine Revisionist Theses on the Picturesque," *Representations*, no. 38 (Spring 1992): 76–100.

8   Ann Bermingham, *Landscape and Ideology: The English Rustic Tradition 1740–1860* (Berkeley: University of California Press, 1986), 83. On a similar subject, see John Barrell, *The Dark Side of the Landscape: The Rural Poor in English Painting, 1730–1840* (Cambridge: Cambridge University Press, 1980).

9   William Gilpin, "Three Essays on Picturesque Beauty; on Picturesque Travel; and on Sketching Landscape: To which is added a poem, on Landscape painting, 2nd ed. 1794," in *The Picturesque: Literary Sources and Documents*, vol. 2, ed. Malcolm Andrews (East Sussex: Helm Information, 1994), 15.

10 Nigel Leask, *Curiosity and the Aesthetics of Travel Writing, 1770–1840* (2002; reprint, Oxford: Oxford University Press, 2004), 168.

11 Ibid., 174.

12 Nicholas B. Dirks, "Guiltless Spoliations: Picturesque Beauty, Colonial Knowledge, and Colin Mackenzie's Survey of India," in *Perceptions of South Asia's Visual Past*, ed. Catharine B. Asher and Thomas R. Metcalf (New Delhi: American Institute of Indian Studies, 1994), 217.

13 William Hodges, *Travels in India during the Years 1780, 1781, 1782 and 1783* (London: J. Edwards, 1793), iii.

14 Ibid., 47.

15 Ibid., 59.

16 Sita Ram illustrated many sites along the Ganges, including the riverfront at Banaras. See illustrations by Sita Ram included in the *Hastings Albums*, British Library, especially *Riverfront at Banaras*, 1814, British Library, Shelfmark Add. Or. 4719.

17 In his sketch of the Mughal emperor Humayun's tomb (completed in 1571) at Delhi, Sita Ram placed the edifice in a pastoral wilderness rather than at the center of its geometric *chahar-bagh*. He depicted it with majestic proportions and irregular edges, suggesting a ruin rather than focusing on the precision of structure and form in imperial Mughal architecture. See Sita Ram, *Tomb of the Emperor Humaioon*, 1815, British Library, Shelfmark Add. Or. 4822.

18 George Valentia, *Voyages and Travels to India, Ceylon, the Red Sea, Abyssinia, and Egypt: In the Years 1802, 1803, 1804, 1805, and 1806*, vols. 1, 2, and 3 (London: William Miller, 1809), vol. 1, 117. Valentia also chose the riverfront for his description, declaring that it was "covered with buildings to the water's edge," adding that it was only from the opposite bank that a viewer could get a "conception of its beauty."

19   Hodges, *Travels in India*, iv.

20   Prinsep, "Preface," in *Benares Illustrated*, 5.

21   Leask, *Curiosity and the Aesthetics of Travel Writing*, 174. See also Christopher
     Pinney, "Colonial Anthropology in the 'Laboratory of Mankind,'" in *The Raj: India
     and the British 1600–1947*, ed. C. A. Bayly (London: National Portrait Gallery
     Publications, 1990), 252–263.

22   Emma Roberts, *Scenes and Characteristics of Hindostan with Sketches of Anglo-Indian
     Society*, vol. 1 (London: Wm. H. Allen and Co., 1835), 228.

23   Fanny Parks, *Wanderings of a Pilgrim in Search of the Picturesque, during Four-and-
     Twenty Years in the East; with Revelations of Life in the Zenana*, 2 vols. (1850; reprint,
     Karachi: Oxford University Press, 1975), vol. 2, 440. British tourism in India followed a
     certain prescribed terrain by the middle of the nineteenth century, and the riverfront
     was well established as an object for the colonial gaze. The "Directory" provided an
     official view of Banaras, picturesque from the river but on closer examination severely
     lacking in hygiene.

24   Ibid., 441.

25   Read (publisher), *Benares on the Ganges*, 1857, British Library, London, accession
     no. 53345 (1).

26   Bernard S. Cohn, *Colonialism and Its Forms of Knowledge: The British in India*
     (Princeton: Princeton University Press, 1996), 7–8. As Cohn describes it, in the context
     of colonial India, the "survey" came to define any investigation of the empire's natural,
     built, economic, as well as social landscape.

27   Prinsep, *Benares Illustrated*, description of plate titled "Madhoray Ghat and
     the Minarets."

28   Enugula Veeraswamy (Veeraswamiah), *Enugula Veeraswamy's Journal (Kasiyatra
     Charitra)*, trans. P. Sitapati and V. Purushottam (Hyderabad: Andhra Pradesh
     Government Oriental Manuscripts Library and Research Institute, 1973), 105.

29   Bholanauth Chunder, *The Travels of a Hindoo to Various Parts of Bengal and Upper
     India*, vols. 1 and 2 (London: N. Trubner, 1869), vol. 1, 260.

30   Prinsep, *Benares Illustrated*, description of plate titled "Eve of an Eclipse of the Moon."

31   Ibid., 49. Prinsep also mentions this event as having occurred in 1805; Regional Archives,
     Allahabad, Benares Collectorate, Pre-mutiny Records, XXIX, file no. 121, "Ranee
     Bhawanee's Estate." The Kapal Mochun tank was built in the eighteenth century and
     construction was sponsored by Rani Bhawani.

32   Reginald Heber, *Narrative of a Journey through the Upper Provinces of India, from
     Calcutta to Bombay, 1824–1825*, vols. 1 and 2 (London: John Murray, 1844), vol. 1, 184.

33   Sen, *Holy City—Benares*, 77.

34   For instance, the committee continued to monitor the *chowk*. When petitioned by one
     Nika Mul, an auctioneer for permission to cover a shed projecting from the arcade
     on the eastern side, the committee resolved that this would ruin the "contours" of the
     building. Instead, the auction site was placed to the north of the *chowk*, where the "line
     of arcades" could not be continued and ruin its urban profile. See Regional Archives
     Allahabad, Duncan Records, Basta no. 96, Book no. 180, "Proceedings of the Committee
     for Local Improvement in the City of Varanasi 1823–1829," minutes of meeting held on
     January 7, 1826.

35   The committee was dissolved in 1829, although its functions and preoccupations
     continued within other arms of the colonial apparatus.

36   Regional Archives, Allahabad, Duncan Records, Basta no. 96, Book no. 180,

"Proceedings of the Committee for Local Improvement in the City of Varanasi 1823–1829," minutes of meeting held on March 22, 1824.

37 Regional Archives, Allahabad, Duncan Records, Basta no. 96, Book no. 180, "Proceedings of the Committee for Local Improvement in the City of Varanasi," minutes of meeting held on May 22, 1824. Amrut Rao Peshwa offered to purchase and repair the temple of Rutneshwur in the Naek Bazaar and to donate a part of this property toward a road-widening scheme on condition that the committee provide him with a written assurance that the temple precinct would never be acquired for subsequent projects.

38 Regional Archives, Allahabad, Duncan Records, Basta no. 96, Book no. 180, "Proceedings of the Committee for Local Improvement in the City of Varanasi, 1823–1829," minutes of meeting held on November 8, 1823.

39 Ibid.

40 For more on the Lat Bhairo incident, see Sandria B. Freitag, *Collective Action and Community: Public Arenas and the Emergence of Communalism in North India* (Berkeley: University of California Press, 1989); also see Gyanendra Pandey, *The Construction of Communalism in Colonial North India* (1990; reprint, Delhi: Oxford University Press, 1997).

41 Regional Archives, Allahabad, Duncan Records, Basta no. 96, Book no. 180, Proceedings of the Committee for Local Improvement in the City of Varanasi, 1823–1829, minutes for meeting held on April 30, 1825.

42 Ibid.

43 Chunder, *Travels of a Hindoo*, vol. 1, 252–253.

44 Baboo Ishuree Dass, *Domestic Manners and Customs of the Hindoos of Northern India or More Strictly Speaking of the North West Provinces of India* (Benares: Medical Hall Press, 1860), 92.

45 Ibid.

46 National Archives India, Central India Agency, Office of the Agent Governor General for Central India, File no. 1823, Letter dated May 15, 1865, from A. Shakespear, Agent Governor General, Banaras, to Lieutenant Colonel R. J. Mead, Agent Governor General for Central India, Indore.

47 Ibid., and National Archives of India, Central India Agency, Office of the Agent Governor General for Central India, File no. 1823, Letter no. 643 of 1885, dated January 19, 1885.

48 National Archives of India, Central India Agency, Office of the Agent, Governor General for Central India, File no. 1823, Letter dated May 27, 1868, from A. Shakespear, Agent Governor General, Banaras, to Lieutenant Colonel R. J. Mead, Agent Governor General for Central India, Indore. Also see National Archives of India, Central India Agency, Office of the Agent Governor General for Central India, File no. 1823, Letter dated January 14, 1885, from the Commissioner, Banaras, to the Agent, Governor General for Central India, Indore.

49 National Archives of India, Gwalior Residency, File no. 93/27 (1861–74), Letter dated September 19, 1863, from the magistrate of Banaras, to the Agent, Governor General, Banaras.

50 National Archives of India, Gwalior Residency, File no. 93/27, Letter dated June 13, 1864, from the Gwalior Durbar, to the Political Agent at Gwalior.

51 National Archives of India, Gwalior Residency, File no. 93/27, Letter dated July 22, 1864, from W. S. Halsey, officiating magistrate, Banaras, to the Agent, Governor General, Banaras.

52   National Archives of India, Gwalior Residency, File no. 93/27, Letter no. 106 of 1867, dated July 12, 1867, from the Agent, Governor General, Banaras, to the Political Agent at Gwalior.

53   National Archives of India, Gwalior Residency, File no. 93/27, Letter no. 52 of 1873, dated April 28, 1873, from W. Kaye, officiating magistrate and President, Municipal Committee, Banaras, to C. P. Charmichael, Commissioner, Fifth Division, and Agent, Governor General.

54   National Archives of India, Gwalior Residency, Benares, Correspondence in File 301 (1911–1921), "Acquisition by the Mysore Darbar of a House belonging to H. H. Benares." My conclusions are also based on my conversation with Smt. Seetabai Jayatirtha Rajpurohit in December 2005. Smt. Rajpurohit, onetime resident of Mysore State and later of the Karnataka State, knew of the *chattra* through a network of family and friends, many of whom stayed at Mysore/Karnataka ghat on their visits to Banaras. For more on modernization and the Mysore State, see Janaki Nair, *Mysore Modern: Rethinking the Region under Princely Rule* (Minneapolis: University of Minnesota Press, 2011).

55   Sen, *Holy City—Benares*, 232–233.

56   Regional Archives, Banaras, List 7, Box 7, File 87, "Kashi Tirtha Sudhar Trust at Benares," letter dated October 21, 1926, from Collector, Banaras, to E. F. Oppenheim, Commissioner, Banaras Division.

57   Kashi Tirtha Sudhar Trust, *Benares and Its Ghats* (Banaras: Kashi Tirtha Sudhar Trust, 1931), 40–42.

58   Ernest Binfield Havell, *Benares, the Sacred City: Sketches of Hindu Life and Religion* (London: Blackie and Son Limited, 1905).

59   Ibid., vii.

60   Ibid., 199.

61   Ibid., 2.

62   Greaves as quoted in Kashi Tirtha Sudhar Trust, *Benares and Its Ghats*, 56.

63   Ibid., 22.

64   Ibid.

65   Saiyyad Marhar Hasan Korvi, *Tarikh-e-Banaras, 3 vols., 1916, 1926* (Banaras: Maharaja Banaras). This historical account was commissioned and published by the Rajas of Banaras. Korvi drew on the region's Indo-Islamic traditions as he compiled this account. At the same time, he relied on a composite format based in colonial constructions, genealogies, and myths to create his account.

66   Regional Archives, Banaras, List 7, Box 7, File no. 87, "Kashi Tirtha Sudhar Trust at Benares," petition dated January 5, 1927, from Babu Motichand, President, Kashi Tirtha Sudhar Trust, to Baron Irwin, Viceroy and Governor-General of India.

67   Ramkrishna Gorji Dikshit, *Kashiyatraprakash* (Banaras: Bengali Shah, ca. 1890), 2.

68   Sherring, "Sacred City of the Hindus," 90. The raja presented four sculptures of lions, representations of the deity's "vehicle," to various temples—namely, "one is in the temple at Durga Kund; a second is in the Chausathi-devi temple, in the Bengali Tola; a third is in the Siddhimata-devi temple, in the Bulhanala; and a fourth is in the possession of the Gujarati Pandit Gor Ji, awaiting its ultimate destination."

69   Dikshit, *Kashiyatrarakash*, 4.

70   Thomas R. Metcalf, *Land, Landlords, and the British Raj: Northern India in the Nineteenth Century* (Berkeley: University of California Press, 1979), 352 (notes).

71   See the Duncani Bandobast survey of 1883–1884 and the inscription at the site.

72   Family recollections suggest that the patrons and masons devised the *panchayatana* plan for this temple as a revivalist gesture. Author's conversation with Shri Shashank Singh in October 2005.

73   Denise Blake Oleksijezuk, *The First Panoramas: Visions of British Imperialism* (Minneapolis: University of Minnesota Press, 2011).

74   R. Burford, "Royal Panorama of the Holy City of Benares and the Sacred River," from *A Description of a View of the Holy City of Benares and the Sacred River Ganges* (London, 1840).

75   The Vizianagaram family's connection with Banaras was sustained over several generations, beginning ca. 1825.

76   British Library, McNabb Collection, photograph by Bourne and Shepherd, 1885, Shelfmark: Photo 752/15(47).

77   British Library, Bellew Collection, photograph by Samuel Bourne, 1860, Shelfmark: Photo 50/2(63).

78   For more on photography as an instrument of colonial knowledge-making, and Indian self-representation see Christopher Pinney, *The Coming of Photography in India* (London: British Library, 2008).

79   "Pandit Bapudeva Sastri, professor of Astronomy, teaching a class at Queen's College, Varanasi (Benares)," Archaeological Survey of India Collections, India Office Series (volume 46), photo by Bromochary, Brajo Gopal, c. 1870, British Library, Shelfmark: Photo 1000/46(4709).

80   "Manmandil Ghat," photograph by Brojo Gopal Bromochary, 1869, British Library, Shelfmark: Photo 984(13).

81   Frederick Oscar Oertel, *Buddhist Ruins of Sarnath near Benares* (Calcutta: Superintendent Government Press, 1908). Copies of Prabhunarain Singh's album of photographs were widely circulated, and one such copy is part of the "Kitchener of Khartoum" collection held by the British Library.

CONCLUSION

1   Mark Twain (Samuel L. Clemens), *Following the Equator: A Journey around the World* (New York: Harper and Brothers Publishers, 1897), vol. 2, 174.

GLOSSARY

adalat court or courthouse
amil revenue collector

bagh garden
bangla/bangaldar curved eave inspired by
    the Bengali thatched hut
baradari open pavilion with twelve arches
bhojan meal
bhumihar member of a brahmin caste who
    also works in agriculture
brahmapuri a neighborhood or settlement
    of Brahmins
Brahmin scholar or ritual specialist in
    Hinduism
brahmin-bhojan a ritual meal for Brahmins
burj battlement tower

chahar-bagh quadripartite garden, usually
    of Persian origin
chattra; chattram resting place for pilgrims
    where charitable meals may be served
chattri pavilion or umbrella
chihil-sutun pavilion supported on forty
    columns
chowk urban square

dakshina gift to a respected individual to
    express gratitude
dana charitable donation
dargah tomb of a Muslim saint
darshan to receive visual benediction from
    a deity or an image
diwan reception room
dharma religion or code of ethics

dharamshala charitable inn or rest house
    for pilgrims
dom funeral specialists
Dom Raja head of the funeral specialists in
    Kashi
Durga *puja* worship and communal
    celebration for the Hindu goddess
    Durga

farman decree; written declaration or order

gandharva celestial musicians
garbha-griha sanctum of a Hindu temple
ghat a stabilized riverbank; also riverfront
    fortress-palace
gunj a residential and commercial
    settlement built for speculation or
    profit
guru teacher or mentor
gurukul scholarly retreat presided by a guru

hasht-behisht pavilion with eight sides and
    internal divisions
haveli mansion
hom-havan offerings in a fire sacrifice
hundi check, bill of exchange

Kashikshetra sacred region of Kashi
Kashi Naresh legendary king or kings of
    Kashi
kothi banking house
kotwal chief of police
kotwali office of the *kotwal* or police
    headquarters

krosa unit of measuring distance
kshatriya member of a warrior caste or group
kshatriya dharma code of conduct for a
    kshatriya or warrior
kund tank or well

linga aniconic symbol of Shiva in the form
    of an erect phallus

madhi chambers on ghat steps facing the
    river
mahal palace
maharaja an enhanced role of a raja or king
mandapa pillared pavilion, usually in a
    Hindu temple
mandi market
mandir Hindu temple
mardana section of house, mansion, or
    palace reserved for men
mansabdar title awarded to a Mughal
    grandee in charge of a battalion or
    troop
masjid mosque
mehfil musical soiree
moksha liberation from the cycle of rebirth
muhallah residential neighborhood
mukti liberation
Muktikshetra sacred zone where the soul
    can attain liberation from reincarnation
muraqqa album
mushaira poetry recital
muth monastery

nach dance
nach girl female dancer or entertainer
naresh king
nawab governor or military leader
    (especially) under the Mughals
nibandha critical summary or essay

padushah king or ruler
pandit Brahmin scholar or priest
pata pilgrimage chart or spatial diagram
pathshala school
pishtaq portal with a pointed (Islamic) arch
pucca built from durable materials
puja Hindu ritual of worship
pura neighborhood or settlement

purana collection of myths (in Hinduism)
purohit priests who are ritual specialists
pushta embankment wall

qasba provincial administratiave town
qazi judge
qila fort or fortress

raja king
rupee unit of currency in India and other
    parts of South Asia

sadhu male ascetic
samadhi cenotaph
sanatan dharma the orthodox Hindu
    religion
sandhya ritual of Hindu worship
saray inn
shastra can refer to a religious prescription
    as well as a religious text
shastrartha explication of a religious
    principle
shikhara tower of a Hindu temple
snan-puja Hindu practice of ritual bathing
    and worship
sultan king
swayambhu self-generating (usually refers
    to a linga)

talao pond or lake (natural or artificial)
tarah a survey or map
Thakurji form of Hindu god Krishna when
    he is worshipped as a feudal chief
thana police station
tirtha pilgrimage site or destination
tirtha yatra pilgrimage
trishtali three Hindu sacred sites of Gaya,
    Kashi, and Prayag

wada mansion

yatra journey or pilgrimage
yojana unit for measuring distance and
    equal to two *krosa*

zamindar landowner or revenue collector
zenana section of a house, mansion, or
    palace reserved for women

BIBLIOGRAPHY

MANUSCRIPTS

BRITISH LIBRARY, LONDON.

Amal-i-Salih. Add. 20735.
Archibald Gough's Journal. MssEur, Biography No. 2, D. Residence in India 1869–1871.
Humphry, Ozias. *Sketch Book in India,* 1786. Additional MS. 15962.
Selections from the *Hastings Albums* (Sitaram's Journey), or *Views by Seeta Ram.* Add. Or.
4719 and Add. Or. 4726.

DISTRICT MAGISTRATE'S OFFICE, BANARAS

Duncani Bandobast (Land Records) of 1883–1884.

DOCUMENTS IN PRIVATE POSSESSION

Documents for Azmatgarh Palace in possession of Shri Shah, Azmatgarh Palace,
Mahmurganj, Banaras.
Documents for Dharamsala at Sheopur in possession of Shri Shah, Azmatgarh Palace,
Mahmurganj, Banaras.
Documents in possession of the Jangambadi Muth, Banaras.

REGIONAL ARCHIVES, BANARAS

List 1
List 3
List 4
List 5
List 6
List 7

UNPUBLISHED PUBLIC RECORDS

Duncan Records
    Pre-mutiny Records
    Proceedings of the Resident of Benares
Foreign Department (Political)
    Central India Agency
    Home Department
    Judicial Department (Civil)
Gwalior Residency
National Archives of India, New Delhi
Political Department
Public Branch
Regional Archives, Allahabad
Uttar Pradesh State Archives

MAPS AND PANORAMAS

All Benares. By Debi Pershad, ca. 1901. From the collection of the Bharat Kala Bhawan. Banaras. Paintings. Accession no. 86.405.

Banaras, India. Compiled by Army Map Service Corps of Engineers. U.S. Army. Washington D.C., 1955 (from Survey of India, 1925–1930).

Benares City, 1928–1929. Public domain. Obtained through courtesy of Mr. Klaus Rotzer, Pondicherry and Vienna.

Cantonments of Sikrol and Pandypoor, Also the Civil Station and the City of Benares 1867– 1868. From the collection of the British Library, London. IOL Shelfmark X/1427/1-2.

The City of Bunarus. By James Prinsep, 1822. From the collection of the British Library, London. Maps, Accession no. 53345. (6).

A Complete View of the Benares City. By Durga Pershad, 1901. British Library, London. Page 761.

Kashidarpana. By Kailasnath Sukul, 1876. From the collection of the British Library, London. Maps, Shelfmark 53345. (2).

Kashidarpanapurti. By Krishnachandra Dharmadhikari, 1877. From the collection of the British Library, London. IOL Shelfmark 53345. (4).

Map of Man Mandir. Ca. 1760. From the collection of the Sawai Man Singh II Museum, Jaipur. Accession no. 130.

Panorama of Bundiparkota ghat. Late seventeenth century. From the collection of the Sawai Man Singh II Museum, Jaipur. Accession no. 7.

Pilgrimage Map of Banaras. Ca. 1820. From the collection of the National Museum, New Delhi. Paintings Gallery. Accession no. 63935.

Pilgrimage Panorama. Late seventeenth century. From the collection of the Sawai Man Singh II Museum, Jaipur. Accession no. 138.

Pilgrimage pata. Ca. 1700. From the collection of the National Museum, New Delhi. Paintings Gallery. Accession no. 56.59/58.

Plan of Benares City, Cantonment and Civil Station. 1879–1880. From the collection of the Bharat Kala Bhawan, Banaras. Paintings. Accession no. 800.

Saptapuriyatradiprakashapatram. 1873. In possession of Mr. Shashank Singh, Banaras.

Srikashichitra. By Jung Bahadur, 1897. In possession of Mr. Shashank Singh, Banaras.

Tarah Kashijiki (Map of Kashi). Ca. 1700. From the collection of the Sawai Man Singh II
  Museum, Jaipur. Accession no. 191.

PUBLISHED RECORDS

*Collection of Treaties and Engagements with the Native Princes and States of Asia Concluded
  on Behalf of the East India Company.* London: United–East India Company, 1812.
*First Appeal Number 58 of 1934, between Sri Mad Jagat Guru, Sri Mahanth Mallikarjun
  Swami Jangam Alias Sri Mahanth Panch Akshar Shiva-Acharya Maha Swami Mahanth,
  and Nishikant Banerji and Others, in the High Court of Judicature at Allahabad.* Record
  of Proceedings.
Fitzjames, Frank. *Preliminary Report on the Sewage and Water Supply of the City of Benares.*
  Allahabad: North West Provinces and Oudh Government Press, 1880.
Imperial Gazetteer of India: Bareilly to Benares. Oxford: Clarendon Press, 1908.
Kashi Tirtha Sudhar Trust. *Benares and Its Ghats.* Banaras: Kashi Tirtha Sudhar Trust, 1931.
Neville, H. R. *Gazetteer of Benares.* Allahabad: Government Press, 1908.
Selections from the Peshwa Daftar. Bombay: Government Central Press, 1930–1933.
*Selections from the Vernacular Newspapers Published in the North-Western Provinces, Oudh,
  Central Provinces and Rajputana, Received up to 4th June 1891.* No. 22 of 1891.
Sources of Maratha History from Marathyanchya Itihasachi Sadhane. 22 volumes. Edited and
  published by Itihasacharya V. K. Rajwade and V. T. Gune, Part 1. Dhule: Rajwade Itihas
  Samshodhan Mandal, 2010.

PERIODICALS

Harishchandra Chandrika
Indu
Kavivachanasudha

PRIMARY SOURCES

Aiyangar, K. V. Rangaswami, ed. *Krtyakalpataru of Bhatta Laksmidhara.* Baroda: Oriental
  Institute, 1942.
Allami, Abul Fazl. *Ain-i-Akbari.* Translated by H. Blochmann. Volume 1. 1873. Reprint,
  Calcutta: The Asiatic Society of Bengal, 1993.
———. *Ain-i-Akbari.* Translated by H. S. Jarrett. Volume 2. 1891. Reprint, Calcutta: The
  Asiatic Society, 1993.
Bahura, Gopal Narayan, and Chandramani Singh. *Catalogue of Historical Documents in
  Kapad Dwara, Jaipur.* Jaipur: Jaigarh Public Charitable Trust, 1988. See document nos.
  200–254.
———. *Catalogue of Historical Documents in Kapad-Dwara Jaipur: Maps and Plans.* Jaipur:
  Maharaja of Jaipur, 1990.
Banarasidas. *Ardhakathanak (A Half Story).* Translated by Rohini Chowdhury. New Delhi:
  Penguin India, 2009.
Barker, Robert. *An Account of the Bramins Observatory at Benares.* London: W. Bowyer and
  J. Nichols, 1777.
Bernier, Francois. *Travels in the Mogul Empire.* Edited by Archibald Constable and translated
  by Irving Brock. 1891. Reprint, New Delhi: S. Chand and Company, 1968.

Bhatt, Nagesh. *Tirthendushekhara*. In *Bhattojidikshitkruta Tristhalisetuh, Nageshbhattakrut Tirthendushekharaha, Sureshwaracharyakrut Kashimokshavicharaha*. Edited by Suryanarayan Shukla. Varanasi: Sampurnananda Sanskrit Vishwavidyalaya, 1997.

Bhatt, Narayan. *Tristhalisetuh*. Edited by R. Gokhale and H. N. Apte. Pune: Anandashram, 1915.

Burford, R. "Royal Panorama of the Holy City of Benares and the Sacred River." In *A Description of a View of the Holy City of Benares and the Sacred River Ganges*. London, 1840.

Burway, Mukund W. *Devi Ahilyabai Holkar*. Bombay, 1920.

Chunder, Bholanauth. *The Travels of a Hindoo to Various Parts of Bengal and Upper India*. Volumes 1 and 2. London: N. Trubner, 1869.

Cunningham, Alexander. *Report of Tours in the Gangetic Provinces from Badaon to Bihar in 1875–76 and 1877–78*. Calcutta: Archaeological Survey of India, 1880.

Curwen, Frederick, trans. *The Bulwuntnamah: Translated from the Tuhfa-i-taza of Fakir Khair-ud-din Khan*. Allahabad: North West Provinces Government Press, 1875.

Dagens, Bruno, ed. and trans. *Mayamata: An Indian Treatise on Housing, Architecture, and Iconography*. New Delhi: Sitaram Bhartia Institute of Scientific Research, 1985.

Damodar, Pandit. *Uktivyaktiprakarana*. Edited by Jinvijaya. Bombay, 1953.

Daniell, Thomas, and William Daniell. *A Picturesque Voyage to India by Way of China*. London: Longman, Hurst, Rees and Orme, Paternoster-Row; and William Daniell, No. 9, Cleveland Street, Fitzroy Square, 1810.

Dass, Baboo Ishuree. *Domestic Manners and Customs of the Hindoos of Northern India or More Strictly Speaking of the North West Provinces of India*. Benares: Medical Hall Press, 1860.

Devtirtha Kashthajivhaswami. *Panchkroshasudha*. Ramnagar, Varanasi: Sarvabharatiya Kashirajanyas, 1997.

Dharmadhikari, Krishnachandra. *Kashidarpanam*. Calcutta: Kavyaprakash Namdheya Yantralaya, 1875.

Dharmadhikari, Krishnapant Sharma. *Kashishvinod Champukavyam*. Varanasi: 1885.

Dikshit, Ramkrishna Gorji. *Kashiyatraprakash*. Banaras: Bengali Shah, ca. 1890.

Dow, Alexander. *The History of Hindostan, from the Death of Akbar to the Complete Settlement of the Empire under Aurangzebe*. London: T. Becket and P. A. de Hondt, 1772.

Duncan, Jonathan. "An Account of the Discovery of the Two Urns in the Vicinity of Benaras." *Asiatic Researches* 5 (London: J. Sewell, 1799): 131–133.

Editor's Report. "Notice of an Inscription on a slab discovered in February 1838, by Capt. T. S. Burt, Bengal Engineers, in Bundelkhund, near Chhatarpur." *Journal of the Asiatic Society*, no. 87 (March 1839): 159–184.

Eggeling, Julius, ed. *Catalogue of the Sanskrit Manuscripts in Library of the India Office, Part VII*. London: Gilbert and Rivington, 1891.

Elliot, Henry Miers. *The History of India, as Told by Its Own Historians: The Muhammadan Period*. Edited by John Dawson. 1867. Reprint, New York: AMS Press, 1966.

Fergusson, James. *History of Indian and Eastern Architecture*. London: John Murray, 1891.

———. "Notes on Babu Rajendralala Mitra's Paper on the Age of the Ajanta Caves." *Journal of the Royal Asiatic Society of Great Britain and Ireland* (new series) 12 (January 1880): 139–151.

Forrest, Charles. *A Picturesque Tour Along the Rivers Ganges and Jumna in India: Consisting of Twenty-four Highly Finished and Coloured Views, a Map, and Vignettes, from Original*

Drawings Made on the Spot; with Illustrations, Historical and Descriptive. London: L. Harrison for R. Ackermann, 1824.

Fuhrer, A. *The Sharqi Architecture of Jaunpur: With Notes on Zafarabad, Sahet-Mahet and Other Places in the North-Western Provinces and Oudh.* London: Trubner and Company, 1889.

Garstin, Lieutenant Colonel. *An Account of the Hindoo Temple of Vissvisshoor or Bissinaut, at Benares.* London: T. Bensley, 1800.

Ghoshal, Jaynarayan. *Kashiparikrama.* 1792 (Manuscript). Calcutta: Bangiya Sahitya Parishad, 1905.

Girvanpadamanjari and *Girvanvanmanjari.* Edited with an introduction by Umakant Premanand Shah. Baroda: Oriental Institute, 1960.

Greaves, Edwin. *Kashi the City Illustrious or Benares.* Allahabad: Indian Press, 1909.

Gune, V. T., ed. *Sources of Maratha History from Marathyanchya Itihasachi Sadhane.* 22 volumes. Edited by Itihasacharya, V. K. Rajwade, part 1. Dhule: Rajwade Itihas Samshodhan Mandal, 2010.

Gurucharitra. Translated by K. V. R. Rao. Bombay: Samartha Vishwa Kalyan Kendra, 1995.

Harishastri, Pandit. *Surjancharitamahakavyam.* Edited and translated by Chandradhar Sharma. Banaras: Banaras Hindu University, 1952.

Harishchandra, Bharatendu. "Bharat Durdasha." In *Bharatendu Granthavali.* Volume 1. Edited by Brajratnadas, pp. 467–597. Kashi: Nagari Pracharini Sabha, 1950.

———. "Bhumika." *Kavivachanasudha* 3, no. 19 (May 22, 1872).

———. "Kashi." In *Bharatendu Granthavali.* Volume 3. Edited by Brajratnadas, pp. 139–146. Kashi: Nagari Pracharini Sabha, 1953.

———. *Premjogini.* In *Bharatendu Granthavali.* Volume 1. Edited by Brajratnadas, pp. 319–354. Kashi: Nagari Pracharini Sabha, 1950.

Havell, E. B. *Benares, the Sacred City: Sketches of Hindu Life and Religion.* London: Blackie and Son Limited, 1905.

Heber, Reginald. *Narrative of a Journey Through the Upper Provinces of India, from Calcutta to Bombay, 1824–1825.* 2 volumes. London: John Murray, 1844.

Hodges, William. *Select Views in India, Drawn on the Spot, in the Years 1780, 1781, 1782, and 1783, and Executed in Aqua Tint.* London: J. Edwards, 1786.

———. *Travels in India during the Years 1780, 1781, 1782 and 1783.* London: J. Edwards, 1793.

Kashirahasyam. Edited by Jagdish Narayan Dubey. Varanasi: Adarsh Prakashan Mandir, 1954.

Kennedy, James. *Life and Work in Benares and Kumaon, 1839–1877.* London: T. Fisher Unwin, 1884.

Khan, Dargah Quli. *Muraqqa-e-Delhi: The Mughal Capital in Muhammad Shah's Time.* Translated by Chander Shekhar and Shama Mitra Chenoy. Delhi: Deputy Publication, 1989.

Khan Gholam Hossein. *Seir Mutaqharin or View of Modern Times.* 3 volumes. Translated by Hadjee Mustapha. Calcutta: James White, 1789.

Khan, Saqi Mustad. *Maasir-i-Alamgiri.* Translated by Jadunath Sarkar. 1947. Reprint, Calcutta: Royal Asiatic Society of Bengal, 1986.

Khan, Shayesta, ed. and trans. *The Holy City of Benares: As Administered by a Muslim Noble: Social, Religious, Cultural, and Political Conditions, 1781–1793: Translations of Letters of Ali Ibrahim Khan Written to the Maratha Chiefs, the Trustees of Mandirs and Others.* Patna: Khuda Baksh Oriental Public Library, 1993.

Korvi, Saiyyad Marhar Hasan. *Tarikh-e-Banaras. 3 vols.* Banaras: Maharaja Banaras, 1916, 1926.

Kurukshetramahatmya. Unnumbered manuscript, composed/copied ca. 1800. Saraswati Bhandar (Library). Ramnagar.

Mandan, Sutradhar. *Devtamurtiprakaranam.* Translated by Bhagvandas Jain and Rima Hooja. Jaipur: Prakrit Bharati Academy, 1999.

———. *Rajavallabhamandanam.* Translated by Shailaja Pandey. Varanasi: Chaukhamba Surbharati Prakashan, 2001.

Mill, James. *The History of British India.* 3 volumes. London: Baldwin, Cradock and Joy, 1817.

Mir, Mir Taqi. *Zikr-i-Mir.* Translated by C. M. Naim. 1999. Reprint, New Delhi: Oxford University Press, 2005.

Misra, Mitra. *Tirthaprakasha of Viramitrodaya.* Edited by Pandit Vishnu Prasad. Benares: Chowkhamba Sanskrit series, 1917.

Misra, Vacaspati. *Tirthacintamani.* Edited by Kamalakrishna Smrititirtha. 1912. Reprint, Calcutta: The Asiatic Society, 1992.

Mitra, Rai Bahadur Rajendralal. "On the Age of the Ajanta Caves." *Journal of the Royal Asiatic Society of Great Britain and Ireland* (New Series) 12 (1880): 126–139.

Mitra, Rajendralal. *The Antiquities of Orissa.* 1875. Reprint, Calcutta: Indian Studies, Past and Present, 1961.

———. *Indo-Aryans: Contributions Towards the Elucidation of Their Ancient and Medieval History.* 2 volumes. London: Edward Stanford, 1881.

Nathan, Mirza. *Baharistan-i-Ghaybi: A History of the Mughal Wars in Assam, Cooch Behar, Bengal, Bihar, and Orissa during the Reigns of Jahangir and Shahjahan.* 2 volumes. Translated by M. I. Borah. Gauhati: Government of Assam, Department of Historical and Antiquarian Studies, 1936.

Newell, Hebert A. *Benares, the Hindus' Holy City: A Guide to Places of Interest with History and Map.* Madras, 1915.

Nicholls, George. *Sketch of the Rise and Progress of the Benares Pathshala (with a Supplement Bringing the Story down to 1906).* 1906. Reprint, Varanasi: Sampurnanand Sanskrit University, 2005.

Oertel, Frederick, Oscar. *Buddhist Ruins of Sarnath near Benares.* Calcutta: Superintendent Government Press, 1908.

"An Old Resident." *All About Benares, Containing a Sketch from the Vedic Days to the Modern Times.* Benares City: K. S. Muthiah & Co, 1917.

"An Old Resident." *The Benares Guide-Book.* Benares: Medical Hall Press, 1875.

[Parks, Fanny]. *Wanderings of a Pilgrim in Search of the Picturesque, during Four-and-Twenty Years in the East; with Revelations of Life in the Zenana.* 2 volumes. 1850. Reprint, Karachi: Oxford University Press, 1975.

Prinsep, James. "Benares Directory." In *James Prinsep: Life and Work.* Volume 1. Edited by P. Thankappan Nair. Calcutta: Firma KLM Private Ltd., 1999.

———. *Benares Illustrated in a Series of Drawings.* Parts 1–3. Calcutta: Baptist Mission Press, 1831–1833.

Roberts, Emma. *Scenes and Characteristics of Hindostan with Sketches of Anglo-Indian Society.* 3 volumes. London: W. H. Allen, 1835.

Rousselet, Louis. *India and Its Native Princes.* New York: Scribner, Armstrong, and Co., 1876.

Ryley, J. Horton. *Ralph Fitch, England's Pioneer to India.* London: T. Fisher Unwin, 1899.

Sarvadhikari, Jadunath. *Tirthabhramana.* Calcutta: Bangiya Sahitya Parishad, 1915.

Sen, Rajani Ranjan. *The Holy City-Benares.* Chittagong: M. R. Sen, 1912.

Sen, Surendranath. *Sanskrit Documents: Being Sanskrit Letters and Other Documents Reserved in the Oriental Collection at the National Archives of India.* Allahabad: Ganganatha Jha Research Institute, 1951.

Sen, Vijayaram. *Tirthamangala.* 1768–1769 (Manuscript). Calcutta: Bangiya Sahitya Parishad, 1905.

Sharma, Narayanapati. *Atha Srikashikhandam Bhashatikasahitam Prabhyate.* Bombay: Khemka Press, 1908.

Shastri, Surendranath, trans. *Shrivenkatadhvaripraneetah Viswagunadarasachampuh.* Reprint, Varanasi: Chaukhamba Vidya Bhawan, 2011.

Sherring, M. A., and C. Horne. "Description of the Buddhist Ruins at Bakariya Kund, Benares." *Journal of the Asiatic Society of Bengal* 34, part 1 (1864).

Sherring, Matthew A. *The Sacred City of the Hindus: An Account of Benares in Ancient and Modern Times.* London: Trubner and Company, 1868.

Shivprasad, Raja. *Itihas Timirnasak: A History of India in Three Parts.* Allahabad: Government Press, 1877.

Shukla, Ravidutt. "Honorable Babu Motichandji." *Indu*, Kala 4, Khand 1, Kiran 4 (April 1913): 389–395.

Shyamaldas. *Veer Vinod: Mewad ka Itihas.* Volume 2. Udaipur: Maharana Ratna Singh and Udaipur Rajyantralaya, 1886.

"The Speech of H. H. The Maharaja of Benares at the Anniversary Meeting of the C.H.C." *Vidya Mandir Patrika* 19 (November 1985): 20–21.

Sundaram, V. A., ed. *Benares Hindu University: 1905–1935.* Benares: Benares Hindu University, 1936.

Tavernier, Jean Baptiste. *The Six Voyages of John Baptista Tavernier (Book III).* London: John Starkey, 1678.

Thambiran, Kumarsami. *Saint Kumaraguruparar and the Two Great Mutts Associated with Him.* Tirupanandal: Sri Kasi Mutt, 1997.

Tieffenthaler, Joseph. *Des Pater Joseph Tieffenthaler's Historische, Geographische Beschreibung von Hindustan.* Berlin: Bendem Berausgeber, 1785.

Tod, James. *Annals and Antiquities of Rajasthan,* 3 vols. Edited by William Crooke. London: Oxford University Press, 1920.

Tripathi, Karunapati. *Srikashikhandaha.* 3 volumes. Varanasi: Sampurnananda Sanskrit Vishwavidayalaya, 1991.

The Tristhalisetuh of Bhattoji Dikshit. In *Bhattojidikshitkruta Tristhalisetuh, Nageshbhattakrut Tirthendushekharaha, Sureshwaracharyakrut Kashimokshavicharaha.* Edited by Suryanarayan Shukla. Varanasi: Sampurnananda Sanskrit Vishwavidyalaya, 1997.

Twain, Mark (Samuel L. Clemens). *Following the Equator: A Journey around the World.* Volume 2. New York: Harper and Brothers Publishers, 1897.

Valentia, George. *Voyages and Travels to India, Ceylon, the Red Sea, Abyssinia, and Egypt: In the years 1802, 1803, 1804, 1805, and 1806.* 3 volumes. London: William Miller, 1809.

Varma, Rameswarprasad. "Baudhha Bharat Ki Pracheen Sabhyata–1." *Indu*, Kala 5, Khand 1, Kiran 1 (January 1914): 17–20.

———. "Baudhha Bharat Ki Pracheen Sabhyata–2." *Indu*, Kala 5, Khand 1, Kiran 1 (January 1914): 118–121.

———. "Baudhha Sthapathya (Architecture) tatha Bhaskarkala (Sculpture)." *Indu*, Kala 5, Khand 1, Kiran 6 (June 1914): 540–544.

Veeraswamy (Veeraswamiah), Enugula. *Enugula Veeraswamy's Journal (Kasiyatra Charitra)*. Translated by P. Sitapati and V. Purushottam. Hyderabad: Andhra Pradesh Government Oriental Manuscripts Library and Research Institute, 1973.

Wheeler, J. Talboys. "Introduction." In *The Travels of a Hindoo to Various Parts of Bengal and Upper India*. By Bholanauth Chunder, xi–xxv. London: N. Trubner and Company, 1869.

SECONDARY SOURCES

Aitken, Molly Emma. *The Intelligence of Tradition in Rajput Court Painting*. New Haven: Yale University Press, 2010.

Alam, Muzaffar. *The Crisis of Empire in Mughal North India: Awadh and the Punjab*. Delhi: Oxford University Press, 1986.

[———]. "The Mughals, the Sufi Shaikhs, and the Formation of the Akbari Dispensation." *Modern Asian Studies* 43, no. 1. *Expanding Frontiers in South Asian and World History: Essays in Honour of John F. Richards* (January 2009): 135–174.

Alam, Muzaffar, and Sanjay Subrahmanyam. *Indo-Persian Travels in the Age of Discoveries, 1400–1800*. Cambridge: Cambridge University Press, 2007.

———. *The Mughal State, 1526–1750*. New Delhi: Oxford University Press, 2011.

———. *Writing the Mughal World: Studies on Culture and Politics*. New York: Columbia University Press, 2011.

Ali, Daud, and Emma Flatt, eds. *Garden and Landscape Practices in Re-colonial India: Histories from the Deccan*. New Delhi: Routledge, 2012.

Almond, Philip. *The British Discovery of Buddhism*. Cambridge: Cambridge University Press, 1988.

Altekar, A. S. *History of Banaras*. Banaras: Culture Publication House, 1937.

Andhare, Sridhar. "Jain Monumental Painting." In *The Peaceful Liberators: Jain Art from India*. Edited by Pratapaditya Pall, pp. 76–87. London: Thames and Hudson, 1995.

Andrews, Malcolm, ed. *The Picturesque: Literary Sources and Documents*. 3 volumes. East Sussex: Helm Information, 1994.

Asher, Catherine B. "Amber and Jaipur: Temples in a Changing State." In *Stones in the Sand: The Architecture of Rajasthan*. Edited by Giles Tillotson, pp. 68–77. Mumbai: Marg Publications, 2001.

———. *Architecture of Mughal India*. 1992. Reprint, Cambridge: Cambridge University Press, 2003.

———. "The Architecture of Raja Man Singh: A Study of Sub-imperial Patronage." In *Architecture in Medieval India*. Edited by Monica Juneja, pp. 370–397. New Delhi: Permanent Black, 2001.

———. "Lucknow's Architectural Heritage." In *India's Fabled City: The Art of Courtly Lucknow*. Edited by Stephen Markel and Tushara Bindu Gude, pp. 121–143. Munich: Prestel Verlag, 2011.

———. "Mapping Hindu-Muslim Identities through the Architecture of Shahjahanabad and Jaipur." In *Beyond Turk and Hindu: Rethinking Religious Identities in Islamicate South Asia*. Edited by David Gilmartin and Bruce B. Lawrence, pp. 121–148. Tampa: University of Florida, 2000.

———. "Sub-Imperial Palaces: Power and Authority in Mughal India." *Ars Orientalis* 23 (1993): 281–302.

Asher, Catharine B., and Thomas R. Metcalf, eds. *Perceptions of South Asia's Visual Past*. New Delhi: American Institute of Indian Studies, 1994.

Asher, Catherine B., and Cynthia Talbot. *India before Europe.* Cambridge: Cambridge University Press, 2006.

Bakker, Hans T., and Harunaga Isaacson, eds. *Skandapurana: The Varanasi Cycle.* Groningen: Egbert Forsten, 2004.

Barrell, John. *The Dark Side of the Landscape: The Rural Poor in English Painting, 1730–1840.* Cambridge: Cambridge University Press, 1980.

Bayly, C. A. "'The Pre-History of Communalism?' Religious Conflict in India, 1700–1860." *Modern Asian Studies* 19, no. 2 (1985): 177–203.

———. *Rulers, Townsmen, and Bazaars: North Indian Society in the Age of British Expansion, 1770–1870.* 1983. Reprint, New Delhi: Oxford University Press, 1992.

———, ed. *The Raj: India and the British, 1600–1947.* London: National Portrait Gallery Publications, 1990.

Beach, Milo Cleveland, and Ebba Koch. *King of the World: The Padshahnamah, an Imperial Mughal Manuscript from the Royal Library, Windsor Castle.* London: Azimuth Editions and Sackler Gallery, 1997.

Belli, Melia. "Keeping Up with the Rajputs: Appropriation and the Articulation of Sacrality and Political Legitimacy in Scindia Funerary Art." *Archives of Asian Art* 61 (2011): 91–106.

Bermingham, Ann. *Landscape and Ideology: The English Rustic Tradition, 1740–1860.* Berkeley: University of California Press, 1986.

Biswas, T. K. "Vestiges of the Past." In *Banaras: The City Revealed.* Edited by George Michell and Rana P. B. Singh, pp. 43–49. Mumbai: Marg Publications, 2005.

Blair, Sheila, and Jonathan Bloom. *The Art and Architecture of Islam, 1250–1800.* 1994. Reprint, New Haven: Yale University Press, 1995.

Blake, Stephen. *Shahjahanabad: The Sovereign City in Mughal India, 1639–1739.* 1991. Cambridge: Cambridge University Press, 2002.

Branfoot, Crispin. "Imperial Frontiers: Building Sacred Space in Sixteenth-Century South India." *Art Bulletin* 90, no. 2 (2008): 171–194.

Brown, Rebecca M., and Deborah S. Hutton. *A Companion to Asian Art and Architecture.* Chichester, UK: John Wiley and Sons, 2013.

Busch, Allison, "Hidden in Plain View: Brajbhasha Poets at the Mughal Court." *Modern Asian Studies* 44, no. 2 (2010): 267–309.

———. "Portrait of a Raja in a Badshah's World: Amrit Rai's Biography of Man Singh." *Journal of the Economic and Social History of the Orient* 55, no. 2–3 (2012): 287–328.

Cassels, Nancy Gardner. *Religion and Pilgrim Tax under the Company Raj.* New Delhi: Manohar Publications, 1987.

Chakrabarti, Dilip K. "The Development of Archaeology in the Indian Subcontinent." *World Archaeology* 13, no. 3 (February 1982): 326–344.

Chakrabarty, Dipesh. "Open Space/Public Space: Garbage, Modernity, and India." *South Asia* 14, no. 1 (1991): 15–31.

———. *Provincializing Europe: Postcolonial Thought and Historical Difference.* Princeton: Princeton University Press, 2000.

Chakravarty, Kalyan Kumar, Maruti Nandan Tiwari, and Kamal Giri, eds. *Khajuraho in Perspective.* Bhopal: Commissioner Archaeology and Museums Madhya Pradesh, 1994.

Chatterjee, Kumkum. "Cultural Flows and Cosmopolitanism in Mughal India: The Bishnupur Kingdom." *Indian Economic Social History Review* 46, no. 2 (2009): 147–182.

———. *Merchants, Politics, and Society in Early Modern India, Bihar: 1733–1820.* Leiden: E. J. Brill, 1996.

Chatterjee, Partha. *The Nation and Its Fragments*. Princeton: Princeton University Press, 1993.

Chattopadhyay, Swati. "Blurring Boundaries: The Limits of 'White Town' in Colonial Calcutta." *Journal of the Society of Architectural Historians* 59, no. 2 (June 2000): 154–179.

———. *Representing Calcutta: Modernity, Nationalism, and the Colonial Uncanny*. London: Routledge, 2005.

Chaudhuri, Jatindra Bimal. *Muslim Patronage to Sanskritic Learning, Part 1*. Delhi: Idarah-i-Adabiyat-I Delli, 1954.

Chopra, Preeti. *A Joint Enterprise: Indian Elites and the Making of British Bombay*. Minneapolis: University of Minnesota Press, 2011.

Cockburn, J. A. "Sanitary Progress during the Fifty Years, 1876–1926—Overseas Dominions and Colonial Aspect." *Journal of the Royal Sanitary Institute* 47 (1926): 89–94.

Cohn, Bernard S. *An Anthropologist among the Historians*. Oxford: Oxford University Press, 1987.

———. *Colonialism and Its Forms of Knowledge: The British in India*. Princeton: Princeton University Press, 1996.

———. "Representing Authority in Victorian India." In *The Invention of Tradition*. Edited by Eric Hobsbawm and Terence Ranger, pp. 165–209. 1983. Reprint, Cambridge: Cambridge University Press, 1999.

Dalmia, Vasudha. "The Establishment of the Sixth Gaddi of the Vallabha Sampraday." In *Studies in South Asian Devotional Literature*. Edited by Alan W. Entwistle and Francoise Mallison. Paris: Ecole Francaise d' Extreme-Orient, 1994.

———. *The Nationalization of Hindu Traditions: Bharatendu Harishchandra and Nineteenth Century Banaras*. New Delhi: Oxford University Press, 1997.

Dalmia, Vasudha, and Heinrich von Stietencron. "Introduction." In *Representing Hinduism: The Construction of Religious Traditions and National Identity*. Edited by Vasudha Dalmia and Heinrich von Stietencron, pp. 17–32. New Delhi: Sage Publications, 1995.

———, eds. *Representing Hinduism: The Construction of Religious Traditions and National Identity*. Thousand Oaks, CA: Sage Publications, 1995.

Dalrymple, William, and Yuthika Sharma. *Princes and Painters in Mughal Delhi, 1707–1857*. New York: Asia Society; New Haven: Yale University Press, 2012.

Desai, Devangana. *Khajuraho: Monumental Legacy*. Delhi: Oxford University Press, 2000.

Desai, Madhuri. "City of Negotiations: Urban Space and Narrative in Banaras." In *Banaras: Urban Forms and Cultural Histories*. Edited by Michael S. Dodson, pp. 17–41. New Delhi: Routledge, 2011.

———. "Resurrecting Banaras: Urban Space, Architecture, and Religious Boundaries." PhD dissertation, University of California at Berkeley, 2007.

Deshpande, Prachi. *Creative Pasts: Historical Memory and Identity in Western India, 1700–1960*. New York: Columbia University Press, 2007.

Dirks, Nicholas B. *Castes of Mind: Colonialism and the Making of Modern India*. Princeton: Princeton University Press, 2001.

———. "Colin Mackenzie: Autobiography of an Archive." In *The Madras School of Orientalism: Producing Knowledge in Colonial South India*. Edited by Thomas R. Trautmann, pp. 29–47. New Delhi: Oxford University Press, 2009.

———. "Guiltless Spoliations: Picturesque Beauty, Colonial Knowledge, and Colin Mackenzie's Survey of India." In *Perceptions of South Asia's Visual Past*. Edited by Catharine B. Asher and Thomas R. Metcalf, pp. 211–232. New Delhi: American Institute of Indian Studies, 1994.

———. "The Policing of Tradition: Colonialism and Anthropology in Southern India." *Comparative Studies in Society and History* 39, no. 1 (January 1997): 182–212.

Dodson, Michael S. *Orientalism, Empire, and National Culture: India, 1770–1880*. New York: Palgrave Macmillan, 2007.

———, ed. *Banaras: Urban Forms and Cultural Histories*. New Delhi: Routledge, 2011.

Doniger, Wendy, ed. *Purana Perennis: Reciprocity and Transformation in Hindu and Jaina Texts*. Albany: State University of New York Press, 1993.

Dow, Alexander. *The History of Hindostan, from the Death of Akbar to the Complete Settlement of the Empire under Aurangzebe*. London: T. Becket and P. A. de Hondt, 1772.

Dumont, Louis. *Homo Hierarchicus: The Caste System and Its Implications*. Chicago: University of Chicago Press, 1974.

Eaton, Natasha. *Mimesis across Empires: Artworks and Networks in India, 1765–1860*. Durham: Duke University Press, 2013.

Eaton, Richard M. *The Rise of Islam and the Bengal Frontier, 1204–1760*. 1993. Reprint, Berkeley: University of California Press, 1996.

———. *A Social History of the Deccan, 1300–1761: Eight Indian Lives*. Cambridge: Cambridge University Press, 2005.

———. "Temple Desecration and Indo-Muslim States." In *Beyond Turk and Hindu: Rethinking Religious Identities in Islamicate South Asia*. Edited by David Gilmartin and Bruce B. Lawrence, pp. 246–281. Gainsville: University Press of Florida, 2000.

Eaton, Richard M., and Phillip B. Wagoner. *Power, Memory, Architecture: Contested Sites on India's Deccan Plateau, 1300–1600*. New Delhi: Oxford University Press, 2015.

Eck, Diana L. *Banaras: City of Light*. 1982. Reprint. New York: Columbia University Press, 1999.

Entwistle, Alan W., and Francoise Mallison, eds. *Studies in South Asian Devotional Literature*. Paris: Ecole Francaise d' Extreme-Orient, 1994.

Farooqui, Amar. "From Baiza Bai to Lakshmi Bai: The Sindia State in the Early Nineteenth Century and the Roots of 1857." In *Issues in Modern History: For Sumit Sarkar*. Edited by Biswamoy Pati, pp. 45–74. Mumbai: Popular Prakashan, 2000.

Faruqui, Munis D. *The Princes of the Mughal Empire, 1504–1719*. Cambridge: Cambridge University Press, 2012.

Feldhaus, Anne. *Connected Places: Religion, Pilgrimage, and Geographical Imagination in India*. New York: Palgrave Macmillan, 2003.

Flood, Finbarr Barry. *Objects of Translation: Material Culture and Medieval "Hindu-Muslim" Encounter*. Princeton: Princeton University Press, 2009.

Foucault, Michel. *The Archaeology of Knowledge and the Discourse on Language*. 1972. Reprint, New York: Pantheon, 1982.

Freitag, Sandria B. *Collective Action and Community: Public Arenas and the Emergence of Communalism in North India*. Berkeley: University of California Press, 1989.

———. *The Public and Its Meanings in Colonial South Asia*. Special Issue of *South Asia* 14, no. 1 (1991).

———. "State and Community: Symbolic Popular Protest in Banaras's Public Arenas." In *Culture and Power in Banaras: Community, Performance, and Environment, 1800–1980*. Edited by Sandria B. Freitag, pp. 203–228. Berkeley: University of California Press, 1989.

———, ed. *Culture and Power in Banaras: Community, Performance, and Environment, 1800–1980*. Berkeley: University of California Press, 1989.

Frykenberg, R. E. *Delhi through the Ages: Selected Essays in Urban History, Culture, and Society*. Delhi: Oxford University Press, 1993.

Gengnagel, Jorg. *Visualized Texts: Sacred Spaces, Spatial Texts, and the Religious Cartography of Banaras.* Wiesbaden: Harrassowitz Verlag, 2011.

Ghosh, Pika. *Temple to Love: Architecture and Devotion in Seventeenth-Century Bengal.* Bloomington: Indiana University Press, 2005.

Gilmartin, David, and Bruce B. Lawrence, eds. *Beyond Turk and Hindu: Rethinking Religious Identities in Islamicate South Asia.* Tampa: University of Florida, 2000.

Gilpin, William. "Three Essays and a Poem." In *The Picturesque: Literary Sources and Documents.* Volume 2. Edited by Malcolm Andrews, pp. 5–60. East Sussex: Helm Information, 1994.

Glover, William J. *Making Lahore Modern.* Minneapolis: University of Minnesota Press, 2007.

Gode, P. K. "The Asvamedha Performed by Sevai Jaysing of Amber (1699–1744 A.D.)." In *Studies in Indian Literary History.* Volume 2, pp. 292–306. Bombay: Singhi Jain Sastra Sikshapith, 1954.

———. "Bernier and Kavindracarya at the Mughal Court." In *Studies in Indian Literary History.* Volume 2, pp. 364–379. Bombay: Singhi Jain Sastra Sikshapıth, 1954.

———. *Studies in Indian Literary History.* 3 volumes. Bombay: Singhi Jain Sastra Sikshapitha, 1954.

Gordon, Stewart. *The Marathas, 1600–1818.* 1993. Reprint, New Delhi: Foundation Books Pvt. Ltd., 1998.

Guha-Thakurta, Tapati. *Monuments, Objects, Histories: Institutions of Art in Colonial and Postcolonial India.* Delhi: Permanent Black, 2004.

Habermas, Jurgen. *The Structural Transformation of the Public Sphere.* Translated by Thomas Burger. 1989. Reprint, Cambridge: Cambridge University Press, 2000.

Habib, Irfan. *Confronting Colonialism: Resistance and Modernization under Haidar Ali and Tipu Sultan.* New Delhi: Tulika, 1999.

Havell, Ernest Binfield. *The Ancient and Medieval Architecture of India: A Study of Indo-Aryan Civilization.* London: J. Murray, 1915.

———. *Indian Architecture, Its Psychology, Structure, and History from the First Muhammadan Invasion to the Present Day.* London: J. Murray, 1913.

Hobsbawm, Eric. "Introduction: Inventing Traditions." In *The Invention of Tradition.* Edited by Eric Hobsbawm and Terence Ranger, pp. 1–14. 1983. Reprint, Cambridge: Cambridge University Press, 2015.

Hobsbawm, Eric, and Terence Ranger, eds. *The Invention of Tradition.* 1983. Reprint, Cambridge: Cambridge University Press, 1999.

Hosagrahar, Jyoti. *Indigenous Modernities: Negotiating Architecture and Urbanism.* London: Routledge, 2005.

Huntington, Susan L. *The Art of Ancient India: Buddhist, Hindu, Jain.* 1985. Reprint, Boston: Weatherhill, 2001.

Inden, Ronald B. *Imagining India.* 1990. Reprint, Bloomington: Indiana University Press, 2000.

Irschick, Eugene. *Dialogue and History: Constructing South India, 1795–1895.* Berkeley: University of California Press, 1994.

Irving, Robert Grant. *Indian Summer: Lutyens, Baker, and Imperial Delhi.* New Haven: Yale University Press, 1981.

Johnson-Roehr, Susan. "Centering the Chārbāgh: The Mughal Garden as Design Module for the Jaipur City Plan." *Journal for the Society of Architectural Historians* 72, no. 1 (2013): 28–47.

Juneja, Monica, ed. *Architecture in Medieval India*. New Delhi: Permanent Black, 2001.

Kafescioglu, Cigdem. *Constantinopolis/Istanbul: Cultural Encounter, Imperial Vision, and the Construction of the Ottoman Capital*. University Park: Pennsylvania State University Press, 2009.

Kaimal, Padma. "Shiva Nataraja: Multiple Meanings of an Icon." In *A Companion to Asian Art and Architecture*. Edited by Rebecca M. Brown and Deborah S. Hutton, pp. 471–485. Chichester, UK: John Wiley and Sons, 2013.

Kale, Yadav Madhav. *Nagpurkar Bhoslancha Itihas*. Nagpur: Vidarbha Samshodhan Mandal, 1979.

Kapur, Nandini Sinha. *State Formation in Rajasthan: Mewar during the Seventh–Fifteenth Centuries*. New Delhi: Manohar Publishers, 2002.

Kaul, Shonaleeka. *Imagining the Urban: Sanskrit and the City in Early India*. New York: Seagull Books, 2011.

Kejariwal, Om Prakash. *The Asiatic Society of Bengal and the Discovery of India's Past, 1784–1838*. Delhi: Oxford University Press, 1988.

King, Anthony D. *Colonial Urban Development*. London: Routledge and Kegan Paul, 1976.

Kinra, Rajeev. *Writing Self, Writing Empire: Chandar Bhan Brahman and the Cultural World of the Indo-Persian State Secretary*. Oakland: University of California Press, 2015.

Koch, Ebba. "The Baluster Column: A European Motif in Mughal Architecture and Its Meaning." *Journal of the Warburg and Courtauld Institute* 45 (1982): 251–262.

———. *The Complete Taj Mahal and the Riverfront Gardens of Agra*. London: Thames and Hudson, 2006.

———. *Mughal Architecture*. Munich: Prestel-Verlag, 1991.

———. "Mughal Palace Gardens from Babur to Shah Jahan (1526–1648)." *Muqarnas* 14 (1997): 143–166.

———. "The Symbolic Possession of the World: European Cartography in Mughal Allegory and History Painting." *Journal of the Economic and Social History of the Orient* 55 (2012): 547–580.

Kulke, Hermann, and Dietmar Rothermund. *A History of India*. 1986. Reprint, London: Routledge, 2006.

Leask, Nigel. *Curiosity and the Aesthetics of Travel Writing, 1770–1840*. 2002. Reprint, Oxford: Oxford University Press, 2004.

Leonard, Karen. "Indo-Muslim Culture in Hyderabad: Old City Neighborhoods in the Nineteenth Century." In *Indo-Islamic Cultures in Transition*. Edited by Alka Patel and Karen Leonard, pp. 165–188. Leiden: Brill, 2012.

Llewellyn-Jones, Rosie. *A Fatal Friendship: The Nawabs, the British, and the City of Lucknow*. Delhi: Oxford University Press, 1992.

Losty, J. P. "Depicting Delhi: Mazhar Ali Khan, Thomas Metcalfe, and the Topographical School of Delhi Artists." In *Princes and Painters in Mughal Delhi, 1707–1857*. Edited by William Dalrymple and Yuthika Sharma, pp. 53–67. New Haven: Yale University Press, 2012.

Losty, J. P., and Malini Roy. *Mughal India: Art, Culture, and Empire*. London: British Library, 2012.

Lutgendorf, Philip. *The Life of a Text: Performing the Ramcaritmanas of Tulsidas*. Berkeley: University of California Press, 1991.

———. "Ram's Story in Shiva's City: Public Arenas and Private Patronage." In *Culture and Power in Banaras: Community, Performance, and Environment, 1800–1980*. Edited by Sandria B. Freitag, pp. 34–61. Berkeley: University of California Press, 1989.

Majeed, Javed. "James Mill's 'The History of British India' and Utilitarianism as a Rhetoric of Reform." *Modern Asian Studies* 24, no. 2 (1990): 209–224.

Markel, Stephen, and Tushara Bindu Gude, eds. *India's Fabled City: The Art of Courtly Lucknow*. Munich: Prestel Verlag, 2011.

Marshall, P. J. *The Eighteenth Century in Indian History: Evolution or Revolution?* Oxford: Oxford University Press, 2003.

McCrea, Lawrence. "Hindu Jurisprudence and Scriptural Hermeneutics." In *Hinduism and Law: An Introduction*. Edited by Timothy Lubin, Donald R. Davis, and Jayanth K. Krishnan, pp. 123–136. Cambridge: Cambridge University Press, 2010.

McDermott, Rachel. *Mother of My Heart, Daughter of My Dreams: Kali and Uma in the Devotional Poetry of Bengal*. Oxford: Oxford University Press, 2001.

———. *Revelry, Rivalry, and Longing for the Goddess of Bengal: The Fortunes of Hindu Festivals*. New York: Columbia University Press, 2011.

McInnis, Maurie D. *The Politics of Taste in Antebellum Charleston*. Chapel Hill: University of North Carolina Press, 2005.

Meister, Michael W., and M. A. Dhaky, eds. *Encyclopedia of Indian Temple Architecture*. Volume 2, parts 1 and 2 (*North India*). Princeton: Princeton University Press, 1986.

Metcalf, Thomas R. *An Imperial Vision: Indian Architecture and Britain's Raj*. 1982. Reprint, New Delhi: Oxford University Press, 2002.

———. *Land, Landlords, and the British Raj: Northern India in the Nineteenth Century*. Berkeley: University of California Press, 1979.

Michasiw, Kim Ian. "Nine Revisionist Theses on the Picturesque." *Representations* 38 (Spring 1992): 76–100.

Michell, George, and Rana P. B. Singh, eds. *Banaras: The City Revealed*. Mumbai: Marg Publications, 2005.

Mill, James. *The History of British India*. Volumes 1–3. London: Baldwin, Cradock and Joy, 1817.

Minkowski, Christopher. "Advaita Vedanta in Early Modern History." In *Religious Cultures in Early Modern India*. Edited by Rosalind O'Hanlon and David Washbrook, pp. 73–99. London: Routledge, 2012.

———. "I'll Wash Your Mouth Out with My Boot: A Guide to Philological Argument in Early Modern Banaras." In *Epic and Argument in Sanskrit Literary History: Essays in Honor of Robert Goldman*. Edited by Sheldon Pollock, pp. 117–141. Delhi: Manohar, 2010.

Moin, A. Azfar. *The Millennial Sovereign: Sacred Kingship and Sainthood in Islam*. New York: Columbia University Press, 2012.

Moitra, A. K. *A Short History of Natore Raj*. Natore: Rani Bhawani Printing Works, 1912.

Motichandra. *Kashi Ka Itihas*. 1962. Reprint, Varanasi: Vishwavidyalaya Prakashan, 2003.

Nair, Janaki. *Mysore Modern: Rethinking the Region under Princely Rule*. Minneapolis: University of Minnesota Press, 2011.

Nair, P. Thankappan. *James Prinsep: Life and Work*. Volume 1. Calcutta: Firma KLM Private Ltd., 1999.

———. *Tercentenary History of Calcutta*. Volume 2. *A History of Calcutta's Streets*. Calcutta: Firma KLM, 1987.

Narain, V. A. *Jonathan Duncan and Varanasi*. Calcutta: Firma K.L. Mukhopadhyay, 1959.

Nicholson, Andrew J. *Unifying Hinduism: Philosophy and Identity in Indian Intellectual History*. New York: Columbia University Press, 2010.

O'Hanlon, Rosalind. "Speaking from Siva's Temple: Banaras Scholar Households and the Brahman 'Ecumene' of Mughal India." In *Religious Cultures in Early Modern India: New

Perspectives. Edited by Rosalind O'Hanlon and David Washbrook, pp. 121–145. London: Routledge, 2012.

O'Hanlon, Rosalind, and Christopher Minkowski. "What Makes People Who They Are? Pandit Networks and the Problem of Livelihoods in Early Modern Western India." *Indian Economic and Social History Review* 45, no. 3 (2008): 381–416.

O'Hanlon, Rosalind, and David Washbrook, eds. *Religious Cultures in Early Modern India: New Perspectives.* London: Routledge, 2012.

Oleksijezuk, Denise Blake. *The First Panoramas: Visions of British Imperialism.* Minneapolis: University of Minnesota Press, 2011.

Pal, Pratapaditya, ed. *The Peaceful Liberators: Jain Art from India.* London: Thames and Hudson, 1995.

Pandey, Gyanendra. *The Construction of Communalism in Colonial North India.* 1990. Reprint, Delhi: Oxford University Press, 1997.

Parodi, Laura. "Darbars in Transition: The Many Facets of the Mughal Imperial Image after Shah Jahan as Seen in the ex-Binney Collection in the San Diego Museum of Art." In *Indo-Islamic Cultures in Transition.* Edited by Alka Patel and Karen Leonard, pp. 87–110. Leiden: Brill, 2012.

Parry, Jonathan P. *Death in Banaras.* Cambridge: Cambridge University Press, 1994.

Patel, Alka. *Building Communities in Gujarat: Architecture and Society during the Twelfth through Fourteenth Centuries.* Boston: Brill, 2004.

Patel, Alka, and Karen Leonard, eds. *Indo-Muslim Cultures in Transition.* Leiden: Brill, 2012.

Pati, Biswamoy. *Issues in Modern History: For Sumit Sarkar.* Mumbai: Popular Prakashan, 2000.

Pauwels, Heidi. "A Tale of Two Temples: Mathura's Kesavadeva and Orchha's Chaturbhujadeva." In *Religious Cultures in Early Modern India.* Edited by Rosalind O'Hanlon and David Washbrook, pp. 146–167. London: Routledge, 2012.

Peabody, Norbert. "Review of *Death in Banaras* by Jonathan Parry." *Modern Asian Studies* 30, no. 3 (1996): 698–701.

Pinney, Christopher. "Colonial Anthropology in the 'Laboratory of Mankind.'" In *The Raj: India and the British, 1600–1947.* Edited by C. A. Bayly, pp. 252–263. London: National Portrait Gallery Publications, 1990.

———. *The Coming of Photography in India.* London: British Library, 2008.

Pollock, Sheldon. *Forms of Knowledge in Early Modern Asia.* Durham: Duke University Press, 2011.

———. "Introduction." In *Forms of Knowledge in Early Modern Asia.* Edited by Sheldon Pollock. Durham: Duke University Press, 2011.

———. ed. *Epic and Argument in Sanskrit Literary History: Essays in Honor of Robert Goldman.* Delhi: Manohar, 2010.

Prakash, Gyan. *Another Reason: Science and the Imagination of Modern India.* Princeton: Princeton University Press, 1999.

Ramaswamy, Sumathi. "Conceit of the Globe in Mughal Visual Practice." *Comparative Studies in Society and History* 49, no. 4 (2007): 751–782.

Rao, Velcheru Narayan. "Purana as Brahminic Ideology." In *Purana Perennis: Reciprocity and Transformation in Hindu and Jaina Texts.* Edited by Wendy Doniger, pp. 85–100. Albany: State University of New York Press, 1993.

Richards, John F. *The Mughal Empire.* 1993. Reprint, Cambridge: Cambridge University Press, 2008.

Rotzer, Klaus. "Mosques and Tombs." In *Banaras: The City Revealed.* Edited by George Michell and Rana P. B. Singh, pp. 51–65. Mumbai: Marg Publications, 2005.

Sears, Tamara I. *Worldly Gurus and Spiritual Kings: Architecture and Asceticism in Medieval India.* New Haven: Yale University Press, 2014.

Sen, Sudipta. *Empire of Free Trade: The East India Company and the Making of the Colonial Marketplace.* Philadelphia: University of Pennsylvania Press, 1997.

Sharma, G. N. *Mewar and the Mughal Emperors.* Agra: Shiv Lal Agarwala and Co. Ltd., 1954.

Shastri, Veda Vrata. *Nagari Pracharini Sabha ka Ardhashatabdi Itihas.* Banaras: Nagari Pracharini Sabha, 1943.

Sinha, Surajit, and Baidyanath Saraswati. *Ascetics of Kashi: An Anthropological Exploration.* Varanasi: N. K. Bose Memorial Foundation, 1978.

Srivastava, Ashirbadi Lal. *Shuja-ud-Daulah.* 1939. Reprint, Delhi: Shiva Lal Agarwala & Co., 1961.

Steadman, J. M. "The Asiatick Society of Bengal." *Eighteenth-Century Studies* 10, no. 4. (Summer 1977): 464–483.

Stewart, Tony K. "Alternate Structures of Authority: Satya Pir on the Frontiers of Bengal." In *Beyond Turk and Hindu: Rethinking Religious Identities in Islamicate South Asia.* Edited by David Gilmartin and Bruce B. Lawrence, pp. 21–54. Tampa: University of Florida, 2000.

———. "In Search of Equivalence: Conceiving Hindu-Muslim Encounter through Translation Theory." *History of Religions* (2001): 260–287.

———. "Replacing Vaishnava Worlds: Organizing Devotional Space through the Architechtonics of the Mandala." In *Religious Cultures in Early Modern India.* Edited by Rosalind O'Hanlon and David Washbrook. London: Routledge, 2012.

Sukul, Kubernath. *Varanasi Vaibhav.* Patna: Bihar Rashtrabhasha Parishad, 1977.

Summerson, John. *Georgian London.* New York: C. Scribner, 1945.

Talbot, Cynthia, "Inscribing the Other: Inscribing the Self: Hindu-Muslim Identities in Pre-colonial India." *Comparative Studies in Society and History* 37, no. 4 (October 1995): 692–722.

———. "Justifying Defeat: A Rajput Perspective on the Age of Akbar." *Journal of the Economic and Social History of the Orient* 55 (2012): 329–368.

Thapar, Romila. "Imagined Religious Communities? Ancient History and the Modern Search for a Hindu Identity." *Modern Asian Studies* 23, no. 2 (1989): 209–231.

———. *Somanatha: The Many Voices of a History.* New Delhi: Penguin Books India, 2004.

Tillotson, Giles H. R. *Rajput Palaces: The Development of an Architectural Style, 1450–1750.* New Haven: Yale University Press, 1987.

———, ed. *Stones in the Sand: The Architecture of Rajasthan.* Mumbai: Marg Publications, 2001.

Trautmann, Thomas, R. ed. *The Madras School of Orientalism: Producing Knowledge in Colonial South India.* New Delhi: Oxford University Press, 2009.

Truschke, Audrey. *Culture of Encounters: Sanskrit at the Mughal Court.* New York: Columbia University Press, 2016.

Upadhyay, Baldev. *Kashi Ki Panditya Parampara.* 1983. Reprint, Varanasi: Vishwavidyalaya Prakashan, 1994.

Van der Veer, Peter. "'God Must Be Liberated!' A Hindu Liberation Movement in Ayodhya." *Modern Asian Studies* 21, no. 2 (1987): 283–301.

———. *Religious Nationalism: Hindus and Muslims in India.* Berkeley: University of California Press, 1994.

BIBLIOGRAPHY

Von Stietencron, Heinrich. "Religious Configurations in Pre-Muslim India and the Modern Concept of Hinduism." In *Representing Hinduism: The Construction of Religious Traditions and National Identity.* Edited by Vasudha Dalmia and Heinrich von Stietencron, pp. 51–81. Thousand Oaks: Sage Publications, 1995.

Waghorne, Joanne Punzo. "The Diaspora of the Gods: Hindu Temples in the New World System, 1640–1800." *Journal of Asian Studies* 58, no. 3 (August 1999): 648–686.

———. *Diaspora of the Gods: Modern Hindu Temples in an Urban Middle-Class World.* London: Oxford University Press, 2004.

Wagoner, Philip B. "In Amin Khan's Garden: Charitable Gardens in Qutb Shahi Andhra." In *Garden and Landscape Practices in Re-colonial India: Histories from the Deccan.* Edited by Daud Ali and Emma J. Flatt, pp. 98–119. New Delhi: Routledge, 2012.

———. "'Sultan among Hindu Kings': Dress, Titles, and the Islamicization of Hindu Culture at Vijaynagara." *Journal of Asian Studies* 55, no. 4 (November 1996): 851–880.

Watters, Thomas. *On Yuan Chwang's Travels in India.* Volumes 1 and 2. 1904 and 1905. Reprint, New York: AMS Press, 1971.

Yang, Anand A. *Bazaar India: Markets, Society, and the Colonial State in Bihar.* Berkeley: University of California Press, 1998.

Ziegler, Norman P. "Some Notes on Rajput Loyalties during the Mughal Period." In *The Mughal State, 1526–1750.* Edited by Muzaffar Alam and Sanjay Subrahmanyam, pp. 168–210. New Delhi: Oxford University Press, 1998.

INDEX

on the Mughals and Kacchawahasn, 224n43

Padmeshwur and Vishweshwur temples, 221n34

on patronage and imperial support for pilgrimage routes, 34–35, 59

Amal-i-Salih, 121–23, *plate3*, *plate4*

Amethi temple on Manikarnika ghat, *170m5.1*, 200, *202f6.7*

bracket with "flying gandharva" on, *202f6.8*

plan of, *201f6.6*

Annapurna temple, *75m3.1*, *76m3.2*, 110

Antargriha zone:

location of, *39m2.1*, *40m2.2*, 41

opening of a fountain for public use in, 167, 249n102

on Prinsep's 1822 map, 86

Asher, Catherine B., 6, 62, 229n106, 230n118, 237n103

Asiatic Society (and Royal Asiatic Society):

and the architectural revival at Banaras, 17–18, 159, 178, 180

members. *See* Chunder, Bholanauth

positivist historical perspectives promoted by, 156–57, 159

Watters translation of Yuan Chwang's (Xuanzang's) travel narratives published by, 17–18

Assi Madhav temple on Assi ghat, *204f6.10*

Assi Stream, and the pilgrimage landscape of Kashi, *71m2.3*

Aurangabad *saray*, 38, *39m2.1*, *40m2.2*, 51, 81, 88

Aurangzeb:

Kumarasway *muth* supported by, 52–56, 88, 227n79

sketches of elite residences built during the reign of. *See* Humphry, Ozias

Aussan Singh, Aussangunj of, 87, 94, 97, *98f3.8*

Badshah Shah Alam II, 195, 241n633, 246–47n63

Bajirao ghat, *75m3.1*, *76m3.2*, *147f4.26*

Baluster Column, 226–27n72

Balwant Singh. *See* Rajas of Banaras

Banarasidas, *Ardhakathanak* (*A Half Story*), 30, 56

Banaras—riverfront:

festivals. *See* Burhvamangal

minarets of, as a favored subject for artists, 194

purana-based interpretation of, 199–200

See also Lat Bhairo incident

Banaras/Varanasi:

as a creation of the imagination, 211–13

on a pilgrimage *pata*, 69, *plate1*

Ganga Arati as representative of that, 211–12, 213

Buddhist identity of. *See* Buddhism; Sarnath

colonial Calcutta compared with, 160

colonial narratives of, depicted in a lithograph "The City of Benares" (1857), *193f6.5*

fluid relationship between history and myth found in guidebooks, 159–60, 200

location of, *4m1.1*, *75m3.1*, *76m3.2*, *plate5*, *plate6*

and the pilgrimage landscape of Kashi, *71m2.3*

as a feature distinguishing it from the Mughal capital of Shahjahanabad, 41

puranic representation of, 199–200

by Bharatendu Harishchandra, 162

and Hodges' Orientalist mission, 189–90

integration within historical outlines, 160

and sanitary conditions, 244n13, 244n15

baradari (pavilions), *137f4.17*, 137

Baizabai's colonnade compared with, 85, *85f3.3*

of Bhonsla ghat, *135f4.15A*, 137, *137f4.17*

of Chet Singh ghat, 123, *125f4.5B*, *125f4.6*, 126

of Devkinandan *haveli*, 102–4, *103f3.15*

placement of:

on rooftop terraces, 104, 123

within *chahar-baghs*, 120

use by late Mughal circles of elite men, 131–32

Barna (Varuna) Stream, and the pilgrimage landscape of Kashi, *71m2.3*

Bayly, C. A., 231n1, 235n64

Bellew Collection, 208

Bernier, Francois, 44, 225n54

Bhatt, Dikshit, *Tristhalisetusarsangraha* of, 33

Bhatt, Nagesh:

on Kashi:

and the *Kashikhand* and the Vishweshuwur tradition, 77

sacred landscape of, linked to narratives
in the *Mahabharata*, 74
Tirthendushekhara by, 74
Bhatt, Narayan:
Adi-Vishweshwur not mentioned by, 25
on the capricious nature of Indo-Islamic
patronage, 56
Gurucharitra pilgrimage tradition not
mentioned by, 26
on Kashi as an ideal site for cremations, 74
and Mughal Vishweshwur temple, 35
on its consolidation of Shaiva and
Vaishnava practices, 62
promotion of, 32–33
and typologies from the *Kashikhand*, 58
Tristhalisetu, 35–38, 223n21
Manikarnika in, 36, 129
on pilgrimage routes, 34–35
Bhawani, Rani:
brahmapuri of. *See* Brahmapuri Rani
Bhawani
Durga temple of. *See* Durga temple
her charities, 79, 87
patronage of, 78, 79
as a patron of temple construction, 94, 130,
239n130
Bhawaneshwur (or Tarakeshwur) built
by, 84
Kardameshwur temple renovations,
88–89, 111–12, 139n130
as a patron of the Panchkroshi pilgrimage
route, 88, 235n67, 235n69, 236n78
as a prominent landowner, 78, 79, 87,
232n19
Bhonsla ghat:
baradari of, 135f4.15B
construction by Raghuji Bhonsle II, 134–35
plan of, 135f4.15A
riverfront view of, 134, 134f4.14
Bhuvaneshwur, 24
Kedar temple compared with temples of,
251n144
Lingaraja temple of, 177f5.10
Bindu Madhav temple:
dismantling of, 227n77
Aurangzeb's order for, 51
Dharhara mosque built to replace it,
6, 51

key formal attributes shared with
Vishweshwur temple, 62
rebuilt version depicted on Prinsep's map of
Banaras, 233–34n42
Blake, Stephen, 41, 224n41
Bombay (Mumbai), location of, 4m1.1
Bourne, Samuel:
image of Sumeri temple at Ramnagar in the
Bellew Collection, 208
images in the MacNabb Collection, 207
influence of, 208–9
Manikarnika ghat photographed by, 207,
207f6.12
Brahmanal and Siddheshwari areas, 37, 39m2.1,
40m2.2, 223n21
Brahmapuri Rani Bhawani, 75m3.1, 76m3.2
location on Dashashwamedha ghat, 87
brahmapuris (residential precincts for
Brahmin scholars as well as Brahmin ritual
specialists), 36
built by the Peshwa family, 87
and notions of public charity, 86
sponsored by Ahilyabai Holkar, 87
British tourism:
individual tourists. *See* Parks, Fanny
riverfront as an object for the colonial gaze
of, 254n23
Buddhism:
and the colonial identity of Banaras/
Varanasi, 17, 158–59, 247n75
and Islamic iconoclasm, 158–59
Sherring's case for the city's antiquity,
158
Watters translation of Xuanzang's travel
narratives, 17–18
Gahadavala royal support of, 22
and Hindu beliefs, 164, 247n75
lack of overt references on pilgrimage maps
based on interpretations of the *puranas*,
185–86
Bundiparkota ghat:
Hada fortress-place at, 48, 225n46
not mentioned in Girvan texts, 57
Burhvamangal, 80, 141, 144, 145f4.25, 200

Calcutta (Kolkata):
Asiatic Society in. *See* Asiatic Society
location of, 4m1.1

and the city's ritual landscape, 155–56
    concern with sanitary conditions, 155,
        244n13
Durga temple:
    construction of Nawabgunj in relation to,
        94–95
    mandapa added to, 182
    plan of, *113f3.25*
    shikhara of, 112, *112f3.24, 114f3.26*

East India Company:
    infrastructure in its conquered territories,
        162
    sanitation as a concern of, 155
    and the Second Anglo-Maratha war, 145–46
    treaty with Amrut Rao Peshwa, 232n14
    See also Duncan, Jonathan; Ghoshal,
        Krishnachandra; Hastings, Warren;
        Mitra family
Eaton, Richard M., 23, 219n47, 225n51
Eck, Diana L., 12, 24, 215n1, 218n35, 219n5
Elliot, Henry Miers, 159

Feldhaus, Anne, 220n8
Fergusson, James:
    survey and classification of Indian
        architecture:
            categories of Hindu and Islamic used
                by, 176–78
            Vishweshwur temple (of Ahilyabai)
                described by, *176f5.9*, 177
Flood, Finbarr Barry, 217n27
Forrest, Charles, riverfront at Banaras
    described by, 236n16
Foucault, Michel, 10
Freitag, Sandria B., on "public arenas," 13, 79

Gahadavalas:
    Ghurid attacks during the rule of, 3–4, 7,
        19, 24–25
    Kashi designated as a capital by
        Govindchandra, 7, 22
Ganesh temple and ghat, *138f4.18*
    Amrutvinayak temple on, 140
    construction by Amrut Rao, 140–41
    mandapa of, 140, *140f4.20*
    plan of, *139f4.19A*
Ganga Arati, 211–12, 213

Ganges River:
    boat-ride views of the riverfront, 199
    foreign travel accounts by boat along. *See*
        Bernier, Francois
    location of, *4m1.1*
    and the pilgrimage landscape of Kashi,
        71m2.3
    ritual bathing in, 199
    See also Banaras—riverfront
garbha-griha (sanctum):
    of Ahilyabai Vishweshwur temple dedicated
        to Vishweshwur and Dandapani, 83–84,
        83f3.2, 114, *115f3.27*
    of Annapurna temple, 110
    formal distinction from the *mandapas*
        (ritual hall), 59, 60
    of the Kedar temple, 64, *65f2.15A*
Garstin, Lieutenant Colonel, plan of Ahilyabai's
    Vishweshwur temple, *115f3.27*
Gautameshwur Mahadev temple, Govind Dev
    temple compared with, 180–81
ghats:
    merger/disappearance of:
        absence from Girvan texts, 118
        renaming of, 228n92
    Sanskritized as *ghatta*, 57
    See also Bhonsla ghat; Bundiparkota ghat;
        Chet Singh Ghat; Dashashwamedha
        ghat; Ganesh temple and ghat;
        Manikarnika ghat; Panchaganga ghat
Ghosh, Pika, 219n43
Ghoshal, Jaynarayan:
    construction of Gurudham temple, 106,
        238n122
    on the Durga temple, 112
    Kasiparikrama of, 6, 89, 245n27
        on the limits of Kashi, 235n66
    scribe of. *See* Sen, Vijayaram
Ghoshal, Krishnachandra, 232n15
    as a partner of the East India Comany, 78
    recording of pilgrimage sites visted by,
        82–83
    shastra-based arguments in assemblies of
        Brahmins presided over, 78–79
Ghurids, 3–4, 7, 19, 24–25
Gilpin, William, 188
Girvan texts:
    Banaras described through Sanskritized

Kardameshwur temple, *111f3.23*
  incorporation into the Panchkroshi
    pilgrimage route, 26, 27, 64, 169
  Rani Bhawani's sponsoring of renovations
    to, 88–89, 111–12
  and urban improvement plans, 239n130
Kashi:
  designated as a capital by Govindchandra,
    7, 22
  idealization of its sacred landscape by
    Brahmin scholars, 33–35
Kashibas, 81, 213
Kashikhand:
  absence of sites from, 24
  composition of, 5, 18
  influence as a source of universal
    knowledge and authenticity, 58, 182
    as a result of political and social
      negotiation, 212
    and its role as the ultimate pilgrimage
      text on Banaras, 69
    spatial descriptions in, 64, 84
  Jnan Mandap of, 85
  Manikarnika in, 129
  pilgrimage routes and related rituals
    emphasized in, 22–24
  and the *puranas*, 18, 184
  translation into Telugu, 215n2
  twenty-five sites identified by Kacchawaha
    surveyors, 37, 86
  and the Vishweshwur *linga*, 5, 24, 28
    and Nagesh Bhatt's views on Kashi, 77
Kashikshetra:
  and the pilgrimage landscape of Kashi,
    71m2.3, 95–96, *plate2*
    and Mughal patronage and protection of
      sites associated with, 64
    purana-based antiquity of, 184
  pre-Islamic ritual landscape of, and the
    Kryakalpataru of Lakshmidhara, 22
Kashirahasya, universal knowledge and
  authenticity of, as a result of political and
  social negotiation, 212
Kashi Tirtha Sudhar Trust:
  formation by Babu Motichand, 167
  and the spatial and ritual order within the
    Antargriha zone, 167
Kavindracharya:

conversations on religious philosophies
  with Francois Bernier, 44, 225n54
  as mentor to Mughal prince Dara Shukoh,
    43
Kavivachanasudha, Bharatendu
  Harishchandra's essay on the Panchkroshi
  route in, 168, 236n76
Kedarasya *mutha*, 25
Kedareshwur temple:
  linga of, 24
Kedar temple:
  compared with temples of, Bhuvaneshwur,
    251n144
  dual relationship with Mughal urbanism
    and Kashikshetra, 64
  location of, *39m2.1, 40m2.2*
  plan of, *65f2.15A, 65f2.15B*
  renovation of, 43, 52–53, 55
Kennedy, James:
  Indic cultural legacy described as an
    amalgam of Buddhist and Hindu beliefs
    and material cultures, 158
  on the practice of Kashibas, 81
  on temple construction in Banaras, 176,
    248n90
Khajuraho temples, 24, 208, 228–29n100,
  239n129
Khan, Ali Ibrahim:
  and the construction of *naubatkahana* of
    Vishweshwur temple, 246n63
  as magistrate of Banaras, 154, 244n8
  repairs of Dharhara mosque, 162
Koch, Ebba, 226–27n72, 237n103
Kolkata. *See* Calcutta
Krishna Govardhanadhara, as evidence of the
  antiquity of Banaras, 17
Krittivaseshwur temple:
  Alamgiri mosque built on the foundations
    of, 18
  depicted on Prinsep's map of Banaras,
    230n19, 233–34n42
Krtyakalpataru of Lakshmidhara:
  influence of:
    at its intended audience, 22, 221n37
    on Narayan Bhatt, 34, 35
  tirthas absent from, 22–23, 223n11
  as a *tirtha* text and a *nibandha*, 220n15
  and Vishweshwur *linga*, 28, 34

Kumarswamy *muth, 53f2.10,* 88
  Aurangzeb support for the construction of,
    52–56, 227n79
  and Dara Shukoh, 227n79, 227n82
  location of, *39m2.1, 40m2.2*
  plan of, 54, *54f2.11*
  refectory of, *55f2.12*
  samadhi (funeral marker) within, 64

Lal Darwaza mosque (Jaunpur), and the
  destruction of Padmeshwur temple, 25,
  221n32
Lat Bhairo incident, 164, 195, 196
Laxmi Narayan temple, *shikhara* of, *136f4.16,*
  136–37
Leonard, Karen, 11
Lingaraja temple, *177f5.10*
Lolark *kund*:
  and colonial government tensions, 166, 174,
    238n127
  construction of, 248n95
  and the Cooch Behar Family, 108, 166,
    238n127
  Mughal support for its refurbishment, 43
Losty, J.P., 239n6
Lutgendorf, Philip, 80

MacNabb Collection, 207
Madhayameshwur *linga,* 77
Madras (Chennai), location of, *4m1.1*
Maidagin:
  location of, 169, *170m5.1,* 171, *171f5.4*
  as Mandakini *tirtha* on pilgrimage routes
    and maps, 169, 171, *plate5, plate7*
  See also Ishwari Memorial Hospital; New
    Kotwali; Prince of Wales Hospital; Town
    Hall
Man Singh, *haveli,* 41–42
mandapas (ritual hall):
  of Devkinandan *haveli,* 105, *106f3.18*
  formal distinction from the *garbha-griha*
    (sanctum), 59, 60
  of Amrutvinayak temple and ghat, 140,
    140f4.20
  of Govind Dev temple, 62, *63f214B*
  preceding *shikhara* on sanctums, 239n128
  roof-types used over, 59
  of the Vishweshwur temple, 25

Manikarnika ghat, *39m2.1, 40m2.2, 149f4.27,*
  207f6.12
  Bajirao ghat located near, 146–47
  transformation into a funeral ghat, 241n31
Man Mandir, *208f6.13*
  as a tourist site, 162, 206
  location of, *39m2.1, 40m2.2,* 42, *42f2.3*
  Mughal fortress-palace architectural style
    of, 45
  plan of, *46f2.4*
mansabdari system, prominent *mansabdar*s.
  See Man Singh; Todarmal
mapping:
  of Banaras/Varanasi, *4m1.1, 39m2.1, 40m2.2,*
    75m3.1, 76m3.2, 170m5.1, plate6
  Durga Pershad's scroll, 206, *plate8*
  of Maidagin, *170m5.1, 171f5.4*
  and the concept of Kashikshetra, 95–96,
    plate2, plate7
  increased accuracy in techniques of, 184,
    plate6
  map of India, *4m1.1*
  pilgrimage panorama (map number 138),
    50, *50f2.8*
Marshall, P.J., 216n12, 216n16
minarets:
  of the Dharhara mosque, 144–45, 206
  as a favored subject for artists, 194
Minkowski, Christopher, 222–23n8, 223n10
Misra, Mitra, *Tirthaprakasha of*
  Viramitrodaya, 33, 64, 223n11
Misra, Vacaspati, *nibhanda* text,
  Tirthachintamani, 33, 34
Mitra family, and the East India Company, 78,
  99
Mitra *kothi* (or the Bengali Deohri):
  construction of, 99
  Durga *puja* pavilion of, 100, *100f3.11*
  Grecian pediment on exterior of, *99f3.10,*
    100
  outer courtyard of, 100, *101f3.12*
  shikhara of Shiva temple within, 102,
    102f3.13
Mitra, Rajendralal:
  on the age of the Ajanta caves, 177
  on temple architecture, 178, *179f5.11,* 251n144
Motichand, Babu:
  Azmatgarh palace of, 174–75, *175f5.8*

as chairman of the Municipal Board, 165, 167

construction of a *dharamshala* at Sheopur sponsored by, 168

and the Kashi Tirtha Sudhar Trust: formation of, 167

hosting of European visitors, 199

Motichandra, 220n18, 221n32

on the historical basis for the military conquest of Banaras, 215n1

Mughal Vishweshwur temple, building of, 35

muhalla structure:

clustering of. *See pucca maholl*

and the construction of *brahmapuris*, 86

significance of, 165

Muhammad Shah, cultural and religious tolerance of, 216n16

Mumbai. *See* Bombay

Nagari Pracharini Sabha, *170m5.1*, 173, 174

Nag Kuan, 196

nai patti, 75m3.1, 76m3.2, 87–88

Nawabs of Lucknow, 216n19

Neville, H. R.:

Gazetteer of Benares:

on Buddhist Banaras, 159

on mandatory use of public latrines, 244n15

on the Lolark *kund*, 248n95

Newell, Hebert A., 159

new *kotwali, 170m5.1*, 173, 174

nibandha, titles of. *See Kryakalpataru of* Lakshmidhara; Misra, Mitra, *Tirthaprakasa of Viramitrodaya*

Nicholson, Andrew J., 22

O'Hanlon, Rosalind, 222–23n8

"An Old Resident," *All About Benares*, 160

Padmeshwur temple:

destruction (possible) by Sharqi sultans, 221n32, 221n34

mention of its building on an inscription in Lal Darwaza mosque, 25

Panchaganga ghat, Dharhara mosque on, *191f6.3*, 192

Panchikroshi pilgrimage route:

Bharatendu Harishchandra on, 168, 236n76

Kashthajivhaswami's poem, the *Panchkroshsudha* on, 89

and the pilgrimage landscape of Kashi, *71m2.3*

Panchkroshasudha, Devtirtha Kashthajivhaswami, 89

Pandit family:

and the East India Company, 128

and the Maratha chiefs, 128

Pandit, Beni Ram, 87, 128, 240–41n22

Pandit, Bishambur, 128, 162, 240–41n22

Parks, Fanny, 148–49, 193

Parry, Jonathan P., 12, 218n35, 218n37

Patankar, Narayan Dikshit, 87, 230n120, 241n31

Patel, Alka, 11, 219n43

Peabody, Norbert, 218n37

Pershad, Durga, *Complete View of the Benares City*, 206, *plate8*

Peshwa family:

eleven *brahmapuris* built by, 87

pilgrimages to Banaras, 230n120

Peshwa, Amrut Rao:

chahar-baghs of, 92–93

patronage of, 78, 138, 143, 146, 242n46

as Peshwa in Pune, 78, 138

and Bajirao Peshwa II, 138

installed as Peshwa by Holkar, 138

repair of the temple of Rutneshwur in Naek Bazaar, 225n37

treaty with the East India Company, 232n14

See also Ganesh temple and ghat

Peshwa, Bajirao I:

mansion near Adi Keshav temple, 126, 128, 147

Peshwa, Bajirao II:

East India Company's domination over, 146

patronage of, 146

replacement of Amrut Rao by, 138

photography:

and colonial knowledge making, 208–10, 257n78

incorporation into guidebooks, 210

individual photographers. *See* Bourne, Samuel

and the representational legacy of a mythically charged panorama, Hindu identity based on, 210

pilgrimage routes:

288   INDEX

as a feature distinguishing Banaras from
  Shahjahanabad, 41
changing practices regarding the inclusion
  of sites, 22–24, 220n22
guides. *See* guidebooks
and the imagination of texts, material
  reality of the city measured against,
  71m2.3, 72, 74, 186
maps based on interpretations of the
  puranas, lack of overt references to
  Buddhist sites on, 185–86
See also Panchikroshi pilgrimage route
pilgrimage *tarah* (*Tarah Kashijiki Ki*), 37,
  224n31
pishtaqs (portals framing pointed arches), 45
Prince of Wales Hospital, *170m5.1, 171–72,*
  172f5.5
Prinsep, James:
  "Benares Directory," 74, 240n22
  Benares Illustrated:
    "Benares, A Brahmin placing a garland
      on the holiest spot in the sacred city,"
      192f6.4
    "Elevation of a Hindoo Temple," 100,
      116f3.28
    "Madhoray Ghat and the Minarets at
      Benares," *191f6.3, 192*
    references only, 253n4, 254n20, 254n27,
      254n30
    "The Temple of Vishveshvur," *32f2.1*
    "The City of Bunarus," 74, 171, *plate5*
  Bisheshurgunj of, 167, 237n96
  on the Burhvamangal festival, 144, *145f4.15*
  on the Lat Bhairo incident as having
    occurred in 1805, 254n31
  map of Banaras:
    rebuilt Bindu Madhav and the
      Krittivaseshwur temple depicted on,
      230n119, 233–34n42
    religious life emphasized in, 247n81
  observation of contemporary masons using
    archaic plans and forms, 115
public spaces:
  access to rituals and festivals within
    buildings, 101, 105, 120–21, 123, 137
  alteration of, by Indian elites, 165–66, 169
  conflict and protest occurring within
    "public arenas," 13, 79

private observance combined with public
  visibility, 134
See also baradari
pucca maholl:
  ancestral *havelis* in, 174
  of the Antargriha zone, 27
  defined, 251n131
puranas on Banaras or Kashi:
  and the *Kashikhand*, 18, 184
  and Narayan Bhatt's *Tristhalisetu*, 35–36
  reconciliation of Sarnath with, 156–58
  as representations of negotiated pasts, 18

qasbas (administrative centers), idealized
  chowk (town square) of "Sher Singh"
  compared with, 94, *95f3.7*
Queen's College, *161f5.2*
  as a tourist site, 162

Rajas of Banaras:
  Singh, Balwant:
    conflict over the Vishweshwur temple,
      81–82
    fortress-palace at Ramnagar built by, 123
    as successor to Meer Rustam Ali, 123
    title "Kashi Naresh," 9
  Singh, Chet:
    dispute with Warren Hastings, 9, 144
    patron of *Chet Sinha Vilas*, 89, 235n71
    succession as Raja of Banaras, 89
  Singh, Ishwariprasadnarain:
    temples on Chet Singh ghat build in
      memory of, 200
    photo album commissioned by, 209
  Singh, Mahipnarain, appointed as "Raja" at
    Ramnagar by Warren Hastings, 9
  Singh, Prabhunarian, 180, 209–10
    Ganga Mahal constructed by, 209
    Gautameshwur Mahadev temple
      constructed by, 180–81
    photo album commissioned by, 209–10
    temples on Chet Singh ghat constructed
      by, 200
Ramnagar:
  chahar-bagh of, 91, *93f3.6*
  Mahipnarain Singh as "Raja" at, 9
  and the pilgrimage landscape of Kashi,
    71m2.3

Ramlila celebrations at, 80

Sumeri temple at, 208

Rana Mahal, *49f2.7*

    absence from the pilgrimage panorama, 50–51

    location of, *39m2.1, 40m2.2*

    syncretic architectural vocabulary of, 49–50

Ranas of Mewar:

    Maharana Jagat Singh I:

        Jagdish temple commissioned by, 60

        and the Rana Mahal, 50, 227n74

    See also Rana Mahal

Razia's mosque, 18, *19f1.1*, 25, 58, 221n33

Red fort at Agra. *See* Agra

Roberts, Emma, 193

Rotzer, Klaus, 227n85

Rutneshwur temple in Naek Bazaar, 255n37

Safdarjung (second Nawab of Awadh), tomb of, 90, *91f3.4, 92f3.5*

sanitation:

    Banaras compared unfavorably to other metropolitan environments, 162

    construction of a pumping station near Lolark *kund. See* Lolark *kund*

    designs for a citywide sewage plan, 161

    and the desire for spaciousness, 167, 249n102

    opening of a fountain for public use in the Antargriha zone, 167, 249n102

    protests against the introduction of public toilets, 155, 244n17

Sanskrit terminology, used by Brahmin authors to define "uncontaminated" spaces, 57

Sarnath:

    antiquities excavated at, *210f6.14*

    discovery of, 245n26

    as evidence of the antiquity of Banaras, 17, 156–58

    image of a "modern temple" at, 208

    its absence from pilgrimage maps based on interpretations of the *puranas,* 185–86

    and the pilgrimage landscape of Kashi, *71m2.3*, 162

Sen, Rajani Ranjan:

    Banaras' lack of visible antiquity tied to violent Islam by, 158–59

    on the Lat Bhairo incident, 195

Sen, Vijayaram:

    Dharhara mosque visited by, 144

    as Krishnachandra Ghoshal scribe, 78–79

    description of his pilgrimages, 82–83

Shahjahan:

    imperial fortress-palaces built by, 49, *120f4.2*, 121, 123, *plate3, plate4*

    Mughal support for Banaras and its ritual traditions during the reign of, 8, 43

Shahjahanabad (Delhi):

    Amber court properties in, 225n44

    havelis of, 41, 224n41

    imperial fortress-palaces at, 121

Sharqi sultans of Jaunpur:

    and the Bakariya *kund,* 220n18

    and the destruction (possible) of Padmeshwur temple, 25, 221n32

    incorporation of Banaras into the Sharqi sultanate, 8

    mosque of. *See* Lal Darwaza mosque

    and Razia's mosque, 25, 221n33

Shastri, Pandit Bapudev, 168, 209, 249n110

Sherring, Matthew Atmore, 239n131

    on Annapurna's public role, 84

    on Buddhist Banaras, 158

    on city festivals, 80

    cultural legacy of Banaras described by, 158

    on the Hindus, 158

    on the Rani Bhawani as a patron of the Panchkroshi route, 79

    on temple construction in Banaras, 176

shikhara (temple towers):

    of Durga temple, 112, *112f3.24, 114f3.26*

    of Govind Dev temple, 62

    of Mitra *kothi,* 102, *102f3.13*

    roof-types used over, 59

    on sanctums preceded by a *mandapa,* 239n128

Shivala ghat. *See* Chet Singh ghat (aka Shivala ghat)

Sita Ram:

    construction of landscapes with visual connections to the built environment, 191–92

    depiction of a *haveli,* 238n116

    depiction of Devkinandan *haveli,* 104, *104f3,16*

depiction of Dharhara mosque on
  Panchaganga ghat, *190f6.2*, 192
and the Marquess of Hastings, 104, 190
riverfront at Banaras illustrated by, 253n16
sketch Humayun's tomb, 253n17
"The temple of Raja Dusserath with the
  house he lived in to the left," *190f6.2*
Sitarehind, Raja Shivprasad, *Itihas
  Timirnashak*, 164, 247n75
state-based support for Hindu institutions,
  216n18
Stewart, Tony K., 11
Subrahmanyam, Sanjay, 216n10, 222n7, 225n50
Sukul, Kailasnath, *Kashidarpana*, 184–85, 205,
  252n160, *plate7*
Sukul, Kubernath, 215n1
Sursand Panch-mandir, *170m5.1*, 182, *183f5.14*
syncretism:
  and Brahmin concerns with ritual purity, 58
  of British colonizers, 59, 171–73, 228n99
  as a flawed concept, 11
  Indo-Islamic architectural forms of South
    Asian religious sites, 12–13
  and the fluid role of Indo-Muslim
    cultural products, 11
  as options for both Hindu and Muslim
    patrons, 58–60
  and politics, 60–61, 62
  Mughal architecture as the marriage of
    Iranian and Indo-Islamic precedents, 45
  and Mughal policies, 14, 33–34, 49, 55–56
    of Aurangzeb, 51, 52–53, 55–56
    of Meer Rustam Ali, 78, 123
  See also Indo-saracenic architecture

Taj Mahal at Agra, 121–22, *121f4.3*, 208
Talbot, Cynthia, 226n68, 230n118
Tarah Kashijiki Ki. See pilgrimage *tarah*
Tavernier, Jean Baptiste, on Govind temple, 62,
  229n104
Thapar, Romila, 217n24
Tilbhandeshwur *linga*, 70
Todarmal:
  haveli of:
    location of, 39–40m2.1–2.2
    "Old Mint" as a name for, 41
    survey *tarah* of the properties of, 38–41,
      38f2.2

Tod, James, 225n46
Town Hall, *170m5.1*, 172, 173, *174f5.7*, 205, 206,
  209
Tristhalisetu. See Bhatt, Narayan
Twain, Mark (Samuel L. Clemens), 211

Varanasi. *See* Banaras/Varanasi
Varma, Rameshwar Prasad, 185
Veeraswamy (Veeraswamiah), Enugula:
  on bazaars in Patna, 248n84
  on Brahmins in Banaras, 79–80
  on Dharhara mosque as symbol of Islamic
    iconoclasm, 194
  description of Banaras as a city filled with
    temples, 73
  description of *Kashikshetra*, 235n66
Vishweshwur *linga*:
  and ideas regarding a sacred zone
    summarized in the *Kashikand*, 5
  location of:
    original location at the Adi-
      Vishweshwur temple, 58, 230n123
    relocation of, 18
  manifestation of Shiva, 5
  pilgrimage traditions associated with, 26, 77
    and the Antargriha *yatra*, 27
    and popular practice, 28
  preeminence of, 25
  and Swai Singh II's Adi-Vishweshwur
    temple, 25
Vishweshwur temple, *32f2.1*
  of Ahilyabai, described by Fergusson,
    176f5.9, 177
  as a tourist site, 162, 206
  dismantling of, 221n34, 227n77
    Aurangzeb's order for, 51
    and its place as the center and fulcrum
      of the city's ritual landscape, 69
    and key formal attributes of Bindu
      Madhav, 62
  evolution of pilgrimage routes around it, 4
    and its dismantling, 69
    and pilgrimage *pata*, 230n123, *plate1*
  and the formal and spatial characteristics of
    Govind Dev temple, 60–62, *63ff2.14A;B*
  Gyan Vapi mosque built as a replacement
    for, 6
  mandapas of, 25

and pilgrimage routes, shaping of, 212–13
See also Adi-Vishweshwur temple;
   Ahilyabai Vishweshwur temple; Mughal
   Vishweshwur temple

Wagoner, Philip B., 217n28, 236n92
Watters, Thomas, 17–18

Xuanzang (Yuan Chwang or Hiuen Thsiang):
   travel narratives by, 159
      Watters translation of, 17–18

Yuan Chwang. See Xuanzang

GLOBAL
SOUTH
ASIA

Padma Kaimal, K. Sivaramakrishnan, and Anand A. Yang, SERIES EDITORS

GLOBAL SOUTH ASIA takes an interdisciplinary approach to the humanities and social sciences in its exploration of how South Asia, through its global influence, is and has been shaping the world.

A Place for Utopia: Urban Designs from South Asia, by Smriti Srinivas

The Afterlife of Sai Baba: Competing Visions of a Global Saint, by Karline McLain

Sensitive Space: Fragmented Territory at the India-Bangladesh Border, by Jason Cons

The Gender of Caste: Representing Dalits in Print, by Charu Gupta

Displaying Time: The Many Temporalities of the Festival of India, by Rebecca M. Brown

Banaras Reconstructed: Architecture and Sacred Space in a Hindu Holy City, by Madhuri Desai